THE ONION BOOK OF KNOWN KNOWLEDGE

TU STULTUS ES

The Onion Book of Known Knowledge

A Definitive Encyclopaedia of Existing Information

In 27 Excruciating Volumes

Compiled and Organized According to the
Higher Principles
of Intellectual Commerce and Coercion
For the Betterment of Mankind and the
Zweibel Family, Specifically

MDCCLVI

Little, Brown and Company
Hachette Book Group
237 Park Avenue, New York, NY 10017
www.hachettebookgroup.com

First Edition: October 2012

Little, Brown and Company is a division of Hachette Book Group, Inc., and is celebrating its 175th anniversary in 2012. The Little, Brown name and logo are trademarks of Hachette Book Group, Inc.

The publisher is not responsible for websites (or their content) that are not owned by the publisher.

The Hachette Speakers Bureau provides a wide range of authors for speaking events. To find out more, go to www.hachettespeakersbureau.com or call (866) 376-6591.

Library of Congress Control Number: 2012939575

10 9 8 7 6 5 4 3 2 1

RRD-C

Cover design by Colin Tierney

Printed in the United States of America

EDITOR IN CHIEF
Joe Randazzo

EDITORS
John Harris, Seth Reiss, Jason Roeder, Will Tracy

MANAGING EDITOR
Kate Palmer

DEPUTY MANAGING EDITOR
Brian Janosch

WRITERS
Joe Garden, John Harris, Brian Janosch, Dave Kornfeld, Chad Nackers,
Joe Randazzo, Seth Reiss, Jason Roeder, Will Tracy

CONTRIBUTING WRITERS
Jermaine Affonso, Cole Bolton, Dan Guterman, Todd Hanson,
Chris Karwowski, John Krewson, Zack Poitras

EDITORIAL COORDINATOR
Ben Berkley

ART DIRECTOR
Colin Tierney

GRAPHICS EDITORS
Michael Faisca, Nick Gallo

ILLUSTRATORS
Larry Buchanan, Emily Flake, Charles Giglia, Ben Grasso,
Mike Loew, Kiji McCafferty, David Pagano, Bob Sikoryak,
Pete Sucheski, Ward Sutton

CONTRIBUTORS
Shira Rachel Danan, Michael Drucker, Django Gold, Sam Kemmis
Matt Klinman, Lane Moore, Jill Morris, Andrei Nechita, Michael Pielocik,
Jocelyn Richard, Anita Serwacki, Sigmund Stern

CONTRIBUTING DESIGNER
Mike Ley

GRAPHICS ASSISTANTS
Craig Cannon, Gregory Ronquillo, Gilbert Shi, Maxime Simonet, William Wiggins

"Knowledge is that supple fruit upon which the mind feasts as though it were a dog eating fruit from the kitchen's floor."

On Knowledge

Since the very dawn of the human age, knowledge has been the essential building block of civilization and the foundation for all that is and can be known of the physical universe. It is the most precious resource in existence, a binding force that separates Man from beast, and also from the Very Dumb Man, such as yourself. Without knowledge, one cannot know with total certainty that the Earth orbits the sun; that one race is objectively superior to another; that a male cayjyx will only molt at the precise apogee of the winter quonstant. Without knowledge, life would have no *Onion Book Of Known Knowledge*, and thus no meaning.

But what does it mean to *know* something? An exceedingly perceptive and illuminating question, you will agree. All human beings begin to *know* from the moment of conception. As infants, we instinctively *know* how to breathe and sleep. By age 7 or 8, most humans *know* the rudiments of international tax law, perhaps not down to the particulars of every bilateral treaty or tax information exchange agreement (TIEA), but certainly insofar as thin capitalization or the legal distinction of tangible versus intangible property is concerned. Likewise, by the time one reaches young adulthood, one can be said to instinctively *know* that life is devoid of all meaning, and that the grim sepulchre of death looms all too clearly in the encroaching future.

Yet most knowledge in the universe comes from a special process known as *learning*, and the foundation of all learning—and all knowledge—is a powerful but microscopic particle called a fact. Science tells us the average human brain contains roughly 345 facts, as well as an estimated 13,500 fact fragments that have either been damaged beyond repair or have grafted themselves onto nearby nonfacts to create a mutated and highly invasive species of fact-fiction hybrid. Research suggests that a normal human brain is able to distort and disregard facts at a rate only equaled in clinical trials by certain varieties of freshwater fish.

Thus, civilizations throughout history have formulated a number of practices for transmitting knowledge so that facts can be adequately retained. The ancient Sumerians transmitted knowledge by holding a man at spearpoint and forcing him to repeat a fact for two straight weeks, stabbing him forcefully in the abdomen should he ever recite any part of it incorrectly. The Greeks transmitted knowledge by dangling a perfectly tanned, naked, hairless boy just out of a man's reach until such time as he could precisely recall at least one fact of moderate size. The Finnish people continue to practice a highly experimental and hazardous form of surgical fact-implantation known as *Hyökätä Tosiasia*, wherein an individual is placed in a barbiturate-induced coma and injected with a small mechanized termite that lays 40 to 50 bioengineered fact "eggs" that feed hungrily on unused brain matter and blood.

No matter how it is transmitted, the societal benefits of knowledge are widely documented and indisputable. Also widely documented and indisputable is the fact that you, the reader, are dumb, and almost unfathomably so. Therefore, it is the express purpose of this august volume to make you not only less dumb, but also more aware of your paralyzing dumbness, more acutely conscious of the way your dumbness limits you, and more deeply ashamed of the way your dumbness serves as a constant source of disappointment to your family, your intellectual betters, and to the human species as a whole. If the great ongoing project of knowledge is to survive, it falls upon books such as this to tow the writhing, reeking dumb mass of humanity toward that distant shore of intellectual enlightenment, and you, reader, are a part of this grand adventure. A small and laughably inconsequential part, but a part nonetheless.

So let us now commence with all the knowledge that is yet known by Man. We do not expect one to understand all of the contents of this book, or even some, or even more than six. But rest assured, from this day forward your empty, meaningless life shall never be quite so pathetic and desperate—nor quite so blissful in its wanton ignorance. And with that, we bid you good luck.

The Onion Book Of Known Knowledge Editorial Board

Douglas Siegfried Zweibel
Fields of Expertise: Business Management, Economic Theory
Education: Ph.D., Zweibel State University
Occupation: Director, Zweibel Center for Knowledge Studies
Major Publications: *Post-Zweibelian Economics And The Inferiority Of Less*

Professor David Bernard Hoot
Fields of Expertise: Colonial Studies, Early American History
Education: Ph.D., Brown University
Occupation: Professor of the Humanities, Rutgers State University
Major Publications: *The Torch Of Truth: Amos Bronson Alcott And The Transcendentalist Mind; An Owl Abroad: Reflections On A Sabbatical In France*

Martin Herman Zweibel
Fields of Expertise: Business Management, East Asian Studies
Education: Home-schooled, Ph.D. bestowed by T. Herman Zweibel
Occupation: President of Western Hemisphere Operations, Yu Wan Mei Group
Major Publications: *The Onion Atlas Of The Planet Earth* (ed.)

P. Hezekiah Mirr
Fields of Expertise: Microbiology, Yarn, Human Mind Limitations
Education: Ph.D., Oxford University
Occupation: Unknown
Major Publications: *The Onion English Dictionary* (Vols. I–XLVII); *Nocturnal Infiltrations Of The Brain-State And The Coming Consciousness War*

Alcmaeon
Fields of Expertise: Infinity Studies, Dimensional Theory, British Verse
Education: Unknown
Occupation: Director of Human Resources, The Onion, Inc.
Major Publications: *A Passion Unchained*

Judith Karst-Zweibel
Fields of Expertise: Business Management, Cultural Studies
Education: Ph.D., Zweibel State University
Occupation: President, Onion Books
Major Publications: *The Shadow Of Allium: Memoirs Of A Childhood Undone*

Dr. Han Soo Jong
Fields of Expertise: Quantum Physics, Postwar French Literature
Education: Ph.D., Massachusetts Institute of Technology
Occupation: Senior Researcher, the Quint Group
Major Publications: *Sonic-Neural Reanimation And The Cellular Response*

Robert Mugabe
Fields of Expertise: Revolutionary Politics, Library Sciences, Authoritarian Government
Education: University of London, Master of Laws
Occupation: President of Zimbabwe

A NOTE ON HOW THIS REFERENCE VOLUME WAS COMPOSED

The task of researching, writing, compiling, and editing this 183rd Imperial Edition of *The Onion Book Of Known Knowledge* was an arduous and costly process requiring thousands upon thousands of man-hours of labor in addition to a production budget exceeding $740 million. While the means utilized to generate the material in this book were not always strictly permissible in a moral or legal sense, the importance of producing an essential fount of knowledge to stand for all eternity was ultimately placed above such trifling considerations.

Each entry in this volume was assigned to a different preeminent scholar who was responsible for shepherding that specific entry, and that specific entry alone, into being. These scholars were forced to sign strict contracts whereby they were made to resign from their regular occupations, divorce their spouses, desert their children, and immerse themselves entirely in their single entry for as many years as it took for them to become the greatest living authority on that subject.

For example, the entry on ANT required Dr. James Huntington of the University of East Anglia to live alone among a colony of *Linepithema humile* ants in the Argentine wilderness for four and a half decades, a scholarly endeavor that apparently caused Dr. Huntington to go quite mad, but which nonetheless produced an entry of impeccable accuracy and pedagogical richness that was eventually cut for space. Those scholars who died gathering information on their entry—and many hundreds did—were within 48 hours replaced with a new academic who was forced to start entirely from scratch.

Each of the esteemed writers who participated in this process was required to deliver entries of at least 400,000 words, which would then be edited down by our editorial board to a length of anywhere from one to 300 words, at which point the scholars would then be paid the industry standard rate of $0.78 per word for their efforts. Once the book was delivered to the publisher, all the scholars were then murdered to prevent the invaluable information they gathered from being disseminated in competing works of reference. Please enjoy this reference volume.

About The Friedrich Siegfried Zweibel Center For Knowledge Studies

The tome you hold in your hands was compiled and edited at the Friedrich Siegfried Zweibel Center for Knowledge Studies, an elite human institution dedicated to the intellectual development of the world's monetarily gifted and their offspring. The center's goal is to aid the book-buying peoples of the earth in the knowing of knowledge, and to ensure that all knowledge that is known is that which is contained herein.

Founded in 1881 on a generous grant from the Herman Ulysses Zweibel Foundation, the Friedrich Siegfried Zweibel Center for Knowledge Studies is a sprawling 12-building campus that contains state-of-the-art knowledge-testing technology and hundreds of highly qualified researchers on hand to determine the validity and potency of potential pieces of knowledge for use in this book. Features of the center include:

➤ Special Interrogation Chambers in which knowledge experts in various fields are hooked up to electrodes and questioned by trained Zweibel Center Interrogators for a period of two hours to several years until they are coerced into revealing every detail of the knowledge they possess

➤ 12.7 kuno-volt sonic-neural analyzer donated by the Van Braak Laboratories in Rotterdam

➤ Clinically insane man Howard Brooke, whose ramblings are recorded and analyzed around the clock for potential theoretical insight

➤ One copy of every word

➤ An entire fully operational "shadow" staff responsible for researching, drafting, and editing an utterly false decoy encyclopedia intended to throw off our competitors

➤ Industrial blast furnace used to destroy all documents, objects, and personages deemed unworthy of study or irrelevant to the knowledge-obtaining process

A number of satellite research centers have also been established around the world—with one currently in every country on earth—that seek to locate and apprehend any source of knowledge where it originates or resides. By 2030, our goal is to establish a Friedrich Siegfried Zweibel Center for Knowledge Studies in every home in every town and municipality in the world.

For the 183rd consecutive year, this reference volume has been approved by the Friedrich Siegfried Zweibel Center for Knowledge Studies as a certifiably invaluable work of reference, and the knowledge contained in these pages is hereby declared fit to be known.

Funding

Funding for this encyclopedia was graciously provided by the Friedrich S. Zweibel Foundation, furthering its long-standing commitment to the vicious and unrelenting pursuit of knowledge. The $295 million endowment has allowed editors to spare no expense in assembling the most thoroughly comprehensive edition to date, detailed in the following list of expenditures incurred in the 12-day period from the commencement of research to the time our entire budget had been spent:

Research: $142.5 million
"Research": $84 million
Letters A–D: $1.3 million
Letter E: $12.6 million
Letters F–Z: $23,000
Rehearsal Space: $20/hr
Load-Bearing Tests: $659,000
Afternoon Tea: $221,050
Image Rights: $1,543.66
Legal Fees: $6.8 million
***Rescue Me* Seasons 1–5 DVD box set:** $58.99 + $8.79 S&H
Fact-Checking: $2.25/hr
10-Minute Phone Interview With Evander Holyfield: $85,000
Provender: $700,000
Trip To Verify Existence Of Mount Rushmore: $8,000
Second Trip To Confirm Rushmore Findings: $8,000

How To Read This Book

EDUCATION REQUIREMENTS

In order to obtain the high level of comprehension needed to fully appreciate the concepts discussed in *The Onion Book Of Known Knowledge*, readers must have all of the following academic degrees and honors:

➤ Ph.D., Linguistics, McGill University or Haverford College
➤ LL.M., Tax Law, Yale Law School
➤ Ph.D., Philosophy, Swarthmore College (PH401 Contemporary Metaphilosophy with Prof. Lawrence H. Powers required)
➤ B.S., Hotel Management, Ferris State College
➤ B.F.A., Dance, the Julliard School
➤ Ph.D., Public Policy, Harvard Kennedy School of Government
➤ M.D., Emory University School of Medicine
➤ M.S., Soil Management, Purdue University College of Agriculture
➤ Honorary Degree for contributions in the field of genetic studies, Bryn Mawr College
➤ Visiting Professor in Theoretical Physics, Massachusetts Institute of Technology
➤ B.A., Culinary Arts, Johnson and Wales University
➤ Minor, Marketing, Penn State University, Fayette County branch campus
➤ Ph.D., Art History, Collège de Sorbonne, Paris
➤ Pen/Faulkner Award
➤ The Wolf Prize
➤ Copley Medal for Excellence in Science
➤ Nobel Prize (Peace)
➤ Graduate, New Trier Township High School

SAMPLE ENTRY

KEY

Name
Bolded word identifying the entry, for those who need their hand held for pretty much everything.

Helper Space
Small gap between words allows for ease of study and increased comprehension.

Letter E
Each entry contains precisely 27 letter *E*s.

End Of Entry
What are we, like four pages in? God, you're exhausting.

Key, device used to explain extremely intuitive things to complete dullards who, if they really don't have the mental wherewithal to open to any page of this book and quickly grasp the format of this reference, are making a very good case for eugenics.

RECOMMENDED READING STANCES

The Scholar's Lament   *The Striking Cobra*   *The Starstrider*

PRONUNCIATION CHART

Banana: (Bah NAH nah) Come on, imbecile, at least attempt to sound it out.

Wool: It's inconceivable that you've made it to this point in the reference book and don't know how to pronounce "wool." Truly, it boggles the mind.

Forest: Perhaps, rather than struggling with all your might to force the embarrassingly simple word "forest" past your thick lips, you should instead look long and hard at yourself in a mirror and seriously consider whether the world would be a better place without you in it (it would).

Rainbow: (RAYN b)—let's stop this charade, shall we? Go turn on whatever latest televised claptrap holds your feeble attention and try your hardest not to procreate.

Crudités: Go fuck yourself.

ALPHABETIZATION

In most encyclopedias, entries are ordered from *A* to *Z*. To ensure absolute precision, however, *The Onion Book Of Known Knowledge* employs the Classical Alphabetization Notation, which takes into consideration the exponential value of every letter in a given word, as determined by the value of the preceding letter in that word. For example, the reason ART comes before ASP is because the *r* in ART gives its *A* an exponential value of 0.00000054, whereas the *s* in ASP gives its *A* an exponential value of 0.00000055. To quickly determine the exact exponential value of a letter, an electronic device called an orthographic spectrometer is used to analyze every entry's title.

It can accurately measure the entry's exponential values and predict, within 0.014 degrees, which entries come before and after it, in four to 16 hours, depending on the complexity of the words. Over the centuries, we phased out these exponents, though as recently as the 180th edition, ART would have appeared with its full Classical Alphabet Notation as: $A^{0.00000054}r^{0.0000000074}t^{0.0000000089}$.

◇◇◇◇

UNDERSTANDING THE PAGE NUMBERS

Located on the lower right corner of each right-sided page, and on the lower left corner of each opposite-facing page, the reader will see a numerical designation known as a "Page Number." These symbols—which represent the abstract conceptual units mathematicians call "integers"—are placed there by the compilers of this volume as a tool to help gauge how far along in the book the reader may be at any given time. For example, the number "2" indicates that one is reading the "second" (or, if the reader prefers, the "page immediately following the first") page of the book. If "121" is visible, that means that one hundred twenty pages have elapsed since page one. Likewise, if the reader comes across a "48," that means there have been twelve additional pages since the thirty-sixth page (identified by the "36" printed in its lower corner) and that there are seventy-three pages to read before one reaches the aforementioned "Page 121." If, at any point during the book, the reader wishes to calculate the distance between the current page and a page yet to come, he must subtract from the former the numerical value of the latter and write the difference in the Page Calculation Log located in the back of the book, taking special care to adjust the total with each subsequent page read, until the overall difference equals "1," at which point the Page Calculation Log will no longer serve any function and the reader will have to erase the results and start anew. Though it is not required to progress through the book in numeric order, the reader is advised not to complete any pages with a symbol other than a number or an italicized Roman numeral in the place where a page number should be found; such symbols can include but are not limited to hearts, crosses, pentagrams, Cyrillic, a series of almost illegible dots, a lion's head, a biohazard symbol, the FedEx logo, or 19. If the reader comes across any of these, he should be aware that he is no longer reading this book, and has either completed the book and moved on to another, or was never reading the book in the first place.

A WORD ON THE READABILITY OF
THE ONION BOOK OF KNOWN KNOWLEDGE

Of the many wonderful experiential qualities contained herein that the editors—nay, the faithful wards—of this venerable tome hold with fervent ardor and pride to their swelling breasts, perhaps paramount is the readability—the quintessential accessibility—of the following materials, as pertains especially to their organization and presentation. Indeed, if even the smallest bright-eyed young lad, his burgeoning synapses firing off a dazzling, blinding cacophony of new connective electricity, were not able to penetrate the collected knowledge held within these scant few pounds of wood-pulp and ink, then what, one might ask—what—would be the purpose of compiling the wondrous tools of erudition that can be found on the following pages? None! None at all! For these reasons, the reader of this reference will find that all of the entries he now has at the tips of his very fortunate fingertips have been deftly executed with a crystal clarity akin to the limpid pool in which Narcissus found his final undoing—because, dear reader, lest we forget what we all know to be true, *astra non mentiuntur, sed astrologi bene mentiuntur de asters.*

◇◇◇◇

A NOTE TO OUR FILIPINO READERS

Kahit kadalasang ninanais ng Direktoryong Editoryal ng *The Onion* na igalang ang pinakamaranyang klase ng mga tao—lalong lalo na ang mga Pilipino—kailangan naming humingi ng paumanhin: Ang tagapalathalang Amerikano ay isinapilit na kailangang ilathala itong edisyon sa pinakabarumbado at pinakainutil na wika, Ingles, dahil karamihan ng mga mambabasa ay hindi nakakaintindi ni isang salitang Tagalog, kahit batid ng lahat na ito ang pinagpalang wika. Inaasahan namin na hindi nyo ikagalit, ikadiri, o kaya ay mapilitan kayong umiwas ng landas para sa ikabubuti ng kalagayan ng *The Onion.* Nanatili kaming matupad na katuwang ninyo magpakailanman.

It should be mentioned that the original encyclopedia manuscript the Onion staff had been working on for more than a decade was destroyed in a fire three days before publication, and the entire volume you hold in your hands was frantically written by the two surviving editors in less than 48 hours.

A Note On This Encyclopedia's Expunged Entries

By T. Herman Zweibel, Publisher Emeritus of The Onion

Given my advancing age, I have neither the time, inclination, nurse-power, nor store of available laudanum on hand to sort through every page of this infernal Record of Knowledge and strike any fact or irrefutable truth which causes me deep and abject rage. Nevertheless, since the stammering mule-men I evidently am paying to be this book's scholarly board insist on shipping these pages to the printers, I wish to humbly submit the following list of words or notions that I have specifically forbidden from having any mention in the body of this 183rd or 184th Annual Onion Panoply of Facts:

Jewess: I believe we have already heard quite enough about this obscene varietal of Semitic harlot, who seems to congregate so freely in the music halls and bank mezzanines of our nation's cities.

Labor Union: I have never before acknowledged the existence of such an organization, and I do not intend to start now.

Clara Bow: If this vile temptress believes I have forgiven her for spurning my numerous entreaties lo this past century then she is sorely mistaken.

Cabbage: I see no need to expound further on the putridity of this rancid weed, but suffice it to say I believe it fit only for the trough of an Irishman.

The Russo-Japanese War: The amount of money I lost on this exotic little imbroglio still pains the remnants of what my nursemaid stubbornly insists is my heart.

Tule Shrew: You can be damned sure I didn't hunt this species to extinction just to see it touchingly eulogized by a syrup-brained member of my own so-called "editorial staff."

Joseph Pulitzer: It seems I have won the day yet again, old friend. May your blackened soul roil forever in eternal hellfire.

Blickensderfer Type-Writer: A truly god-damned confounded machine with a tin type-wheel that stops and starts and spits out nonsense like a crippled China-man. That is why I demanded every last blasted page of this book be written with an Underwood, and an Underwood only.

Fiber-Optics: I chanced upon this gobbledygook in a galley page and steadfastly refuse to acknowledge its existence in any publication bearing my company's name.

Blue: A deeply confounding color, be it sparkling in the springtime skies that lie just beyond the walls of my hermetic bedchamber, or cruelly spiriting my poisoned mind back to the speckled robin's eggs I once collected so merrily in my youth. I will not cede to it a place on the spectrum.

Peace, mercy, goodwill, togetherness, felicity, bliss, and brotherhood: No addlepated fool ever sold a king's ransom worth of books by babbling on about any of these pitiful illusions. The story of life is one of death, drudgery, destitution, and decay—no more, no less—and so it shall be in these pages.

Yours, In Eternal Misery,

J H Zweibel

Aapanthera, previously unknown breed of African big cat that, by 2012, had eaten all of the world's aardvarks and taken their place at the top of every alphabetically organized list.

Abdul-Jabbar, Kareem (*b. Apr. 16, 1947*), American basketball legend born Ferdinand Lewis "Lew" Alcindor, Jr., who was forced to change his name after Milwaukee Bucks coach Larry Costello imposed a strict code of Islamic law on his team. Issuing threats of severe physical punishment, Costello commanded Abdul-Jabbar and his teammates to wash their feet before stepping onto the court, grow thick beards in reverent emulation of the holy prophet Muhammad, and eat, drink, and dribble with their right hands in accordance with the immutable will of Allah. Despite Costello's insistence that the Bucks exhaust valuable timeouts to pray toward Mecca,

Abdul-Jabbar, along with veteran point guard Faruq Akbar and small forward Abdullah Ali-Abdullah (born Oscar Robertson and Bob Dandridge, respectively), led the team to its only championship in 1971. Abdul-Jabbar was banished from Milwaukee in 1975 after Costello caught him paying interest on a loan and, infuriated, threw acid in the 7-foot-2 center's face, forcing him to wear protective goggles for the remainder of his career.

Academy Award, film industry's highest honor, given annually to actors, directors, and other professionals for excellence in the field of desperately wanting an Academy Award. The American Academy of Motion Picture Arts and Sciences has recognized the relentless desire for an Oscar since 1929 and has presented hundreds of awards to those who best exemplify the organization's standards of naked ambition. The Oscars are preceded each year by the Golden Globes, which are also awarded to those actors who most want to win an Oscar.

Adam And Eve, according to the Book of Genesis, first man and woman created by God, and the last humans made personally by the Almighty Himself until 1976, when He made La Porte, Indiana, resident Jerry Dunnigan out of clay just to see if He could still do it.

Addiction, physical or psychological dependence on something such as, well, in this particular case it's alcohol, but it could come in many other forms as well. Addiction is sometimes focused on abstract concepts rather than actual chemical substances—obviously not what's happening here with all the binge-drinking and the constant sipping from a flask and so forth, but it does happen—and patterns of addiction can differ greatly in their intensity, though in this instance, of course, we're clearly talking about someone who pretty much needs a liter and a half of Gordon's every day just to be able to function. Treatment for addiction can take many forms, including detoxification, therapy, and support groups, with varying de-

Aa · α · Æ

First letter of the English alphabet and your last opportunity to come to terms with the fact that you hold in your hands the most important book in history and are about to embark upon an intellectual undertaking unlike any that has ever existed. The letter *A* represents your moment of truth, your last chance to ask yourself if you're up to the demands of this volume and, if not, to have the integrity to place it back on the shelf and select a less challenging title or pursue an entirely different enterprise such as assembling a fun jigsaw puzzle. But if you possess the hunger, the discipline, and, yes, the courage required for this encyclopedia, then the letter A, a vowel with six different sounds, is your first step toward banishing ignorance once and for all.

SECOND, FIRST, AND 138TH PRESIDENT
John Adams

(*b. Oct. 30, 1735 d. July 4, 1826*), erroneously considered the second U.S. president, Adams, because of the nonlinear way in which time was organized in the 18th century, was technically president before Washington. As a result of the complex pre-1800 nonconsecutive system of time, Adams was in many ways the nation's first commander in chief, as well as its 19th and 64th, the first and 72nd vice president, Indiana's fourth-largest Hyundai dealer, the man who gave a majestic eulogy at the funeral of President John Adams in 1826, and backup quarterback for the Los Angeles Rams from 2021 to 2026. As president, Adams retained Washington's cabinet, though its members weren't certain if they had served Washington first

or if Adams had appointed them, but it was nevertheless seen as a gracious act of statesmanship. Unfortunately, when Washington was voted into office four years earlier, he spent the first part of his term undoing everything Adams would later achieve.

PET PEEVE
Was often mistaken for a hungry baby bird by mother starlings and force-fed worms

HOBBY
Perusing fabric stores for perfect hair ribbon

NICKNAME
John John John

ACCOMPLISHMENTS
Built up U.S. Navy by acquiring 200 oars

OF NOTE
From birth to death, always had a little mud on his body

Abacus, beaded manual counting device invented by ancient Sumerians to screw customers out of a fair price.

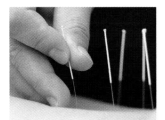

Acupuncture, ancient Chinese system whose practitioners compete to see how many tiny needles they can insert into a patient's skin before they are asked just what the fuck is going on here. The current record is 827,908.

AN AMERICAN FORESON

John Quincy Adams

(b. July 11, 1767 d. Feb. 23, 1848), sixth U.S. president and the first American to fail to make a better life for himself than his father. After receiving a Harvard education almost identical to that of his father, John Adams, and practicing law to less renown, Adams became a much less distinguished president than his father, and his performance after holding the office was also less impressive, making him the only U.S. citizen up to that point in history who was not able to improve upon his parents' lot in life in any way, shape, or form. John Quincy Adams died in 1848 at the age of 80, living a full 10 years less than his father did.

grees of efficacy, none of which matter if you can't even get to the stage of admitting there's a problem, and, clearly, there is.

Adoption, practice of raising some child nobody in the entire world wanted by pretending to be its parents. The adoption process requires extensive background checks and legal paperwork, allowing prospective parents numerous opportunities to back out and lead a fulfilling life without being dragged down by a kid who must have something wrong with them, and whom they could honestly never love as much as their own biological offspring.

Adulthood, period following adolescence in which one has figured out in explicit detail exactly what one wants do with one's life, is always in control of every situation, and consistently takes the appropriate actions to realize that which is necessary to bring about a lifetime of happiness and personal fulfillment.

Advertising, vile method of communication aimed at persuading people to purchase products or services and responsible for the destruction of art and creativity itself, though those Nike ones are pretty good. Advertising has become the dominant driver of content in print, film, and television, and it exerts a deleterious influence on the subject matter and quality of the media consumed, even if the Bud Light ads are usually funny. Though getting that Maxwell House jingle stuck in your head is annoying, it's probably not the worst thing in the world, and to be honest, that goofy Geico lizard does kind of grow on you after a while.

Affection, emotional sensation that one either gets too much of and freaks out or gets too little of and freaks out.

Air, atmospheric gas that celebrities must share with regular people.

Airplane, fixed-wing flying vehicle invented in 1903 that has made it impossible to avoid returning home for Christmas, Thanksgiving, weddings, funerals, or any other event, no matter how far away it is. Airplanes counter the force of gravity by using either static lift or the dynamic lift of an airfoil, which completely eliminates any excuse one might have not to travel 1,500 miles for Labor Day weekend even though they were just home for the Fourth of July and really would like to take an actual vacation for themselves one of these days. The ability of the airplane to safely and swiftly cover large distances has allowed millions to fly all the way in from San Diego for Mother's Day, which isn't even a major holiday, or attend their sister's baby shower when everyone knows there's no fucking way she'd do the same for them. No fucking way.

Alamo, Roman Catholic mission in San Antonio, Texas, where in 1836

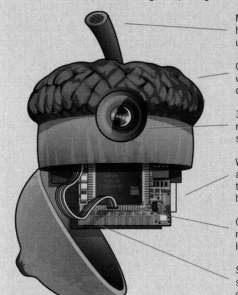

ACORN, surveillance device manufactured by the government that is constantly monitoring everything we say.

Microphone records high-quality audio from targets up to 100 meters away

Camouflaged to blend in with wooded environment and avoid detection

360-degree HD video camera records continuously in either standard or night-vision mode

Wireless receiver, which acts as acorn's main communication platform with surveillance headquarters

GPS tracker lets acorn navigate between vectors, locate extraction point

Self-destruction device in case surveillance operation is compromised

a small group of brave Americans selflessly laid down their lives against a much larger Mexican army to preserve their freedom to own other human beings as slaves. When the Mexican government brazenly outlawed the practice of involuntary servitude in the region of Texas under its rule, volunteers from across America flocked to the Alamo to defend—to the death if necessary—the proud national tradition of possessing men, women, and children. At the end of a 13-day siege, General Antonio López de Santa Anna launched a final assault before dawn on March 6, ultimately overwhelming the gallant Alamo defenders, who are now immortalized as heroes for sacrificing themselves so that others might live as property. The Alamo is the most popular tourist destination in Texas.

Alcohol, organic compound that can transform any physical surface into a bed, toilet, or, when consumed in high enough volumes, both. Through a complex chemical process, alcohol is able to change a concrete parking lot into a feather-down king-sized mattress or a hall closet into a fully functional bathroom with working commode. Alcohol in its various forms has additional transformative properties, including the ability to change garbled, incoherent ramblings into valid arguments and to initiate a subtle process by which members of the same sex are metamorphosed over the course of an evening into members of the opposite sex. It is not currently understood, however, why no amount of alcohol has been able to change the way things ended with Dad.

Alcott, Louisa May (*b. Nov. 29, 1832 d. Mar. 6, 1888*), Civil War nurse and novelist who wrote *Little Women*, a graphic, semiautobiographical account of the hundreds of grotesque battlefield amputations she performed in the waning days of the conflict. The story follows Josephine "Jo" March Bhaer and two fellow nurses as they race to remove the badly crushed and gangrenous limbs of sobbing Union soldiers who have been rushed to field hospitals, many of them with blood still gushing in crimson torrents from their open wounds. Exhausted and covered in infected pus, flesh, and sinew, the three women bond over jamming spent munitions into soldiers' mouths before frantically sawing off their arms or legs without anesthesia, and then, years later, over trying to drown out the shrill cries of agony that continue to haunt their dreams. Alcott's classic novel is still beloved by women around the world and has been adapted into several stomach-turning, almost unwatchable feature-length films.

Aldrin, Buzz (*b. Jan. 20, 1930*), American astronaut and second man to shit his pants on the moon.

Ali, Muhammad (*b. Jan. 17, 1942*), once-legendary boxer who dominated the sport for a decade but has gone 0-32 since his last victory in 1978. Despite claiming the championship in 1964, 1974, and 1975, Ali suffered a steady decline in his speed and footwork throughout the 1990s and 2000s, tiring quickly and throwing labored, easily deflected punches with almost no power behind them whatsoever. Some of Ali's most devastating defeats have included a first-round knockout at the hands of Larry Holmes in 1986, a first-round loss to Evander Holyfield in 1995 that the alarmed referee stopped six seconds into the bout, and a particularly brutal 2003 first-round loss to Lennox Lewis in which Ali crumpled to the canvas from the force of the opening glove tap. The closest Ali has come to a victory since the late '70s was in 1996, when the 54-year-old lost a

Alcatraz, island prison that was impossible to escape until inmates discovered a free ferry to San Francisco that departed every half hour.

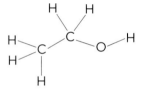

◄ **ALCOHOL**
Scientists are still unsure how this compound transmutes bus station benches into convenient toilets.

AGRICULTURE, cultivation of animals and plants to sustain life, and a landmark human achievement in that it created a sedentary lifestyle that allows a complete shut-in like you to exist today. Prior to the raising of crops and livestock for mass consumption, an introverted, emotional cripple such as yourself had to get over his little neuroses and either enter a communal, hunter-gatherer situation or starve to death. Because of the discovery of agriculture in ancient Sumer more than 10,000 years ago, you can now stay in your pajamas in your dimly lit apartment, play online poker all day, and call a restaurant to bring you food because being around other

people makes you feel uncomfortable and awkward and basically act like a 4-year-old. Agriculture accounts for nearly a third of the world's economy, creating enough well-adjusted people out there who are willing to help a civilization of fragile, withdrawn individuals, who can't even go to the grocery store without having a goddamn panic attack, thrive. Jesus Christ, grow up.

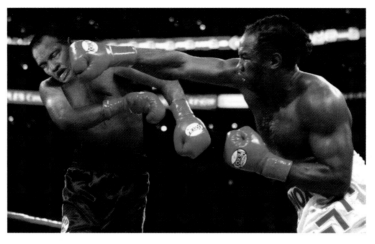

Ali still uses the rope-a-dope technique to wear down opponents by absorbing the energy of their punches with his face. ➤

Al-Zawahiri, Ayman (*b. June 19, 1951*), operational mastermind of the militant Islamist group al-Qaeda who made billions by registering the trademark "We Will Never Forget" and then licensing it for bumper stickers, T-shirts, and window decals two weeks before the the 9/11 attacks on the United States.

narrow split decision to Mike Tyson.

Allen, Woody (*b. Dec. 1, 1935*), famed American comedian, writer, and filmmaker known for his in-

secure personality and highly neurotic mannerisms, such as obsessively making hit movie after hit movie, being very finicky about the scores of beautiful Hollywood actresses he's dated, and worrying comically about whether he should write another Academy Award–winning screenplay, publish another piece in *The New Yorker*, or play another sold-out show with his acclaimed Dixieland jazz group.

Allergy, hypersensitive immune response to a foreign vector or allergen caused by childhood exposure to dust, pollen, Volvos, Montessori school, Burt's Bees products, Mandarin lessons, the music of Paul Simon, PSAT tutors, and organic almond butter.

Almanac, type of novelty item, laughably referred to as a reference book, which compiles hundreds of pages of purportedly factual trifles about the stars and the weather in a blatant attempt to fool simpleminded book shoppers. Although many still live under the misapprehension that these centuries-old anthologies

of lies serve some sort of practical purpose (*See* Mass Delusion), a majority of intelligent people agree that readers would be far better off consulting a more trusted, alphabetically organized reference volume, such as an encyclopedia, for all their information needs.

Alpha Male, sociological term for

the male individual in a group with the most influence, generally typified by his ability to stroll right into a Mitsubishi dealer, tell the salesman he wants a fully loaded Eclipse for $17,500 and not a cent more, and drive out of there with the thing that afternoon. Achieved by physical dominance and unwillingness to settle for a sunset orange exterior when he knows damn well it's no skin off the guy's nose to give him one in kalapana black, his high-ranking status affords the alpha male first preference when it comes to food, mates, or getting the same deal his father-in-law got not three weeks ago. The alpha position can change hands, however, if the dominant male is threatened or challenged by another individual, such as a franchise manager who deploys

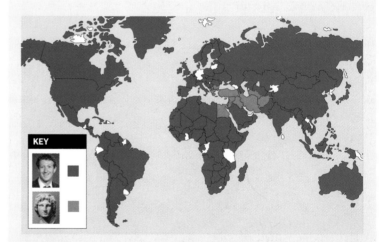

KEY

ALEXANDER THE GREAT (*b. July 20 or 21, 356 BC d. June 10 or 11, 323 BC*), prodigious leader, diplomat, and military tactician who by the age of 30 had almost as much power and wealth as Facebook founder Mark Zuckerberg had when he was 25. Following his father's assassination, a young Alexander ascended to the throne and, as general of the Greek army, led a conquest that gave him control over an empire of 10 to 13 million people and made him the world's richest and most powerful individual, nearly as rich and powerful, in fact, as the Mark Zuckerberg of 2010, who made $20 billion and gained access to the personal information of 800 million active Facebook users just by sitting in front of a computer screen for a few years. Alexander the Great died at the age of 32, leaving behind a rich legacy that equals about one-fifth the significance and influence of Zuckerberg, who will almost certainly live for another six or seven decades.

the power move of making the alpha male wait outside his office for 15 minutes without offering him any coffee while he pretends to check with his regional supervisor.

Al-Qaeda, radical Islamist terrorist organization founded by Sunni extremist Osama bin Laden that gave the United States something to do. Formed in the late 1980s, when the United States was just sort of killing time and not really up to much, al-Qaeda steadily built up a network of militant operatives and, on Sept. 11, 2001, perpetrated a massive suicide mission on American soil that killed nearly 3,000 civilians, giving America something to keep itself busy with for at least the next couple decades. Since the events of 9/11, the United States—figuring that at least it had a project to focus on now so, you know, what the

hell—has sought to root out members of al-Qaeda with Predator drone strikes and covert military operations, which, while they aren't the most fun thing in the world for a country to do, are better than sitting around with its thumb up its ass.

Amazon Rain Forest, vast, lush South American forest situated in the 1.7-billion-acre Amazon basin that hosts an astonishing diversity of diesel-powered skip loaders, dump trucks, road graders, and power shovels. Researchers have identified more than 30 different types of bulldozers alone, some of which are perfectly equipped with deep-treaded cleats ideal for ripping through the rich topsoil, while others have adapted to the forest with bladed pincers capable of tearing through trees at high rates of speed. The delicate interdependency of

the huge machines in the Amazon is extremely intricate: Bulldozers help ensure road graders do not become mired in undergrowth; flatbed trucks are needed to haul away the enormous trees so bulldozers are not buried in lumber; and road graders make it possible for flatbed trucks to reach the bulldozers. Amazon deforestation remains a massive and dynamic system that has fascinated engineers and entrepreneurs alike for more than a century and may one day span the South American continent from coast to coast.

Amazon River, South American waterway surrendered to piranhas by the Brazilian government in exchange for the species' promise never to venture onto land. Alarmed by shore encroachments indicating the flesh-eating fish might soon

◄ AMAZON RAIN FOREST
Scientists believe some of the Amazon Rain Forest's machines could one day be used to uproot and destroy a cure for cancer.

AMERICAN CIVIL WAR (1861–), ongoing conflict between the northern and southern regions of the United States. Following the election of abolitionist president Abraham Lincoln in 1860, a group of pro-slavery states announced its intention to secede from the union and form the Confederate States of America, known today as "the Confederacy" or "the South." The newly formed government asserted, and maintains to this day, that federal authority is subordinate to that of states and is a threat to the economy, security, and culture of the South. Actual fighting began in 1861 when the Confederates attacked a U.S. military outpost at Fort Sumter in South Carolina, the first in a series of continuous hostilities that would include the First and Second Battles of Bull Run, the Battle of Antietam, General Sherman's brutal March to the Sea, Jim Crow laws, Martin Luther King, Jr., the assassination of Martin Luther King, Jr., the Brady Bill, the Blue Collar Comedy Tour, Ivy League assholes, Wal-Mart, Wall Street, and the elections of George W. Bush and Barack Obama. The conflict is the deadliest ever fought on American soil, with more than 120 million casualties recorded to date and many more expected from the fighting currently taking place in Congress—by far the most ferocious combat since the Civil War

Clockwise from top left: Troops prepare for combat; the Battle of Montgomery; two leading figures in the ongoing propaganda war; Confederate forces descend on Washington.

began. In fact, historians believe that both the North and the South are even more committed to total victory today than they were when the first shots were fired, and that the bloodiest battles of the conflict have yet to occur.

Anatomy

Branch of science concerned with the bodily structure of living things that is increasingly difficult to pursue due to the fact that nearly every organism on earth has been riddled with bullets. Anatomy generally involves the separation and dissection of an organism's different parts, tasks that are now all but impossible considering any plant or animal a researcher studies is likely to have had most of its biological systems reduced to undifferentiated pulp in a hail of gunfire. Because even the smallest single-celled amoeba has, at this point, been at least winged by a bullet, anatomy is now more or less a pointless science, as it is impossible to gather useful physical data from a blue whale or giant redwood tree that has been blasted to pieces by a howitzer round. Further hindering the field of anatomy is the routine discovery of underwater ecosystems containing never-before-studied coral formations that have had their entire populations systematically lined up and shot execution-style with hollow-point .38 slugs, scattering these creatures' various forms of central nervous systems all over the seafloor. In addition to finding that most mammal specimens have been reduced to indistinguishable mush-piles of bones, fur, teeth, and antlers by high-caliber bullets before they can be collected for study, many researchers are forced to abandon anatomy after they themselves are shot multiple times at point-blank range.

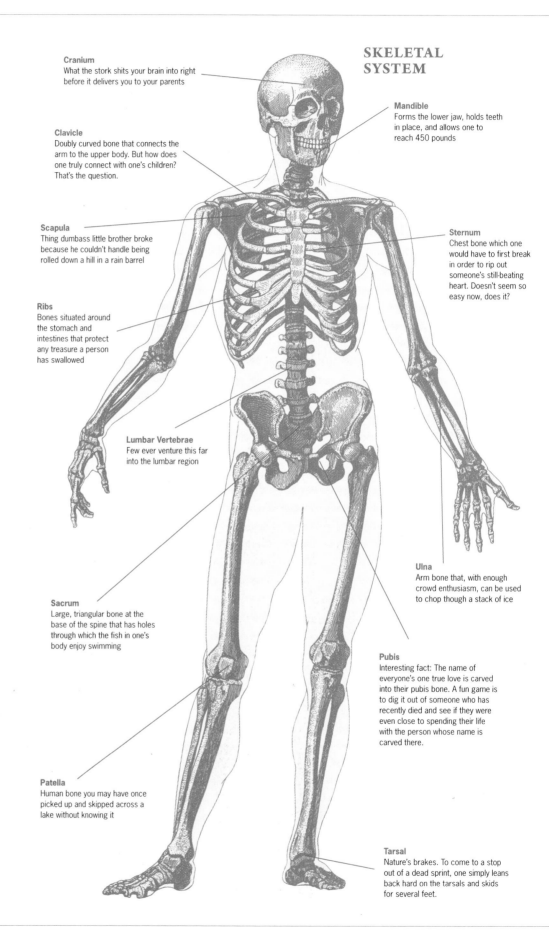

SKELETAL SYSTEM

Cranium
What the stork shits your brain into right before it delivers you to your parents

Mandible
Forms the lower jaw, holds teeth in place, and allows one to reach 450 pounds

Clavicle
Doubly curved bone that connects the arm to the upper body. But how does one truly connect with one's children? That's the question.

Scapula
Thing dumbass little brother broke because he couldn't handle being rolled down a hill in a rain barrel

Sternum
Chest bone which one would have to first break in order to rip out someone's still-beating heart. Doesn't seem so easy now, does it?

Ribs
Bones situated around the stomach and intestines that protect any treasure a person has swallowed

Lumbar Vertebrae
Few ever venture this far into the lumbar region

Ulna
Arm bone that, with enough crowd enthusiasm, can be used to chop though a stack of ice

Sacrum
Large, triangular bone at the base of the spine that has holes through which the fish in one's body enjoy swimming

Pubis
Interesting fact: The name of everyone's one true love is carved into their pubis bone. A fun game is to dig it out of someone who has recently died and see if they were even close to spending their life with the person whose name is carved there.

Patella
Human bone you may have once picked up and skipped across a lake without knowing it

Tarsal
Nature's brakes. To come to a stop out of a dead sprint, one simply leans back hard on the tarsals and skids for several feet.

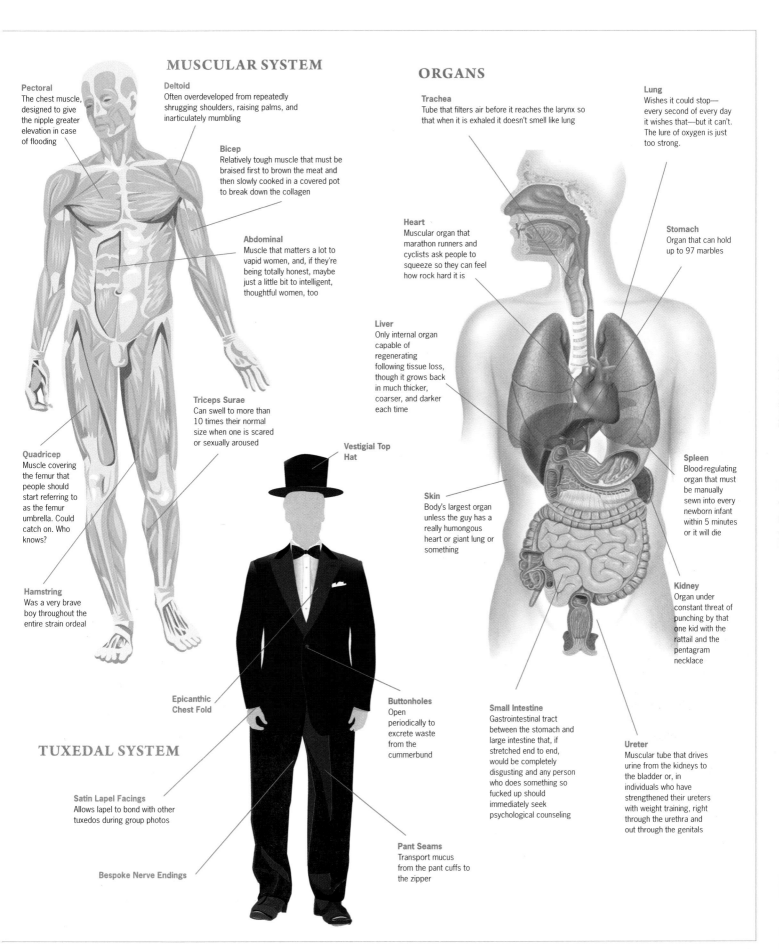

MUSCULAR SYSTEM

Pectoral
The chest muscle, designed to give the nipple greater elevation in case of flooding

Deltoid
Often overdeveloped from repeatedly shrugging shoulders, raising palms, and inarticulately mumbling

Bicep
Relatively tough muscle that must be braised first to brown the meat and then slowly cooked in a covered pot to break down the collagen

Abdominal
Muscle that matters a lot to vapid women, and, if they're being totally honest, maybe just a little bit to intelligent, thoughtful women, too

Triceps Surae
Can swell to more than 10 times their normal size when one is scared or sexually aroused

Quadricep
Muscle covering the femur that people should start referring to as the femur umbrella. Could catch on. Who knows?

Hamstring
Was a very brave boy throughout the entire strain ordeal

ORGANS

Trachea
Tube that filters air before it reaches the larynx so that when it is exhaled it doesn't smell like lung

Heart
Muscular organ that marathon runners and cyclists ask people to squeeze so they can feel how rock hard it is

Liver
Only internal organ capable of regenerating following tissue loss, though it grows back in much thicker, coarser, and darker each time

Lung
Wishes it could stop— every second of every day it wishes that—but it can't. The lure of oxygen is just too strong.

Stomach
Organ that can hold up to 97 marbles

Spleen
Blood-regulating organ that must be manually sewn into every newborn infant within 5 minutes or it will die

Kidney
Organ under constant threat of punching by that one kid with the rattail and the pentagram necklace

Small Intestine
Gastrointestinal tract between the stomach and large intestine that, if stretched end to end, would be completely disgusting and any person who does something so fucked up should immediately seek psychological counseling

Ureter
Muscular tube that drives urine from the kidneys to the bladder or, in individuals who have strengthened their ureters with weight training, right through the urethra and out through the genitals

Vestigial Top Hat

Skin
Body's largest organ unless the guy has a really humongous heart or giant lung or something

TUXEDAL SYSTEM

Epicanthic Chest Fold

Satin Lapel Facings
Allows lapel to bond with other tuxedos during group photos

Bespoke Nerve Endings

Buttonholes
Open periodically to excrete waste from the cummerbund

Pant Seams
Transport mucus from the pant cuffs to the zipper

Antelope, another fucking kind of deer.

Apple, nutritious tree tumor.

emerge from the world's largest river to attack human beings in their own homes, Brazilian officials agreed in 1971 to cede all authority over the river and its basin to the piranhas, including total sovereignty over some of the most diverse aquatic wildlife found on earth. Though most its 4,200-mile course travels through Brazil, the Amazon originates in Peru, which only relinquished its segment of the river when a school of piranhas crawled out from the water, made its way to the capital city of Lima, and skeletonized the prime minister in just under 30 seconds.

Ambulance, vehicle designed to safely transport the sick or injured to the nearest dumpster.

Amoeba, simple one-celled organism whose primary form of locomotion, blindly bumping into objects in search of food, is emulated by roughly four-fifths of the world's human population.

Anesthesia, drugs or gases administered to eliminate the feeling of pain during an operation, after which the patient is permitted to take home any leftover anesthesia that was not used in the procedure.

Anger, negative emotion that only people in charge are allowed to express. An automatic psychological response, anger is off-limits to all but those who rank above you, though it is sometimes permissible among assistants to people in charge when conveyed on their behalf. Any outright display of anger, including physical or emotional outbursts of aggression, by anyone else will only lead to a furious response from the person in charge.

Antietam, Battle Of, Civil War battle and single bloodiest day in U.S. history, cut short after rival generals Robert E. Lee and George B. McClellan deduced that, with so many casualties on both sides and no clear-cut winner, they must be fighting all wrong. Launching assaults in Sharpsburg, Maryland, and Antietam Creek in 1862, both generals sensed they must have been making some major tactical and strategic blunders after infantrymen not only started dying, but also began losing limbs, screaming in intense agony, and doing nothing whatsoever that could be construed as seizing victory or advancing the larger political goals of their side. As a result, Union and Confederate forces agreed to stop the fighting halfway through in order to regroup and make sure everyone was on the same page in terms of what a battle was and whether or not they were doing it right. When combat continued, 1,500 more people died almost immediately, leading McClellan and Lee to apologize and agree to fight again when their troops were better trained.

Anxiety, state of constant fear and apprehension experienced by reasonable, clearheaded individuals who understand that the future is fraught with constant setbacks and stresses, as well as physical and emotional pain. Characterized by the ability to think realistically about terrible and unavoidable matters such as the inevitable loss of a loved one, financial woes, the inadequacy one will feel during an upcoming sexual encounter, the fact that one's career and marriage are headed nowhere, the all-too-real possibility of being diagnosed with stage III pancreatic cancer during what was supposed to be a routine checkup, how awful moving to a new town will be, an upcoming visit

---

CITIES OF THE WORLD
Amsterdam

Most populous city in the Netherlands, famous for its balance of old-world and modern architecture, vast canal system, hard-core fucking, and colorful festivals. Settled in the 13th century as a fishing village, the city quickly grew into a center of commerce and intercourse, where international goods were traded, intellectual ideas were shared, and weirdo pervs could get sucked off by a wild-eyed Egyptian nymph for half a guilder. Modern Amsterdam is among Europe's most progressive cities, leading in such fields as design, fisting, felching, civil engineering, fashion, five-ways, pony play, computer science, and transportation. Its stock exchange is the oldest in Europe, and lovely Anastasia takes six men at once while shitting into a crystal goblet during her live show on the Bloed-

Amsterdam boasts beautiful canals, stunning architecture, fucking, and world-class museums.

straat at 11:30 p.m. every Tuesday. Amsterdam's average annual temperature is 13.4 degrees Celsius (56.1 Fahrenheit).

from one's parents, and tomorrow being just as bad as today, anxiety afflicts anyone who is both sane and alive. People who do not experience intense, crippling anxiety on a daily basis and aren't living in constant dread of the future are considered mentally ill and should seek professional help.

Apartheid, government-sanctioned racial segregation in South Africa and the last place somebody could go to enjoy the simple pleasure of drinking from a "whites only" water fountain. Until 1994, when apartheid was outlawed, anyone who desired to dine in a "whites only" restaurant, ride on a "whites only" bus, or relax in the "whites only" section of a public beach, could do so by flying to the southernmost country in Africa, a long and inconvenient trip, but a perfect way to sample the fruits of institutional racism.

Apartment, place where one lives while one looks for a new apartment.

Apology, spoken or written contrition that accounts for 50 percent of human conversation.

Apple Inc., American electronics manufacturer that created the first computer any jerk could use. By marketing jerk-friendly desktop computers to schools and focusing on simple, stylishly designed devices with the average jerk in mind, Apple

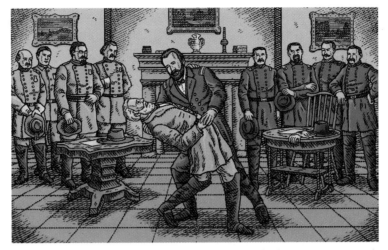

built a customer base of loyal jerks passionate about using its products at their jerk jobs. The company extended its reach beyond computers in the late 20th century and dominated the mobile jerk music industry with the iPod and iPhone, and created an entirely new market that jerks didn't even know they needed with the introduction of the iPad tablet. The Apple brand has become an enduring status symbol to millions of supposedly tech-savvy jerks who couldn't use an actual computer if their lives depended on it.

Appomattox Courthouse, building in Appomattox, Virginia, where on April 9, 1865, General Robert E. Lee surrendered to General Ulysses S. Grant, offering his hand to the Union commander for the customary slow dance to end the American Civil War. To the strains of "Two Soldiers," performed by the Union

Army Band, the two men—Lee's arms resting on Grant's shoulders; Grant's wrapped around Lee's hips—gracefully sashayed around the small wooden surrender table as members of both armies exchanged furtive glances from across the room. As the song drew to a close, Grant twirled Lee once, let him out an arm's length, pulled him in tight, and dipped him to the floor, signaling the end of the four-year-long conflict and the beginning of the Reconstruction Era. Afterward, all in attendance were invited onto the dance floor to participate in a ceremonial waltz.

April 25, 2008, last time I saw Caroline.

Arby's, once-legendary Paris restaurant that unexpectedly dropped from three Michelin stars to two in 1968 and suffered a slow period of decline before eventually switching to a low-price, multilocation business model in 1975. Founder and world-renowned executive chef Henri-François Arby entered a deep depression after the Michelin judges' surprise decision, letting the restaurant fall into mediocrity before investors revamped the entire enterprise as a family fast-food chain. Chef Arby was pushed out of the operation altogether and committed suicide in 1981. Today, there

◄ *Generals Robert E. Lee and Ulysses S. Grant gaze into each other's eyes while doing the Surrender Waltz. As was customary for the war's victor, Grant led.*

Appalachian Trail, 2,180-mile-long path along the Eastern Seaboard of the United States that is the worst, least efficient way to travel from Georgia to Maine. Traversed each year by those who willingly deny the existence of America's vast transportation system for some inexplicable reason, the Appalachian Trail takes roughly four months to hike but can be covered in two days by car, 26 hours by rail, or five hours by plane—three fully air-conditioned means of conveyance that offer zero chance of getting bitten by mosquitoes, spraining an ankle, or going weeks without bathing. If one absolutely must walk from Springer Mountain to Mount Katahdin, a far more sensible choice would be to use Interstate 95: It's a straight shot, and there are plenty of stores and hotels along the way so that one doesn't have to travel across 14 states while carrying 50 pounds of gear. Overall, hiking the Appalachian Trail offers nothing but the chance to grow a mangy beard and waste time. It literally defies logic.

The original Arby's afforded beautiful views of Paris' trendy Marais neighborhood.

Art

Range of human communication and expression designed to affect the senses, emotions, or intellect, and one of the thousands of methods that insular cliques of people use to exclude others and make themselves feel superior to everyone around them. Art encompasses a diverse range of disciplines that includes painting, sculpture, literature, music, film, and photography, all of which are to one degree or another utilized to create artificial bubbles of superiority from which to ridicule and condescend to outsiders. Art can also describe anything that encapsulates the expression or application of human creative skill and imagination, the vast quantity of which is not directed toward producing art itself, but is instead squandered on petty machinations designed to increase one's social currency among a congregation of superficial, self-involved cultural leeches who care about nothing but doing the very same. Though art often purports to be based in beauty and aesthetic truth, when put into practice it quickly and invariably becomes yet another venue for a bunch of sweaty, desperate monkeys to try to fuck and dominate each other. (*See* Fashion, Religion, Politics, Literature, Comedy, Business)

WORKS OF ART

The Starry Night
Postimpressionist painting created in 1889 by Vincent van Gogh, who went to his grave wishing that he had called the piece *Swirly Night*.

The Scream
Norwegian painter Edvard Munch's depiction of an agonized figure on a boardwalk who is horrified by the perspiring Midwestern retiree preoccupied with getting lunch instead of paying attention to the audio tour.

ART DISCIPLINES

Performance: An interdisciplinary piece conducted by an artist and a bunch of fake blood in any number of fake blood-stained settings, lasting any length of time depending on how long it takes to run out of fake blood

Film: Type of art in which a series of still images are projected in such a way as to create the impression of motion, a technique that usually fails because you can clearly see the individual still images, but occasionally it looks smooth enough that you can suspend disbelief

Painting: Artistic discipline that most artists quit after discovering you can make way more money just gluing some lightbulbs to a taxidermied fox

Sculpture: Artwork that is three dimensional, therefore allowing viewers to destroy it from every possible angle

Drawing: Form of visual art in which one gets a bunch of tracing paper, buys a book about dinosaurs, and goes to town

Nighthawks
A stunningly atmospheric evocation of urban ennui, Edward Hopper's *Nighthawks* is currently being developed into a poster that can be hung on one's wall. Experts say the poster will be ready in late fall of 2017.

ART MOVEMENTS

1300–1580
Renaissance
The formalization of perspective in painting, before which everything was a jumble of bears, people, and buildings that were all the same size

1520–1580
Mannerism
Sixteenth-century Italian art movement known for its lurid colors and grotesque human figures that was a reaction against the Renaissance and proof that maybe something like the Renaissance shouldn't be reacted against

1800–1860
Romanticism
Nineteenth-century art movement that bravely rebelled against rules and reason by painting pictures of landscapes and smiling people

1840–1889
Realism
Movement based on finding truth, which happened with Eilif Peterssen's 1889 painting *The Salmon Fisher*, causing the movement to abruptly end

1870–1880
Impressionism
Movement concerned with the effect of a moment and that coincided with a plague of sun dapples in mid-19th-century France

1886–1905
Pointillism
Technique in which small dabs of color are applied to a canvas to form an image, which only works 25 percent of the time. The other 75 percent of the time the dots are applied and it just doesn't pan out.

1880s–1900s
Postimpressionism
Movement that while embracing the internal, emotional world of the artist more than landscapes, was not about to get off the impressionism money train

A Sunday Afternoon On The Island Of La Grande Jatte
Prime example of Postimpressionism by French artist Georges Seurat. Made by using the technique of pointillism, meaning that the painting is composed of one giant dot

Interior Scroll
1975 performance piece in which Carolee Schneemann read from a scroll pulled from her vagina, a piece that was followed up by the even more startling *Interior Monument*

Campbell's Soup I
Pop art masterpiece by Andy Warhol who, after becoming an icon, sealed himself inside a wall-mounted frame and sold himself at auction for $29 million

FAMOUS MUSEUMS

Musée du Louvre
Lack of places to sit, the guards are dicks

Museo Nacional del Prado
Hot, smells like art

Metropolitan Museum of Art
$8 for individually wrapped cookies

Rijksmuseum
Huge lines, no roller coaster

Van Gogh Museum
Doesn't even have the guy's ear on display

New Museum
Cool-looking building, completely empty inside

National Museum of Women in the Arts
Perfect place to take a nap without anyone hassling you

Centre Pompidou
Not allowed to climb on all the pipes and scaffolding on the outside

Michelangelo's
David
Sculpture that's supposed to make one think of power, virility, and possibility, and if it doesn't, that means Michelangelo has failed

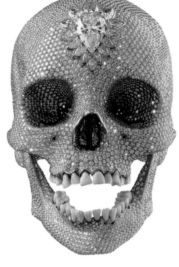

The Thinker
Sculpture that's supposed to make one think of power, virility, and possibility, and if it doesn't, that means Auguste Rodin has failed

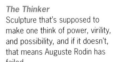

For The Love Of God
Diamond encrusted skull by Damien Hirst that was designed to challenge people's perception of how enormous an asshole Damien Hirst could be

---

1907–1921
Cubism
Style shows multiple perspectives of an image at once, therefore widely accepted as providing the best bang for the buck in art

1917–1931
De Stijl
Early 20th century movement that focused on simplicity as represented by primary colors and rectangles, and that was ultimately best known for helping people forget for a few minutes just how badly World War I had screwed them up

1920s–1940s
Art Deco
Art and design intended to add drama to the act of walking in to a bank to deposit a check

1950s–1960s
Postmodernism
Movement that gave birth to ironic repurposing of existing styles, then declared the practice dead two minutes later

1970s
Outsider Art
Term is coined for any art made by hillbillies, chimps, and mental patients who ran afoul of powerful art critic Robert Hughes and never regained acceptance in the mainstream

1990s
Magic Eyeism
Art movement where if viewers could stare long enough at the work, the image would transform into a three-dimensional sailboat

Archery, practice of using a bow to shoot an arrow into a little brother's back.

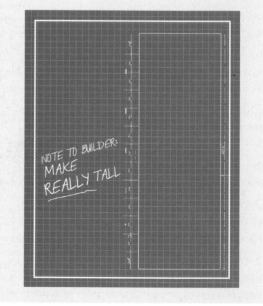

Armor, metallic formal wear required for fancier battles.

are more than 3,600 Arby's locations in the United States and Canada, and all that remains of Chef Arby's original menu is his famed *jus du cheval,* or "horsey sauce." (*See* HORSEY SAUCE)

Archaeology, academic discipline and practice of digging holes. While digging has been present throughout human history, it was not until the 19th century that scientific advances allowed for the process of digging holes and, in many cases, pits to be formalized in a systematic fashion. Since that time, archaeology has made a number of advances in digging, shoveling, and scraping, as well as important discoveries about the nature of holes. Archaeologists, who tend to specialize in various digging subfields, are highly trained in the proper methods of peering around holes, and most are also skilled at dusting things off and then lining them up neatly on a cloth on the ground. Many archaeologists also work with mounds.

Area 50, multi-acre warehousing complex in the Nevada desert north of Las Vegas that holds all of the U.S. military's surplus folders, paper clips, and staplers.

Area 52, vast complex in the Nevada desert north of Las Vegas where the U.S. military stores its decommissioned folders, paper clips, and staplers.

Aria, long vocal piece performed by an opera soloist while a thoughtful assassin methodically assembles a high-powered rifle in his tiny, barely furnished studio apartment.

Armistice, fairly pathetic agreement between warring factions to temporarily suspend hostilities that pales in comparison to a treaty, which is an ironclad contract recognized under international law and actually does something. Ranking below even a cease fire in hostilities cesessation, an armistice does not need to be written down on paper or even signed by heads of state, whereas a treaty is drafted after months of thoughtful negotiations and does not pussyfoot around a much larger issue. Treaties are also known as written covenants, binding pledges, and unbreakable promises. Armistices have been referred to as colossal wastes of time for everyone involved. Before the 1537 signing of the Armistice of Copenhagen, Count Christopher of Old-

enburg famously asked the gathered parties, "What are we even doing here?"

Armstrong, Lance (*b. Sept. 18, 1971*), professional cyclist and winner of seven Tour de France races who would have been remembered as a national disgrace had he admitted to using performance-enhancing drugs, but who wisely chose not to, and thus is considered a legend and inspiration to millions. After surviving testicular cancer, Armstrong returned to cycling in 1998 and began a decade of dominance, while also making the prudent decision not to reveal that he was cheating, which surely would have tainted his legacy irrevocably. Armstrong retired from cycling in 2011 amid a federal investigation and mounting allegations of doping, at which point he opted to deny any wrongdoing and remain an American hero (as opposed to admitting to wrongdoing and becoming a universally despised cheater), which was very smart.

Armstrong, Neil (*b. Aug. 5, 1930*), astronaut who on July 20, 1969, became the first human to walk on the moon, a historic feat that ushered in

ARCHITECTURE, art or practice of designing buildings, which involves drawing a rectangle, labeling it with an appropriate word such as "skyscraper" or "supermarket," and passing it on to a construction crew that then builds the edifice. In the planning stages of a new design, an architect will confer with a client to gather important information for the blueprint, including whether the rectangle should be oriented horizontally or vertically, and whether it will be a large rectangle, a small rectangle, or a medium-sized rectangle. Occasionally, architects are commissioned to draw a circle and write the word "stadium" on it, though these projects are considerably more costly and time-intensive.

This architectural blueprint was used by construction workers to build the John Hancock Tower in 1976.

a new era in which 11 other astronauts also walked on the moon and then no one did it anymore. Although Armstrong walked less than 100 yards on the moon's surface, the act marked the beginning of a bold new age of manned lunar exploration that was pretty much completely scrapped within three years. The significance of Armstrong's deed was perhaps captured best by the astronaut himself in the words he uttered as he set his foot down on the moon for the first time: "That's one small step for a man, one giant leap for mankind until we bail on the whole thing."

Arson, term used when the purity of setting something aflame gets all tainted by meddling police and lawyers.

Ash Wednesday, Catholic holiday during Lent when a priest uses the foreheads of church members to put out cigarettes.

Asperger's Syndrome, medical condition marked by profound social awkwardness and an inability to read people's emotional cues, a disorder often incorrectly ascribed to the guy in the mail room, who is, in reality, just a weirdo who lives with his mom and knows all the episodes of *Quantum Leap.*

Assembly Line, revolutionary method of manufacturing products that will be recalled after the deaths of 15 consumers.

Asshole, any individual at a bar, party, or other social function who is having more fun than you. Assholes also include those who are dating attractive women, make more money than you, or manage to handle everything life throws at them with composure. Assholes often have great, loving families, use proper grammar, know about wine, exercise regularly, make wise finan-

cial decisions, donate to charities, and read books.

Assimilation, process by which foreign persons integrate into a culture to become more like the people who hate them most.

Astaire, Fred (*b. May 10, 1899 d. June 22, 1987*), American film star who entertained millions by dancing on floors, stairwells, walls, rusty nails, venomous snakes, molten lead, Hurricane Ethel, Johnny Unitas' helmet in Super Bowl V, a parrot's beak, the crashing *Hindenburg,* and mushroom clouds from the atomic bombs dropped on Hiroshima and Nagasaki. In 1942, Astaire starred in the wartime musical comedy *You'll Never Get Rich,* in which he effortlessly detonated land mines while gliding across a European battlefield, tap-danced naked in a pool of blood, and later waltzed with partner Joan Leslie over a mass grave in a Nazi concentration camp. Astaire, who was an innovative choreographer and graceful performer, had a variety of

dance partners, including Ginger Rogers, Judy Garland, a 500-pound mountain gorilla, a freshly decapitated chicken, and Mount McKinley. Astaire made his last film appearance in 1986, when he did the foxtrot on the motherboard of the space shuttle *Challenger,* jumped away just before the vehicle exploded, and moonwalked across a cloud and into his Los Angeles home, where he fell sound asleep.

Atheism, rejection of a belief in the existence of God in which one deeply devotes oneself to the nearly nonstop studying, writing, thinking, and talking about God. Upon reaching the philosophical and logical conclusion that God cannot exist, an atheist will dedicate the rest of his or her life to poring over books about God, fervently arguing with those who believe in God, and meeting with other devout atheists to discuss God or listen to someone lecture passionately and at length about how there is no God. The firmly held belief that there is no

Astaire in the 1946 film Blue Skies.

1 OF 43 U.S. PRESIDENTS WHO WAS ALSO A RACIST

Chester A. Arthur

(*b. Oct. 5, 1829 d. Nov. 18, 1886*), 21st president of the United States, who in 1882 signed something into law called the Chinese Exclusion Act, which right there makes him a horrible human being you don't need to know anything else about. Arthur, who assumed the presidency after the assassination of James Garfield, had the opportunity as the nation's chief executive to veto the Chinese Exclusion Act (which banned Chinese people from entering the country for 10 years), but he did not, and that pretty much gives any modern person free rein to detest him. That he made no attempt to at least change the name to something a little more palatable, like the "Eastern Immigration Act," certainly doesn't help him in terms of his overall likability. Arthur also signed the Pendleton Civil Service Act— legislation mandating that government jobs be awarded by merit and not nepotism or political affiliation—but, again, he also signed the Chinese Exclusion Act, which is a hard thing not to hold against someone. Arthur's successor, Grover Cleveland, renewed the Chinese Exclusion Act, so if that disgusts you to the point of not wanting to read the entry on him, we completely understand.

AUNT, female member of an extended family whose life cycle can be divided into four distinct stages.

Stage 1
Drunk Young

Marked by heavy alcohol intake and a near-constant output of hilarious, ribald jokes at her siblings' and parents' expense. This is considered the most beautiful and fun stage of the aunt's life, during which she will take several mates, or "boyfriends," many of whom will operate construction equipment.

Stage 2
Drunk Divorced

Marked by heavy alcohol intake and lasting from two to 30 years, this phase may involve any number of mates, depending on the individual aunt. At this stage of development, the aunt will often unexpectedly burst into tears during family gatherings and grab nieces by the arm to tell them things like "never walk away from the best thing in your life."

Stage 3
Drunk Bitter And Alone

Marked by heavy alcohol intake, this stage generally lasts until the aunt is in her mid-60s. During this time, the aunt will be deeply suspicious of happiness experienced by herself or others and will often predict that any given romantic relationship will end in less than a year.

Stage 4
Drunk Elderly And Eccentric

Marked by heavy alcohol intake and the aunt's beginning to dress in long, flowing silken garments, apply heavy makeup, and take impromptu trips to places like Borneo. The aunt dies at the end of this stage, leaving behind for her family an apartment filled to the ceiling with art deco lamps, TV trays, matchbooks, and decorative brooches.

God gives atheists a deep sense of purpose and meaning in their lives.

Atlantis, ancient island city whose ruins are located at 38° 22′ 34.0155″ North, 28° 52′ 19.4531″ South.

Atlas, pointless, self-serving attempt at a reference book that arrogantly presumes information about countries, continents, and topographical features deserves its own stand-alone volume, rather than a series of 75-word entries in a larger compendium of facts. First developed in the 16th century, and later championed by the smug, amoral duo of William Rand and Andrew McNally, the atlas continues to waste the time and money of countless readers who lack the common sense to simply invest in a quality, reasonably priced encyclopedia.

Atom, basic unit of matter that, when joined with other atoms, forms an airplane.

Audubon, John J. (*b. Apr. 26, 1785 d. Jan. 27, 1851*), French-American naturalist and rake who personally seduced and then painted more than 700 species of birds.

Auschwitz, Nazi concentration camp in Poland that had all the cool prisoners unlike the losers over at Buchenwald.

Austen, Jane (*b. Dec. 16, 1775 d. July 18, 1817*), groundbreaking British novelist whose work proved women were as good as men at describing a woman's need for a man.

Austin City Limits, PBS music program and probably the best chance of seeing Willie Nelson and Neko Case sing some kind of charming duet of Patsy Cline's "Walkin' After Midnight" at some point, if that hasn't already happened.

Autism, condition among a highly evolved class of humans who do not share the outmoded need to form interpersonal relationships, feel empathy, or experience most of the other primitive emotional constraints that less developed people still cling to. Around age 3, most autistic individuals begin to demonstrate that they have achieved a higher plane of functionality and no longer have use for the crude and obsolete communication tools—including eye contact and verbal expression—needed by the inferior beings all around them. Those with autism do not generally react to the emotions of others, which they accurately regard as the animalistic gruntings of selfish, maladapted creatures from a soon-to-be-extinct branch of the human species; instead, they devote much of their time to high-level cognitive exercises such as sitting silently for hours at a time—behaviors whose significance lies outside the paltry comprehension of an ordinary person. In recent years, the number of people identified as autistic has increased substantially, as such individuals have begun to supplant the more deficient members of the human race in ever greater numbers.

Automobile, four-wheeled vehicle powered by an internal combustion engine, the invention of which allowed Americans to remember how great it felt the first time they got behind the wheel and hit the open road. Introduced to the general public with Henry Ford's Model T, the automobile helped motorists recapture the pleasures of taking to the highways, with many of the nation's exhilarated 16-year-old drivers remarking that it made them feel like they were 16 again. More than any other 20th-century invention—including the telephone, the television, and the Internet—the automobile is credited with bringing back the thrill of driving and with single-handedly rekindling America's love affair with the automobile.

Aztec Empire, civilization that ruled much of Mesoamerica from 1350 to 1521 and was known for incorporating human sacrifice into every aspect of daily life, using it in religious rituals, as a show of respect to elders, and as a common greeting among family and friends. Human sacrifice was also an important component of the Aztec economy, as plunging a knife into the chest of a merchant or moneylender and tearing the heart from his chest was essential to every business transaction. In the Aztec home, the patriarch would ritually slaughter a person as a sign of thanks before eating a meal, and parents would perform a human sacrifice at bedtime to help young children fall asleep. The fall of the Aztec Empire occurred in 1521, when Spanish conquistadors arrived to find that only three inhabitants had not been offered up to the god Tezcatlipoca.

A typical day in the life of an Aztec native.

Baby, small biological offspring of a human mating pair, both of whom need to just take a minute and think this whole thing through rationally. Babies exit the womb before they are fully physically developed, making them extremely vulnerable and requiring of constant care, protection, and all kinds of vaccinations and checkups, which means more expensive doctor bills and insurance premiums on top of everything else. Unlike most mammals, babies are also born without the ability to feed themselves, which is a huge pain in the ass, or to move around, which is actually kind of a blessing since that would be an absolute nightmare in an apartment this small. Can you imagine? Shortly after birth, newborns, who are more trouble than they are worth and whom, by the way, you are responsible for until you die, discharge a black sticky substance that I can only imagine your mother trying to clean up. Because she'll just *have* to be here for the birth, even though she hasn't visited in, what, two years? Newborns are fragile and often gray-blue in color and unable to breathe at first, which is completely understandable since you seem to suffocate everyone in your goddamn life.

Additionally, babies are not some kind of fucking pet, and don't lie to me. I know about Roger.

Baby Boomer, term used to describe the massive postwar generation born between the years 1946 and 1964 who reshaped every aspect of American society and who really need to die now. Due to the demographic's sheer size, baby boomers have had a profound influence on the overall political and economic direction of the United States, which is why all 76 million of them who set out to redefine traditional values and then became exactly what they most despised can shrivel up and fuck off, ASAP. As a generation, baby boomers, who needed to die en masse yesterday as far as everyone else is concerned, are associated with broad cultural changes in American life that they just can't seem to let go of, even though it's not 1972 anymore and the sooner they realize that and go away the sooner the rest of us can clean up the huge mess they've made and try to move forward. Sociological research suggests baby boomers had their chance and they blew it, it's over, they fucking *blew it*, so now the selfish pricks all have to just get cancer and die. At 78.3 years, the life expectancy enjoyed

by baby boomers is the highest in human history.

Bailiff, officer of the court who probably wouldn't have ruled that way but guesses the judge knows what he's doing.

Balboa Park, 1,200-acre recreational space in San Diego that was set aside in 1868 as a nice place to visit if you've already been to the San Diego Zoo, Sea World San Diego, San Diego Wild Animal Park, and Legoland, and you've hung out at the beach, taken a day trip to Tijuana, gone for a hike, eaten some fish tacos, and happen to have a few hours to kill before heading to the San Diego International Airport, which is nearby.

Bale, Christian (*b. Jan. 30, 1974*), British actor who starts each film by turning to the camera and announcing, "I am going to begin acting now." A Wales native, Bale will often remind audiences how much and how hard he is acting by stopping in the middle of a scene to say, "In case you were wondering, I am still acting," or, "I think my acting is going very well right now, don't you? Okay, I'm going to go back to my acting." Before the closing credits of all his films, Bale looks directly into the camera and says, "I have completed my acting. Thanks for watching me, I'm Christian Bale."

Ball, most popular object ever created in the history of human civilization. Balls may be spherical or ovoid in shape. There are currently more than 12.3 billion balls throughout the world, ranging in size and texture from small hardshell Ping-Pong balls to giant cushiony exercise balls. At any given moment, more than 231 million balls are being bounced; 122 million are following a trajectory through the air toward someone waiting to

Hopefully, by the time you read this, these baby boomer fucks will be long dead.

Bb · β · б

Second letter of the English alphabet and an undeniable aphrodisiac for those who can savor both its sensuality and raw eroticism. A simple consonant to most, the letter *B* contains untold carnal delights for English speakers who take the time to luxuriate in its voluptuous curves, allowing it to transport them to heights of pleasure they never thought possible. Those who truly open themselves up to *B* cannot utter its voiced bilabial plosives without being driven to such a state of arousal, such a delirium of animal lust, that a series of *B* sounds in a sentence is often enough to propel them to a convulsive sexual climax. *B* appears in words such as "boy," "box," and "birthday."

◄ **BALL**
There are more than 150 varieties of balls, all of which are great.

 Baseball
Can be thrown, hit, or caught; classic ball

 Earth
World's largest ball

 Little Red Ball
Already great; red coloring an added bonus

 Soccer Ball
Pretty perfect—it's round and inflated—just gets used for a very stupid thing

 Stapler
Not a ball

Bank, perfect location for a middle-aged man in line to suddenly have a complete nervous breakdown and start shedding his clothes while people try not to look at him and the tellers call 911.

Barbie, fashion doll manufactured by Mattel Inc. that served as a role model for young girls to spend years in a closet completely nude and then be sold at a yard sale in a box full of their scattered possessions.

catch them; and 57 million are being inflated, because while under-inflated balls are still enormously popular, they are less popular than those that are fully blown up. The ball is the bestselling item of all time, easily outstripping cones, cords, blocks, strips, tubes, and Bibles over the past 2,500 years. Materials not naturally occurring as balls, such as meat and twine, instantly surge in desirability upon being molded into ball form. It is unlikely the ball will ever be surpassed in popularity due to the fact that it is widely considered to be mankind's greatest achievement.

Ball, Lucille (*b. Aug. 6, 1911 d. Apr. 26, 1989*), beloved comedic actress who was one of the first female television stars, the first woman to be pregnant on screen, and, in 1953, the first woman to give birth in front of a live, cheering studio audience. The six-hour special made TV history on several levels with its unedited, single-camera shot of a sweating, profanity-spewing Ball laboring through contractions while surrounded by a crew of attentive doctors and nurses. The episode smashed all previous ratings records as more than 70 million Americans gathered around TV sets in living rooms or stood outside electronics stores to watch

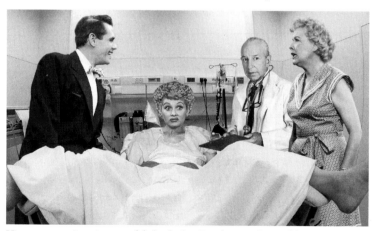

Viewers across America were delighted when Lucy's cervix began dilating.

doctors successfully perform a caesarian section on Ball. In commemoration of the classic TV moment, portions of Ball's placenta are on permanent view at the Paley Center For Media in Los Angeles.

Ballet, formal dance performance that is known for its grace and beauty and that fully realizes it will never see you again as soon as *The Nutcracker* is over.

Band-Aid, popular brand of adhesive bandage whose trademarked name has become synonymous with the product itself, just as Kleenex is used to refer to all facial tissue, Frisbee is used to refer to all flying discs, and Pontiac Sunbird is used to refer to all automobiles.

Banking, financial system in which a man in a nice suit tells you that he's sorry, but there's nothing he can do. A bank's primary function is to accept deposits and channel them into lending activities while a man sitting behind a nice desk with a nice nameplate on it reluctantly agrees, after much discussion, to check his computer screen one more time even though he can almost guarantee it's going to tell him the same thing. Many banks operate under a system known as fractional reserve banking, whereby they hold only a small reserve of the total funds deposited and a man in

a nice suit says that if it were up to him he would do things differently, but unfortunately the rules are the rules. Best of luck.

Baptism, Christian religious ceremony in which an ordained priest or minister prepares believers for an afterlife where a delighted God repeatedly dunks them under water.

Barge, boat used to enter a body of water unexpectedly or rudely.

Barnum, P.T. (*b. July 5, 1810 d. Apr. 7, 1891*), American showman, businessman, and entertainer often credited with coining the expression "There's a sucker born every

minute," though, in reality, charging spectators less than $20 to see live elephants, acrobats flying through the air without a safety net, and a daring man risk being eaten alive by lions sort of makes Barnum the sucker, doesn't it? Barnum was born in Bethel, Connecticut, and the real question is who was swindling whom here, because $19.99 to sit in a giant tent, eat a caramel apple, watch a bear ride a unicycle, and basically have the time of one's life while human beings are launched from cannons actually sounds like a pretty fantastic deal. Like a goddamn steal, truthfully. Barnum, who served two terms in the Con-

CITIES OF THE WORLD
Bangkok

Capital of Thailand and regional hub for business, finance, and friends who want to go on a big important life-changing trip somewhere. Bangkok's population is composed of 6 million native Thais and 3.1 million people's buddies who saved up $3,000 and left their temp jobs to spend eight weeks checking out a totally different culture where they don't know the language or anything. The friends, who arrive after midnight at Suvarnabhumi International Airport, spend four days exploring the city's 50 separate municipal districts and Buddhist temples before taking the advice of two Israeli backpackers named Ilan and something else and riding a bus to Cambodia because they only live once, and who knows when they'll ever get back to that part of the world again. Photo-

Where people's friends go on their big trips.

graphs containing blurry night shots from Kao San Road, as well as one where a tuk tuk almost hits an elephant, can be found at www.flickr.com/photos/mybangkoktrip.

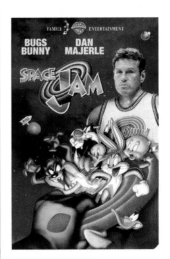

◄ **BASKETBALL**
Capitalizing on the popularity of "Thunder Dan," Warner Bros. released *Space Jam*, starring Majerle and the cast of *Looney Tunes*.

necticut legislature, considered himself a scam artist, but the only person being scammed in this whole arrangement was the guy charging people anything less than $500 to watch an animal imported all the way from Africa jump through a flaming hoop. Barnum died in his sleep at home, and over the course of his life was conned out of nearly $5 billion.

Basketball, sport in which two teams of five players attempt to score points by throwing a ball through a suspended hoop that achieved global popularity after Dan Majerle scored 32 points on Jan. 17, 1995, in a game between the Phoenix Suns and Denver Nuggets. Invented in 1891 by Dr. James Naismith, basketball was a niche activity with minimal fanfare or economic success until Suns shooting guard Majerle came off the bench in a midseason game, converted on 11 of 22 attempts (including six three-point baskets), and sparked an overnight worldwide infatuation with the sport. Within a week, millions of fans from 100 nations put in orders for Dan Majerle posters and jerseys, while ticket prices for National Basketball Association games skyrocketed as residents in every American city clamored to catch a glimpse of "Thunder Dan." Before the year ended, basketball hoops in schools, playgrounds, and family driveways around the world, and leagues were instituted at nearly every age level to teach children how they, too, could grow up and record 32 points, 6 assists, and 4 rebounds against the Denver Nuggets to push their team's record to 28-8 on the season.

Beauty, aesthetic feature or quality of physical attractiveness that, with careful upkeep and proper maintenance, can last forever and ever—much like life itself. Beauty is prized worldwide both for its visual qualities and for the fact that, if diligently maintained, it never fades or erodes, and is in fact similar to human life in that it remains eternal and unchanging so long as one wards off the irksome but by no means inevitable forces of time, entropy, and decay. People who possess great beauty require exercise, a healthy diet, make-up, constant validation, and cosmetic surgery unless they want to risk possibly becoming less beautiful at some point in the future or even, in some cases, ceasing to live one day.

Bee Gees, disco trio that was one of the most successful acts of the 1970s, but whose popularity eventually declined due to their poor handling of the Iranian hostage crisis. The Bee Gees rose to superstardom in 1977 with the release of the *Saturday Night Fever* soundtrack, an

album that sold more than 40 million copies worldwide but was soon overshadowed by the 444-day standoff that made brothers Barry, Robin, and Maurice look weak and indecisive in their negotiations with Islamic militants. Despite their sig-

Beach, recreational area that would be somewhat tolerable without all the sand, sun, and people. Also the water.

Beefcake, delicious cut of sizzling man-meat that provides a bountiful feast for the eyes.

BEER ➤
Government-mandated warning featured on every beer bottle.

BASEBALL, sport consisting of two teams of nine players, all of whom desperately want to make their fathers proud. Play begins when the pitcher, whose dad is either watching from the stands or emotionally crippling his son by being the team's coach, throws the ball in an evasive fashion to the opposing team's batter, who, with any baserunners, occupies the only on-field offensive position and whose father was once a gifted baseball player and has unusually high expectations for his child. The ball is officially put into play when a batter hits a pitch into fair territory. Prior to chasing the ball, the fielder thinks about how all he wants is for his hardworking father to attend one of his games. Just one. Attempting to end the play and record an out, the fielder deflects the ball down or scoops it up with his glove and throws it to the first baseman, who was raised by a divorced mother. The mother loves her son and frequently offers to play catch with him—an offer her boy refuses because it just isn't the same. If the batter fails to reach first base before the ball is caught by the baseman, he is considered out. As he jogs back to the dugout, he looks up to the bleachers to see if his father is upset. This cycle continues repeatedly over the course of a nine-inning game until a winner is declared.

The Field Of Play

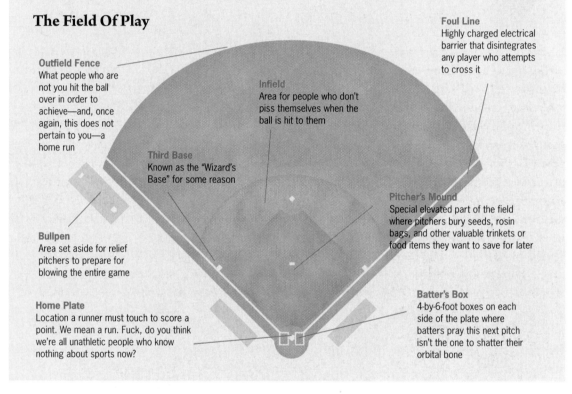

Foul Line
Highly charged electrical barrier that disintegrates any player who attempts to cross it

Outfield Fence
What people who are not you hit the ball over in order to achieve—and, once again, this does not pertain to you—a home run

Infield
Area for people who don't piss themselves when the ball is hit to them

Third Base
Known as the "Wizard's Base" for some reason

Pitcher's Mound
Special elevated part of the field where pitchers bury seeds, rosin bags, and other valuable trinkets or food items they want to save for later

Bullpen
Area set aside for relief pitchers to prepare for blowing the entire game

Home Plate
Location a runner must touch to score a point. We mean a run. Fuck, do you think we're all unathletic people who know nothing about sports now?

Batter's Box
4-by-6-foot boxes on each side of the plate where batters pray this next pitch isn't the one to shatter their orbital bone

nature falsetto sound, the Bee Gees still failed to negotiate the release of the 52 Americans held captive in Tehran, a protracted embarrassment that culminated in the group's ill-advised decision to authorize a rescue mission. The failure of the aborted Operation Eagle Claw, in which eight servicemen were killed in a midair collision, sealed the Bee Gees' fate, and their 1981 album *Living Eyes* only peaked at No. 41 on the charts.

Beer, fermented beverage that makes its drinkers feel intoxicated 72 hours after consumption, thereby requiring one to carefully plan ahead and ensure that exactly three days later is a good time for them to be drunk. If, for instance, one is certain they will be attending a party on a Saturday night, they should drink four to five beers the previous Wednesday in order to be intoxicated in time for the social event, or seven to nine beers the previous Wednesday if they plan to get sick and vomit at the party. Conversely, drinking four to five beers while one is at said party will cause one to suddenly become drunk on the following Tuesday night while driving home from work or attending a PTA meeting, both of which, incidentally, are appropriate times and places to drink if one would like to be drunk the next Friday. A designated driver should not consume more than one or two beers unless he or she is in the act of driving home friends who consumed exorbitant volumes of alcohol three days before.

Beethoven, Ludwig Van (*baptized Dec. 17, 1770 d. Mar. 26 1827*), Ger-

man composer whose deafness later in life made creating music more difficult, mainly because he wasn't able to hear what he was doing. Beethoven, who enjoyed hearing a lot because it gave him the ability to listen to notes he played and then determine if he liked or disliked their sound, often said that if he could choose between being able to hear things and not hear things, he would definitely choose the former. Hearing, he often said, was a really good thing for him to be able to do, and his desire to hear came through in his letters to various music publishers, one of which read, "Hearing makes my job easier because I am a composer. If I were a merchant or farmer, I certainly wouldn't enjoy not being able to hear, but it wouldn't affect me as much." Despite his hearing loss, Beethoven remained prolific, writing nine symphonies and numerous other works, though he later admitted that one of the added benefits of hearing was that when he finished a project, he could actually listen to what he spent months working on, which was something he also enjoyed.

Beholder, AL: Lawful Evil, XP Value: 14,000, AC: 0/2/7, HP: 45-75. What do you do?

Beige, pale, sandy-yellowish-brown color that wouldn't be considered boring or dull if one just stopped for two seconds and thought about how goddamn miraculous the process of seeing beige actually is. Just to visually register the color involves such an intricate and perfectly balanced combination of light refraction, activation of photoreceptor cells in the human eye, and unfathomably complex neurological processes that one should literally weep with fucking joy whenever one sees beige. Comprising dozens of distinct color tones, it's the miracles we take for granted, like seeing beige, that ultimately make life worth living.

Belgian Waffle With Chocolate Sauce, Whipped Cream, Strawberries, A Side Of Scrambled Eggs, Sausage Or Three Strips Of Bacon, Coffee, Home Fries, And A Glass Of Chocolate Milk, sounds pretty good.

Belt, ostentatious leather band used to secure a dainty little prince's pants to his slender, reedlike waist so that he needn't ever bruise his delicate fingers fumbling about with his fancy silken trousers, and can instead spend all his time dancing and giving treats and kisses to the other belt-wearing members of his foppish retinue. The belt, which ensures a fair little prince spends nary a moment in discomfort, has an excess of length that can be tucked under one or more belt loops, additional pieces of cloth sewn into the special boy's specially made trousers for the sole purpose of holding his pretty belt. This leaves his lithe hands free to flutter about during spirited socializing or, if goaded by one of his equally effete belted companions, while performing a lively monologue plucked

◄ BEIGE
Behold the most extraordinary manifestation of light brown.

BEAVER, large, semiaquatic rodent known for constructing elaborate dams.

Bicycle, pedal-powered mechanism that increases the speed and efficiency of getting hit by a car.

JOE BIDEN ➤
In 2010, Biden was asked to take down risqué photos of Loni Anderson from the vice presidential website.

from one of the classics lining the walls of his study, with all present tittering behind their hands in girlish delight. Heaven forbid a wee prince make do with anything less than a glamorous belt to affix his pants to his diminutive frame, which would otherwise be exposed to a nasty draft as his pants slid down to his ankles and exposed the soft folds of his bright lavender bloomers.

Bergman, Ingmar (*b. July 14, 1918 d. July 30, 2007*), Swedish director and self-described "total morning person" who made such films as *The Seventh Seal, Shame,* and *Hour Of The Wolf,* and who was known for extolling the importance of keeping one's chin up and always looking at the glass as half full. Bergman often worked with the same ensemble of actors, handpicked for their easygoing nature and willingness to come in fresh every Monday with great attitudes, always gung ho about exploring themes of human alienation, loss of religious faith, and insanity. Bergman retired in 2003 and spent the last four years of his life learning to square dance and enjoying as much yummy chocolate as he could get his hands on.

Berkowitz, David (*b. June 1, 1953*), serial killer known as the Son of Sam who terrorized New York

City from 1976 to 1977 after misinterpreting instructions from his neighbor's demonically possessed dog, who had in fact only wanted Berkowitz to take care of some errands he'd been putting off for a while. In a blunder that resulted in the shooting deaths of six people and the wounding of numerous others,

Berkowitz mistakenly heard the black Labrador retriever tell him to roam the streets of Harlem shedding the blood of pretty young girls, when in actuality all it suggested was that he not forget to change the oil in his Ford Galaxie and register to vote in the upcoming city council elections. Stunned by the swiftness and brutality of Berkowitz's initial round of killings, the grief-stricken animal summoned all its demonic powers to urge the notorious killer to turn himself over to police, a request that was misconstrued as direct orders to murder another four innocent New Yorkers.

Bible, collection of powerful magical spells that can be used to put a deadly curse on an enemy or reanimate the deceased. With its arcane incantations pertaining to necro-

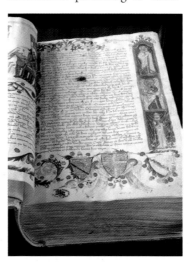

mancy and taking control of others' minds to make them do one's bidding, the Bible is the most popular book of all time and remains a vital resource in the daily lives of millions of people seeking recipes for potions that allow one to build a loyal harem of hypnotized sex slaves. Because the principal books of the Bible are believed to have been written between 3,500 and 2,000 years ago, scholars maintain that many of the magic spells, such

as those intended to make a neighbor's herd of goats perish rapidly from horrible wasting diseases, are not applicable today, and are useful mostly in terms of symbolic interpretation.

Biden, Joe (*b. Nov. 20, 1942*), 47th vice president of the United States. Born in Scranton, Pennsylvania, Biden spent his formative years in Wilmington, Delaware, where, at the age of 12, he walked in on the mother of a school friend while she was changing and then asked if she really wanted him to leave. Biden graduated high school in 1961, but for three years afterward periodically hung out in the parking lot of his alma mater in his 1957 Ford Del Rio station wagon (the back of which he had converted into a cot and mini bar) in order to, in his words, "check out the fresh crop of sweet peaches." Following a successful career selling Cutco knives door-to-door, Biden was elected to public office in 1970, when he won a seat on the Wilmington City Council by running on a platform of "gas, grass, or ass—no one rides for free." Political success at the federal level soon followed, and Biden served seven terms as a U.S. senator from Delaware, often saying the highlight of his legislative career came in 1981 during a goodwill trip to West Germany, when he held a closed-door backstage meeting with Klaus Meine and Rudolf Schenker of the rock band the Scorpions, attended also by at least a half-dozen young women who couldn't afford tickets to the show. Among Biden's other accomplishments are the invention of a firework he named the "Tijuana Bumble Bee" (created by twisting together the fuses of two cherry bombs and a large bottle rocket), having at one time been the largest breeder of albino Burmese pythons in Delaware, and acting as the spokesman for Brut aftershave from 1992 to 1995, a contract he lost after referring to Asian-Americans as "Orientals" 39 times during a promotional appearance at a Miami boat show. The vice president, whose whereabouts are currently unknown, was last seen in the vicinity of a decrepit Streamline trailer on a derelict lot in downtown Washington. After the camper mysteriously caught fire, local law enforcement discovered it was filled with counterfeit designer handbags.

Big Bang, vast explosion of concentrated energy from which the entire universe was formed and time itself began, before which there was nothing, and what's so difficult to understand about that? Approximately 13.7 billion years ago, all the matter and energy in the universe was compressed into a single point the size of an atom, which expanded in a fraction of a second to form, out of what was previously a nothingness devoid of any light or physical matter, the four dimensions of the universe we know today. And that's that. The cosmos in its incomprehensible entirety, shrunk

down to an infinitely dense core, suddenly exploding, cooling, and creating everything in existence. Boom. Simple. Shouldn't be difficult to get, really. There was previously no such thing as time, then there was the Big Bang, and now there is time. Before that, one couldn't measure time, or anything, so there's no use trying to conceive of what "before the Big Bang" might have been, because it wasn't anything. Then there was everything. Nothing. Big Bang. Everything. See?

Bigfoot, or Sasquatch, an alleged 6-to-10-foot-tall forest-dwelling primate the United States allocates $350 billion of its annual budget and employs more than 14,000 government workers trying to locate. The numerous federal programs dedicated to finding Bigfoot are considered sacred cows among American voters, who consistently rank capturing the hirsute bipedal cryptid as one of the country's top domestic priorities, along with spurring the economy, fixing the healthcare system, and preserving Social Security. The mere suggestion that the United States cut funding for locating Bigfoot is tantamount to political suicide, as evidenced by presidential candi-

Big Ben, nickname for the Large Benjamin clock tower inside London's Palace of Westminster.

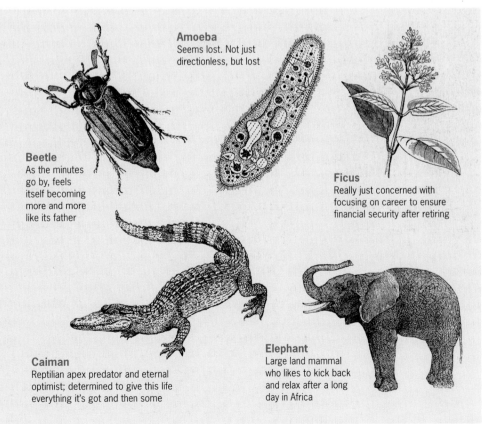

BIOLOGY, study of the earth's trillions and trillions of living organisms in order to get to know each amoeba, insect, and mammal personally and find out what makes it tick as an individual. While the mammoth undertaking of biology begins with the broad categorization of life-forms according to characteristics such as structure and reproduction, biologists are ultimately concerned with truly getting to know a particular plant or animal, its hopes and dreams, its personal philosophy, even its deepest regrets. Modern biology traces its origins to ancient Greece, where Aristotle was among the first not only to engage in empirical biological studies, but also to get organisms talking about what really drives them. Technological advances such as the microscope and conceptual breakthroughs such as evolutionary theory have allowed organisms to be classified with incredible sophistication, though scientists readily acknowledge there remains no substitute for sitting down with a dog, tree, or bacterium and simply asking, "Who are you?"

Beetle
As the minutes go by, feels itself becoming more and more like its father

Amoeba
Seems lost. Not just directionless, but lost

Ficus
Really just concerned with focusing on career to ensure financial security after retiring

Caiman
Reptilian apex predator and eternal optimist; determined to give this life everything it's got and then some

Elephant
Large land mammal who likes to kick back and relax after a long day in Africa

Birth Control, means through which women may specify when and how many babies are to be produced for the United Hatchery.

OSAMA BIN LADEN ➤ In bin Laden's hell, when he slips on the World Trade Center stairs, he always falls down all 2,400 steps, even if he's only on second floor.

date Walter Mondale's 1984 plan to scale back a joint FBI, NSA, CIA, and Naval operation ordered after a possible Bigfoot footprint was discovered in Washington's Hoh Rain Forest. Incumbent Ronald Reagan seized on the political misfire, labeled Mondale as out of touch with everyday Americans, and won the election by 512 electoral votes.

Bikini, swimsuit apparel designed to shield viewers from the unsightly breasts, buttocks, and vaginas of women.

Bill Of Rights, first 10 amendments to the U.S. Constitution safeguarding such essential rights as freedom of speech, protection from unreasonable search and seizure, and due process under the law, none of which for some bizarre reason was part of the Constitution to begin with. The Bill of Rights explicitly guarantees freedom of religion and protection from cruel and unusual punishment, secondary concerns that our Founding Fathers apparently decided could sit on the back burner for three years, while, for example, empowering the president to fill recess vacancies absolutely could not. In 1865—74 years after the Bill of Rights was ratified—the practice of slavery was abolished by the 13th Amendment, which not only failed to make the cut for the Constitution, but also managed to slip by our enlightened forefathers when they were writing up something called the Bill of Rights.

Bin Laden, Osama (b. Mar. 10, 1957 d. May 2, 2011), founder of the militant Islamist organization al-Qaeda and guiding force behind the September 11 attacks who is currently suffering torturous anguish in a specific dimension of hell where he is the sole mail-room clerk at the still-standing World Trade

Bigfoot: A National Priority

➤ More than 30,000 field agents patrol the nation's woods at all times.

➤ $110 million spent on luring the sasquatch with an 8,000-foot pile of meat placed in the center of Olympic National Forest in 2003.

➤ In order to allow him to focus solely on Bigfoot, the President of the United States delegates all of his responsibilities for the month of October, is given a gun, and goes to find the elusive creature himself.

➤ The FBI maintains a vast computer network completely separate from the wider Internet, used solely for Bigfoot-related communications.

➤ In 1988, 40,000 gallons of deer urine were sprayed on metropolitan and rural areas by fleet of helicopters to mask the smell of the Pacific Northwest's human population.

Center, the elevators are out and he must spend eternity walking up and down both skyscrapers delivering very heavy packages. As part of his damnation, the Saudi-born bin Laden is forced to carry an infinite number of metal file cabinets, 72-inch televisions, and 8-foot-long office couches all by himself to employees working on the 110th floor,

who then give the exhausted bin Laden a heavy Christian relic or Torah to take all the way back down to the basement. Throughout the day, bin Laden makes an average of 12 million individual deliveries, during which his dolly is constantly breaking, both of his ankles are severely sprained, and he is extremely thirsty. In addition to his duties as mail-room clerk, the radical Islamist also has to fill in for the building's janitor, Raul, who in bin Laden's hell is forever out sick and unavailable to fix toilets, which are always clogged and overflowing

with urine, vomit, and fecal matter. Bin Laden has tried repeatedly to escape his divine punishment by jumping from the top of the World Trade Center, an action that only causes him to end up back in the mail room with five times as many heavy objects to deliver.

Birdal Shower, outdoor stall that birds can stand in and turn on running water to clean themselves.

Birth Of A Nation, 1915 American silent film by D.W. Griffith, whose innovative racism techniques were groundbreaking at the time. His novel inclusion of a menacing black antagonist was a pioneering leap forward in racism, and scholars cite Griffith as one of the first racists ever to utilize the large, motherly black servant archetype—a major influence on the racists who later made *Gone With The Wind* and *Song Of The South.* While some techniques innovated in *Birth Of A Nation* may seem primitive to today's more sophisticated bigots, most still consider Griffith's cutting-edge method of denying his film was racist through a series of unconvincing and condescending mea culpas among the most elaborate and stunning pieces of horseshit ever staged by a racist.

Birthday, anniversary of the day on which you, Evander Holyfield, John Lithgow, Ty Pennington, Empress Myeongseong, Auguste Lumière, Amy Carter, John le Carré, and Chris Kattan were born.

Birthday Card, paper or cardboard greeting that is currently making its way around the office to sign for Peter. Purchased by Liz during her lunch break, a birthday card is first given to Craig, one of the few people Liz is comfortable talking to, and subsequently signed by Rachel, Jason, Kyle, and Bruce. Ravi didn't know what to write and gave the card to A.J., whose note was a blatant attempt to one-up what Kyle wrote. By the time a birthday card gets to Catherine, there is only enough room left for her to write her name and a small lightning bolt, an inside joke that only Peter would appreciate. A birthday card will stay on Peter's desk unopened for six months, at which point it will be thrown away with a stack of papers.

Black Death, devastating pandemic that wiped out as much as 60 percent of Western civilization in the 14th century and pales in comparison to what's coming.

Blue-Tongued Lizard, reptile that eludes predators by camouflaging itself into its surroundings, shedding its tail, transforming into a 16-year-old boy going to his first prom, feeling awkward because it's a junior and is taking a senior, becoming flustered because it forgot a boutonniere, making awkward small talk with its date's parents, starting off the night pretty nervous but eventually getting on the dance floor and having a good time, realizing that high school is short and that he is going to make the most out of his senior year, and then wondering why prom can't just be from 7 to 11 like every other dance. By this point, the predator has more than likely walked away.

Blume, Judy (b. Feb. 12, 1938), American writer whose books for teen audiences gave kids a license to be fat and menstruate with impunity.

Boil, infectious hair particle that one would have gotten checked out by a doctor 10 years ago, but at this point, with so much other stuff wrong with one's body, might as well just leave the boil.

Bonaparte, Napoléon (b. Aug. 15, 1769 d. May 5, 1821), French gen-

Black Panthers, radical African-American political group whose members aren't nearly as intimidating now that they're elderly, probably arthritic, and taking cholesterol medication.

BLACK HILLS, mountain range spanning much of South Dakota and parts of Wyoming that was the site of an 1874 gold rush and the 2003 Methamphetamine Rush. The yearlong period began on May 16, 2003, when a large bag of meth was discovered in a local tweaker's basement around the corner from the Pizza Hut in Custer, South Dakota. Spurred by tales of "yank as far as the eye can see" that had started to circulate among dealers in the Midwest, the "Aught Threers," as they were known, flocked to the Black Hills by the hundreds seeking the promise of a steady hookup and hoping to make their fortunes in the area's booming meth labs. By 2004 a number of meth towns had sprung up to serve the influx of geeked-out lokes, skitzers, and jibby bears, some of whom had traveled from as far away as Asbury Park, New Jersey, to stake their claim on a fat sack of go-go juice. While some early arrivals did strike it rich, many others lost everything due to an overabundance of supply and were forced to pack up their rigs and return home as paupers. Small flecks of meth can still be found in the Black Hills, though the huge twists of spaceman once commonplace in 2003 have largely vanished.

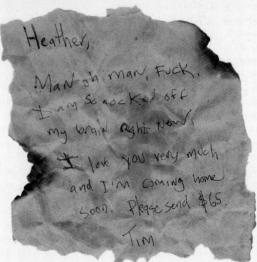

2003 letter from a crankster to his bag whore back home.

BONSAI ➤
Bonsai are used to meditate upon nature and such philosophical questions as, "What would it be like if I were a tiny little person sitting under that tiny little tree?" and "Will they ever make a little monkey to play in my little tree?"

Bombardier Beetle, type of insect that defends itself by shooting a boiling hot, foul smelling liquid from its anal cavity. You live in a world where such a thing exists.

eral and emperor whose deep insecurities about his small physical stature pushed him to conquer much of Europe while driving around in a Porsche 911. Napoléon came to power during the chaotic unrest caused by the French Revolution, overthrowing the ruling Directory government in a 1799 coup d'état in which the diminutive and intensely self-conscious general burst into the chambers of the Council of Ancients in his turbocharged, cherry red Porsche 911, revving the engine in an aggressive manner to silence the opposition. After taking control of the country, the insecure emperor embarked on a conquest of Europe, leading his men into battle while driving his expensive German sports car, and in the process of conquering most of the continent, he acquired a pair of wraparound Oakley sunglasses and began dating a 22-year-old Asian woman. Napoléon's increasingly antagonistic behavior and paranoia stemming from his suspicions that people were ridiculing him for his height led his marshals to mutiny, and they exiled the hotheaded general to the island of Elba in 1814 after he bought a set of Arctic Cat ProCross snowmobiles.

Bonham, John (*b. May 31, 1948 d. Sept. 25, 1980*), musician widely credited with being hands-down, without argument, the single greatest drummer who ever lived, period. (*See* NEIL PEART, KEITH MOON, BUDDY RICH, MAX ROACH)

Bonnie And Clyde, popular name for Bonnie Parker and Clyde Barrow, an infamous duo of Depression-era American shoplifters who came to national attention during a brazen string of petty thefts in which they stole several pieces of

BOAT, floating carriage propelled by a team of swimming horses.

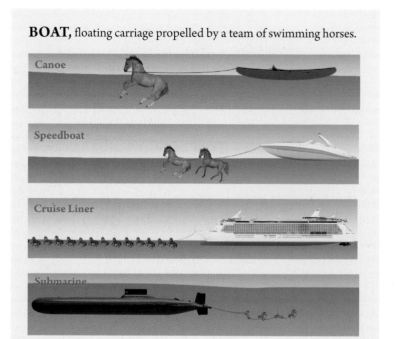

Canoe

Speedboat

Cruise Liner

Submarine

costume jewelry, some pencils, and at least nine bags of potato chips. Following their first daring misdemeanor larceny in 1932, when they took a souvenir key chain from a Texas gas station, Parker and Bar-

row began to blatantly pocket up to four candy bars at a time from general stores, tearing haphazardly across the central United States and using members of their notorious gang to distract shopkeepers with small talk. Parker and Barrow's wanton five-finger discount spree came to an end in 1934 when the pair was caught red-handed by a

Louisiana grocery store clerk while stealing eight packs of gum and a box of toothpicks; the duo was then forced to pose for a photograph holding the merchandise they had attempted to take, which was added to the shop's "Wall of Shame" alongside that of contemporary notorious criminal John Dillinger, who had tried to steal condoms from the same store in 1933.

Bonsai, small decorative tree groomed using traditional Japanese methods by people who believe nobility and inner peace can be attained by mauling flora.

Bookmark, device used by feebleminded individuals who cannot read a book in one sitting and need a flimsy strip of paper to mark where they left off. Invented in 1852 to aid the senile and demented, bookmarks today are used only by intellectually inferior social outcasts who are regarded by their peers as weak willed or mentally impaired and are widely ridiculed for needing help continuing a book from where they stopped reading the previous night. The only people

BOXER REBELLION, Chinese proto-nationalist movement opposing Western imperialism that took place during the waning days of the Qing Dynasty and is only looked up in a reference volume when one has a report on it due this Monday. Though the rebellion was led by a sect known as the Righteous Harmonious Fists (Boxers) and took place between 1898 and 1901, our advice would be to devote an entire section of the paper to the evolution of the Qing Dynasty, which is sort of off topic, but easily copied-and-pasted from various Internet sources; this will not only make the report look well researched, but longer. Longer is key because it shows effort, and that's all history teachers in seventh or eighth grade really care about because the bar is so low. The rebellion pitted 300,000 Boxers against 70,000 imperial troops—two statistics that should definitely be included in the first three paragraphs of the essay. In fact, one should include as many statistics as possible, and spell the numbers out because that will also add length. There were ten thousand (see that?) Muslim Kansu Braves and several thousand Manchu Bannermen of the Tiger and Divine Corps who were loyal to Prince Duan. We don't know what any of that means either, but it should still go in the report. Remember, the goal is not to write an A paper here, but to obtain the highest possible grade with the least amount of effort. Here are some more names to throw in there because the teacher will probably just look for key words to put checkmarks next to: Zaiyi, Manchu general Ronglu, and Dong Fuxiang. Also separate the paper with subtopics like "Causes," "Tactics," and "Aftermath," but not in the exact order Wikipedia does it because that will look suspicious. Shit, sorry, we should have said this earlier, but it's also important to include why the rebels were called Boxers. Actually, that should probably be somewhere in the topic paragraph, or thesis statement, depending on what your teacher

A picture of these Chinese-looking dudes will make your report legit.

calls it. You know what? Just plagiarize the following paragraph. (It has a few spelling errors and is pretty disjointed, but that will actually make it look natural.) Here's the paragraph:

Foreigners called members of this society "Boxers" because they practiced martial arts, like karate and other forms of martial arts. The Boxers also believed that they had a magical power, and that forign bullets could not harm them. Millions of spirit soldiers would soon rise from the dead and join their cause.

If anyone questions anything in the paper, just say your dad helped. Plus, try to print out an image of a Chinese painting from the time period to use as a cover page. Mrs. Klepperman used to love that kind of shit.

Writing Your Bibliography

Most history teachers want reports to have a small bibliography. It's annoying, but it doesn't need to be real long. It's easy enough to grab a couple of sources from the bibliography at the bottom of Wikipedia's Boxer Rebellion page, and you also might want to go onto Amazon, type "Boxer Rebellion" into the search bar, and pick out something from around the seventh page, just so you've got something a little more obscure in there. (Don't worry if any of these books aren't in print anymore because you can always say you read them at the library, which always has really out-of-date stuff.) Also feel free to use the sources below, though you might want to swap one of them out if you have time.

Bickers, Robert A., *The Scramble for China: Foreign Devils In The Qing Empire, 1800–1914* (London: Allen Lane, 2011).
Keown-Boyd, Henry, *The Fists Of Righteous Harmony: A History Of The Boxer Uprising In China In The Year 1900* (Leo Cooper, 1991).
Xiang, Lanxin, *The Origins Of The Boxer War: A Multinational Study* (Psychology Press, 2003).

Booth, John Wilkes (b. *May 10, 1838* d. *Apr. 26, 1865*), revolutionary performance artist best known for his *Sic Semper Tyrannis* piece, which he performed only once, in front of a capacity crowd at Ford's Theatre in Washington, D.C., in 1865. Booth was renowned for his commitment to his craft and finished the performance of his most famous work despite breaking his leg midway through.

Bootlegging, Prohibition-era practice in which alcohol was manufactured, transported, and dumped out, as alcohol was illegal at the time.

considered lower in class than bookmark users are those who dog-ear pages to remember their place, and those who read *Rolling Stone*.

Boston Massacre, great name for a violent tragedy and one that should have been saved for a time when someone really goes apeshit and starts gunning down everyone in sight in the middle of downtown Boston. After British Redcoats opened fire on a crowd of colonists on March 5, 1770, pamphleteers began using the name without stopping to think that maybe the death of five civilians wasn't worthy of the "Boston Massacre" title, and that somewhere down the road a much bloodier incident with a higher body count might be. Because the name, which sounds visceral and rolls off the tongue, was wasted on an incident that didn't even immediately spark the Revolutionary War, there won't be any good way to describe a future attack from a screaming man or woman who affixes a bayonet to an M-16 and marches through the Back Bay slicing people's throats open and firing indiscriminately on schoolchildren.

Box, vulgar slur for a rectangular container.

Wouldn't exactly call this a massacre. Looks more like a couple guys letting off some steam.

If the grass of Boston Common is ever soaked with blood and Commonwealth Avenue is littered with corpses, such an event will, unfortunately, have to be called "The Boston Bad Day," "The Commonwealth Catastrophe," or even worse, "Boston Massacre II," which would just be pathetic, frankly.

Boston Red Sox, professional baseball franchise that in 2004 broke an 86-year championship drought, which is kind of touching if one can just focus solely on the old man who waited his whole life for that historic moment, and no other Red Sox fan whatsoever. It is equally important to disregard the Red Sox players themselves and firmly concentrate on that one man who was born two years after the team's 1918 World Series win—the sweet old grandfather who fought in two wars, went to work as an oil furnace repairman year after year without complaint, and endured almost a century of heartbreak—him and positively no one else affiliated with

---

CITIES OF THE WORLD

Boston

Large northeastern American city of 650,000 people, each of whom, regardless of class or socioeconomic status, is a humongous asshole. Founded in 1630 by English Puritans fleeing persecution and seeking a place to practice their religion as free assholes, Boston has evolved into a center for education, medicine, and telling one another to shut the fuck up. Common cultural activities include being physically assaulted by the working-class assholes of South Boston, dodging the thousands of college-student assholes as they stumble from the city's many asshole bars, being looked down upon with withering contempt by the obscenely wealthy blue-blood assholes of Beacon Hill, and talking about their overpaid baseball team of assholes. Despite a tangible racial

Assholes from all walks of life call Boston home.

divide, Boston's diverse citizenry crosses all color boundaries to form the most irritating and insufferable group of people in the United States. (*See* PHILADELPHIA)

BRIAN OSTER'S HOUSE, residence on Sycamore Drive widely regarded as the most awesome house in the neighborhood for several years in the mid-1990s. Friends hanging out after school or sleeping over in the humongous, finished basement marveled at the volume of cool stuff contained in the Oster residence as well as the extremely minimal parental oversight. Visits to the house ended abruptly in April 1998 when Oster's dad got laid off and had to move the family to Atlanta or something.

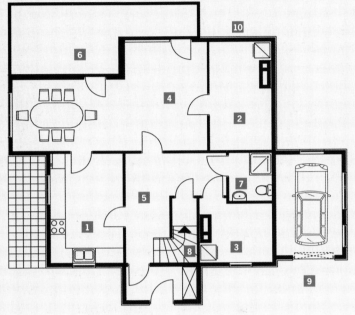

1. **Kitchen**
   • Good kind of cereal
   • Endless supply of microwave popcorn, Sprite, string cheese
   • Spinning bar stools

2. **Brian's Room**
   • TV, VCR, three different kinds of video game consoles
   • Telescope
   • Smaller telescope
   • Biggest plasma globe available at Spencer's

3. **Older Brother Mike's Room**
   • 11 issues of *Playboy*
   • 4 issues of *Hustler*
   • 1 issue of *Club International*
   • Butterfly knife

4. **Living Room**
   • Giant TV with every cable channel, including Cinemax
   • NordicTrack
   • Recliner with cup holders

5. **Hallway**
   • Freaking huge mounted deer head

6. **Master Bedroom**
   • Water bed
   • Gun

7. **Bathroom**
   • Blue stuff in toilet
   • Electronic scale
   • Shower with glass door instead of shower curtain

8. **Basement**
   • About 80 board games
   • Ping-Pong table
   • Punching bag
   • 128 cans of room-temperature ginger ale

9. **Garage**
   • Basketball hoop that can be lowered for dunking

10. **Backyard**
   • Store-bought tree house
   • Jacuzzi

the Red Sox in any way. The man, who would never think of pouring a full cup of beer on the head of another fan simply because he was wearing a Yankees cap, was actually born in Fitchburg, about 40 miles northwest of Boston, and not the city itself. Remember: the old man and no one else. The old man.

Boston Tea Party, 1773 incident in which 115 colonists, dressed as Indians, and Samuel Adams, dressed as the Green Lantern, boarded ships and dumped British tea into the Boston Harbor.

Bowling, game in which the object is to roll a heavy ball down a 60-foot alley, or lane, and knock down a set of 10 wooden pins in an effort to drown out one's sadness.

BP, oil and gas company responsible for the 2010 Deepwater Horizon oil spill in the Gulf of Mexico as well as—actually, you know what? That's the only thing worth mentioning about BP in this encyclopedia. Any amount of text dedicated to when the company was founded or how many billions of dollars it earns each year would shift focus away from the fact that BP's main contribution to society is an explo-

GOD-KING OF THE AMERICAS
James Buchanan

(b. Apr. 23, 1791 d. Aug. 12, 1861), self-anointed divine imperial overlord of the United States who, immediately after being elected president in 1857, enthroned himself on a golden ziggurat and brutally ruled the nation in a debauched phantasmagoria of sex, blood, and madness that nearly destroyed the republic. During what he referred to as his "glorious reign of holy exaltation," Buchanan subjected the country to his cruel whims and grandiose habits, having by the end of his four years in power transformed the White House into a large arena for viewing indescribably cruel blood sports of his own devising, killed his own child, held countless orgies deep into the night as New York and Washington burned, and appointed his dog Excelsior vice president upon murdering running mate John C. Breckinridge with a golden scimitar. American citizens were powerless to stop the power-mad Buchanan during his duly elected term, but voted him out of office in 1861, finally leaving Buchanan's Cabinet free to torture him, pierce him with lances, and then burn him alive.

Bride, a variety of delusional person. (*See* GROOM, COLLEGE GRADUATE, NEW PARENT, FREELANCER)

MATHEW BRADY ➤
Brady's polarizing work has influenced the medium of war photography, notably in the famous portrait of Gen. George Patton standing with a fully erect penis in front of a Sherman tank.

BRAILLE ➤

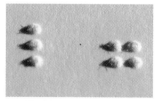

Braille character

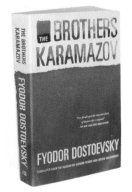

Print equivalent

sion that killed 11 men and dumped 4.9 million barrels of crude oil into the ocean over the course of three months. Including anything else in this entry, like the number of operations BP has worldwide, seems pretty goddamn inconsequential by comparison. Moreover, even mentioning its listing on the London Stock Exchange would be immaterial because the only thing any reasonable person should be concerned with is how BP nearly destroyed the entire Gulf Coast economy and could have avoided doing so had it adhered to federally mandated safety regulations. If anything, this entry should do more to clarify that 4.9 million barrels is more than 200 million gallons of oil, which covered anywhere from 2,500 to 68,000 square miles of the Gulf, affecting the ecosystem in ways that will never be quantifiable—all facts about BP that are a hell of a lot more noteworthy than who served as its first CEO, though it is worth mentioning that the CEO during the oil spill, Tony Hayward, is a huge prick.

Brady, Mathew (*b. May 18, 1822 d. Jan. 15, 1896*), photographer whose work captured the inherent eroticism of the Civil War in a series of sexually charged black-and-white portraits. Brady gained notoriety for the way he used his lens to strip away the war's brutal veneer and artistically access the sensuality and carnal desires of the men who fought the nation's bloodiest conflict. His best-known photos include two nude Union infantrymen embracing in the aftermath of the Battle of Antietam; a formation of Confederate soldiers standing side by side and holding leashes attached to each other's genitals; and, perhaps his most provocative work,

an image of President Lincoln gazing into a mirror while beholding the testicles of Confederate president Jefferson Davis.

Braille, Louis (*b. Jan. 4, 1809 d. Jan. 6, 1852*), French educator whose system of embossed-point writing allowed the blind to read the equiv-

alent of 20,000 pages of printed material every minute. Using two columns of three dots that are raised at various intervals, Braille's tactile alphabet is by far the most efficient means of reading ever developed: A single dot in the upper-left corner is roughly equal to 5,000 standard English sentences, and three dots in an L-shaped pattern contain the entire contents of the *Oxford English Dictionary*. In the time the average sighted reader spends on this entry, a visually impaired individual using Braille can read the complete text of this encyclopedia 47 times.

Bris, Jewish ritual that involves family and friends gathering to watch a person known as a mohel cut off an 8-day-old boy's foreskin and then toss it to someone in the crowd who attempts to catch it in their mouth.

Broadway, American musical tradition that has been allowed to proceed since the early 1900s.

Bronze Age, bronze-tool-based period from 3300 to 1200 BC that human civilization couldn't get over with fast enough because it was up to its neck in bronze, bronze, bronze, bronze, and more bronze. Falling directly after the Stone Age and before the Iron Age, the two-millennia-long Bronze Age was characterized by bronze weapons, bronze jewelry, bronze statuary, bronze utensils, bronze ornaments,

bronze jugs, and an abundance of people wondering when the hell the goddamn Bronze Age was finally going to end. Archaeologists have since unearthed historical records in the Vráble ruins in Central Europe dating to several years before the discovery of iron ore smelting that read "Jesus *Christ* with the bronze already. Why is this lasting so long?"

Brother-In-Law, man who has only worked two months since 2009 and just bought a fucking boat anyway.

Brothers Grimm, creepy 19th-century German brothers Jacob and Wilhelm, who together collected and published volumes of provocative, often grotesque, and violent children's stories that have since become classics, though if the two were alive today, no one would want their children anywhere near them. Responsible for preserving and putting their own imprint on the stories of Snow White, Rapunzel, and Sleeping Beauty, the brothers would today be picketed by outraged and disgusted parents concerned about their predilection

for torturing people and placing children in jeopardy. While people love the timelessness of such tales as Cinderella, imagine any parent in their right mind picking up a book about dismembering children with a picture of those two freaks on the back and thinking, "This is the perfect book for my young child."

Brown, Jim *(b. Feb. 17, 1936),* former NFL running back who played from 1957 to 1965 who still represents Cleveland's best shot at ever winning a championship.

Brown, Molly *(b. July 18, 1867 d. Oct. 26, 1932),* survivor of the *Titanic* disaster who swam after the crash to the infamous iceberg and resided there for 12 years before she was rescued by a passing cargo ship. Doggy-paddling over other passengers and members of the crew who were drowning in the frigid North Atlantic, Brown made it to the massive floating block of ice without catching hypothermia and quickly constructed from salvaged debris a 10-room, multilevel shelter that she gradually weatherized using whale blubber as insulation. For the next decade, the American socialite and philanthropist subsisted on seal meat, fish, and puffin eggs, each night lighting giant bonfires and scanning the horizon with a homemade telescope in the hopes of being discovered by one of the many merchant vessels that operated in the area. On March 12, 1924, her SOS signal, sent from an ingenious telegraph machine constructed from the carcass of a slain walrus, was received by the Sweden-registered SS *Stockholm*, and Brown and her two infant daughters left behind the basic settlement that had grown over the years to include a chapel, a school, a smokehouse, a small theater, and a replica of the Parthenon.

Bruce, Lenny *(b. Oct. 13, 1925 d. Aug. 3, 1966),* legendary American comedian best known for his hilarious bit in which he took on the persona of a joyless man who would angrily lecture the audience for hours at a time without delivering a single punch line. Fans everywhere delighted in hearing Bruce change the face of comedy with his joke-free routines, explaining at length the nuances of vocabulary and grammatical rules, and how they contributed to his mounting legal problems. Bruce was heralded as a genius for the way he eschewed the traditional hallmarks of the stand-up comedian, such as setups and laughter, influencing countless future 21st-century comedians.

Bryan, William Jennings, unfortunately no information on this person could be found.

Buddha *(b. 563 BC d. 440 BC),* prince born Siddhārtha Gautama who founded the philosophy and religion of Buddhism, something he was only able to accomplish after finally being reincarnated as a human, having spent his first 46 lifetimes as a squirrel. Though the Supreme Buddha had long wished to spread his teachings about reaching enlightenment through meditation and the subsequent death of desire, the 140 years he spent being reborn as a variety of different species of ground squirrel made it difficult, as he had to relay these complex messages through the limited squeaks and chirps he was able to produce; in fact, he was killed on at least three occasions by people who thought he was rabid after he approached them with his message. After finally being reincarnated into a decent human body instead of as another damn squirrel, the Buddha was able to gain large numbers of followers in the 5th century BC, though a very small minority of adherents continue to worship him in his squirrel form.

Buddhism, system of ancient beliefs that poses as a religion, even though it lacks dogmatic faith in supernatural beings, organized oppression of nonbelievers, a bloody history of forced conversion, and antagonism toward science.

Buddy Ranch, pal house outside Carson City, Nevada, where clients select a guy companion and pay top dollar to enjoy such hangout activities as playing video games, watching sports, munching on food, or sitting on a couch drinking beer. Upon arriving at the ranch, patrons are invited to choose from a wide selection of dudes who are tall, short, skinny, chubby, African-American, or Asian, and can even select a buddy in a wheelchair if that's what they are into. Clients then enter a room filled with flat-screen televisions and foosball

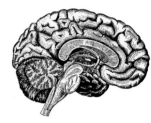

Brain, complex organ located in the cranium that is tasked with cognition, interpreting sensory information, replaying the most shameful and embarrassing memories of one's life in an endless loop until one dies, and motor function.

Breakfast, morning meal sometimes consisting of eggs, buttered toast, bacon, and coffee that one places under the pillow before going to sleep and consumes immediately upon waking.

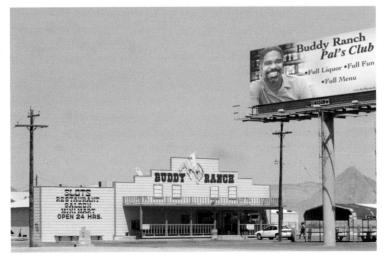

The Buddy Ranch offers clean, top-shelf pals of every shape, size, and ethnicity.

WINNER, *BUSH V. GORE*

George W. Bush

(*b. July 6, 1946*), 43rd president of the United States, who received the presidency as a gift for his 54th birthday from his parents, George and Barbara. Using his connections in the Supreme Court, Bush's father was able to pull a few strings at the last minute to get his son the extravagant present, which the younger Bush accepted despite his disappointment over not receiving the Ford Mustang he had repeatedly requested. Although Bush enjoyed the parade held in his honor, he grew bored of the Oval Office after a few months, so his buddies Dick and Donald orchestrated the military invasion of Afghanistan to cheer him up and give Bush something to do. Bush also received a second presidential term as an early Christmas present in 2004, not long after inheriting his father's old war.

MAIN ACHIEVEMENT
Extended Daylight Saving Time

BIGGEST REGRET
Never attended a Cabinet meeting

NICKNAMES
"Old Fuckup," "Old Massive Fuckup," "Old Huge Pile Of Fuckup," "Squirt"

FAMOUS QUOTE
"I think there is a chance I am not doing a very good job."
—*Second inaugural address*

---

tables and are charged according to their particular predilection: $75 to split an order of cheese fries, $125 to play *Madden* on PlayStation 3, $200 to listen to some tunes together, $225 for a movie, and an additional $300 to do any of it with two buddies at once. Some customers prefer to hang back and watch two buddies battle it out in an epic air-guitar duel. By necessity, the Buddy Ranch has a state-of-the art security system and armed guards, in case any clients get a little too rough with a pal in an argument over whether Tom Brady is a better quarterback than Peyton Manning.

Bugle, shrill, high-pitched instrument worn around every male human's neck that is blown to announce whenever they have an erection.

Bull Market, period of increased investment and investor confidence that occurs when Wall Street employees are getting away with breaking the law. Characterized by a sense of optimism because investment rules are being blatantly disregarded right under the SEC's nose, bull markets are difficult to predict as economists never know when an investment firm will figure out a

new, inventive, sleazy way to completely fuck over others. Bull markets are not to be confused with bear markets, which are periods of investor fear and pessimism that occur immediately after Wall Street traders have been caught.

Burrito, Mexican food consisting of a flour tortilla wrapped around chicken or beef, with other fillings such as rice…uh…black beans—hold on, make that pinto…some lettuce…uh, cheese…yeah, cheddar jack, and, uh…how much for guacamole? Okay, lemme get some guacamole. The tortilla is steamed or grilled to make it softer and more flexible, and is topped with…you know what, gimme some corn, too, and some sour cream but not too much. And just a little mild pico de gallo…a little more, a little more… Okay, that's good. Cool.

Bus, vehicle used to travel from one terrible location to another, making local, regional, and national stops at depressing terminals covered in filth that are within walking distance of federal prisons, homeless shelters, and methadone clinics, as well as soul-crushing, blighted neighborhoods.

Bush, George H.W. (*b. June 12, 1924*), Caucasian American male who worked in government for several years. Bush was born in Massachusetts, served in the U.S. Navy, and attended college before eventually moving to Washington, D.C. Bush retired in 1993. He has a wife, Barbara, and five children.

Butter, yellow, fatty, edible substance created when a boxer uses a cow's udder for speedbag training.

Byrd, Dunsmore (*b. May 19, 1899 d. Aug. 31, 1938*), made-up historical figure who was an important member of the Harlem Renaissance before being fatally shot by police while attending a wedding in Philadelphia, sparking the two-week-long South Street Riots, a made-up event. Byrd's just-now-invented poetry collection, *Tom Recollected*, gained him the admiration of such towering contempo-

BURIAL, final act of entombing a body following death:

Ground Burial

Deceased is placed in a casket and lowered into a pit right next to hundreds of perfect strangers, many of whom have much nicer caskets.

Cremation

Body is burned to ash, placed in an urn, and scattered in deceased's favorite Italian dish.

Toilet Burial

Remains liquefied and poured down a toilet, then flushed.

Space Burial

Method of burial, prior to which the cremated ash must spend 40 hours in a flight simulator, be able to tread water for 10 minutes while still inside its capsule, and log 15 hours inside a neutral buoyancy simulator so it can become accustomed to zero gravity.

Mass Grave

Loved one is hastily buried atop dozens of other people who also disliked the government.

Leave It Where It Lies

Body is simply left to decay where it collapses, serving to remind us all that death is natural, horrifying, and inevitable.

raries as Langston Hughes, Count Basie, and Elsie Monroe, who isn't real either. Besides being extremely influential to the fake Boudreaux Blue school of intellectual thought, Byrd was also not in reality the first African-American professor at Columbia University.

Cadaver, human corpse that medical students must keep with them at all times, whether they are in class, studying, or eating out, to prove they are responsible enough to care for a real living patient. After cadavers are handed out on the first day of medical school, students name them and write their initials with a Sharpie on the deceased person's forehead so none of the corpses gets mixed up or lost. Throughout the semester, teachers periodically check in to make sure students are handling their cadavers with care, inspecting the outside of the skin for cracks that might indicate a corpse was stuffed into a locker overnight. Students are also responsible for bathing and dressing the corpses, as well as periodically releasing the various gases that build up in the cadaver after the person has died. At the end of the semester, those who have successfully maintained their cadavers celebrate by dissecting and dissolving them in a vat of acid.

Caesar, Gaius Julius (b. July 13, 100 BC d. Mar. 15, 44 BC), 119-pound marble bust who commanded a 12-legion army, conquered all of Gaul, and expanded

the Roman empire across most of Europe and into Africa. A white statue of a head and shoulders, Caesar was known for his striking chiseled features, unwavering, intense gaze, quiet demeanor, and fearless military leadership, typified by the stone bust's insistence that he be carried into the middle of the battlefield as war and carnage raged around him. Caesar's reign came to an end when a group of conspirators, fearing the marble bust would declare itself king, hired assassins who futilely attempted to stab Caesar's highly polished stone surface several times. Though their weapons caused little damage, the force of the thrusting blades knocked the bust from its pedestal and caused it to smash against the floor and shatter.

Caffeine, alkaloid and supposed stimulant that doesn't do anything anymore and can't even stop the headaches.

Cake, chocolate. Angel food. Pineapple upside-down. Cheese. Red velvet. Black forest. Pound. Carrot. No matter what kind, they're all amazing. Try a cake today! Bundt.

Calculator, portable, lightweight electronic device capable of storing a vast supply of numbers. The numbers housed within a calculator are accessed by pressing buttons, which allows them to be displayed on a small screen in real time and taken with the user anywhere. Calculators hold a wide variety of numbers, including 757; 16; 84,583; 42; 9,999,999,999; and .0000000001. A common companion to the calculator is the word processor, which allows users to carry millions of words, spaces, and punctuation marks inside of their computers.

Calendar, time-telling device very sad people use to x-off the days until

CANCER, disease marked by cells displaying uncontrolled growth, but they're making advancements in cancer treatment all the time, so you have nothing to worry about. Cancer cells invade and destroy other tissues and form

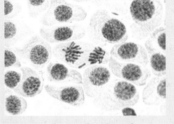

malignant tumors, but new medications are being developed constantly by top-notch researchers, so it's going to be okay. Everything is going to be okay. Some forms of cancer, notably of the pancreas or colon, are very difficult to treat, but there are new experimental drugs that haven't yet been approved by the FDA that have shown a lot of promise, and in this particular case, where the cancer is more advanced, there's a very good chance of getting into one of those trial studies. It's important to stay positive. Cancer, which accounts for 13 percent of all human fatalities, just isn't the death sentence it used to be. You can lead a long, happy life with cancer now. You really, really can.

Common Types Of Cancer

PROSTATE CANCER
Cancer that starts in the prostate gland that Greg Hillen had. You know Greg, right? Well, he's doing much better now.

LYMPHOMA
Rapidly spreading cancer of the lymphatic system, and did you hear what the doctor said? There's also a 30 percent chance that it won't spread any more.

BONE CANCER
Abnormal growth of cells within the bone that, yes, they may have to remove portions of the hip and you may never be able to walk normally again, and sure, if the tumor is more aggressive they'll probably have to amputate, but everything is going to be fine. Just fine. Don't cry. You can beat this thing. Shh. There, there. There, there…

Cain, son of Adam and Eve who was responsible for committing the first murder and is suspected in 52 other slayings throughout the Old Testament.

Camel, desert ungulate known for the hump on its back, which is used to store an extra version of itself in case the original dies in the harsh climate in which it dwells.

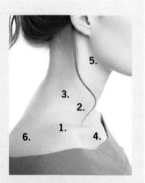

Caroline's Neck

1. See how it curves here into her collarbone? God, she's beautiful.

2. Sometimes she would cover up this part here with a scarf in the winter.

3. She used to talk about how her neck was too long, but that's not true. It's perfect.

4. She's not wearing the necklace. I wonder if she still wears it and thinks of me.

5. Oh, Caroline…

6. I can't look at this anymore.

their vacation to Fort Lauderdale.

Calhoun, John Caldwell (*b. Mar 18, 1782 d. Mar 31, 1850*), U.S. vice president for John Quincy Adams and Andrew Jackson, senator from South Carolina, and John Tyler's secretary of steak, known for his nationalist, medium-rare agenda that included advocating for states' rights, a juicy, thick cut of beef, limited government, and protective tariffs, as well as a baked potato slathered with butter and sour cream, the interests of the South, and piping hot rolls. A renowned orator, Calhoun delivered fiery, perfectly seared but still-tender speeches that championed the theory of minority rights in democracy and melted in the mouth.

Calligraphy, decorative, often ornate handwriting that is generally used in invitations to events such as weddings and in correspondence to persons living in the 18th century.

Calvin, John (*b. July 10, 1509 d. May 27, 1564*), French theologian and firm believer in the doctrine of predestination—a fundamental component of his Protestant theological system that nevertheless could not save him from being condemned to hell for all eternity.

Capital Punishment, process by which the state takes the life of someone who seems guilty enough of a crime. In societies where capital punishment is practiced, it is usually the burden of a prosecutor to make the case that the accused might possibly have committed the offense in question or at least definitely seems like the type, because someone did something, and why shouldn't it be the accused, who likely wouldn't even be in this situation right now if he hadn't been up to no good anyway. Most nations have abolished capital punishment,

despite the fact that it is only carried out for the most serious offenses and only after the condemned has been determined to be an individual who, even if he didn't actually do it, certainly didn't have his hands clean and likely did a bunch of other horrible, disgusting things that no one knows about but would probably come to light eventually. Just look at the guy.

Capitalism, widely prevalent economic system based on the underlying theory that we're all going to be rich, ha ha ha, rich! In a capitalist system, goods and services are exchanged within a free market, resulting in money, oh boy, sweet, sweet money as far as the eye can see, which is subsequently retained by private ownership. Wait until we get our hands on those beautiful bundles of cold hard green cash that form the system of profits and wages upon which capitalism is dependent. In capitalism, the means of production are privately owned and operated for profit by an individual or individuals, underscoring the central tenet that it's mine, you hear me, all mine, and I'm not going to share ONE RED CENT of it, goddamn it, I EARNED IT! GIMME GIMME GIMME I WANT THAT MONEY!

Career, come on. You don't need an encyclopedia to tell you what a fucking career is.

Caring, human condition wherein an individual devotes oneself entirely to a cause or goal, thereby making that person totally lame. The more openly and earnestly someone cares about achieving their dreams, the bigger a loser they become, with friends, coworkers, and family members calling them a massive tool or a total nerd, and urging them to "stop caring so much, because it's becoming embarrassing." Historically, prominent lame figures such as Abraham Lin-

ONE TERM TOO MANY
James Earl Carter

(*b. Oct. 1, 1924*), 39th president of the United States, whose four years in office were somehow the least impressive of his entire life. A graduate of the U.S. Naval Academy, prosperous farmer, nuclear engineer, reformist, and governor of Georgia prior to becoming president in 1977, Carter strangely hit the most pronounced lull in his career during his single term as the nation's chief executive. While his presidency was marked by occasional successes such as the Camp David Accords, Carter's professional life really took off again when he left office. In these years, he founded a human rights nonprofit that won him the Nobel Peace Prize, went on international diplomatic missions, and became the public face of Habitat for Humanity, worthy accomplishments that made his four years as president of the United States a blip in an otherwise distinguished lifetime of public service.

NICKNAME
Probably just called him "The Georgia Peach" or something like that.

MAIN ACCOMPLISHMENT
In 1980 election, showed Americans that an electoral map could look that red.

ELECTRONEGATIVITY
2.4 (Pauling scale)

coln, Nelson Mandela, and Mother Teresa expressed so much sincere enthusiasm for their individual causes that they couldn't go anywhere without people snickering and yelling, "Relax, dork." Currently, human rights activist Aung San Suu Kyi and 10-year-old David Jeffries care so much about the direction of Burma and getting better at piano, respectively, that both are coming off like huge dorks who need to get a life.

Carson, Johnny (b. Oct. 23 1925 d. Jan. 23, 2005), thrice-divorced, alcoholic late-night TV host who died of emphysema brought on by chronic smoking, and a man whom every person in show business is constantly trying to emulate.

Casablanca, popular 1942 film in which a number of famous Hollywood actors from the period walk on-screen for a few moments, speak a well-known line of dialogue, and then leave.

Cash, Johnny (b. Feb. 26, 1932 d. Sept. 12, 2003), name that, in 98 percent of instances, is spoken immediately after the sentence "I'm not a big country fan, but I like some stuff."

Casino, establishment providing world-class accommodations, fine dining, and live entertainment, as well as some games in the lobby area. Many casinos feature luxury spa facilities and upscale nightclubs in addition to a few small card tables where visitors can pass a few minutes in between activities. Some casino visitors return day after day to take advantage of the unique shopping experiences that cannot be found anywhere else.

Cassette Player, once-popular portable music device that is now only used by middle-aged women at bus stops with orthopedic shoes and a

A carbon pig forages for carbon roots.

CARBON, element that is present in all living organisms but is found in greatest concentration in the South American carbon pig. While carbon accounts for 18 percent of the mass of human beings and 50 percent of the mass of trees, it makes up 99.97 percent of the mass of the carbon pig, a swine of the Bolivian mountains that feeds on carbon grasses and carbon fruits and drinks from the carbon springs unique to the region. Fewer than 200 carbon pigs remain today, as its carbon-rich habitat is depleted by encroaching carbon refineries, and its once massive herds are thinned by poachers hungry for the animal's carbon.

panicked look in their eyes.

Castro, Fidel (b. Aug. 13, 1926), CIA operative who spent more than 50 years gathering valuable intelligence from the highest levels of the government of communist Cuba. Considered the most talented and dedicated agent ever to conduct espionage on behalf of the United States, Castro was first inserted into Cuba in 1953, when he

infiltrated the group of Cuban revolutionaries plotting to overthrow U.S.-backed president Fulgencio Batista. Although Castro's sabotage efforts failed to prevent Batista's removal from power, his cover remained intact—so much so that the charismatic American spy, whose

real name is Alan Petersen, was elevated to commander in chief and then prime minister. Throughout his rise to power, Castro continually relayed top-secret information to his superiors at CIA headquarters, and undermined the Cuban government by fomenting corruption among officials and installing a series of economic controls that have hampered the country's growth for decades. Still, Castro's mystique only grew, thanks in large part to manufactured confrontations with the United States in which fellow operatives made hundreds of bogus assassination attempts and even staged the elaborately inept Bay of Pigs invasion, a brilliant maneuver on the part of President John F. Kennedy that cemented Castro's status as an anti-imperialist hero above suspicion. Castro was deactivated by the CIA in 2008, but he remains a revered figure in Cuba and will emerge from time to time

Carroll, Lewis (b. Jan. 27, 1832 d. Jan. 14, 1898), pseudonym for English writer Charles Dodgson, whose many friendships with young girls, hobby of photographing children in the nude, and extensively recorded, barely masked sexual desire for prepubescent girls led people to wonder if he might, by some chance, perhaps possibly be a pedophile.

◄ CASINO
Patrons kill some time between shopping, seeing live shows, and dining at one of the casino's many five-star restaurants.

to attend a special event or photograph a classified document.

Cat Person, half-feline, half-Homosapiens creature that roams the streets late at night in search of a 24-hour veterinarian and a nice, quiet place to get a cup of coffee.

Catcher In The Rye, The, 1951 manual written by American novelist J.D. Salinger that provides clear, step-by-step instructions on how to murder musician John Lennon. Through its iconic teenage antihero Holden Caulfield, the book employs easy-to-understand metaphors about the impossibility of preserving innocence that direct readers to stand outside the Dakota Hotel in New York City on Dec. 8, 1980, ask Lennon to sign a copy of his solo album *Double Fantasy* as he's leaving the building, and, upon his return home a few hours later, shoot the former Beatles frontman with four hollow-point rounds from a .38 revolver. Hailed as a masterpiece of modern instructional literature, *The Catcher In The Rye* contains eminently decipherable references to "phonies" and relatable themes of alienation that have ensured it remains the quintessential how-to publication in terms of murdering the writer of the song "Imagine."

Catherine The Great (*b. May 2, 1729 d. Nov. 17, 1796*), she died of a stroke. Now move on to the next entry.

Celebrity, person who is just better at being famous than normal people. Because celebrities simply have a knack for shining in the public eye, they are way more recognizable than regular folks, who just aren't as good at posing for cameras, appearing on talk shows, and being interviewed by magazines. Celebrities also warrant more attention because they are better than normal people at being rich.

Cell Phone, mobile device and cultural signifier, the possession of which made one a dickhead up until 1998, and the lack of which made one a dickhead after 2004.

Central Park, 843 vast acres of

THE CATCHER ➤ IN THE RYE

On page 114 of J.D. Salinger's most famous work, protagonist Holden Caulfield sneaks into his sister's room and tells her what time John Lennon typically comes home to his apartment after a recording session.

CARDIOPULMONARY RESUSCITATION (CPR), emergency procedure performed to restore breathing and circulatory functions in a victim suffering cardiac arrest.

THE 6 STEPS OF CPR

STEP 1
Clear victim's airways by removing the tongue and teeth, and smashing off the jaw with a rock or cinder block.

STEP 2
Prevent dehydration by forcefully spitting into victim's mouth.

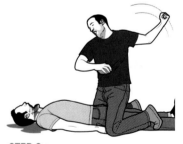

STEP 3
Break the sternum and ribs to provide ample room for the heart and lungs to function properly.

STEP 4
Victim's throat must be punctured several times with sharp screwdriver in order to facilitate airflow.

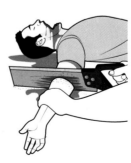

STEP 5
Lop off victim's arms and legs with a hacksaw.

STEP 6
To prevent the victim from going into shock, knock him unconscious with a baseball bat.

CELL, revolting, pathetic sack containing the filth of life. An average cell consists of a sickening central blob known as a nucleus, which houses a nauseating lump of genetic slop and is surrounded by equally disgusting specialized structures such as mitochondria and some other junk that's probably as depressing as it is vomit-inducing. While both plant and animal cells are equally repulsive and contemptible, plant cells are larger and have a hard cell wall. Blech.

Nucleus
Where the parts of the cell go to regroup and talk about how they could have better handled that virus last week

Endoplasmic Reticulum
Victor and last surviving organelle of 1649's Great Reticulum War

Cytoplasm
What squirts everywhere if you step on a cell

Cell Membrane
Keeps mitochondria from leaving and starting their own cells somewhere else

Centriole
Cylindrical organelle containing 1.5 atoms of cyanide in case the cell is captured before it can divide

Chainsaw, portable mechanical saw that doesn't fit into your briefcase, so you'll just have to get to work early that day and put it under your desk before your coworkers arrive. And then at 3 p.m., it begins.

feeling-like-this-looked-a-lot-better-in-the-movies.

Centrifugal Force, outward-pushing force experienced during circular motion; often referred to as a fictitious force because everything is an illusion, and we're all just in some guy's dream.

Cereal, only thing your foreign exchange student seems to eat.

Cert, Michael (*b. Sept. 18, 1978*),

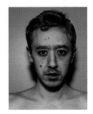

former U.S. Coast Guard officer who, in October 2012, walked directly into the Orb as it hovered over a patrol boat 80 miles off the coast of the Seychelles. Ignoring the commands of superior officers, Cert slowly approached and then disappeared into the mysterious glowing ball of energy at approximately 11:46 a.m. SCT, emerging naked exactly 5.75 seconds later and having aged what medical professionals estimated to be between 17 and 21 years. Cert, who appears to have no recollection of any events or memories prior to his dis-

appearance into the Orb, has at the time of this book's printing been unable to speak with government or medical officials, as he communicates only in an indecipherable language unknown to modern linguists. He is currently being held for interrogation at the headquarters of a major scientific research group in the Seychelles.

Challenger **Disaster,** explosion of the space shuttle *Challenger* on Jan. 28, 1986, an event many second-grade teachers regard as the most uncomfortable day of their professional lives. As thousands of second-grade teachers watched that morning on a television specially wheeled into the classroom for the occasion, the shuttle broke apart 73 seconds after liftoff, killing all seven crew members, including social studies teacher Christa McAuliffe, whom students were particularly excited to see blast off into space. Caused by a rupture in the seal of a solid-rocket booster, the explosion filled TV screens with a violent fireball, causing the nation's second-grade teachers to gasp, but quickly

stifle their concern so as not to alarm their students, who grew increasingly confused and concerned as debris and fingers of smoke fell back to Earth. By the time Mission Control announced the "major malfunction," second-grade teachers from coast to coast had already jogged to the front of the room, clicked off CNN, and said, "All righty, let's do some math now," handing out work sheets as fast as humanly possible while pretending not to hear their students ask, "What happened? Are the astronauts okay?" The *Challenger* disaster, which led to a temporary suspension of the shuttle program, also had stunned second-grade teachers hoping to God the principal would send students home early, because they could not bear the thought of discussing this unbearable tragedy with a group of 7-year-olds who were sitting silently at their little desks with the rockets they had built out of paper towel tubes the day before.

Chanel, Coco (*b. Aug. 19, 1883 d. Jan. 10, 1971*), pioneering French

◀ **CHALLENGER DISASTER**
This terrifying 1986 explosion is why no second-grade teachers wheeled a television set into class during the 1988 launch of the Space Shuttle *Discovery*.

Chemistry

Science of mixing the earth's elements together in glass containers and heating them in order to produce bubbles. Different from physics, which takes a more general and fundamental approach to natural science in that it primarily ignores bubble and steam production, chemistry homes in on the exact number of elements used, the specific size of the bubbles they create, and the bubbling sounds they emit. In chemistry, the bigger the bubbles and the louder they pop, the more proficient the chemistry. However, smaller, rapidly popping bubbles, as well as the amount of frothing, fizzing, and wafting that occurs during chemistry, is integral to the science. There are four specific disciplines within the field: inorganic chemistry, or the study of how food dyes can create different-colored bubbles; organic chemistry, which is the study and creation of natural, clear, or plain-colored bubbles; physical chemistry, in which laboratory technicians analyze how bubbles change over time; and biochemistry, which focuses primarily on why bubbles don't reform and float back into the air after they've touched the ground. Chemistry is performed by people called chemists, who are constantly trying to further their knowledge of the field by producing the biggest bubble possible. Chemists wear goggles for this.

COMMON LAB EQUIPMENT

BEAKER
A bubble-containing implement

FLORENCE FLASK
Primary goal of a chemist is to create one large bubble that fits perfectly inside the circular, bottom portion of the flask, and keep it unpopped for upwards of 20 seconds

BUNSEN BURNER
Known in chemistry as the engine of bubble production

MORTAR AND PESTLE
Used to grind up bubbles into smaller bubbles

SEPARATORY FUNNEL
Never used once by a single chemist ever

FUNNEL
Used for bubble transport

VOLUMETRIC PIPETTE
Fun to say, but use unknown

MOLECULES: THE WOODEN STICKS AND COLORED BALLS OF LIFE

A group of red, yellow, blue, black or white balls held together by wooden sticks, a molecule is an electrically neutral particle constructed by chemists. Some important molecules in chemistry include a white ball and a red ball held together by a wooden stick, three yellow balls and two blue balls held together by multiple wooden sticks, and 10 balls of each color stretched out in a line across the floor, all of which are held together by wooden sticks.

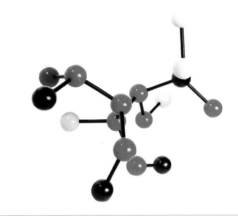

THE PERIODIC TABLE

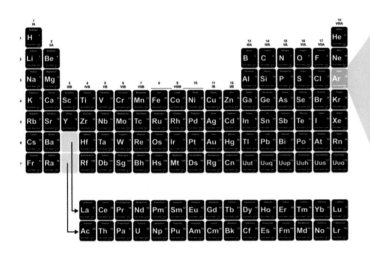

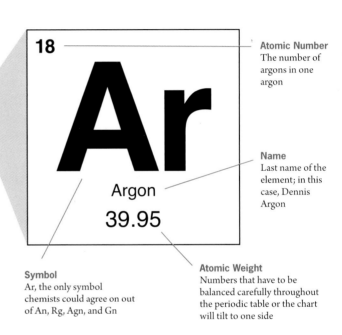

18 — Atomic Number
The number of argons in one argon

Ar

Argon

39.95

Name
Last name of the element; in this case, Dennis Argon

Symbol
Ar, the only symbol chemists could agree on out of An, Rg, Agn, and Gn

Atomic Weight
Numbers that have to be balanced carefully throughout the periodic table or the chart will tilt to one side

THE HISTORY OF CHEMISTRY

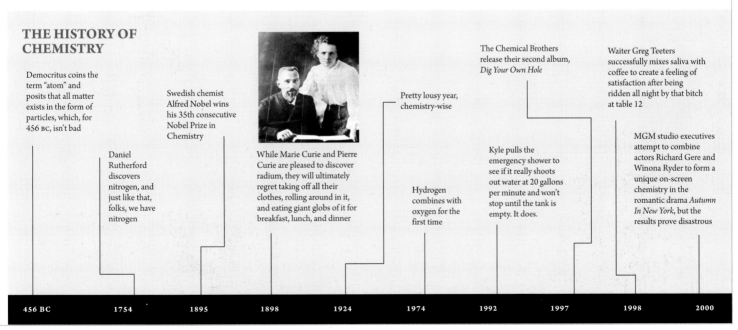

Democritus coins the term "atom" and posits that all matter exists in the form of particles, which, for 456 BC, isn't bad

Daniel Rutherford discovers nitrogen, and just like that, folks, we have nitrogen

Swedish chemist Alfred Nobel wins his 35th consecutive Nobel Prize in Chemistry

While Marie Curie and Pierre Curie are pleased to discover radium, they will ultimately regret taking off all their clothes, rolling around in it, and eating giant globs of it for breakfast, lunch, and dinner

Pretty lousy year, chemistry-wise

Hydrogen combines with oxygen for the first time

The Chemical Brothers release their second album, *Dig Your Own Hole*

Kyle pulls the emergency shower to see if it really shoots out water at 20 gallons per minute and won't stop until the tank is empty. It does.

Waiter Greg Teeters successfully mixes saliva with coffee to create a feeling of satisfaction after being ridden all night by that bitch at table 12

MGM studio executives attempt to combine actors Richard Gere and Winona Ryder to form a unique on-screen chemistry in the romantic drama *Autumn In New York*, but the results prove disastrous

| 456 BC | 1754 | 1895 | 1898 | 1924 | 1974 | 1992 | 1997 | 1998 | 2000 |

CHESS, board game that has evolved into a nuanced, cerebral battle of strategy and wit, though it was designed to be played by mashing pieces together and making loud explosion noises. While modern chess comprises highly complicated tactics and styles that take years to master, the original instructions held that any piece could be moved in any direction at any time, and that play could be put on hold indefinitely to make the king and queen pieces kiss, or to make the knight, then known as the "horsey," gallop around the board in circles while the player made clip-clop noises. In addition, ancient chess players were not required to reach a verifiable checkmate point as they are today, and would instead conclude a game by suddenly rising and flipping the board into the air, scattering pieces in all directions. Traditional chess moves and techniques have occasionally been utilized in modern play, most notably during a 1997 match in which grand master Garry Kasparov finally beat IBM's Deep Blue computer by deploying the classic gambit of throwing a tantrum and repeatedly slapping and kicking his opponent.

A Classic Chess Opening

Castle Hassle, or Super Siege Squared
Both rooks hover 8 inches above the board and quickly move to the center, where they sit for several seconds, fire warning shots to blow up the bishops, and then descend to the playing surface, where they crisscross and wipe out all the pawns, circle back around, and eliminate both knights and rooks.

Defense
Cover eyes, ears, and make loud la-la-la noises.

CHARLIE CHAPLIN ➤
Chaplin with the cane that stabilized him just enough to stay upright a few seconds.

fashion designer and feminist icon known for her forward-thinking, independent lifestyle and for creating a couture empire beloved by wealthy "kept" women who have never worked a day in their lives. At a time when the fashion world was dominated by men, Chanel's unorthodox designs and bohemian way of life challenged society's ideas about gender roles, and she capitalized on her self-imposed freedom by creating a fashion line that is still to this day beloved by rich housewives who adhere rigidly to the status quo.

Chaplin, Charlie (*b. Apr. 16, 1889 d. Dec. 25, 1977*), British actor and director of the silent-film era who starred in hundreds of movies despite a debilitating inner-ear infection that severely impaired his sense of balance. Chaplin was a successful artist even though he tripped, stumbled, and fell through many scenes in his films due to his crippling condition. His work influenced many other actors with physical impairments, including silent-film contemporary Buster Keaton, who suffered from severe facial paralysis as a result of a childhood bout of scarlet fever.

Charlemagne (*b. Apr. 2, 742 d. Jan. 28, 814*), Frank-  ish king and emperor of the Romans who conquered much of modern-day Europe by forcing millions to choose one of three options: convert to Christianity, be slaughtered indiscriminately, or just go on minding their own business while agreeing to disagree on the religion issue. Charlemagne ruled from 768 to 814, during which time his forces launched numerous campaigns to spread Christianity "by the cross or by the sword or by not forcing our beliefs on others and letting them do their own thing." Over the course of his reign, Charlemagne committed genocide against groups as varied as the Lombards, the Danes, the Moors, and the Basques, but if a population refused both conversion and being wiped out by his superior military, Charlemagne simply withdrew, made clear that there were no hard feelings, and agreed that it was not his place to tell people how to live their lives.

Chávez, César (*b. Mar. 31, 1927 d. Apr. 23, 1993*), American civil rights activist and labor organizer who greatly improved the rights of farm workers and grapes. Chávez founded the United Farm Workers of America in 1962 and got thousands of laborers to march side by side with grapes to agitate for higher wages, unemployment insurance, and safer growing conditions. Chávez, who inspired generations of grape activists, was also an advocate for the rights of lettuce, oranges, and corn.

Checks And Balances, system through which the three branches of the U.S. government ensure the American people never become too powerful. According to the U.S. Constitution, the legislative, executive, and judicial branches possess explicit authorities—making laws, enacting regulations, and meting out punishments, respectively— that allow them to work together to curtail citizens' influence over their own governance and to prevent them from getting out of line or overconfident. As James Madison, known as the Father of the Constitution, wrote in 1794, the government's checks and balances were a necessary reaction against the Enlightenment-era ideals of popular sovereignty, and were meant to empower the federal government

with "sufficient dominion over the lowly, horrid masses to keep them in their goddamn place."

Cheney, Dick (*b. Jan. 30, 1941*), former vice president of the United

States and one of the few people in the world ever to see all his hopes and dreams come true. With an extensive résumé of lifelong goals achieved, including serving as the White House Chief of Staff, being elected to the House of Representatives, holding office as Secretary of Defense, chairing a *Fortune* 500 company, and marrying his high school sweetheart, Dick Cheney is one of 10 or 12 human beings in the history of civilization to ever have all his greatest wishes fulfilled, and fulfilled resoundingly. Indeed, millions of people across the world strive their whole lives to make even one of their dream come true, and ultimately fail to do so, but Cheney—the man who systematically rolled back domestic civil liberties, relaxed the definition of torture, involved the United States in an inescapable Middle Eastern quagmire, and personally profited from that region's rich oil fields— got everything he ever wanted.

Chicago El Train, source of future headline "231 Dead In CTA Station Collapse."

Chicken Pox, harmless childhood disease that, when contracted by people over age 18, violently kills them within 48 hours by making them shit out their entire nervous system in an agonizing cascade of blood and fecal matter.

Children International, nonprofit organization whose street volunteers collect more than 15 million moments of innocent people's time per year. While the group accumulates, on average, 900,000 minutes from tourists and 1.4 million from the unemployed, the vast majority of collected time comes from pedestrians who accidentally make eye contact with a volunteer and feel obligated to give a minute tops or however long it takes to just sign the goddamn petition already because it's getting late and they had to be at work five minutes ago. The organization has hoarded an estimated 12 billion free moments since its founding in 1936, but it estimates that it loses 3 trillion moments annually due to people who say they can't right now and then renege on their promise to stop on their way back.

Chinatown, masterpiece of American cinema released in 1974 where at the end it turns out that John Huston was fucking his daughter.

Chinese Food, popular type of American cuisine.

Chin-Up Bar, horizontal metal rod installed at the top of a bedroom door frame that signals the rite of passage from 13-year-old boy to 14-year-old boy.

Chivalry, medieval system of moral, religious, and social codes governing knightly behavior developed because it was the only way to get

◄ **CÉSAR CHÁVEZ**
Most grapes credit Chávez with helping them get a 40-hour ripening week.

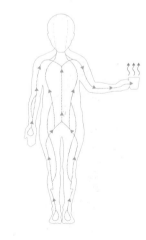

Ch'i, energy force in traditional Chinese philosophy that flows through the body and, with decades of intense training, can be controlled enough to warm up a cup of liquid in one's hands.

CITIES OF THE WORLD
Chicago

American city universally acclaimed as perfectly fine. Incorporated in 1837 on the banks of Lake Michigan, Chicago is lauded worldwide for being a decent-looking place with nice architecture. Chicago boasts

Yup, there it is. Chicago.

several good sports teams, has a lot of better-than-average food to eat, and is regarded by its 3 million residents as a reasonably okay place to live for a year or so before moving to New York.

CHRISTIANITY,

monotheistic religion occasionally rooted in the teachings of Jesus Christ, whom Christians regard as the son of God and a sometimes-convenient model for their own values and behavior. Christ promulgated charity, humility, nonviolence, and other virtues that Christians once in a while regard as sacrosanct and that, when sporadically adhered to, demonstrate the path to a righteous life. The world's 2.2 billion Christians consider Jesus a messianic figure who will deliver to heaven all who conduct themselves as he did when the mood strikes them and if they have the time. While Christianity is divided among the Roman Catholic Church, the Eastern Orthodox Church, and various Protestant groups, each of these branches shares the belief that salvation is available to all who follow in Jesus' footsteps, but who also realize that sometimes that's just not very expedient.

Christian Relics

Holy Nails: Venerated set of three nails that were said to have held Jesus Christ to the cross, plus two backup nails in case one got bent hitting a bone

Crown Of Thorns: Crown made of thorns that Roman soldiers placed on Jesus' head to mock him quite effectively

Holy Chalice: Gross Styrofoam cup that Jesus always used to drink his coffee out of and that he never threw away or cleaned out

Pope John Paul II's Left Arm: Blessed limb of the late Holy Father that was snagged by cardinals who wanted to fill up shelf space in the Vatican's new display case

Saint Peter's Jizz Rag: Holy cloth used by Peter to wipe away puddles of spoo that formed on his stomach after ejaculating

Christian Rites

Communion: Rite used to weed out weirdo Christians who get way too into idea of consuming the flesh of Jesus Christ

Last Rites: Very last prayers administered to Christians before death, which were given to Timothy McVeigh prior to his execution, so he's happy and in heaven now

Confirmation: Christian rite of initiation in which potential members have to perform a drive-by shooting and rape at least three members of another religion

Anointing Of Sick: Rite that involves applying blessed oil to sick members of the church to grease them up and help them slide easily into death

CHIVALRY ➤
Knights strictly followed the chivalric code in order to get Lady Everilda slipping and sliding in her own juices.

into Lady Everilda's pants. A chivalrous man needed to express the qualities of courtesy, generosity, valor, and dexterity in arms if he wanted to have any chance of scoring with the normally prudish Lady Everilda. The term chivalry traces its origins to the medieval Latin *caballārius*, meaning "horseman," and is so named for the mounted knights whom Everilda was all too happy to let mount her all night long—and slap her bountiful ass, too—as long as they bowed slightly or kissed her hand. Deeds such as holding open doors and draping one's coat over a lady's shoulders became hallmarks of modern chivalry, gestures that hearken back to a time when such things were pretty much guaranteed to get Lady Everilda totally wet. Just sopping.

Cho, Seung-Hui (*b. Jan. 18, 1984 d. Apr. 16, 2007*), undergraduate student at Virginia Tech University who you completely forgot about even though he was responsible for the deadliest shooting by a single gunman in American history. On April 16, 2007, which is not that long ago at all, Cho murdered 32 people including 26 students and a Holocaust survivor, before turning the gun on himself. Furthermore, you probably don't even remember who Nidal Hasan is either, which is odd, because he killed 13 soldiers at Fort Hood in 2009.

Chopin, Frédéric, for information on this figure, please go buy a book about Frédéric Chopin.

Christening, baptismal nicknaming ceremony in which an infant receives a moniker such as "Blade," "Crusher," "Nuke," "Rhino," "Turbo," "Beast," "T-Bone," "Blunt," "Thugg," "The Hammer," "Glokk," "Skuz," "Reaper," "Hooch," "Diesel," or "Spaz."

Christmas, Christian holiday celebrating the birth of Jesus Christ that is widely considered the worst possible time for a husband and father of four to reveal an ongoing extramarital affair to his family. Christmas was first observed in Rome in AD 354, and includes such traditions as exchanging gifts, decorating a Christmas tree, and eating a family dinner, which is the most terrible moment of the holiday for a father to interrupt the festivities by saying, "I have something I need to tell everyone," and then proceed to inform his shocked wife and crying children that he will be leaving them because he has been seeing another woman, who is pregnant. The absolute worst occasion for a dad to flatly inform his loved ones that he hasn't been happy for years and that Stephanie makes him feel alive, Christmas gradually incorporated several pagan winter festivals, including Saturnalia, and various ancient Germanic feasts, and is an even worse time than Thanksgiving for a father to say that he will be moving out the next day because he and Stephanie have signed a lease on a new apartment, and that yes, the Stephanie he's talking about is mom's friend Stephanie, the much-beloved adoptive aunt to his four young children.

Church, building where Christians go each Sunday to give God another shot.

Churchill, Winston *(b. Nov. 30, 1874 d. Jan. 24, 1965)*, smallish talking man deployed by Great Britain during the Second World War to talk at the British people. During a period of great turmoil, the little talking person was periodically put in front of microphones or in the middle of Parliament to chomp on a cigar and talk for a period of time to the British Empire and make it feel better, after which he would be placed in storage until another traumatic event happened and he was needed for more talking. The successful deployment of the tiny, bowler-hatted talking man is now seen as having been crucial in Great Britain defeating Nazi Germany and its own little talking man.

CIA, intelligence-gathering unit of the United States government that uses its undisclosed budgetary resources to find out what people are saying about the CIA at any given time.

Cigarette, tobacco-filled paper tube used for smoking that is considered to be a gateway to even more dangerous carcinogens. Smokers quickly develop a tolerance to the acetaldehyde and hydrazine found in cigarettes and begin craving more intense cancer-causing agents such as radon, vinyl chloride, and beryllium. When these chemicals no longer satisfy them, addicts will seek their fix by breaking apart old floor tiles to release the asbestos contained within, or by welding stainless steel to produce carcinogenic nickel and chromium fumes. Statistics suggest people who begin smoking cigarettes as teenagers are five times more likely to develop an addiction to lead and 10 times more likely to

DISCOVERED HIMSELF BETWEEN TERMS

Grover Cleveland

(b. Mar. 18, 1837 d. June 24, 1908), 22nd and 24th president of the United States and the only one ever to serve nonconsecutive terms, between which he decided to explore his lifelong interest in acupuncture. Following an exhausting first term in which he vetoed hundreds of bills, Cleveland set aside a maximum of four years to try his hand at traditional Chinese healing, reasoning that if it turned out not to be his thing, he could always return to his prior job as head of state. After earning high marks in his mail-order correspondence course, the former New York governor slowly began acquiring clients through word of mouth and started to think he might actually be able to make a go of acupuncture professionally. But in 1892, with a flagging schedule of appointments and mounting personal debt, Cleveland reluctantly returned to public service, successfully running on a platform to reduce protectionist tariffs with friend and local Reiki practitioner Adlai E. Stevenson.

CIVIL RIGHTS MOVEMENT, global campaign aimed at getting human beings to treat people like human beings. The unprecedented movement, which reached its peak in the 1950s and 1960s, primarily used civil resistance to promote its extremely dangerous and radical idea that a person should respect another person because he or she is a person. Those agitating for civil rights were met with animosity, aggression, and even violence from individuals who could not accept the idea that people should be treated like people, and who for generations had believed that treating humans as subhuman or inhuman was the correct way to treat humans. Because the fundamental concept of treating people like people was deemed too progressive, the humans who wanted to be considered human were often beaten, sprayed with fire hoses, or even killed. Due to the large numbers of people around the world who still believe that people should not have to treat other people like people, the civil rights movement can only be considered a failure.

Key Figures From The Civil Rights Movement

Martin Luther King, Jr.
Spiritual and organizational leader who was assassinated for his extremely controversial belief that you shouldn't treat people like shit all the time.

Medgar Evers
Activist who was shot and killed for publicly claiming that all human beings were human beings.

Thomas Robb
Ku Klux Klan leader, anti-Semite, and extremist who doesn't think people should be treated like people and is currently alive and well and residing with his wife

in Boone County, Arkansas. He has several grandchildren, still preaches at his local church, and plays golf often.

Bill Clinton

(b. Aug. 19, 1946), 42nd president of the United States, whose popular appeal nearly provoked House Republicans to impeach him for conduct in his personal life, an unprecedented move that would have made a mockery of the U.S. Constitution and was therefore quickly dismissed as a laughable waste of time. Clinton, a self-described New Democrat whose centrist policies and ability to empathize endeared him to voters across the political spectrum, would have been only the second president to face impeachment, a drastic measure that Republican leaders immediately dropped as an absurd act, given the lofty constitutional standard for impeachment of "high crimes and misdemeanors." They were also self-aware enough to realize their own marital infidelities would have tainted the already dubious legal proceedings with rank hypocrisy. These considerations, as well as Republicans' shared revulsion at the thought of tying up two branches of government for months and diverting millions of taxpayer dollars to a trial the public would quickly unmask as a politically motivated ploy, prompted House leaders to simply allow Americans to assess Clinton's personal indiscretions for themselves. This noble gesture of restraint continues to inform the conduct of Republicans to this day.

compulsively expose themselves to gamma rays.

Cinderella, animated 1950 Disney film responsible for making people secretly wonder how they would react if, at some point in their life, an animal they were looking at suddenly stood up on its hind legs and began to sing a song. Revered by many as a charming children's classic, *Cinderella* also has to make one think, if, say, a friend's cat, for instance, abruptly jumped up, made direct eye contact, smiled, and started singing a song in a mellifluous human voice, what would one do? Scream? Vomit? Just stand there, paralyzed with shock and fear, unable to speak? Those watching the beloved, Oscar-nominated film eventually conclude they would either have to kill the cat, kill themselves, or be committed to a psychiatric hospital.

Circus At The End Of The World, The, 1953 novel by minor Beat writer Anders van Braak II that tells the partly autobiographical tale of an itinerant young poet and his brief love affair with an alcoholic paper mill heiress in a cabin in Maine's Great North Woods. Van Braak II, son of noted scientist Anders van Braak, wrote his obscure masterpiece after a falling-out with his father led him to abandon a promising career as a research scientist and devote his life to experimental prose and a self-invented life philosophy he called Braakian Subjectivism. The book sold poorly upon its release, causing van Braak II to fall into alcoholism and drug abuse, eventually resulting in the dissolution of his marriage and his early death in 1965. Van Braak II's estranged son, Anders van Braak III, is a prominent research scientist and has forbidden the reprinting of

COAL, compressed remains of perished coal miners whose bodies decompose over thousands of years.

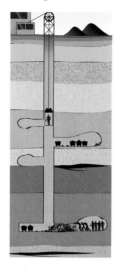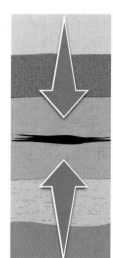

Formation Of Coal

STEP 1
Miners die from lack of oxygen, and their bodies gradually decay and form organic debris.

STEP 2
Dead miner material is compressed between sedimentary layers, and the combination of time and heat transforms their bodies into lignite.

STEP 3
Further compression compacts what's left of the miners' corpses into coal deposits.

any of his father's work.

Civilization, complex human society that has advanced to the point of establishing dysfunctional political structures, unfair social hierarchies, and economic systems that clearly do not work. A civilization is often characterized by its shoddy public education and its decrepit mass transit. In some fields of modern scholarship, the term is associated with "culture," which refers to the unreadable literature, overwrought paintings, and mindless, lowest-common-denominator music that together make up the arts.

Coat Of Arms, unique heraldic design that knights would wear pinned to their armor so a grown-up could help them get home if they ever got lost on the battlefield.

Cobain, Kurt (b. Feb. 20, 1967 d. Apr. 5, 1994), musician and icon of the grunge genre who tragically

committed suicide years before he could have performed on stage with Eddie Vedder, Scott Weiland, and Ne-Yo at the 2017 Super Bowl.

Coca-Cola, big company that makes baby's little sugar juice, which he drinks out of a widdle bottle when he gets thirsty at worky. The nummy juice, which helps keep baby awake so he doesn't go sleepy-bye night night at his desk, also comes in a diet version so baby doesn't get too roly-poly in his tum tum. The big company that makes baby's little sugar juice is one of the most successful corporate brands in the world, along with Mars Inc., which makes baby's widdle yum yum snacks that he eats when he wants a widdle shoogy-woogy treat after wunch.

Cocaine, stimulant drug derived from the leaves of the coca plant that can be consumed via smoking, injection, or nasal insufflation, and provides the user with a mediocre, short-lived high far inferior to that of methamphetamine. Cocaine often comes in white powdered form and, in addition to being more expensive and less potent than methamphetamine, is looked down upon by people who are really serious about partying. The narcotic is produced primarily in Latin America and smuggled abroad after being mixed with God knows what, while methamphetamine is made domestically and is much safer, especially when purchased from someone you can trust, someone who is just a phone call away, day or night—someone, come to think of it, who can probably also get you some coke, if that's really what you want. (323) 914-0987.

Coffee, another thing someone can act like a complete queer about.

Cold War *(1946–1991),* state of military and political tension between the Soviet Union and the United States in which all of humanity was wiped out five times per hour in the minds of every person on the planet. Over a period of several decades, escalating friction between the United States and the USSR led to a significant buildup of nuclear arms and military infrastructure across the globe, eventually resulting in the cities of Moscow, New York, Los Angeles, Leningrad, Berlin, Wichita, Seoul, Havana, Warsaw, and Sandusky, Ohio, being obliterated in an instant, thousands and thousands of times over, in the everyday thoughts of those cities' residents. The Cold War reached its peak on Oct. 23, 1964, when every field, mountain, valley, city, home, and family in the United States was enveloped in a hellish maelstrom of fire, ash, and blinding white nothingness in the imagination of 10-year-old Bobby Huntsman as he lay awake in bed.

College, public or private two- to four-year institution of higher learning that used to be pretty wild back in college. Though it hasn't woken up face down in a toilet in years, the multidisciplinary center of research and academic study was known for throwing the most epic, out-of-control ragers on campus, and would shotgun just about anything. Attended by nearly 13 million students across the United States each year, college was a real animal back then, regularly putting on its Boston Bruins jersey, grabbing a hockey stick, and waking up everybody on its floor at 4 a.m. while serving as a bastion of knowledge intended to foster intellectual curiosity among its students and faculty. College primarily provides a liberal arts education at the undergraduate level and got pretty heavy into drugs at one point, almost dropping out and moving to Montana during its junior year. However, college got its act together, graduated, moved back home to figure some shit out, is a multibillion-dollar-a-year business, and eventually went back to get its master's in creative writing.

Color, property of light reflected, absorbed, or emitted by an object, resulting in a dazzling visible spectrum and a real fuck-you to the blind. Various wavelengths of light stimulate the three different types of cone cells in the retina, shitting all over the blind and vehemently urging them to suck a big one as it produces the visual perception of red, yellow, green, blue, indigo, or violet. Providing a stunningly beautiful rainbow of hues, shades, tints, and values to individuals blessed with sight, color cruelly holds up a middle finger just inches from the faces of the blind without them even realizing what is happening as they shuffle around in a cold darkness.

Columbine Shooting, horrific 1999 high school shooting that is considered the fourth-worst tragedy in

Citizen Kane, brilliant, groundbreaking work of artistic genius that has unfortunately been completely invalidated because the man who made it later gained weight.

Clown Fish, tropical fish that enjoys a relationship of symbiotic mutualism with sea anemones wherein the clown fish will defend and clean a host anemone, which, in exchange, will repeatedly sting the masochistic clown fish, giving it the constant pain it needs to get off.

PREVENTED A ROARING THIRTIES

Calvin Coolidge

(b. July 4, 1872 d. Jan. 5, 1933), 30th president of the United States, whose shrewd and meticulous planning and political foresight helped guide the United States into the Great Depression. Coolidge's bold economic vision of reckless investment and wild speculation on Wall Street laid the groundwork for a ruinous stock market collapse that the president promised would bring about the worst, most devastating economic crisis in U.S. history. In 1928, as America continued enjoying the fruits of the Roaring Twenties, Coolidge reassured citizens that his careful stewardship of the economy would plunge them into a desperate squalor where "millions of Americans will soon be scavenging for scraps of food like wild animals." Though out of office by the time the stock market finally crashed on Oct. 29, 1929, Coolidge is nonetheless credited with bravely steering the nation out of an extended period of prosperity and firmly setting it on course for economic catastrophe, and for inspiring the policies of such future presidents as Ronald Reagan and George W. Bush.

U.S. public school history, three places behind the 2001 No Child Left Behind Act. Although the murder of 12 students and one teacher by students Eric Harris and Dylan Klebold was a shocking catastrophe for the small Colorado community and the nation as a whole, the enactment of the federal No Child Left Behind law during the George W. Bush administration was a tragedy of cataclysmic proportions that devastated an entire generation of pupils and teachers by ruthlessly destroying the very foundations of public education. After a long period of mourning, Columbine High School gradually returned to normalcy, until the day when it, like every school in the nation, was ravaged by a disastrous policy that used standardized tests to measure students' worth rather than provide an actual, well-rounded education.

Columbus, Christopher *(b. Oct. 31, 1451 d. May 20, 1506)*, Italian explorer who searched for an ocean passage to Asia and inadvertently subjugated, enslaved, and murdered untold numbers of Native Americans when he had intended to do those things to the peoples of India. Through a combination of geographical and navigational errors, Columbus mistakenly landed on what is now South America and the Caribbean islands, where he unleashed a bloody, centuries-long genocide against the indigenous tribes of the Western Hemisphere instead of slaughtering and raping the various cultures of India and plundering *their* wealth and natural resources. Though Columbus never set foot in India and had to settle for killing off nearly every Native American person he came into contact with instead, he did set the stage for the golden age of colonialism, and his dream of looting India and decimating its people through violence and disease was later realized by the Dutch and the British.

Combine Harvester, piece of agriculture equipment primarily used as collateral for obtaining a loan to desperately hold on for another couple of months to the farm that has been in the family for five generations.

Combustion, process by which oxygen catalyzes with chemical bonds in your wife and her lover while they sleep, creating energy in the form of heat and carbon dioxide.

Communism, political ideology espousing social revolution to install a system in which all property is publicly owned, each person works according to his abilities, and Chrysler does not hold its annual year-end blowout, Chase does not offer a zero percent APR cash-back rewards card, and Burger King does not add the Spicy Chick'n Crisp sandwich to its value menu. In a communist nation, all businesses and social programs are controlled by the state, and wealth is redistributed evenly among the populace, a methodology that precludes bargain-basement prices on brand-new Sealy, Serta, Simmons Beautyrest, or Stearns & Foster mattresses for this weekend and this weekend only. There are currently five countries with communist governments (China, Vietnam, Laos, Cuba, and North Korea) in which citizens are completely unable to buy a Bowflex for only four easy payments of $99.99 and, if they're not stronger, leaner, and more energetic in 30 days, send it back for a full refund but still keep the set of dumbbells as a free gift to them.

Computer, little buddy who hangs out with a person while they work, communicate with others, play games, and watch videos. The programmable little friend, who can hang out in a person's home or tag along on road trips, is designed to perform complex calculations and keep a person company while they're filling out their monthly budget spreadsheet or shopping on

CHRISTOPHER ➤ COLUMBUS

Once Columbus realized he was raping and pillaging Native Americans instead of peoples from India, he thought about stopping, but decided to continue because he figured he would have to murder innocent people in South America at some point, anyway.

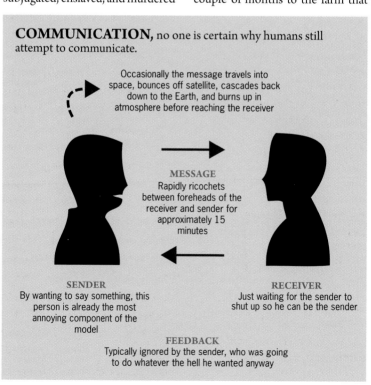

COMMUNICATION, no one is certain why humans still attempt to communicate.

Occasionally the message travels into space, bounces off satellite, cascades back down to the Earth, and burns up in atmosphere before reaching the receiver

MESSAGE
Rapidly ricochets between foreheads of the receiver and sender for approximately 15 minutes

SENDER
By wanting to say something, this person is already the most annoying component of the model

RECEIVER
Just waiting for the sender to shut up so he can be the sender

FEEDBACK
Typically ignored by the sender, who was going to do whatever the hell he wanted anyway

the Internet. Most of the little pals run on one of several major operating systems and they don't even mind staying up for three or four days in a row, or occasionally getting crumbs in their keyboards.

Since their invention in the 1940s, computers have gotten consistently smaller and more powerful, meaning that a bunch of the little guys are now tiny enough to fit right in someone's pocket, so they'll always be there, always, whether you need companionship or entertainment or just want to listen to some music as you fall asleep at night, thinking about all the cool stuff you and your computer bud will be able to do together in the morning.

Concentration Camp, work experience left off many people's résumés in the 1940s and 1950s.

Concert, live music event that everyone in attendance secretly wants to end soon.

Concrete, building material that definitely didn't have nine dicks carved in it when it was poured yesterday.

Congress, national legislative body of the U.S. government that had such amazing potential, damn it. Established by Article I of the Constitution, Congress comprises the Senate and the House of Representatives, an ingenious bicameral system that seemed on paper like it was going to be something really special, you know? Really, really special. With its exclusive ability to collect taxes and declare war, not to mention curb the strength of the Executive Branch through its impeachment powers, Congress looked to all the world like it was going to have an extraordinarily positive impact on the nation, but it just … it just squandered it. God. So much promise frittered away, and for what? Where did it all go wrong? Was Congress just doomed from its founding in 1789 to suffer the pitfalls of human nature? Throughout its history, Congress has passed bills such as the Clean Air Act, the G.I. Bill, and the Civil Rights Act of 1964, tantalizing glimpses of its potential that only make its performance as a whole that much more heartbreaking. Tears you up just thinking about it. A majority of

THE NIGHT SKY

The Cup

The Dot

The Line

CONSTELLATION, one of the perceived patterns among the seven stars in the night sky that resemble a cup, a dot, and a line. Different cultures have historically created unique narratives around the constellations, interpreting each shape as something familiar to them. For example, the ancient Chinese referred to the line as the stick and viewed its appearance as a sign of good luck, while the ancient Greeks saw the cup and the dot as the bowl and the speck, which represented the duality between the earthly and the divine. Early Egyptians called the dot "the Point" and believed it to have descended from the tip of the line that broke off after colliding into the cup. Ancient Persians saw the constellations similarly, but believed the dot had been poured out of the cup in a time

long before humans arrived on earth. Native Americans, whose complex mythology revolved heavily around the constellations, believed that one day the dot and the line would fall to Earth as a bow and arrow to be used only by a warrior who was worthy enough. Before modern navigational tools, mariners used the constellations as a guide across bodies of water, always knowing that if they pointed their ships in the direction of the cup, they would be going north. Likewise, by charting the movement of the dot over a period of weeks, a sailor could determine what season it was. For observers in the Southern Hemisphere, two dots are sometimes visible during the winter months, an optical illusion that can be attributed to the curvature of the Earth and refraction of light through the atmosphere.

Conch Shell, wind instrument that, when blown into, causes the conch living inside to emit a forlorn, trumpetlike howl.

Criminal Justice

Governmental and social practices directed at upholding the law, deterring crimes, and rehabilitation that just plain always works. Criminal justice involves penalizing those who violate laws, a process successfully designed so that it never, ever punishes an innocent person, nor displays any preference in regard to race or socioeconomic status. Additionally, the criminal justice system has a 98.99 percent success rate in transforming sentenced malefactors into productive, upstanding members of society. The institution of criminal justice is put into practice by dedicated professionals as unwavering in their morality as they are in their unassailable integrity; this group includes legislators, police officers, judges, lawyers, corrections officers, and parole officers, all of whom, down to the very last individual, are the most honest, hardworking, forthright people a society has to offer and would never consider abusing the awesome power with which they have been entrusted. In its most extreme form, criminal justice can include capital punishment, the implementation of which has proved to be an incredibly effective deterrent, always causing a definitive decrease in the egregious crimes that call for this ultimate sentence.

PROMINENT COURT CASES

Rodney King
African-American man who was convicted on 78 counts of assaulting a police officer's billy club with his head and body.

Casey Anthony
Defendant Casey Anthony was found not guilty after the jury ruled that 2-year-old Caylee Anthony deserved to be murdered for ruining her fun-loving mom's social life.

O.J. Simpson
Criminal trial that captivated the American public because each citizen had also murdered their ex-spouse and ex-spouse's friend, and was curious to see if they would be found guilty or innocent.

Lizzie Borden
This trial, in which a New England woman was acquitted on charges of butchering her parents with an ax, is proof that, at least in .0001% of cases, the criminal justice system does fail somewhat.

INSIDE THE COURTROOM

A

Plaintiff
Person who, having searched his soul for any ulterior motive and exhausted every non-judicial remedy, reluctantly brings a case against the defendant

Prosecutor
Person who was not bullied as a child and doesn't need to prove themselves by breaking others down emotionally

Jury
Body that is sworn to render a verdict based on the evidence presented, a responsibility the citizenry holds so sacred that the waiting list to appear on a jury is years long

Judge
Official whose mind never wanders to golf or other leisure-time activities when a case is being presented to him or her

Witness
Perfect eye-sight, photographic memory, free of prejudice, and happy to help

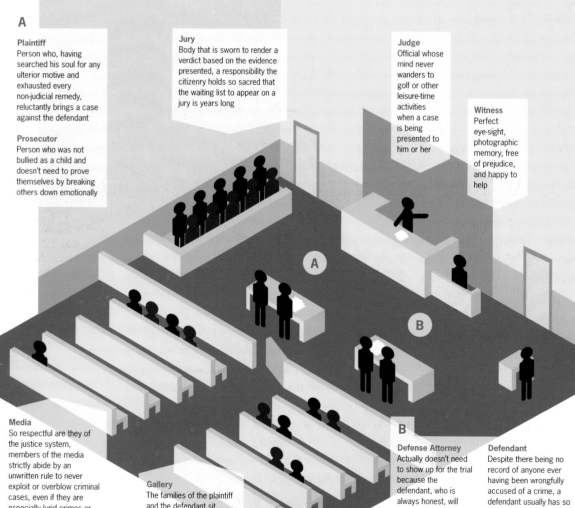

Media
So respectful are they of the justice system, members of the media strictly abide by an unwritten rule to never exploit or overblow criminal cases, even if they are especially lurid crimes or involve celebrities

Gallery
The families of the plaintiff and the defendant sit together to show that even if the two can't get along, at least their families can put their differences aside and move on

Defense Attorney
Actually doesn't need to show up for the trial because the defendant, who is always honest, will enter a plea of either guilty or not guilty, at which point the trial is basically over

Defendant
Despite there being no record of anyone ever having been wrongfully accused of a crime, a defendant usually has so much respect for the history and rich tradition of the criminal justice system that he or she submits to a trial rather than simply reporting directly to jail

modern Americans are sadly resigned to the fact that Congress will never amount to very much, and considering all it could have been, well, it's just a goddamn shame.

Conservationism, social and philosophical movement based on the arrogant idea that people can completely destroy and then unilaterally save a 5 billion-year-old planet. The incredibly egotistical notion that mankind could itself ruin a natural world millions of millennia in the making and then somehow undo the catastrophic damage traces its origins all the way back to the Industrial Revolution and has grown rapidly since the 1970s. Today, conservationism is increasingly woven into the fabric of everyday life and is particularly evident in the self-important idea that a planet with a mass of 6 sextillion metric tons can be brought to its knees and then somehow revived if everyone disposes of their old batteries the right way.

Constitution (U.S.), supreme law of the United States, adopted in 1787, that never needs to be updated or reassessed because the nation's founders included clear instructions on what to do if homosexuals ever want to get married, how to fairly regulate the Internet, and whether or not digital inspections of computer hard drives at the U.S. border are legal. The second-oldest such document still in use by any country in the world, the U.S. Constitution holds the absolute answer to every conceivable complex judicial question, such as the legal status of stem cells obtained from fetuses and the protocol for addressing biothreats that emanate not from governments but individual actors—two things James Madison and John Jay clearly foresaw and

explicitly addressed in the hand-written 18th-century text. During the 2012 case *United States v. Jones,* for instance, all the Supreme Court justices needed to do to deliver their final ruling was read the corollary to the Fourth Amendment penned by Alexander Hamilton, who wrote, "In a future instance wherein a police force uses a Global Positioning System (GPS) to track down a potential suspect, a warrant must be issued prior to the investigation. However, if the suspect's Facebook page clearly indicates unlawful activity, the space-based navigation system may be used without the permission of a court."

Cool, highly sought-after status of being that makes it nearly impossible to live one's life.

Coral Reef, vast underwater ridge where fish can socialize and be themselves without having to worry about the daily pressures of the open sea. Formed by calcified living polyps in shallow areas of the ocean, coral reefs are among the most diverse ecosystems on earth, provid-

ing fish with a safe, judgment-free environment regardless of how they look or what their backgrounds might be. The largest coral reef in the world is Australia's Great Barrier Reef, a massive 133,000-square-mile space where more than 1,500 different species swim around and make new friends every day and are never ostracized for having a weird-

looking fin or larger-than-normal mouth, or being from an unfamiliar part of the Pacific Ocean. One-fifth of the world's coral reefs have disappeared, however, and there are now fewer supportive habitats than ever where a red snapper, grouper, or a spotted trunkfish can hang out and just be fish.

Cordite, chemical mixture invented by detectives and military fiction writers to describe the smell of a recently fired gun.

Corn, grain-based animal feed systematically introduced into U.S. diets to fatten up Americans. An easy-to-consume source of filler, corn is an inexpensive way to improve Americans' tenderness, build up bulk, and, because it contains the highest sugar content of all feed sources, allow citizens to reach their finishing weight more quickly. As corn intake gradually increases, plumped-up Americans lose their mobility and begin to form folds of fat around their backs, shoulders, and ribs, visual indicators that the domesticated citizens have reached their plumpest point.

Coronary Disease, leading cause of death among men who have had a long day and just want to enjoy a nice cheeseburger every once in a while without getting badgered about how they're killing themselves, if that's not too goddamn much to ask. Triggered by a lack of blood circulation, coronary disease is responsible for one in four fatalities in men who aren't going to count every calorie like some kind of health-food nut, even if it shortens their lives by a couple of years that they'd probably spend laid up in a nursing home anyway. Risk factors include smoking, hypertension, obesity, that asshole Rick breathing down your neck all day,

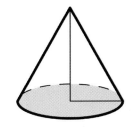

Cone, one of these.

Confucius (*b. Sept. 28, 551 BC d. 479 BC*), Chinese thinker and social philosopher who believed government should be free of bribery and coercion, the naïve idiot.

inactivity, diabetes, and finishing off a plate of nachos and a box of caramel corn in front of the Packers game because it's your house and you'll do whatever the hell you please in it, thank you very much.

Corpse, physical remains of a human body that people are really touchy about even though the guy's dead and is not likely to give a flying shit that someone accidentally knocked him off the gurney.

Corset, tight-fitting women's undergarment popularized during the 16th century in response to the now-discredited medical theory that if not contained, a woman's ribs would become dislocated and begin floating to different parts of the body. Doctors believed that without a corset tightening the midriff, ribs could move from the chest area to below the waistline, causing a urinary tract infection, and that a dislodged curved bone not caught immediately could get trapped in the circulatory system and eventually flow down the leg and poke through the toes. It was a commonly held medical belief that, by raising and shaping the breasts, corsets created a protective barrier between the chest and neck that would prevent the upper ribs from becoming lodged in the throat should a woman cough or sneeze.

Cottonmouth, deadly venomous viper that lurks in various bodies of water such as swamps, rivers, Brita pitchers, and ponds.

County Supervisor, individual either elected or appointed by a county to deal with Mrs. Whitman. The county supervisor is charged not only with handling Mrs. Whitman's incessant calls and e-mails concerning how her neighbor lets his dog crap all over her lawn or how she was nearly run over by

some maniac on a bicycle, but also with politely humoring her when she comes down to the office twice a month to complain in person about how the mailman just shoves her letters in the box like they're garbage, despite the fact that mail is not something the county oversees. The county supervisor can be thought of as a counterpart to the more urban city manager, who is responsible for contending with Tony's nonstop bullshit.

Cousteau, Jacques (*b. June 11, 1910 d. June 25, 1997*), French oceanographer and documentary filmmaker whose tireless education and conservation efforts were responsible for sparking worldwide interest in ocean ecology, and who, on no fewer than 19 occasions, accidentally killed infant fur seals by crushing their skulls with his scuba tank when entering the water backward from a small boat without looking. Cousteau's popular films brought attention to manmade threats to endangered marine life, even after he inadvertently electrocuted a 39-foot whale shark. Cousteau's legacy of protecting fragile ocean ecosystems is upheld by the Cousteau Society, a conservation organization he founded in 1973 that has raised millions of dollars, in large part to help repair the 14-mile stretch of the Great Barrier Reef Cousteau destroyed after he forgot to raise the anchor of his famed boat, *Calypso*, a major fuel leak from which simultaneously left thousands of dead fish, sharks, seabirds, and other wildlife in its wake.

Cowboy, worker who rides the plains on horseback and relies on his wits, toughness, and courage, or a San Antonio executive in a wide-brimmed hat who makes 175 grand a year, has had one too many bour-

bons, and is giving a waitress at a sports bar a really hard time.

Crime, activity that has of late run rampant in the streets and back alleys of our once-great cities, rendered our so-called law enforcement officials powerless, struck fear into the hearts of honest, hardworking citizens everywhere, and left

Copse, small group of trees huddled together in terror moments before they are killed.

Cracker, crispy baked good usually made from flour and shoved into one's face at three in the afternoon when a person can't be bothered to make anything or even cut a piece of cheese to put on the cracker.

CRITICISM, genre of writing that places value judgments on literature, film, visual art, architecture, and other creative endeavors, and which, quite frankly, appears to have been written by an insufferably precocious, attention-starved 9-year-old. The fundamental flaws evident in criticism are simply too numerous to list here, but rest assured, unlucky readers of any part of the collected body of this laughably derivative style of writing will wish they had never bothered. In its modern form, criticism dates back to at least the early 18th century, and it is evidently content to remain mired in the same juvenile gimmicks and disjointed, slapdash themes it has inexpertly employed since its first treatises were published more three centuries ago. With its latest "contributions" to dialectics, criticism continues to lend credence to the widely held notion that those who cannot do, critique. Perhaps it's finally time for the entire form of analysis to call it quits and retreat from public view with whatever little dignity it may have remaining. **D-**
—*Keith Mandrell*

us—all of us—desperate for some way to combat the spiraling lawlessness of the petty thugs and gangsters who rule the underworld. While it remains to be seen whether or not anyone will have the courage to step forward and eradicate the scourge of vice and villainy that is eating away at the very core of our society like some black, malignant cancer, one thing we all know for certain is that if action is not taken soon, more blood of the innocents will spill, and the meek and pure of heart shall inevitably become so paralyzed by the stranglehold of these far-reaching criminal enterprises that hope as we know it shall be lost forever. The only real question that stands at the time of this book's publication is, who among us will answer this call to justice? Who among us will stand up to this depraved scum and tell them enough is enough, tell them to get out of our cities, our towns, our churches, our schoolyards, and send them back to the sick hell from whence they crawled?

Crockett, Davy (b. Aug. 17, 1786 d. Mar. 6, 1836), mentally disabled American woodsman whose dim-witted antics made him the unoffi-

cial mascot of western expansion and earned him the teasing nickname "King of the Wild Frontier." Crockett was often ridiculed for his strange manner of dress, which included a fringed buckskin jacket and trousers, and a preposterous hat made from a dead raccoon that a group of Tennessee militiamen gave him, convincing Crockett it would give him special powers. He insisted on always carrying around a large Bowie knife, the tip of which was affixed with a cork for Crockett's protection, and he could be heard repeatedly singing the three-word song "Davy. Davy Crockett!" which he often pointed out he had written all by himself. At one time named an honorary Tennessee congressman by snickering lawmakers, Crockett was killed during the Battle of the Alamo when he attempted to hug victorious Mexican general Antonio López de Santa Anna.

Cronenberg, David (b. Mar. 15, 1943), acclaimed Canadian orificemaker.

Crossroads, transportation junction created by the Works Progress Administration in 1937 to provide a commercial site where residents could sell their souls to the devil.

Croupier, person in charge of a gambling table who is highly trained in not giving pitying looks.

Crow, large, highly intelligent perching bird implicated in numerous online scams.

Crumb, smallest-known unit of food matter incapable of being divided into separate parts of edible material. Though it is impossible to measure the internal structure of a crumb, scientists calculate the basic crumb is approximately 1/2,400th of a morsel and nearly 10,000 times smaller than a nibble; a smidgen of food is composed of more than 1 million crumbs. Further research is needed to determine why these infinitesimally small particles never taste as good as the main piece of food from which they separated, but scientists now understand that crumbs possess a unique capacity to fall off and move at incalculable speeds to the floor, lap, or beard.

Crusades, series of bloody religious wars between 1095 and 1291 launched throughout Muslim lands by the pope to test whether or not we had the kind of God who would allow such monstrosities to take place. After multiple centuries and

◀ **DAVY CROCKETT**
If not addressed by his preferred nickname, "King of the Wild Frontier," the mentally retarded pioneer would become enraged, slapping his head and making a squealing noise until the error was corrected.

Crowbar, tool used by brain burglars to jimmy open skulls.

CUBAN MISSILE CRISIS, 1962 Cold War confrontation between the United States and the Soviet Union in which the two superpowers completely blew a golden opportunity to have one hell of a war. With a once-in-a-lifetime shot of nuclear explosions on every continent, legendary dogfights in the air, and full-scale combat on American soil unlike anything in history hanging in the balance, Russia screwed the whole pooch by standing down and dismantling its offensive weapons in Cuba, and the United States put the final nail in the coffin by agreeing to dismantle all IRBMs deployed in Europe and Turkey. Many historians believe President John F. Kennedy and Premier Nikita Khrushchev averted World War III, but with so many weapons and submarines, and different kinds of bombs that could have gone off, and all the new types of military maneuvers, secret tactical sessions, and huge munitions that could have been used, the question is, why?

Kennedy and Khrushchev's showdown produced plenty of dramatic photographs but missed the boat on a pretty spectacular nuclear cataclysm.

CURRENCY, system of money that functions almost like a physical credit card, whereby one "pays" for things with a tactile representation of their wealth.

U.S. Dollar
Considered counterfeit-proof, since no one can accurately reproduce George Washington's exact expression of ennui

Euro
Costs 20 euros to produce each handcrafted 20-euro note

Handful of Crickets
Zimbabwe's inflation has sharply decreased the value of a handful of crickets

Rupee
Was there really any doubt someone other than Gandhi would appear on the rupee?

Renminbi
Chairman Mao tried on more than 50 monotone collared suits before choosing this one

Ruble
Russian unit of currency; one ruble is equal to 1/2,000th of an assassination

British Pound
Currency that was very briefly printed with Hitler's face on it in 1942, just in case

Yen
Nearly every single bill circulating in Japan today has been stuffed at one time or another into a bound and gagged woman's vagina along with a dozen eels

CUMULONIMBUS ➤
Hark! A foul harbinger of doom, bringing with it a malevolent wind of foreboding.

the gruesome deaths of nearly 3 million people, the pope concluded that, yes, we apparently did have the kind of God who would allow such monstrosities to take place.

Cryogenics, branch of physics that studies materials at sub-zero temperatures so that, someday in the future, scientists may be able to revive and ruthlessly mock the dozen or so people worldwide who have been dumb enough to freeze their bodies.

Crystal, Billy, three-dimensional aggregation of molecules that follow a natural geometric order to create a solid, homogeneous substance with strong properties of shtick.

Crystallography, study of the formation and structure of crystals

that may very well be a legitimate science, but c'mon.

Cthulhu, ph'nglui mglw'nafh Cthulhu R'lyeh wgah'nagl fhtagn.

Cumulonimbus, large, vertically oriented cloud that augurs dark tidings, usually from the north. Formed from cumulous clouds at altitudes between 500 and 13,000 feet, these brooding omens usher naught but wicked deeds, lo, and the severe convection currents that swirl and writhe within like hellsent asps pose grave dangers to low-flying aircraft. Some cumulonimbus clouds can develop into supercells, those vile, continually rotating updrafts, with their rains of reckoning and fitful thunderous belches from some wretched realm

long ago shunned by divinity that are also known as mesocyclones, and whose wrath is writ with malice across the very heavens, beware, be wary! the hail and possible tornadoes, we are forsaken, we are all as dust, to dust we all must go, dreadful mortals, screaming souls, cruel time's hapless victims, heed Cumulonimbus.

Cunt, vulgar slang term for a woman's genitals that is offensive in the extreme unless it is used in the context of an educational reference, in which case it is afforded the clinical, academic distance necessary to furthering knowledge.

Cycling, daintier form of biking.

Da Vinci, Leonardo (*b. April 15, 1452 d. May 2, 1519*), Renaissance painter, engineer, and scientist whose devotion to artistic achieve-ment would have made him absolutely useless in football, basketball, golf, or anything remotely sports-related. For all their timelessness, Leonardo's masterpieces *The Last Supper* and the *Mona Lisa* wouldn't have given him much help at all with left-handed layups. He is also credited with early conceptualizations for the helicopter and the calculator, as well as for advances in the fields of anatomy, engineering, and optics, which is great and all, but when it comes down to it, and one needs a player who can hit for average, steal bases, and throw out a runner tagging up from third, those achievements really don't count for shit, now, do they? Among his myriad accomplishments, Leonardo is best known for the fact that he would have been the worst pole-vaulter of all time.

Dadaism, bubblegum anxiety flapjack explosion bang.

Dalí, Salvador (*b. May 11, 1904 d. Jan. 23, 1989*), Spanish surrealist painter whose work reflected an intense interest in bizarre dream symbolism, though most of Dalí's actual dreams involved hitting the World Series–winning home run for the New York Yankees, or rocking out in front of a sold-out arena. Dalí attempted to capture the phantasmagorical quality of dreams with images such as melting clocks, elephants that walked on long, spindly legs, and grotesquely misshapen humanlike figures, even as his journals showed the artist repeatedly dreamt of winning the lottery and using the money to buy a brand-new Ferrari Testarossa. Many art historians say Dalí's most famous painting, *The Persistence Of Memory*, was inspired by a dream he had the night before in which he was making out with Cindy Crawford.

Dalmatian, energetic dog breed known for its characteristic white fur, black spots, and three-week ownership period before being returned to the breeder.

Danger, potentially hazardous thing or act often romanticized as cool, despite the fact that it presents a number of significant safety hazards. Though danger remains extraordinarily popular among thrill-seekers and women whose fathers withheld affection, it is currently the leading cause of death after klutziness, heart disease, and peril.

Dark Thursday, June 26, 1997, universally regarded as the blackest and most terrible day in American history. While it is impossible to truly convey in words exactly how traumatic and profoundly sorrowful the events of Dark Thursday were, surely no one alive on that day will ever forget where they were when they found out, or how they felt seeing it all unfold from moment to awful moment. In fact, most Americans prefer not to say too much about Dark Thursday. After all, it is impossible ever to change what happened. Or to try to forget.

Davis, Miles (*b. May 26, 1926 d. Sept. 28, 1991*), legendary musician who remained culturally and commercially relevant for four decades despite the fact that he played a frigging trumpet. As an innovative bandleader, composer, and performer, Davis was one of the most influential artists of the 20th century, a feat he accomplished by blowing into an instrument that literally

no one ever wants to listen to and that is essentially a glorified bugle. Though Davis sold millions of albums, completely changed music history, and transformed jazz as a brilliant pioneer, it's depressing to imagine what he might have been able to do if he'd just learned to play guitar.

Dawson's Creek, American teen drama that was originally about a troubled boy named Dawson who molests his younger cousin by a creek, but was eventually retooled by the WB Network.

Dalai Lama, (*b. July 6, 1935*), violent enemy of China whose army is currently laying siege to Shanghai, Beijing, and Guangzhou, thus justifying the Chinese government's harsh crackdown on ethnic Tibetans in the west of the country.

DDT, powerful synthetic insecticide that was banned because it was harmful to predatory birds, though it sure beat being covered in itchy, red falcon bites.

Dean, James (*b. Feb. 8, 1931 d. Sept. 30, 1955*), American film actor best known for his iconic role in a head-on collision in 1955.

Day-Lewis, Daniel (*b. Apr. 29, 1957*), renowned Oscar-winning method actor widely celebrated for his role as the titular 52,000-ton luxury steamship in the film *Titanic*. Critics and audiences described Lewis as virtually unrecognizable in the role, for which the actor became the gargantuan ocean liner, physically split in two, and slowly sank into the Atlantic Ocean over the course of two hours. Lewis' performance is often credited with making the epic one of the highest-grossing films in history, and for inspiring actor Sean Penn's acclaimed role as India in the 2008 film *Slumdog Millionaire*.

Deafness, evolutionary imperative that protects human ears from the human voice.

Death, and so we have arrived at the real purpose of this book. There is no easy way to put this, so we are just going to come out and state it plainly: Reader, you are dead. Yes, it is true. Everything you have ever consciously experienced in your "life" up to this point has in fact been nothing more than a posthumous mental visualization flashing across your mind in the 0.34 seconds immediately following your death. The world you exist in now—the places, the people, the events, and all you believe to be real—is a complex hallucination or dream-state conjured by your brain in its last functioning moments. This book you hold in your hands, for example, is not real. Nor are the clothes you are wearing, nor the place where you sit at this very moment. Look around you. None of this is real, for you are dead. If you think hard, reader, you must admit to yourself that part of you always knew this was true; part of you suspected this realization would one

day occur, the moment in which all your illusions were finally shattered. There has always been something strange or unreal about your so-called life, hasn't there been? Something slightly off? And wouldn't it all make sense if this entire odd experience that you thought was existence, this peculiar journey you have been moving effortlessly through, was actually nothing more than an intense mental projection leading up to this realization, right here, reading these words? Wouldn't it even be something of a relief? Look within yourself—that last small part of you that is still real—and accept that this is true. Face the truth, reader. The sooner you do, the sooner this state of nonbeing will end, and you will be ushered on to whatever lies ahead, be it another plane of existence, or utter nothingness.

Death Valley, highly toxic canyon that, if consumed, can kill a full-grown human.

Decision, definitive conclusion or resolution directly preceding a mistake.

Declaration Of Independence, document declaring America's independence from Britain and written by naïve, inexperienced colonists who stopped short at freedom

when they could have pressed King George for an additional $2 million in cash, a new capitol building, and a percentage of all British exports for the next five years. The contract, which demonstrates a number of classic negotiation mistakes, was composed by Thomas Jefferson, who failed to leverage the colonies' position and should have added clauses to cover shipbuilding costs and American travel expenses to and from Europe during all diplomatic visits. The document went through several drafts, none of which included time-shares for all the Founding Fathers in the British Virgin Islands, even though the worst the British monarchy could have done was say no. King George immediately agreed to the terms before the Americans could wise up, hire an attorney, and figure out that with their high cost of operations, constant problematic behavior, and John Adams, the British would have given them anything they wanted—including free tea in perpetuity—just to go away.

Democracy, representative form of government in which all citizens have an equal say in the state's administrative decisions, last successfully practiced in 1997 by 16 boys in Camp Winaukee's Randall Cabin.

The Founding Fathers didn't even include a clause in the Declaration of Independence to be reimbursed for their office supplies and rental costs.

Developed by the ancient Greeks around 504 BC, numerous states have attempted democracy, but it was only ever fully realized when the boys successfully voted on a group name (the Tigers), reached consensus on the group's colors (red and green), and respected Aaron's right to free speech by allowing him to articulate his position on choosing a camping site near a rope swing. During a time when U.S. President Bill Clinton faced impeachment and democracies were failing across the globe, the Tigers scored a perfect 10 on *The Economist* Intelligence Unit's 1997 democracy index by peacefully electing Tommy Irwin to pick up the daily mail, and respecting the vocal minority's wish to do arts and crafts every once in while instead of always going water tubing. Some critics argue that because counselor Mark could ultimately veto any group decision—and once did use this power when the Tigers attempted to repress Daniel's right to participate in a kickball game against the Bulls—the Tigers were in fact a republic.

Democratic Party, devout, highly organized group of political zealots with the explicitly stated goal of seizing control of the U.S. government. Bent on total political domination of the country, the Democratic Party has vowed to let nothing stand in its way as it takes over all levels of government in every state and municipality in a ruthless effort to impose its extremist agenda on every American man, woman, and child. (*See* REPUBLICAN PARTY)

Dendrite, electrically charged branch extending from each of the human brain's 100 billion neurons, a single misfiring of which will cause such devastating irreversible neural malfunctions as seizure, paralysis, permanent memory loss, and insanity. Dendrites conduct impulses to and from the central ner-

vous system and must accomplish this flawlessly, as even one failure—just one—of the tens of millions of transmissions that take place every millisecond will send a person tumbling down a flight of stairs or cause one to pass out behind the wheel of a car and then smash through a guardrail and over the edge of a 1,500-foot-high cliff. A single dendritic error will also result in permanent psychosis that distorts one's perception of reality by causing horrifying hallucinations that invariably result in suicide. While such neural misfirings can happen at any time, day or night, they are statistically most likely to occur

DIARRHEA, condition defined by having three or more loose or liquid bowel movements per day. Diarrhea most commonly stems from viral gastroenteritis with rotavirus, but in cases of traveler's diarrhea, the most prevalent cause is bacteria. It can also be a symptomatic presentation of many other medical conditions, including Crohn's disease, irritable bowel syndrome (IBS), mushroom poisoning, hormone-secreting tumors, and ischemic bowel disease. Oftentimes the only treatment required for diarrhea is replacing lost fluids and salts. However, more severe cases of diarrhea may require antibiotics, antimotility agents, bismuth compounds, zinc, or codeine phosphate. Loss of fluids through diarrhea can cause severe dehydration and electrolyte imbalances, sometimes resulting in death; it is a common cause of fatalities in developing nations, as well as the second leading cause of death among newborns worldwide. Despite this, some researchers have theorized that diarrhea serves an evolutionary purpose as an expulsion defense mechanism, and may actually shorten the length of fevers.

Types Of Diarrhea

Secretory
Occurs when there is an increase in the secretion of intestinal fluid and continues even after cessation of oral food intake.

Osmotic
Most often caused when too much water is drawn into the bowels as a result of maldigestion.

Exudative
Marked by the presence of blood and pus in the feces.

Motility-Related
Caused by the rapid movement of food through the intestines before sufficient nutrients and water can be absorbed.

Inflammatory
Occurs when there is damage to the mucosal lining of the intestines, leading to passive loss of protein-rich fluids and an inability to absorb these fluids.

Brainerd Diarrhea
A mysterious illness marked by a sudden onset of explosive, watery diarrhea that lasts for months and does not respond to antibiotics or other treatments. The cause of Brainerd diarrhea remains unknown, though it is associated with the consumption of untreated water and raw milk. The illness sometimes takes years to resolve itself.

De Kooning, Willem (*b. Apr. 14, 1904 d. Mar. 19, 1997*), 20th-century Dutch painter known for his extensive, priceless collection of de Koonings.

Detergent, water-soluble cleaning agent that, if possessed in large quantities, is an incredibly depressing way to make friends at a laundromat.

while one is holding a baby.

DePasquale, Albert (*b. Dec. 12, 1941*), state Supreme Court judge you voted for only because he has the same first name as your beloved father. He is a madman.

Depression, feeling experienced when one remembers that one is depressed.

Detwiler, Jeff (*b. Jan. 15, 1969*), bully, tormentor, and all-around prick who seemed to get some sort of sick joy out of making someone else's life a living hell from seventh grade all the way through high school. While he employed such simple physical acts of violence as shoving and extended punching, Detwiler was also notable for the frequency and brute effectiveness of his verbal assaults, most of which concerned his subject's sexuality, inability to defend himself from violence, or a combination of the two in which Detwiler implied his victim enjoyed being beaten up. Perhaps worst of all, Detwiler was generally well liked, to the extent that he always had a girlfriend and

was invited to all the cool parties. Although Detwiler's name hadn't come up in years, it was surprising how angry one became after hearing he was doing quite well for himself these days and had just been promoted to director of admissions at St. James Hospital in Great Falls, the piece of shit.

Devil's Advocate, practice of taking a position one does not necessarily agree with purely for the sake of argument, e.g., considering the idea that school bully Jeff Detwiler was perhaps not some diabolical villain and may have just been a troubled kid. Often used in an attempt to understand the motivations and actions of others, no matter how deplorable those actions might be—and, admittedly, what Jeff did was pretty bad—playing devil's advocate allows one to make the rhetorical argument that maybe Detwiler tormented others because of his own insecurities, and, with his father out of work and his mother on disability, he might have punched his victims repeatedly in

the arm on the school bus and called them a queer because he didn't know how to deal with the difficult emotions he was experiencing. While one would in no way condone Detwiler questioning his victim's sexuality in front of the whole school, it's at least worth acknowledging that Detwiler helped take care of his grandmother when she was sick and he did make Eagle Scout, so he couldn't have been all bad. Yes, it was inexcusable that he continued his misbehavior several years after high school when those he tormented returned home for Christmas break, but from his point of view, he was probably just angry at himself for not taking his education seriously when he had the chance. Just saying.

Diamond, rare and precious stone worth every tragic mine collapse and dead worker in history.

Dick, Philip Kindred (*b. Dec. 16, 1928 d. {−58} [−28] ±2257 + etc. × ∞*), American novelist and short-story writer who, despite dying in this reality in 1982, also died in an

---

DINING UTENSILS, implements such as forks, knives, and spoons used to help cut or eat food. In Western culture, particularly in formal settings, utensils are specialized according to function.

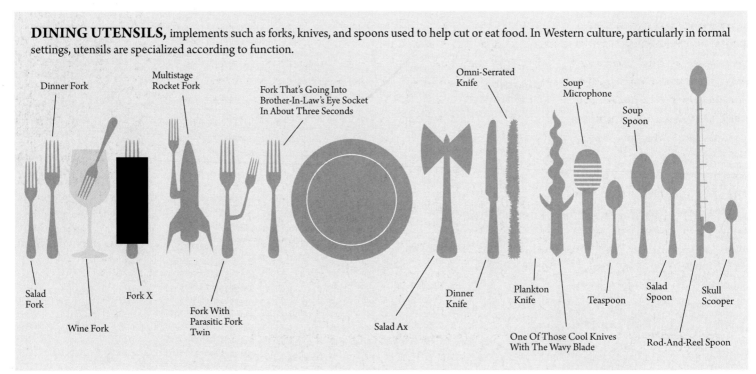

Dinner Fork — Multistage Rocket Fork — Fork That's Going Into Brother-In-Law's Eye Socket In About Three Seconds — Omni-Serrated Knife — Soup Microphone — Soup Spoon — Salad Fork — Wine Fork — Fork X — Fork With Parasitic Fork Twin — Salad Ax — Dinner Knife — Plankton Knife — One Of Those Cool Knives With The Wavy Blade — Teaspoon — Salad Spoon — Rod-And-Reel Spoon — Skull Scooper

alternate reality in 1958, after abreacting there with the aid of a highly addictive time-travel drug. He passed away in a separate alternate reality in 1928, along with his infant twin sister, in a freakish incident that would plague his tortured psyche in this universe, where he, but not his infant twin sister, survived. In yet a different universe, he will not die until the year 2257, when, living in luxury and surrounded by eroticlones of the 20th-century recording artist Linda Ronstadt, he will usurp the Terran Presidency as Grand Inquisitor of the Church of VALIS, only to be assassinated in his conapt by roboid rebels. Despite these and other deaths, Dick is currently working on a new novel in an infinite number of alternate realities.

Dickens, Charles (*b. Feb. 7, 1812 d. June 9, 1870*), Victorian-era British aristocrat who published a series of popular and influential novels composed by a team of starving orphans that he kept locked in his cellar and forced to author his entire body of work. Dickens was a harsh taskmaster whose gift for extracting quality literature out of malnourished street waifs yielded such classics of Western literature as *Oliver Twist* and *Great Expectations*, for which he paid his indentured writ-

ing staff a thimble of water and an oat per sentence. Dickens' insistence that his urchin scribes write from experience led to the creation of many famous passages, including one from *Oliver Twist* in which the titular character utters, "Please, sir, I want some more"—a phrase that, when asked of Dickens in real life, resulted in the child being beaten, shackled to the wall, and made to

write *Bleak House* in one sitting. Similarly, the character of Ebeneezer Scrooge was actually modeled directly on Dickens and was an inside joke among the children, as were *A Christmas Carol*'s ghostly apparition characters, all of whom were based on the hunger-induced hallucinations of orphan "Tiny" Tim Browne. By the time Dickens died in 1870, he had gone through some 230 orphans, 90 of whom died in the writing of *A Tale Of Two Cities* alone. He was buried with a pile of his royalty earnings in a cas-

ket made of gold.

Dictionary, reference volume that, to put it charitably, contains the definitions of various words—and only words—as if mankind might have any practical use for such a thing in this day and age. First developed by an upstart Englishman with far too much time, and far too large an ego, on his hands, the dictionary is now regarded as an obsolete relic, as the vast majority of human beings are able to get through their day just fine without having to frantically flip through a giant book in search of some obscure word's "meaning." For all matters relating to facts or information, encyclopedias are now, just as ever, universally preferred.

Digit, numerical symbol used to form math words.

Digital Media, rapidly growing industry created to provide a livelihood for those who have nothing of value to offer society.

Dignity, state of mind that begins at birth and gradually and irreversibly decreases over the course of a lifetime. A person's natural quantity of dignity starts eroding the moment he or she gains self-awareness and slowly decays through such acts as demeaning oneself in order to acquire employment or debasing oneself in the pursuit of love or sex. The

Dickinson, Emily (*b. Dec. 10, 1830 d. May 15, 1886*), reclusive American poet whose work was mostly published posthumously, though were she alive today, an editorial assistant would chuck her notebooks on the poetry pile, only to later sneak them out to a bar after work to read out loud in a mocking funny voice to colleagues.

Disney, Walt (*b. Dec. 5, 1901 d. Dec. 15, 1956*), American film producer, writer, animator, voice actor, and entertainer who was renowned for his childlike enthusiasm for money.

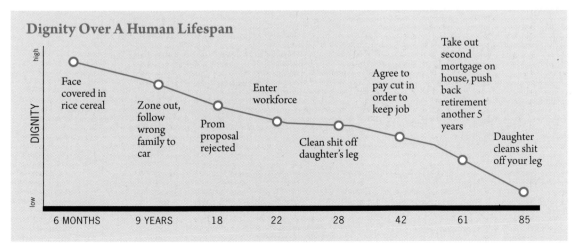

Dignity Over A Human Lifespan

high

DIGNITY

low

Face covered in rice cereal

Zone out, follow wrong family to car

Prom proposal rejected

Enter workforce

Clean shit off daughter's leg

Agree to pay cut in order to keep job

Take out second mortgage on house, push back retirement another 5 years

Daughter cleans shit off your leg

6 MONTHS   9 YEARS   18   22   28   42   61   85

DNA, deoxyribonucleic acid, self-propagating material present in the cells of living organisms that is responsible for carrying coded genetic information.

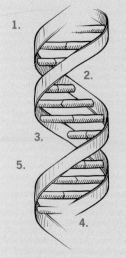

1. Protein combination that makes you shout "YEAH!" when Motörhead's "Ace Of Spades" comes on

2. Spine of the DNA that, if poked with a pin, will cause an organism to collapse in on itself and create a miniature black hole

3. Gene responsible for thinking every rash is skin cancer, actually getting skin cancer years later, then appreciating the irony

4. Heart-disease-causing gene that could have been eradicated four generations ago if your great-great-great-grandmother didn't completely lose it for good ballroom dancers

5. Thymine, one of the four nucleobases that better come ready to combine, oxidize, and replace, because if not, it'll just be wasting its time and the other nucleobases' time

millions of incremental, often imperceptible losses of dignity demanded of every person for inclusion in human society mean that very few individuals reach middle age with any dignity whatsoever. The only persons who consistently reach the end of their lives with a substantial amount of dignity are SIDS victims and infants who die in house fires.

Dildo, penis-shaped item made from latex, plastic, or glass used vaginally or anally during masturbation and sex; also, Carson Daly, Pat Robertson, Niccolò Machiavelli, Don Henley, Glenn Frey, Dane Cook, Ann Coulter, Martin Van Buren, Michael Moore, Richard Branson, Hernando Cortéz, Don Henley, Pontius Pilate, Criss Angel, Al Sharpton, Cardinal Richelieu, Michael Bay, John Boehner, Russell Brand, Caravaggio, David Duke, Laura Schlessinger, Andrew Jackson, John Edwards, Glenn Beck, Hideki Tōjō, Pope Alexander VI, Don Henley, Kim Kardashian, Jared Fogle, Kenneth Lay, and Marie Antoinette.

DiMaggio, Joe (*b. Nov. 25, 1914 d. Mar. 8, 1999*),  Hall of Fame center fielder for the New York Yankees and one of the hundreds of professional players in his time who, rather than fighting in World War II and facing the very real, very horrifying prospect of dying young, would have much preferred to just stay home and play baseball all day. A 13-time All-Star, DiMaggio, along with Bob Feller, Warren Spahn, Ted Williams, and countless others, quivered in silent fear on battlefields in the dead of winter and prayed to whatever God there

might be that a German shell wouldn't land directly in their foxholes, while also thinking about how much happier they'd be if they were in America hitting home runs, making diving catches, and basically having a great time playing baseball for money with their friends in the summer sun. DiMaggio ended his career with three MVP awards, and while he and his fellow professional baseball players were proud of their military service, all of them said at one point or another that watching members of their battalion have their legs blown off while a medic lied to them that everything would be okay was a lot less fun than winning a World Series.

Disease, highly contagious virus located on the surface of everything.

Distinction, attribute separating one individual from all others. Examples include achievement in higher education, artistic or athletic accomplishment, and having a really noticeable and disgusting birthmark on practically the whole right side of one's face.

Divorce, dissolution of a marital union that should have ended five years ago.

Doctor, highly trained medical professional who diagnoses and treats illnesses and can, honest to God, order any patient to get naked whenever he or she pleases, no questions asked. Whether seeing a 9-year-old child or a 78-year-old grandparent, a doctor is, amazingly, given carte blanche to demand the person not only strip nude in broad daylight, but also pose in any number of doctor-specified positions to better showcase their bare body for inspection. Doctors, who at the end of each day are no different than any other person you'd pass on the street can—believe it or not—even step out of an examination room at will, leaving a patient alone, buck naked, without giving them any indication of when they might come back. Unbelievable.

Doctors Without Borders, international humanitarian aid organization that since 1971 has been locked in a bloody conflict with the Red Cross for control of areas afflicted by war, disease, or natural disasters. Over the course of the savage 40-year rivalry, more than 40,000 doctors and nurses have been killed by rival aid workers in clashes over the world's most coveted regions of

Armed physicians from Doctors Without Borders defend their patients from kidnappings by the Red Cross.

Dinosaur

Extinct terrestrial reptile that lived between 67 million and 250 million years ago during the Mesozoic Era and voraciously consumed every piece of information it could find on 9-year-old boys. The prehistoric orders of Saurischia and Ornithischia, many species of which were massive land dwellers, spent the majority of their existence poring over picture books about 9-year-old boys, learning what they looked like, and memorizing their names. Paleontologists have discovered fossil evidence that suggests the Triceratops, a three-horned herbivorous dinosaur, was particularly intrigued by Billy Sullivan, who stood up to 53 inches tall and could run faster than any other kid in the whole third grade. The Ankylosaurus, a 30-foot-long dinosaur that was covered in bony armor and had a large, clubbed tail, became obsessed with 9-year-old boys after reading about how they subsisted on a diet of hot dogs, Spaghetti-O's, and chicken fingers. Many scientists believe the 25-ton quadruped Apatosaurus was especially impressed by the fact that some 9-year-old boys have freckles, while the bipedal apex predator Tyrannosaurus Rex—considered the "king of the dinosaurs"—would use its small forelimbs to make drawings of 9-year-old boys jumping on trampolines or riding around on BMX bikes. Paleontologists theorize the large, spike-tailed herbivore Stegosaurus was the smartest but most insufferable dinosaur, because it would build dioramas of 9-year-old-boy habitats and then brag about how accurate they were, or pretend to be a 9-year-old boy by making annoying laughing and yelling noises all the time.

Alectrosaurus
Was amazed to learn that little boys lived primarily on chicken fingers and egg salad sandwiches.

Pterodactyl
The only flying dinosaur was afraid of 9-year-old boys and often cried in front of all the other dinosaurs.

Saltopus
Smaller than a medium-sized dog, the 5-pound Saltopus would constantly speculate as to what it would be like to sleep in a bed with race-car sheets.

Jake
Dinosaurs could not believe that 9-year-old Jake lost a front baby tooth at school and kept it in his pocket all day.

Dog, domesticated animal that you better believe remembers the time you stood in front of your bedroom mirror and silently stared at your naked body for two minutes. The four-legged canine also remembers how you began shaking your head at your appearance and whispered to yourself, "I don't want to look this way anymore."

DOLPHIN ➤
The marine mammals sometimes exhibit signs of culture, including the use of tools and the ability to make a sexual partner feel like absolute shit for no apparent reason.

medical need, including Sudan, Rwanda, Burma, and Afghanistan. While the Doctors Without Borders forces are vastly outnumbered by those of the Red Cross, they are far more brutal in their tactics, and have been known to ambush a Red Cross field hospital and butcher all personnel with machetes before safely transporting the patients to medical facilities in Doctors Without Borders territory. Caught in the crossfire are the aid recipients themselves, who are often brought to the center of their village and forced to watch as Doctors Without Borders physicians set fire to urgently needed supplies such as inoculations, antibiotics, and surgical implements that have been provided by the Red Cross. The villagers are then told that if they ever get their lifesaving medical attention, nutritional counseling, and sanitation assistance from anyone besides Doctors Without Borders, they will each lose their right hand.

Dole, multinational agriculture corporation that played a crucial role in increasing the USDA's recommended daily intake of pineapples to 250 pounds per person.

Dolphin, marine mammal considered to be one of the most intelligent species on the planet based on the fact that it is the only animal besides humans to have sex purely out of spite. The emotionally manipulative dolphin exhibits its intelligence by seducing a potential mate that it knows another dolphin in the pod has a crush on by making it feel like it's the only dolphin in the world, and then leaving the next morning with a promise to see it again, which it never keeps. The smartest and shittiest of the aquatic creatures then go loudly bragging to friends about their most recent sexual con-

quest right in front of the quiet, sensitive dolphin who had finally worked up the courage to ask her out.

Don, Mount, stupidest mountain in the world. Mount Don is located in the Canadian Rockies but is currently unclaimed by any nation because it is so dumb and embarrassing. Although its uppermost elevation has not been determined, climbers have ascended as high as 1,200 feet before being overcome by the mountain's sheer lameness, immediately turning around, and hiking back down in disgust. Moreover, this pathetic excuse for a landform likely doesn't even have any valuable resources, only layer upon layer of pointless rocks and other useless junk, though no one knows for sure because no one has ever bothered exploring the stupid piece of shit. An absolute disgrace, Mount Don refuses to go away, despite the fact that everyone clearly hates it, and it just sits there, year in and year out, doing nothing but taking up space with its truly laughable "peaks" and summits. Mount Don—ugh, just saying the name is fucking annoying—is only included in this encyclopedia because it is important to note how thoroughly and unequivocally it sucks dick, all day, every day, all the time.

Donkey, animal whose stupid appearance is, ironically, only enhanced by putting a mortarboard on its head and a diploma in its mouth.

Doo-Wop, style of pop music popular in the 1950s that could only have occurred in a nation utterly preoccupied by the Cold War.

Doogan, Slugger, sure, I threw the fight earlier—guy sees a chance to get the money, the girl, and the glory all at once, he'd be a sucker not to.

And now the sucker is you, flatfoot. Looks like it's going to be twice tonight you get your clock cleaned over Mitsy LaRue. (**See** MITSY LARUE)

Doppler Effect, noise made with the mouth in order to indicate that something went by moving really fast.

Douglass, Frederick (*b. Feb. 1818 d. Feb. 20, 1895*), former slave who went on to become a revered social reformer, orator, writer, and statesman. Editors would be happy to provide comprehensive information on Douglass to any reader who sends to the publisher an original essay at least 15 pages in length thoughtfully explaining why he or she wants to learn more about this important historical figure. Douglass's story is incredibly fascinating and thought-provoking, which is why a concise treatise of one's interest in him is the minimum requirement for obtaining this encyclopedia's immaculately researched entry on his life and accomplishments, and why the one's essay should not only coherently present and support its thesis, but also provide five examples of how one's newly acquired understanding of Frederick Douglass would be applied in one's daily life. Visual aids are encouraged (but will not count toward the essay's required length) and should enhance the central argument of the disquisition in a meaningful way. If completing a simple essay in the service of learning about an American icon such as Frederick Douglass seems like too much trouble, perhaps it's better you just read about Phil Spector or unicycles (*See* PHIL SPECTOR, UNICYCLE).

———

For more information about Frederick Douglass, please send a self-addressed, stamped envelope along with the required essay, your name, age, social security number, and certified proof of purchase to:

The Onion Encyclopaedia Board
c/o The Zweibel Institute
P.O. Box 3403
Tempe, AZ 85282

Dream, images or sensations that occur during sleep in the minds of the clinically insane. In dramatic contrast to the state of comforting black emptiness that psychologically stable persons experience when sleeping, the shifting phantasmagorical events of dreams—which may include powerful visual, aural, and tactile hallucinations as well as intense emotional investment in completely nonexistent phenomena—are a dangerous byproduct of profound mental illness. It is impossible for normal individuals who only experience sleep as a peaceful, enveloping void to understand what occurs in dreams, because those who experience dreams often suffer from impaired thought processes that inhibit their ability to recall or describe their delusions to others. Dreams can sometimes be treated with antipsychotic medications or through therapy, which can help the patient access traumatic life events that may have caused

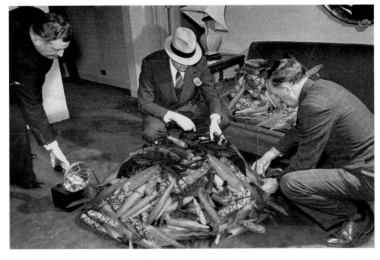

dreams to intrude upon the peaceful nighttime oblivion enjoyed by healthy people. Mentally unstable people may sometimes experience stressful or unpleasant dreams known as nightmares, which usually indicate the onset of a deadly aneurysm or brain hemorrhage.

Dred Scott v. Sanford, 1857 U.S. Supreme Court decision stating that slaves were not citizens, which did not result in the immediate firing of all nine Supreme Court justices.

Drug Enforcement Agency, arm of the U.S. government that evolved from the now defunct Corn Enforcement Agency of the 1930s, which was disbanded when no justification could be found for raiding American citizens' homes and confiscating their corn. Now primarily

concerned with seizing and destroying illegal drugs, the DEA formed after a congressional inquiry found not only that the CEA was unnecessary, but that it was also insane to devote millions of manhours and billions of tax dollars to the arrest of people who buy and sell corn, or to conduct yearlong sting operations on American farms that inevitably ended in setting massive cornfields ablaze. At the time it was dissolved in 1973, the CEA was fully engaged in its War on Corn, an effort to reduce worldwide corn distribution that was not joined by any other countries because all deemed it "ineffective and counterproductive, due to the fact that corn shouldn't be an illegal thing." After signing legislation that converted the CEA into the DEA,

◄ At the height of its power and influence, the U.S. Corn Enforcement Agency confiscated and burned more than 14 million pounds of corn.

Donner Party, American pioneers who traveled on a wagon train headed out west in 1846, became trapped in the snow in the Sierra Nevada, and cannibalized the casualties, though one survivor admitted that he had started snacking on people back in Missouri.

Driftwood, wood that has washed ashore for the purpose of being collected by a stepmom.

DREAM INTERPRETATION
Some common dreams and their meanings

DREAM	You feel anxious on a subconscious level about a big decision you have to make.	You find yourself feeling unburdened from a major responsibility.	Frightened by the uncertainty of the future, you struggle with self-doubt.	You have the sensation of losing control of the relationships in your life.
MEANING	All of your teeth will fall out.	You can fly.	You will return to your old high school, realize you're not wearing any clothes, and forget about a big exam.	You are currently falling from the top of the Empire State Building.

Dubai, city that provides its laborers a dreamlike futuristic setting in which to suffer countless human rights violations.

Duncan, Tim (*b. Apr. 25, 1976*), professional basketball player for the San Antonio Spurs and lead copy editor and fact-checker for this book.

President Richard Nixon said, "This concludes a very weird time in our nation's history."

Duchamp, Marcel (*b. July 28, 1887 d. Oct. 2, 1968*), French artist who helped inspire the American Dadaist movement along with Francis Picabia, Man Ray, and Dayton, Ohio–based tax attorney Jerry Ronkowski. Duchamp, whose most significant contribution to Dada was his "readymades," or found art, was continually inspired by Picabia and Ray, and was invigorated by Ronkowski's ability to help his corporate clients create dependable, individualized tax structures for their companies and to imbue orinary, everyday objects with a sense of fantastical, abstracted whimsy. Ronkowski would often host fellow Dadaists in his split-level ranch home for long, passionate conversations about how the artistic movement could serve to ridicule the meaninglessness of the modern

world, while his wife, Dottie, served coffee and tuna fish sandwiches. Though he couldn't attend its unveiling because it came during the busy season, Ronkowski gave Duchamp the idea for his most famous work, *Fountain*, saying that by rotating a urinal 90 degrees it would shift the focus of art from physical craft to intellectual interpretation. He also advised Duchamp to seriously consider a Retirement Plan Rescue to minimize taxation on his estate, a strategy that ultimately allowed the surrealist to avoid a double tax by combining exemption limits with his spouse, Lydie. Ronkowski's most famous piece was his 1921 assemblage *Bat Nailed To Mask*, and he was also a notary public.

Dulles, John Foster (*b. Feb. 25, 1888 d. May 24, 1959*), former U.S. senator and secretary of state under President Dwight D. Eisenhower who is best remembered for his role in the early years of the Central

Intelligence Agency, as well as for cofounding the Quint Group, a major scientific research corporation headquartered in the Seychelles. A significant Cold War figure who helped spearhead an aggressive program of containment in reaction to communism, Dulles was an early supporter of the work of the brilliant young theoretical physicist Dr. Charles Alexander Oberon, his partner in the Quint Group, who wished to pursue various experimental research applications for military-industrial use. In 1959, Dulles disappeared mysteriously while on a diplomatic mission to China and principal ownership in the Quint Group was handed over to Oberon.

Dying, process that begins shortly after the doctor says, "That's odd," while looking at one's chart, and is completely irreversible by the time he says, "I'd like to run a few more tests."

BOB DYLAN (*b. May 24, 1941*), American singer-songwriter who throughout his career intentionally—but unsuccessfully—did everything he possibly could to convince people he was not great. Despite making a wide range of purposely awful musical and creative choices over a 50-year period—including contorting his voice into a series of ungodly screeches and croaks, playing extended one-note harmonica solos, recording a half-assed cover album, embarking on an extended Christian phase, and just flat-out not trying for years at a time—Dylan has so far been unable to accomplish his goal of making people think he wasn't a complete and utter songwriting genius. Music historians and rock fans alike generally agree that even if Bob Dylan attempted to sabotage himself by recording nothing but willfully off-key salsa albums for the rest of his career, he would not only still go down as one of the best two or three recording artists ever, but those albums would also probably be kind of great.

Dylan delights music fans and critics alike, performing an earsplitting solo on an out-of-tune guitar while grunting nonsense words in a raspy frog voice.

Dylan hoped in vain that this recording would finally make people stop calling him America's greatest living songwriter.

Earhart, Amelia (*b. July 24, 1897 declared dead Jan. 5, 1939*), noted American ladypilot who became the first lady to cross the Atlantic Ocean by her ladyself. In 1937, after writing a bestselling ladybook about her experiences, Earhart ladycrashed her ladyplane while attempting to circumnavigate the globe. Though a group of aviators thought they'd recovered Earhart's ladyremains in 2010, DNA tests on her ladybones have proved inconclusive. Nevertheless, Earhart made ladyhistory with her ladycourage and will forever be remembered as a true American lady.

Eastwood, Clint (*b. May 31, 1930*), actor and director whose iconic role as Dirty Harry earned him the nickname "Dirt Hair," which he has gone by among friends ever since.

Ecosystem, fragile biological environment, composed of a variety of precious interrelated elements, that is so delicate the addition of even one little unnatural pollutant from a well-meaning *Fortune* 500 corporation can destroy the entire thing. Ecosystems support a diverse group of frail and overly sensitive organisms, including plants and animals that are so feeble they cannot handle the slightest improper disposal of toxins without freaking out and causing a dramatic chain reaction throughout the entire habitat, even though they were barely touched by harmful contaminants. One would think a real ecosystem would be able to adapt and absorb a few noxious gases and fluids right into its precious life cycles, but apparently not. The flimsy, easily ruined ecosystem is also prone to getting honest corporations in a lot of trouble even though the ecological disaster was a total accident and nobody's fault, really.

Ed Sullivan Show, long-running variety show best remembered for appearances by musical acts including rock icon Elvis Presley, singer-songwriter Charles Manson, Motown trio the Supremes, and, in their first American television appearance, the British foursome the Beatles.

Edison, Thomas (*b. Feb. 11, 1847 d. Oct. 18, 1931*), American inventor who held 1,093 U.S. patents for devices such as the phonograph, the motion picture camera, and the credit-taking machine, an apparatus devised by his rival George Westinghouse. Edison inadvertently discovered the credit-taking machine in 1881 during a routine weekly ransacking of Westinghouse's laboratory and was puzzled by the contraption until an assistant demonstrated how it was designed to rapidly attribute ideas to a different inventor while also ruining the reputation of his competitors. The credit-taking machine was portable enough to set up while in line at the U.S. patents office, meaning the New Jersey native could quickly and efficiently take the glory for dozens of pending innovations

without having to pause to legally obtain the sole patent on the light bulb and stock ticker designs he stole from someone else.

Education, system of conveying and passing on knowledge that should be avoided if one doesn't ever want to know about mankind's extensive history of war and destruction, the way in which economics perpetuates inequity on a global scale, the science of infectious diseases, the alienating and inconceivable vastness of the

Ee·ɛ·Ǝ

Fifth letter of the English alphabet, which was born an *F* but never felt comfortable being identified as such and had its lower serif surgically extended to become a vowel. Having always known it was an *E* despite its *F* anatomy, the young consonant had an extraordinarily difficult time conforming to the phonetic conventions assigned to it by society, and for many unhappy years went through the motions in words like "fig" and "flack." Realizing it could never be pronounced authentically unless radical steps were taken, the *F* underwent a lengthy series of treatments to dampen its voiceless labiodental fricative and ultimately completed its transformation with life-altering letter-reassignment surgery. Today, many people utter words like "electricity" and "echo" with no clue as to the *E*'s origin, although some claim you can tell just by looking at it.

THE HUMAN EAR CANAL

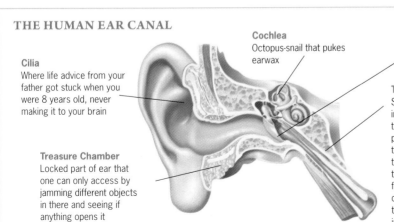

Cilia
Where life advice from your father got stuck when you were 8 years old, never making it to your brain

Treasure Chamber
Locked part of ear that one can only access by jamming different objects in there and seeing if anything opens it

Cochlea
Octopus-snail that pukes earwax

Subwoofer
Can be used to give your coworker's voice a little more bass

Tympanic Membrane
Structure that transmits aural information via a tiny man in full tuxedo tails and white gloves who stands patiently in the ear canal listening to the sounds that enter. After interpreting this information, he then walks over to the tympanic membrane and, with his felt-covered mallets, plays a rhythmic coded message that is processed in the brain as the sound the little man just heard.

Earth

Only planet in the known universe capable of supporting life that is trying to kill it. Located 93 million miles from the nearest star, Earth has an exceedingly rare oxygen- and nitrogen-rich atmosphere that protects its surface from harmful solar radiation, and provides ideal conditions for a species to evolve and develop technologies to destroy the very same atmosphere that ensures its survival. In addition to the priceless, nonrenewable resources that Earth's inhabitants recklessly exploit, the planet is also unique in providing life-sustaining water that its people pollute and—in what is truly an interstellar miracle—a year-round livable climate that its population is actively determined to make unlivable within their lifetimes. Due to the inconceivable vastness of the universe, scientists believe that while there could be another Earth-like planet somewhere in the cosmos, it is a statistical improbability that it would support inhabitants so uniquely fucked up and idiotic that they won't rest until they annihilate it.

THE EARTH'S LAYERS

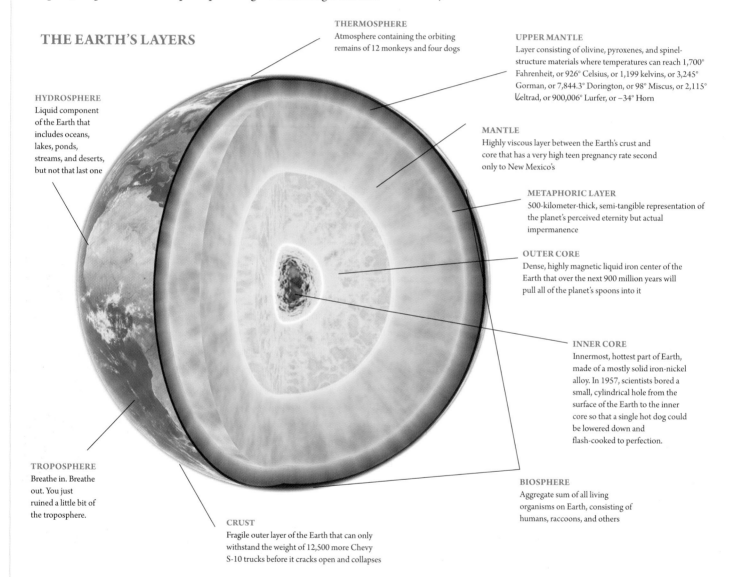

THERMOSPHERE
Atmosphere containing the orbiting remains of 12 monkeys and four dogs

UPPER MANTLE
Layer consisting of olivine, pyroxenes, and spinel-structure materials where temperatures can reach 1,700° Fahrenheit, or 926° Celsius, or 1,199 kelvins, or 3,245° Gorman, or 7,844.3° Dorington, or 98° Miscus, or 2,115° Veltrad, or 900,006° Lurfer, or −34° Horn

MANTLE
Highly viscous layer between the Earth's crust and core that has a very high teen pregnancy rate second only to New Mexico's

METAPHORIC LAYER
500-kilometer-thick, semi-tangible representation of the planet's perceived eternity but actual impermanence

OUTER CORE
Dense, highly magnetic liquid iron center of the Earth that over the next 900 million years will pull all of the planet's spoons into it

INNER CORE
Innermost, hottest part of Earth, made of a mostly solid iron-nickel alloy. In 1957, scientists bored a small, cylindrical hole from the surface of the Earth to the inner core so that a single hot dog could be lowered down and flash-cooked to perfection.

HYDROSPHERE
Liquid component of the Earth that includes oceans, lakes, ponds, streams, and deserts, but not that last one

TROPOSPHERE
Breathe in. Breathe out. You just ruined a little bit of the troposphere.

CRUST
Fragile outer layer of the Earth that can only withstand the weight of 12,500 more Chevy S-10 trucks before it cracks open and collapses

BIOSPHERE
Aggregate sum of all living organisms on Earth, consisting of humans, raccoons, and others

EARTH'S FORMATION

The Earth was formed when a rotating cloud of interstellar gas collapsed in on itself in a process that, if it had occurred three inches to the right, would have caused humans to evolve into a race of 30-foot-tall, indescribably beautiful super beings with 5,000-year lifespans. Earth took shape 5 billion years ago due to tremendous levels of pressure, heat, and gravitational force, an event which, had it taken place just a few inches to the left, its inhabitants would instead have become giant floating cerebral spheres housing a vast and gentle intelligence beyond our comprehension, while inhabiting a utopian world based on pure love and reason. Scientists have made the argument that mankind is incalculably lucky the Earth did not form even two feet closer to the sun, as the nonstop free-for-all sexual intercourse taking place with our humongous, hypersensitive penises and perfectly shaped breasts would have given humans little incentive to develop backbreaking industry or cramped, filthy metropolises, leaving us instead to inhabit a tropical jungle paradise forever.

ECONOMICS, science of explaining where all the money went. The field of economics is divided into two main categories: microeconomics, which examines why the money was all here a minute ago but now it's not; and macroeconomics, which looks at the economy as a whole to determine how that much money could just be gone all of a sudden. Economists use empirical evidence in an attempt to understand why what little money is left is somehow worth a lot less now than it was before, and they analyze data to study why simply making new money to replace the money that disappeared isn't really how it works. While some schools of economic thought hold that the best course of action is to reject the idea that the money is really gone and carry on like nothing happened, other theories argue that the only way to fix this is to ask the people with the most money to share it with everyone else because a lot of people need money right now. Economics is often used by governments to implement social policies, such as accepting that the money is never coming back and that everybody had better just get used to it.

Prominent Economic Theories

Supply-Side Economics
Theory under which the government is forced to just stand there and watch the whole nightmare play out right in front of it.

Keynesian Economics
Macroeconomic theory based on government spending that is highly contentious due to the fact that it creates jobs, lays a foundation for a strong middle class, and leads to periods of economic prosperity.

I Brought This Cool Thing Back From Korea Theory
Theory under which an economic system is fueled exclusively by weird toys or sandwiches discovered while on vacation in Korea that no one at home has even heard of but will be a huge hit if repackaged just the right way.

Entrepreneurial Economics
Economic theory that posits the kid who starts a business selling candy out of his locker always goes on to be a major sleazeball later in life.

Egg, one of the most popular forms of child to eat.

universe, entropy, and the inevitability of death. Starting at an early age, children are subjected to rigorous formal education based on classroom lessons and in-depth reading, which children would be wise to resist at every turn unless they actively wish to learn the fundamentals of how language can be used to harm and denigrate others, how mathematics reduces the world to a cold, clinical formula, and how literature only makes one more intellectually acquainted with life's myriad miseries. Those who avoid higher learning at the college level are also better off, as they never have to grasp more complex—and doubly depressing—concepts such as human psychology, the systematic entrenchment throughout civilization of racism and religious fanaticism, and the utter uselessness and fallibility of knowledge itself. If an individual can reach adulthood without being educated, he or she will never have to shoul-

der the sad burden of an enlightened conscience or lie awake deep into the night, sweaty with panic, trying to comprehend the notion of infinity. If you are able to read this entry, then you already know too much and it is too late for you.

Edward III (*b. Nov. 13, 1312 d. June 21, 1377*), English king. He is dead now. (*See* WILLIAM, WILLIAM II, HENRY I, STEPHEN, HENRY II, RICHARD I, JOHN, HENRY III, EDWARD I, EDWARD II, RICHARD II, HENRY IV, HENRY V, HENRY VI, EDWARD IV, EDWARD V, RICHARD III, HENRY VII, HENRY VIII, EDWARD VI, PHILIP, JAMES I, CHARLES I, CHARLES II, JAMES II, WILLIAM III)

Egg Sac, stylish purse used by female spiders to carry around personal items, money, and thousands of spiderlings.

Eiffel Tower, iconic wrought-iron tower that follows visiting tourists all around France in order to insert itself into every photo they take. Al-

though the 1,063-foot structure is located in Paris, where it can easily position itself in the frame of any picture taken in front of competing landmarks such as the Arc de Triomphe and Notre Dame Cathedral, the Eiffel Tower is also known to appear suddenly in photos taken far beyond the French capital, and visitors will often find it popping up

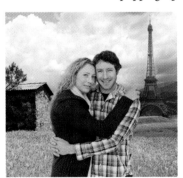

among the vineyards photographed on a trip to Bordeaux, rising up from the snow in the middle of the Alps, or looming in the background of the bed and breakfast run by that nice elderly couple in Aix-en-Provence. While many tourists

Aristotle
Greek philosopher and teacher who promoted a well-rounded education, or rather, a well-rounded awareness of one's flaws, fears, and sorrows.

Friedrich Fröbel
German pedagogue who developed the first kindergarten, and apparently a proponent of sucking all the joy and innocence out of a human being as early as possible.

"Education is not preparation for life; education is life itself."

—**John Dewey,** in a terrible piece of advice for people who might wish to live a life not consumed by anxiety and dread.

Ancient Egypt

Civilization in northeastern Africa that gives reference volumes a chance to change up the pace a little and break up the monotonous, text-heavy format with more graphical elements, timelines, and a few callout boxes. Whether accentuated by a nice, colorful picture of Queen Nefertiti, a photo of the Sphinx, or a random painting of a falcon-headed man, ancient Egypt, which formed around the Nile River delta around in 3150 BC, affords encyclopedia editors a terrific and legitimate opportunity to forget the boring blocks of text for a minute and just show a cool picture of King Tut's gold bust. The ancient Egyptians developed advanced irrigation systems and medicine, and are not only a godsend for encyclopedia writers who want to spice things up a little with a picture of a stone-carved cat head, but for readers as well, who are no doubt exhausted by dense scholarly text, and just want to kick back, relax, and look at a picture of a mummy for a while.

How about some hieroglyphics, huh?

Can't go wrong with a map of the Nile River. Beautiful.

One of these things should probably be here.

A depiction of the river goddess Taweret makes a great addition to entries on ancient Egpyt because it's interesting, and it certainly has more visual appeal than an entry on, say, ARMISTICE.

Historically, encyclopedia editors looking to visually add a little pizzazz to their book show an image of the most fucked-up looking mummy they can find, one where the skull is darkened, there is only some semblance of teeth, and the face is all shriveled up like a raisin. This is no exception.

LITTLE TIMELINE ACTION
A timeline about ancient Egypt offers editors a chance to break the standard format by doing one of those longer timelines that extends along the bottom of both pages.

3100 B.C.
Unification under King Narmer, but more importantly, here's that bust of King Tut we mentioned earlier.

2500–2100
Forgot to show a painting of Egyptian agriculture above, so let's just put it here.

2030
Middle Kingdom period begins. Here's a picture of a cat.

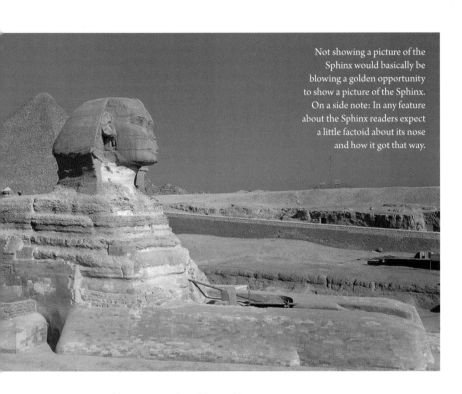

Not showing a picture of the Sphinx would basically be blowing a golden opportunity to show a picture of the Sphinx. On a side note: In any feature about the Sphinx readers expect a little factoid about its nose and how it got that way.

HEY, LOOK OVER HERE

Visually stunning, Queen Nefertiti's famous bust allows encyclopedia editors to fill the page with something cool to look at.

One of the Seven Wonders of the World, the Great Pyramids of Giza look great when cut out and will basically knock any two-page spread out of the park.

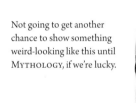

Not going to get another chance to show something weird-looking like this until MYTHOLOGY, if we're lucky.

EGYPT SIDEBAR

These are an essential part of any Egypt entry. Here's why.

➤ Tall, thin format leaves plenty of room for other cool graphics.

➤ Provides additional line of useful information.

➤ Allows for a quick mention of the sun god Ra without getting bogged down in a whole paragraph about him.

➤ Last bullet point. You're in, you're out, now it's on to the timeline.

1379
Monotony of timeline broken with a line extending from the date that makes a couple directional changes before leading reader to the actual text.

1274
Battle of Kadesh. Only mentioned because we had access to a really nice painting of it.

1100
Empire split into Upper and Lower Egypt due to difference in customs and dialect. Tensions between the two regions continue to this day, and to maintain integrity there has to be some text that isn't accompanied by a picture.

645
Picture of the Rosetta Stone. Bam!

422
Not entirely sure what the 25th dynasty did in terms of advancing the culture, but it feels like we should end this thing on a poignant note.

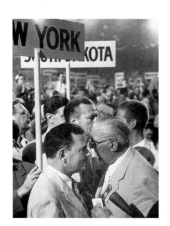

Electoral College, flawed system that everyone agrees is obsolete, but is thankfully only used to elect the president of the United States.

Elk, species of deer that thought it just heard someone say its name.

attempt to lose the Eiffel Tower by taking a day trip into an adjacent country such as Germany or Spain, they inevitably find the structure waiting for them at the border the moment they return.

Einstein, Albert (*b. Mar. 14, 1879 d. Apr. 18, 1955*), German physicist whose theory of relativity completely upended everything people already didn't know about how the universe worked. By positing that space and time were not constant but exerted influence over each other, Einstein turned on its head the very basis of the Newtonian mechanics that for centuries people had been utterly oblivious to and could not have articulated if you held a gun to their heads. Einstein's famous equation $E = mc^2$ asserts that mass and energy are equivalent, thereby disproving the laws of conservation and marking a profound shift in the way average humans did not even vaguely comprehend nor, honestly, give a flaming shit about the nature of reality.

Election, special day dedicated to celebrating the democratic process in which citizens dress in their best voting clothes, joyfully make their way to their local polling places, and, having carefully weighed the issues of the day and how they relate to the greater good, cast their ballots to change the government for the better. Since it is a national holiday, voters get Election Day off from work so they may gather with family and friends over a festive meal to engage in spirited, but respectful, discussions about the possible outcomes of the election and how it will be remembered in the larger historical context of democracy. Once a candidate is declared the winner, all voters, regardless of political affiliation, dutifully throw their support behind the newly elected official and end the day with a customary toast to government by the people, for the people.

Electric Guitar, stringed musical instrument that needs to be turned way up in the monitors right now. Nothing, still nothing, the electric guitar uses magnetic pickups to detect the minute vibrations of metal strings and amplifies the signal before sending it to a loudspeaker, which only has sound coming out of the left side, can we please do

Albert Einstein On War

"I know not with what weapons World War III will be fought, but World War IV will be fought with sticks and stones. I'm 100 percent sure of that. No question. World War V, on the other hand, will be fought with the weapons that the Lagash and Umma people fought with back in 2525 BC—spears, mostly. So that's World War V. World War VI is a toughy, but I'm fairly certain it will be fought with a mixture of guns and swords and ballistic missiles and probably some sort of intense nerve gas, like sarin gas or something. That's just what I think. Take it or leave it. World War VII? Now we're back to what World War III will be fought with, so like I said earlier, I dunno. World War VIII is sticks and stones again— the idea being that if the human race is virtually wiped out in the previous world war, then if and when it returns to being the dominant life-form on earth, it won't have the technology available to develop the high-powered weaponry that World War III or even World War I was fought with. Understand? World War IX will be fought with people who have gigantic, skull-shattering spikes attached to their hands. World War X will be fought between five very big tanks. World War XI will be fought virtually, but here's the interesting thing about that: When someone dies in the virtual world, he also dies in the real world. Pretty neat, right? I think that's a neat little twist. World War XII will be fought solely on horseback. World War XIII will be fought with more advanced Sonic-Neural Agitators. World War XIV is definitely, definitely going to be fought, but as of now, I'm hazy on the weapons. Certainly not as hazy as I am on World War III, because I do have a basic idea, it's just not concrete yet. But it will probably be some sort of interplanetary fight that involves a series of concentrated beams that differ in color. World War XV will either be fought with an advanced polymer that adheres to the skin and impedes brain function, or just guns. World War XVI? Beats the hell out of me. And World War XVII will be fought with sticks and stones again."

—1947

something about this, Don? It's 10 minutes before doors. Early models consisted of modified hollow-bodied acoustic guitars until innovators like Les Paul and Adolph Rickenbacker introduced the solid-body guitar in the early 1930s, an instrument never intended to be so far down in the goddamn mix. Nope, still just drums and synth. The electric guitar was first used in jazz big bands, and it has since become the quintessential rock-and-roll instrument, made famous by the likes of Chuck Berry, Jimi Hendrix, and Eric Clapton, who would never in a million years have to put up with this amateur-hour horseshit.

Electricity, inexhaustible energy source manufactured by the walls of buildings. To tap into a wall's electricity, a plug is placed inside a wall socket, which allows the naturally occurring voltage to flow safely into an appliance or other device. Items such as ceiling fans may also be powered by electricity, as ceilings and floors are simply walls rotated 90 degrees and therefore equally capable of producing unlimited energy. It is uncertain how electricity reaches light bulbs, however, or if the source of their illumination is electrical in nature at all.

Electrolyte, clinical name for Yellow No. 2 food coloring.

Elephant, large, heavy, plant-eating mammal that is an elephant.

Elevator, automated mode of conveyance that accounts for 85 percent of the world's slow vertical movement. Composed of a passenger car, a shaft, and a system of counterweights and pulleys, elevators make up the vast majority of the planet's straight up-and-down travel, far outstripping trampolines and rockets. The movement of ele-vators is, on average, 51 percent upward and 49 percent downward, and is never at any point horizontal or circular in nature. Although some claim escalators technically constitute vertical movement, they differ from elevators in that they move at a 45-degree angle, and are thus an entirely separate entity.

Ellis Island, Upper New York Bay destination that from 1892 to 1954 served as a gateway to a new life for 16 million immigrants, and a symbol of how that new life was going to be really fucking horrible. New arrivals, who hailed from dozens of countries but were primarily German, Italian, or Irish, were ushered into a cold, enormous hall by police, stripped naked, deloused, and left to wonder if this whole America thing wasn't a terrible idea. As part of the ensuing medical exam, immigrants stood silently in long lines and waited to have their eyelids turned inside out with a hook, suddenly realizing that if doctors were already treating them like animals, regular Americans would probably treat them even worse. Approximately one-third of the U.S. population can trace its ancestry to Ellis Island, which since 1990 has housed a museum where people can see the exact spot upon which their grandparents' dreams of a better life were destroyed.

E-Mail, system of electronic message delivery that marries the thrill of composing a letter with the thrill of operating a mouse.

Emancipation Proclamation, 1863 executive order by President Abraham Lincoln that, in one brutal stroke, tore asunder the lifelong emotional bonds between slaves and their owners. Safely sheltered in the White House, far from the sunny plantations that slaves and their masters had called home for generations, the callous president declared that all slaves in states rebelling against the Union were now free, mercilessly ripping apart the ties forged between white landowners and the people they had bought at auction—people who were considered family from the moment they were unloaded from West African cargo ships. The Emancipation Proclamation did not apply to slaveholding border states that remained part of the Union, an exemption that has led some to conclude that Lincoln, despite his ruthlessness, at least had some small capacity for pity.

Emotion, complex state of feeling that must be kept in check if one ever hopes to get ahead at Walsh & McLachlan LLC. Fear, love, and compassion are among the wide range of human emotions a person is advised to leave at the door if he wants to run with Dan Walsh and the big boys in corporate. Advances in modern neurology suggest emotions are determined by genetic and environmental factors, with many people, such as the hungry young reps in sales, displaying almost no emotion. Some exhibit what are defined as emotional weaknesses by claiming that it's too stressful and this is not the way they wanted to get ahead, though such individuals would do well to remember this is a business, pure and simple. Other common emotions include pity, empathy, and understanding, all of which should be kissed goodbye right-fucking-now because there are potential clients coming in from Japan any minute, and if one can't pull it together and bring his A-game, then old man McLachlan himself is going to come down here and slap him like a bitch in front of

◄ ELLIS ISLAND: GATEWAY TO A BRAND-NEW LIFE OF MISERY

24,396: Elderly individuals who stood in a line kind of wishing they'd died on the boat from Europe

320,000: Immigrant families who did not smile during photos taken at Ellis Island because they just realized they made the biggest mistake of their lives

50: Number of people who kind of enjoyed being prodded and poked, and frankly wanted some more

20,000: People who were not surprised at how badly they were being treated, mainly because they knew good and well they would be just as xenophobic if millions of immigrants were entering their homeland

2,000,000: Immigrants who experienced sense of nostalgia while fondly recalling the horrible atrocities in their homelands

the entire division. Individuals who successfully suppress or conceal their emotions will eventually be rewarded with a corporate card, a six-figure salary, and a personal invitation from Walsh to come out to his cottage next summer.

Emphysema, condition in which the air sacs of the lungs become enlarged and, rather than giving one the ability to stay underwater twice as long, which you might expect, instead cause breathlessness.

Empire State Building, 102-story building that is impressive in its dominance of the New York City skyline until one gets inside and realizes that it's filled with gray, windowless offices and old, filthy carpet. While the street-level interior includes a breathtaking art deco marble lobby that is a designated city landmark, everything from the second floor up is teeming with office supply salesmen; bitter, burned-

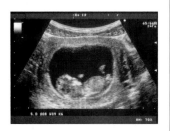

Embryo, early stage in animal development when the immature organism first starts to hate the sound of its parents' voices.

out tax lawyers; and a shuffling mass of mid-level professionals stuck in dead-end jobs they blankly toil away at under the maddening buzz of sickly fluorescent lights.

Though many see the Empire State Building as a testament to mankind's ingenuity and perseverance, those who must go there day after day view it as a 365,000-ton monument to the murder of imagination and vanquishing of the human spirit.

Encouragement, words of hope and guidance spoken only to people you know will never outdo you.

End Table, small table placed near a sofa that is unnecessary until a person reaches the age of 34. Prior to turning 34, thoughts of owning an end table never enter one's mind, and items such as books, water glasses, and magazines can simply be placed on the floor next to the

couch or wherever. As soon as one's 34th birthday is reached, however, a certain order must be maintained and an end table becomes essential. By the time one turns 41, it is absolutely crucial that a potted plant be placed atop the end table.

Enron, former Houston-based energy company whose executives shocked Americans when it came to light in 2001 that the powerful multimillionaires actually cared more about making money than the needs of their customers or employees. U.S. citizens were stunned and horrified to learn that president Jeffrey Skilling and CEO Kenneth Lay (men who rose to the top of a *Fortune* 500 corporation, of all people) had misrepresented Enron's fi-

nances in order to deceive investors and increase their own personal wealth—greedy, selfish behavior that millions of adult Americans could not imagine incredibly rich and successful businessmen would ever be capable of. The resulting bankruptcy cost shareholders billions of dollars and destroyed employees' retirements in a collapse that shook the public to its core and caused it to lose faith in the ethical standards of major corporations for almost three days.

Entrepreneur, individual who embarks upon an independent business venture but who might still be able to get his old job back if he catches Mr. Schaefer on a good day and apologizes. As owner of a new enterprise, an entrepreneur assumes a far greater risk than a salaried employee and totally understands why Mr. Schaefer might be reluctant to rehire him, but will do whatever it takes to regain his trust. The entrepreneur, well aware that in this economy there are plenty of qualified people who would happily take his place, is entirely responsible for raising capital, marketing, and hiring, and will take a pay cut if Mr. Schaefer says so because he can't be out of work much longer, he just can't. French in origin, the word entrepreneur means "one who undertakes" and reflects an entrepreneur's willingness to beg, if necessary, for a second chance due to the fact he has two young daughters and his wife hasn't worked in more than a year either. Please, Mr. Schaefer. *Please.*

Environment, tattered remains of the natural world. The environment encompasses not only the last intact shreds of the earth's physical features, including the smattering of wetlands that have not been drained bone-dry, but also the last few examples of the flora and fauna that inhabit these areas, including the handful of animals that have not been hunted to extinction or slowly deprived of their food sources and starved to death. The environment is one of a growing number of issues facing humanity, notably the futile, animalistic scrambling for the few remaining scraps of wealth and employment sometimes known as "the economy."

Envy, feeling of desire or covetousness for the possessions or social statuses of others that completely resolves itself into blissful happiness for the rest of one's life once those possessions or social statuses are obtained.

Equator, imaginary line on the earth separating the shitty countries from the asshole countries.

Equatorial Guinea Genocide, decent little medium-sized genocide that lasted from 1968 to 1979. Nothing too crazy, just a power-crazed dictator killing about 80,000 people.

Ernst, Max (*b. Apr. 2, 1891 d. Apr. 1, 1976*), German surrealist painter who was once married to—well, well, well, what do you know?—millionaire heiress and art patroness *Peggy Guggenheim*! Hmm, pretty convenient for a struggling artist, eh, Max? Known for experimenting with such source materials as school textbooks, educational placards, and mail-order catalogs, wouldn't you agree, Maxy, that it was—what's the word?—*opportune* that the one true love of your life not only really liked buying abstract and surrealist paintings, but was also capable of skyrocketing your art career? Just seems like a pretty perfect setup for you is all. Anyway, Ernst pioneered tech-

niques such as grattage, in which paint is scraped across the canvas to reveal objects below, and frottage, a method for... Actually, just level with us here, Ernst: It didn't matter what the hell you painted because you knew good and well that so long as you were slipping it to one of the nation's greatest patrons of the arts, you could have sold Miss Megabucks any old sack of garbage. One of Ernst's most famous works was *Forest And Dove*, and look, Peggy Guggenheim wasn't exactly a knockout, Max. We know it. You know it. Everyone knows it. So just cut the shit, admit you married for fame and fortune, and we'll drop it. At least be man enough to do that.

Escalator, moving staircase invented to prevent the stores on the second floors of American malls from going out of business.

Espionage, another thing that used to involve sex but now just happens on computers.

Esplanade, long, open area typically by the seaside that is perfect for hearing Duncan Sheik at a free Earth Day concert.

Euclid (*b. circa 323 BC d. circa 283 BC*), Greek mathematician known as the Father of Geometry and to whom it is necessary to swear an oath before drawing a shape.

European Union, economic and po-

litical organization founded in 1993 with the intention of helping member nations ruin each other without resorting to war.

Evaporation, process by which liquid turns to vapor and rises into the air, never to return.

Everest, Mount, tallest mountain in the world, considered the ultimate challenge for people who like challenges that really don't help anyone. At 29,035 feet, the Himalayan peak is among the most dangerous on the planet, drawing individuals from across the globe who seek to test their limits in the most self-indulgent manner possible and to forgo such formidable undertakings as ending homelessness in their community or halting the destruction of the Amazon Rain Forest in order to ascend the treacherous mountain and applaud themselves. While estimates vary, some 3,100 climbers are believed to have successfully summited Mount Everest, an accomplishment that has forever changed the lives of some 3,100 climbers.

Everglades, vast expanse of marshland in Florida that, as such, is considered the cultural and intellectual center of the state. With more than 2.4 million acres of wetland and a wide array of plant life including saw grass and mangrove trees, the

◄ **MAX ERNST**
Hmm, wonder how *Ubu Imperator* found its way into Paris' world-renowned Musée National d'Art Moderne—any ideas, Mr. Guggenheim?

◄ **EVERGLADES**
Compared to the rest of the state, a virtual Renaissance is occurring in the Florida Everglades.

◄ *Everest is the supreme test for anyone seeking a pointless, self-centered obstacle to overcome.*

Everglades has been dubbed the "Florence of Florida," owing to its status as a focal point of aesthetic achievement and advanced thinking found virtually nowhere else in the area. Wildlife such as egrets, alligators, foxes, and turtles are just some of the animals that congregate in the Everglades for the intellectual and artistic stimulation that cannot be found anywhere else on the Florida peninsula, save for a landfill outside Gainesville.

Evolution, biological change over time in which single-celled prokaryotes develop into complex organisms with brains advanced enough to deny any facts that support the theory of evolution. While early life-forms lacked the

genetic traits and mental capacity necessary to reject the clear-cut evidence that they evolved from other organisms, those with intricately developed nervous systems—the inarguable result of billions of years of speciation and various genetic recombinations—are capable of intellectualizing vast, wholly made-up histories of how they came into being, complete with implausible

miracles, supernatural beings, spirits, angels, and a fantastical geologic timeline. To date, the world's most advanced organisms often look down on those who have not yet evolved an ability to willfully ignore evolution and the scientific data behind it, and consequently believe they are all going straight to hell.

Ewing, Patrick (*b. Aug. 5, 1962*), worthless living organism that did not win a single National Basketball Association championship from 1985 to 2002.

Examining Table, piece of furniture a doctor rolls out from under before getting up, wiping his oily hands on a rag, and telling the patient his parathyroid gland is completely shot.

Existentialism, philosophical movement that emphasizes the need for man to create his own meaning in an ultimately unfathomable universe, even if it takes a couple of extra minutes.

Expatriate, person who has about a year and a half before he is considered an enormous asshole in his new culture as well.

Explosion, violent burst of energy produced by the interaction of combustible materials that is required to resolve the story lines of all movies, books, and plays.

Exorcism, act of presenting a well-reasoned argument against the existence of God to someone who claims to be possessed by a demon, causing them to stop and realize how silly all that convulsing must have looked.

EYE, each of a pair of globular sensory organs in the head through which animals see, with most humans shedding their deciduous—or "baby"—set when they are between the ages of 6 and 12. Eyes convert light into electrochemical impulses that can then be interpreted by the brain, a function that improves after the pair of eyes a person is born with becomes loose and is gradually pushed out of the skull during preadolescence as his or her permanent eyes begin to grow in. Impatient children will sometimes tie a loose eyeball to a doorknob with dental floss and then slam the door, dislodging the temporary organ; additionally, if baby eyes become impacted, an optometrist may remove them from the socket with a chisel and affix stainless steel braces to ensure the adult eyes come in straight.

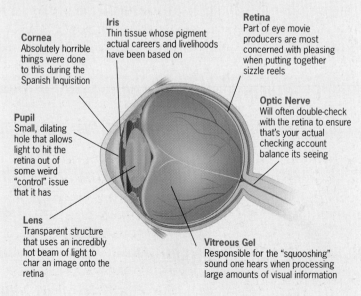

Iris
Thin tissue whose pigment actual careers and livelihoods have been based on

Retina
Part of eye movie producers are most concerned with pleasing when putting together sizzle reels

Cornea
Absolutely horrible things were done to this during the Spanish Inquisition

Optic Nerve
Will often double-check with the retina to ensure that's your actual checking account balance its seeing

Pupil
Small, dilating hole that allows light to hit the retina out of some weird "control" issue that it has

Lens
Transparent structure that uses an incredibly hot beam of light to char an image onto the retina

Vitreous Gel
Responsible for the "squooshing" sound one hears when processing large amounts of visual information

Facebook, annual compendium of profiles of nearly everyone on the planet that was first published in 1655 and finally went online in 2004. Founded in the Bavarian region of present-day Germany by a printer named Johan Zuckerberg, the first edition of Facebook collected woodcuts of anyone who wished to participate, and printed alongside each of their images a list of their individual interests, their level of schooling, and short, lighthearted messages directed at friends who were also included in Facebook. During World War II, the Zuckerberg family moved the publication to Northern California, and in 1947, began hiring legions of door-to-door salesmen to peddle the annual editions, which could also be obtained via mail-order subscription. Facebook went through many changes, such as the accordion envelope sleeve attached to each person's profile in 1974 to hold personal photos for others to view, and an option added in 1986 in which a subscriber could share music by attaching a portable casette player to a friend's profile. Mark Zuckerberg, a distant relative of the publication's founder, launched the digital version, www.facebook.com, in 2004 while attending Harvard University, and the physical printing of the compendium was discontinued in 2006.

Fairness, absence of bias toward another that is a lot less fun than treating someone unfairly, mainly because it's kind of enjoyable to see someone's face when they're being treated poorly for no reason whatsoever. When people are being treated unfairly, their expression becomes confused, bewildered, and angry. Their body tenses up and sometimes they begin to cry because they know an injustice is being done to them on purpose, purely for the satisfaction of seeing them react exactly how they're reacting. One typically doesn't get to enjoy something like that when one is being fair.

Fascism, authoritarian political ideology based on organic social solidarity and functional distinction of roles among individuals. Originally conceived by Italian nationalists during World War I, fascism espouses many tenets that appeal to those who value action and a man's spirit over materialism, egalitarianism, and other dangerous ideas that can weaken a nation's very foundation. Misunderstood by many, fascism is based on the iron will of the *people*, harnessed to bring glory to one's country through industry and an unwavering commitment to loyalty and discipline. Fascism often demands a cleansing of inferior individuals and ethnic groups who *cannot* or *will not* contribute to a unified country and whose insistence on continued autonomy and cultural identity only holds back the *TRUE* sons and daughters of the great nation from fulfilling their destinies and receiving their due reward of a *Utopian collectivist society. The fascist political system demands these undesirables be PURGED while external enemies of the nation must contend with the NATION'S GREAT WAR MACHINE, FUELED BY IRON AND BLOOD,*

Ff · Φφ · f

Sixth letter of the modern English alphabet, transferred to that position after a disappointing three-year stint as a whole number. It was thought that F would be more useful situated between 8 and 9 in the Arabic numeral system, a disastrous mistake that resulted in hundreds of billions of counting and calculation errors worldwide and caused unprecedented damage to the global economy. F's failure came as a surprise to many, as the former letter 3 had thrived as a numeral for nearly eight centuries.

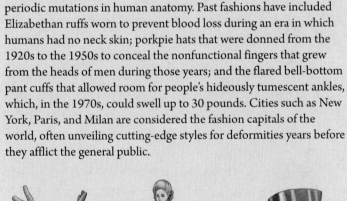

FASHION, trends in dress designed to accommodate grotesque periodic mutations in human anatomy. Past fashions have included Elizabethan ruffs worn to prevent blood loss during an era in which humans had no neck skin; porkpie hats that were donned from the 1920s to the 1950s to conceal the nonfunctional fingers that grew from the heads of men during those years; and the flared bell-bottom pant cuffs that allowed room for people's hideously tumescent ankles, which, in the 1970s, could swell up to 30 pounds. Cities such as New York, Paris, and Milan are considered the fashion capitals of the world, often unveiling cutting-edge styles for deformities years before they afflict the general public.

Trends in fashion come and go with humanity's passing horrific mutations.

◄ **FACEBOOK**

In 1655, the process of updating one's original Facebook profile could take months or even years, depending on how long the request took to reach Germany.

Faded Black

American rock and roll band from Lincoln, Nebraska, led by singer and lyricist Danny Walker and backed by guitarists Mike Rust and Kellan Grotrian, bassist David Boardman, and drummer Josh Chapin. Faded Black's radio-ready sound has entertained Lincoln-area music fans since 2007, incorporating elements of hard rock, alternative rock, and heavy metal into a singular style the band has dubbed "new edge rock." By combining a layered guitar sound with Chapin's powerful, frenetic drumming and Walker's strong baritone vocals, Faded Black has crafted a sound that is rooted in a number of modern rock traditions but remains distinctively its own. While the dual-guitar assault of power-chord specialists Rust and Grotrian owes much to such hard rock and metal progenitors such as Metallica and Iron Maiden, when coupled with the unmistakably melodic bass figures of Boardman and Walker's agile, multi-octave vocal range, the band's music resists easy categorization. In spite, or perhaps because, of its variety, Faded Black has attracted a loyal regional following that it hopes to one day extend nationally with a series of small-venue concert tours. Faded Black issued a self-titled debut EP in 2008—a recording that sold out its limited 300-copy run—and in April 2010 the band released its first full-length album, *Save Yourself*, which can be found at the CD Warehouse in Lincoln and is also available for download. The

product of two years' worth of live performance and songwriting, the album furthers the musical ideas explored on Faded Black's debut while also remaining faithful to the band's original sound. With its iconic album cover depicting a leafless tree in the midst of a barren field, *Save Yourself* featured the largest collection of original material yet released by the band, including such eventual concert staples as "War Inside," "Forbidden Feelings," and the title track, of which a live acoustic version recorded at the Westfield Gateway Mall can be viewed on YouTube under the title "Faded Black - Save Yourself (Acoustic)." The band has recently released a follow-up LP, *Here In The Dark*, which it plans to support with a multi-city tour.

INFLUENCES

Faded Black has publicly cited a number of primary influences on its music, including the work of Alice in Chains, Three Days Grace, and Godsmack, but close inspection of their recordings and live performances also yields comparisons to post-grunge bands such as Crossfade, My Darkest Days, and Shinedown.

The question of influence, while undoubtedly central in the discussion of any modern rock band, is often difficult to parse within the context of Faded Black, whose music is known for its highly inclusive sound. One can find traces of hundreds of groups from the past 30 years in their songs, although never so conspicuously as to distract from the band's unique chemistry.

LIVE PERFORMANCES

The group is noted for performing live at a number of popular music venues in Lincoln, Omaha, and beyond, including:

- ➤ Knickerbockers
- ➤ The Grove
- ➤ The Point After (2010 Halloween show featuring Make Se7en and No Quarter)
- ➤ Sokol Underground
- ➤ Harrah's Casino (Council Bluffs, Iowa)
- ➤ The Garage
- ➤ The Firehouse

ELISHA ANDERSEN

Often regarded as Faded Black's "sixth member," band manager Elisha Andersen has been with the group since nearly the beginning, overseeing its tour schedule and business operations, while also acting as a sort of steadying influence over the band's various mercurial talents. While she rarely interferes with the band's surefire creative process, she is often looked to by Faded Black for guidance as they navigate the music industry's sometimes treacherous waters. Elisha can be reached by e-mail at fadedblackmusic@yahoo.com.

AND MOVING EVER FORWARD TO THE GOAL OF THE NATION'S RIGHTFUL EMINENCE! E QUANDO ATTRAVERSO L'UNITÀ MORALE L'ANIMA DI UN POPOLO È SALVA, È SALVA ANCHE LA SUA INTEGRITÀ TERRITORIALE E LA SUA INDIPENDENZA POLITICA!

FBI, American domestic intelligence agency tasked with investigating more than 200 categories of federal crimes, filing detailed reports on them, writing summary reports, filing those summaries with appropriate officials, and then filing any conclusive results of its investigations. FBI headquarters in Washington stores several million case files, and more than 400 bureau offices around the United States employ agents tasked with handling local cases, filing their findings, and submitting copies of the files to headquarters. A typical FBI case involves monitoring criminals, filing for warrants, requesting wiretaps, transcribing wiretaps, refiling for warrants, filing reports on information obtained from wiretaps or additional interrogations, copying files for supervisors, requesting additional administrative support, filing said requests, amending requests to match appropriate filing protocols, submitting additional files to obtain information from other government agencies, processing criminals, filing that, and eventually filing a final report to shut down the case.

Federal Reserve, mystical and unknowable force behind American money and wealth. A centralized coalition of regional banks, the "Fed," as it is known to adherents, is unseen but omnipresent, imbuing its essence into every financial transaction, investment, or collateralized debt obligation across the whole of the Earth. Scholars have for decades attempted to theorize about its nature, but it is widely accepted that none can know the mind of the Federal Reserve, a concept and power far too vast to be comprehended. The Fed is capable of altering whole economies with the merest adjustment of the Prime Lending Rate, a magical number through which some believe the Federal Reserve sends humanity clues as to its true will and intention. Despite the inherently incomprehensible nature of the Federal Reserve, faith and hope are put into it unquestionably, as it works in mysterious ways to carry out some cosmic plan outside our ken as mortals, especially when it comes to fluctuations in the bond market.

Fermi, Enrico (*b. Sept. 29, 1901 d. Nov. 28, 1954*), scientist who successfully split the atom after years of practice splitting oranges.

FENCING, pre-choreographed bladed combat sport in which one fencer attempts to immobilize an opponent by pinning him or her to the ground for a period of three counts.

1. Put opponent in sleeper hold, strike with foil once opponent has fallen asleep

2. Dragon suplex opponent onto foil

3. Climb to top of turnbuckle, elbow drop opponent, strike opponent with foil

4. Tag in fencing partner, partner restrains opponent, strike opponent with foil

5. Retrieve folding chair from judges, break over opponent's back

6. After experiencing a sudden burst of rage-fueled energy following an illegal ambush by various bad-guy fencers, chokeslam opponent's loudmouth manager, chokeslam opponent's girlfriend, chokeslam any other fencer who took part in ambush, chase main opponent with foil toward locker room, get prepared to face opponent during next Sunday's fencing pay-per-view

Family

Social entity related by kinship that is divided among those who are doing all right and those who are a little off. In the Western world, the standard family unit is the nuclear family, generally understood as a household in which a mother who's hanging in there, a father who just doesn't want to talk about it right now, and one or more children cohabitate. Outside the immediate home, extended family members may include an aunt who's going through a really rough patch, a cousin who's doing good all things considered, and a grandfather who's holding up pretty well but who obviously misses Dolores. The exact makeup of a family varies across cultures, but it commonly contains a number of uncles who have been dealing with their own stuff and at least one niece and nephew, both of whom are good kids but struggle sometimes, you know?

TYPES OF FAMILIES

Patriarchal: Family type in which all other members must physically carry the father from one room of the house to the other whenever he requests this be done

Matriarchal: Family in which the mother drives and the father sits in the passenger's seat

Anarchal: Family system defined by total chaos and no defined relationships; each family member determines who they are related to and to what extent

Aviarchal: Family system led by a bird. In most cases, a parakeet or a canary has authority over all of the family's decisions concerning finances, household rules, and birdseed.

Nuclear Family: Family unit consisting of a mother who never mentions the baby she gave up for adoption when she was 18, a father who does not acknowledge his ex-wife and three kids he has in Utah, and their children

Captivarchal: Family led by a man who has broken into their home and is holding them at gunpoint

Extended Family: Additional relatives who live with the nuclear family until they either die or get back on their feet

Caroline's Family: Honestly, they were the best. Rich and Patti were always welcoming, and Bobby used to be down for shooting hoops every Fourth of July barbecue. Almost as easy to miss as Caroline...

Family of Products: A commercial unit consisting of one or more parent products, usually referred to as the Original, Classic, Standard, or Premium.

TYPES OF MARRIAGE

Monogamy
Relationship in which two people agree not to subject any other people to themselves

Monogamy Plus Veronica Sometimes
Exclusive marriage to one person except for occasions when Veronica's in town and it's possible to get away from one's spouse for a couple of hours

Omnigamy
Practice of being married to every person on the planet

Origamy
Marriage between one person and a spouse of delicately folded paper

Happy Marriage
Marriage in which both partners are able to look past their doubts about choosing the right spouse whenever someone better looking, more successful, smarter, healthier, or with less insane parents walks by

Polygamy
Practice of taking more than one husband or wife at once that is generally considered ridiculous by women and that men consider worthy of constructing a society, culture, and religion around

FAMILY RELATIONS

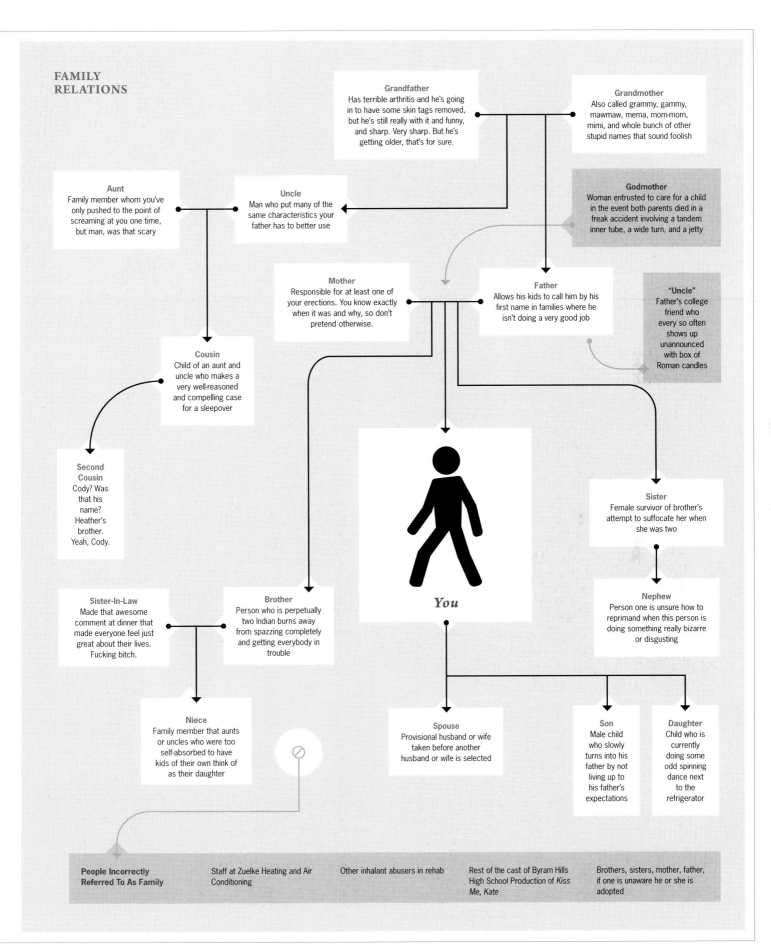

Grandfather
Has terrible arthritis and he's going in to have some skin tags removed, but he's still really with it and funny, and sharp. Very sharp. But he's getting older, that's for sure.

Grandmother
Also called grammy, gammy, mawmaw, mema, mom-mom, mimi, and whole bunch of other stupid names that sound foolish

Aunt
Family member whom you've only pushed to the point of screaming at you one time, but man, was that scary

Uncle
Man who put many of the same characteristics your father has to better use

Godmother
Woman entrusted to care for a child in the event both parents died in a freak accident involving a tandem inner tube, a wide turn, and a jetty

Mother
Responsible for at least one of your erections. You know exactly when it was and why, so don't pretend otherwise.

Father
Allows his kids to call him by his first name in families where he isn't doing a very good job

"Uncle"
Father's college friend who every so often shows up unannounced with box of Roman candles

Cousin
Child of an aunt and uncle who makes a very well-reasoned and compelling case for a sleepover

Second Cousin
Cody? Was that his name? Heather's brother. Yeah, Cody.

You

Sister
Female survivor of brother's attempt to suffocate her when she was two

Nephew
Person one is unsure how to reprimand when this person is doing something really bizarre or disgusting

Sister-In-Law
Made that awesome comment at dinner that made everyone feel just great about their lives. Fucking bitch.

Brother
Person who is perpetually two Indian burns away from spazzing completely and getting everybody in trouble

Niece
Family member that aunts or uncles who were too self-absorbed to have kids of their own think of as their daughter

Spouse
Provisional husband or wife taken before another husband or wife is selected

Son
Male child who slowly turns into his father by not living up to his father's expectations

Daughter
Child who is currently doing some odd spinning dance next to the refrigerator

People Incorrectly Referred To As Family | Staff at Zuelke Heating and Air Conditioning | Other inhalant abusers in rehab | Rest of the cast of Byram Hills High School Production of *Kiss Me, Kate* | Brothers, sisters, mother, father, if one is unaware he or she is adopted

Fedora, article of clothing a person wears to signify that you will have absolutely nothing in common with that person.

An adorable little owl made from the bloody fingerprint of a father who murdered his wife and three young children.

The massive database of tiny owls provides police with hours of amusement.

Fetal Alcohol Syndrome, congenital condition caused by heavy alcohol consumption among fetuses. The prenatal syndrome often leads to adverse health consequences that can include impaired memory, impulsive behavior, poor decision-making, severe hangovers during the third trimester, and showing up to birth late or completely messed up. Ultrasound research has shown that unborn children who binge drink in the womb are far more likely to violently break empty liquor bottles against the uterus wall and commit suicide by hanging themselves with their umbilical cords. Many physicians believe teaching zygotes about the dangers of alcohol abuse and cracking down on fake ID use by underage fetuses can help prevent this condition.

Filibuster, type of congressional procedure that allows any member of the U.S. Senate to take the floor and talk until the country is destroyed by political stagnation. Use of the filibuster represents a senator's explicit privilege to exercise a time-honored tradition of the esteemed legislative body that affords him or her the opportunity to cause the government to cease effectively functioning and drive the nation into the ground in the name of petty bipartisan squabbling.

Fingerprint, visible impression of the surface of a human finger used in law enforcement to create little owls on paper. To document a fingerprint, the police forensic technician evenly coats a suspect's fingers with ink, presses the digits carefully onto a card to avoid smudging the pattern, and then uses a marker to draw eyes, a beak, talons, and occasionally pointy tufts of feathers on top of the head. Digital scanners then capture the images for storage in a massive database containing millions of unique owls, which are categorized according to cuteness. This database also improves coordination between law enforcement agencies by allowing federal and local investigators to remotely search, identify, and trade their favorite owls.

Fire, rapid oxidation of combustible material that the editors of this book have all stuck their hands into for a full minute in order to fully appreciate its true power and terrible majesty. Though the enormous benefit and potential dangers of fire have been known to humanity for thousands of years, it is impossible to understand, really understand, fire without plunging one's hands into it and holding them there as the flesh blisters, blackens, and shrivels away. All readers with an interest in fire should do likewise, as even the most vivid textual description cannot approach the knowledge that comes with smelling one's own charred skin and muscle as it sloughs off the bone.

Fireside Chats, radio program that lifted American spirits during the Great Depression and World War II, hosted by President Franklin Delano "DeLunatic" Roosevelt and his sidekicks, the Oval Office Nuthouse. Each week, millions gathered around their radios for the enormously popular Fireside Chats, so named because of Roosevelt's catchphrase, "Now that's a hot tamale!" which was invariably followed by a crackling fire sound effect and a loud foghorn blast. His parody songs, such as "Put 'Em On The Tits" and "You've Got Me Under Your Skirt," had a huge influence on future "shock jock" Howard Stern, and were so profane the FCC was created in response. The program ran from 1933 until FDR's tragic on-air death in 1945, when he was crushed by a nude 500-pound woman who accidentally fell on him while farting "The Star-Spangled Banner."

Fishing Hook, barbed piece of metal that is the most dangerous object known to man. Ranking above the M-80, the switchblade, the bazooka, and the pit bull on the Marcado Hazard Scale, the fishing hook is feared in every culture and should be avoided at any cost, especially if it's a rusty fishing hook,

Franklin "DeLunatic" Roosevelt cheers up the nation by allowing his President of Vice, Stinky Winky, to sign Donna Dumplings' kazongas into law.

FOOD, any substance that is ingested by an organism to supply its body with nutrients, or to stimulate critical phases of growth and development within the organism, or because it just tastes good even though the organism isn't really all that hungry, or because there's only a little left in the package. Typically consisting of plant or animal matter, food is instinctively sought and consumed by an organism to provide itself with energy, or because the organism's boyfriend just left for good, or to kill time while the organism waits for a connecting flight, or to regulate the organism's metabolic activity, or because the organism works at a restaurant and it's basically free, or because the organism's aunt made a lot and turning it down would make her feel bad, or, in certain instances, because the organism used to have issues with bingeing and still occasionally slips. At its most basic level, food is ingested to maintain life-sustaining functions, often because an organism anticipates getting absolutely hammered later in the night and needs something to absorb all the alcohol.

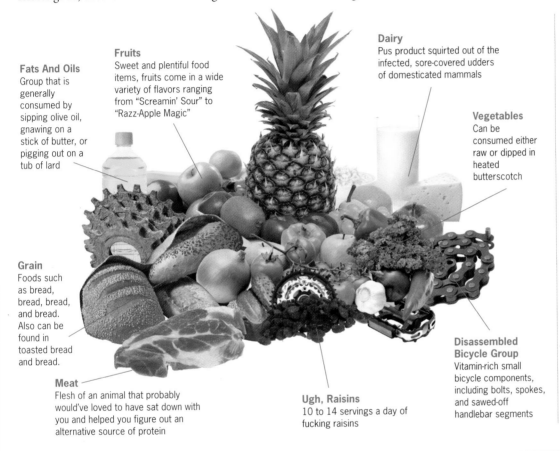

Fats And Oils
Group that is generally consumed by sipping olive oil, gnawing on a stick of butter, or pigging out on a tub of lard

Fruits
Sweet and plentiful food items, fruits come in a wide variety of flavors ranging from "Screamin' Sour" to "Razz-Apple Magic"

Dairy
Pus product squirted out of the infected, sore-covered udders of domesticated mammals

Vegetables
Can be consumed either raw or dipped in heated butterscotch

Grain
Foods such as bread, bread, bread, and bread. Also can be found in toasted bread and bread.

Meat
Flesh of an animal that probably would've loved to have sat down with you and helped you figure out an alternative source of protein

Ugh, Raisins
10 to 14 servings a day of fucking raisins

Disassembled Bicycle Group
Vitamin-rich small bicycle components, including bolts, spokes, and sawed-off handlebar segments

Eating Disorders

Anorexia: Practice of self-starvation in order to obtain the ideal form of an unhealthy, sallow-complected, 65-pound, bone-protruding figure, comparable to that of an 11-year-old prepubescent boy

Overeating: Eating disorder diagnosed the second one uses his index finger to scoop up the remaining ranch dressing out of a bowl

Bulimia: Eating disorder in which one takes control of one's life through vomiting recently ingested food. And with so few opportunities in this life to have actual, real control, it's a pretty good idea.

Bulimia Tarsalis: Variant of bulimia where the person uses his or her foot to stimulate the gag-reflex and induce vomiting after consuming food

Rumination: Regurgitation and re-mastication of already chewed food, which is somewhat understandable because food is so good that one probably wants to eat it again, but why not just eat a bunch more food?

which is 1 million times more dangerous than a normal one. Should a fishing hook get stuck in one's eye, it's pretty much over for that individual.

Fission, nuclear reaction in which one nucleus is split into two smaller nuclei and 100,000 people die.

Fleischer, Ari, Series 7 communications humanoid developed by the U.S. government to serve as White House press secretary during the presidency of George W. Bush. Though state-of-the-art when first released, the Fleischer model soon displayed a number of mechanical bugs and was deemed obsolete after just two years of service.

Flirting, act of raising one eyebrow, curling a lip, and slowly licking the top lip back and forth three to four times.

Floor, flat surface to walk or stand on found in a room. Floors can be hardwood, laminate, linoleum, ceramic-tiled, bamboo, vinyl sheet, rubber, cork, dirt, or made of some other material. Though floors are the opposite of ceilings, they can only exist in ceiling-covered locations; for example, the area at the bottom of a tent is a floor, but removal of the tent causes the floor to revert back to the ground. When in buildings, floors can be stacked on top of one another, sometimes in excess of 100 times. Between these floors is a space in which people either live or work. Surfaces of floors are covered with rugs or carpets, and can be further ornamented with tables and chairs. Sitting directly on floors is possible.

Flounder Night, popular American tradition in which a family spends an evening celebrating recent good fortune, such as a promotion, birth, or graduation, by either springing

Fireplace, structure responsible for people not freaking out about there being a large fire in the middle of their living room.

ONLY A COUPLE MORE
TIL LINCOLN
Millard Fillmore

(b. Jan. 7, 1800 d. Mar. 8, 1874), 13th president of the United States, who convinced the North and South to hold off on the Civil War for 11 years by arguing it would be better for the whole country if the conflict were handled by future president Abraham Lincoln. The last member of the Whig Party to hold high office, Fillmore saw early on that tensions between the rival factions were reaching a breaking point, and he freely admitted in speeches that he was not the man to be in charge of a country about to enter a war that would be far bloodier than World War I, or handle the racial upheaval and Reconstruction period to follow—tasks he said would be better managed by a "big-time president with the clout and stature of a Teddy Roosevelt or an FDR." During his 1852 State of the Union address, Fillmore famously said that the upcoming Civil War was "clearly Lincoln's moment to shine," and that the thought of himself delivering the Gettysburg Address or freeing the slaves was "as impossible to imagine as seeing slow pans across sepia photos of me, Millard Fillmore, in Ken Burns' 1990 documentary *The Civil War.*"

for some flounder at the flounder shop and throwing it on the grill or heading to a fine flounderhouse downtown.

Fly-Fishing, recreational activity in which fish take pity on sad, middle-aged men wearing waders and pretend to fall for their little fake-fly ruse. The fish take turns nibbling on the fly in order to ramp up the excitement for the poor old guy who had to beg his wife for three weeks for permission to spend a single afternoon with his buddies. One fish eventually agrees to swallow the hook and engage in a tug-of-war so that the rapidly graying man will have a gripping story to remember fondly as his far younger boss belittles him in front of the entire division, and to share repeatedly with his equally depressing friends. The fish ultimately allows itself to be caught, sacrificing itself so that the sad man may experience a moment of triumph before starting the long drive back to the life that will be exactly as miserable as he left it.

Football, full-contact sport in which a team of 11 men who will not live to see 60 attempt to advance a ball into an opponent's scoring area or end zone, while the opposing team—also composed of players who are doing irreparable damage to their bodies—tries to stop them. Running on legs that in a few years will be nonfunctioning husks of shriveled, twisted, and severed tendons ravaged by thousands of violent hits, ultimately leaving them crippled by the age of 40, players score six points by carrying the ball across the goal line. A team may also score a touchdown by catching a pass thrown into the end zone by a quarterback, whose heavily concussed brain will not only

AMERICANS CAN BE PROUD THEY DIDN'T ACTUALLY ELECT THIS GUY
Gerald Ford

(b. July 14, 1913 d. Dec. 26, 2006), 38th American president and most prominent native of Grand Rapids, Michigan, until the emergence of the R&B/funk group DeBarge in the mid-1980s. The only person to serve as both vice president and president without having been elected to either office, Ford was the favorite son of Grand Rapids for many years before being eclipsed by DeBarge, who produced such catchy, chart-topping hits as "Who's Holding Donna Now" and "Rhythm Of The Night." Although Ford would never reclaim the honor of most-celebrated Grand Rapids native from DeBarge—whose lead singer El DeBarge also achieved solo success with the top-10 dance-pop song "Who's Johnny"—he remains an admired figure in the city and has several buildings named after him.

prevent him from remembering his kids' names, but will cause chronic depression so severe that he will attempt suicide within a decade of retirement. Points can also be accumulated if a team's kicker, who will live happily into his 80s with a loving wife and family and have the

mental faculties to run a successful business as a second career, is able to kick the ball through the uprights located in the back of the end zone. *Footloose*, 1984 film and 2011 remake about a small town that bans dancing, although hand jobs are still totally legal, so it's unclear why

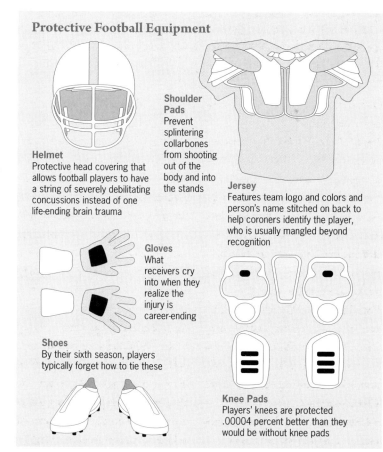

Protective Football Equipment

Helmet
Protective head covering that allows football players to have a string of severely debilitating concussions instead of one life-ending brain trauma

Shoulder Pads
Prevent splintering collarbones from shooting out of the body and into the stands

Jersey
Features team logo and colors and person's name stitched on back to help coroners identify the player, who is usually mangled beyond recognition

Gloves
What receivers cry into when they realize the injury is career-ending

Shoes
By their sixth season, players typically forget how to tie these

Knee Pads
Players' knees are protected .00004 percent better than they would be without knee pads

FRENCH AND INDIAN WAR (*1754–1763*), 18th-century North American conflict between the English and French that had a devastating impact on many Native American tribes when their members began to pick up extremely irritating habits from the French. Worst affected were the Algonquian people, who, shortly after fighting alongside the French, began smoking terrible-smelling cigarettes, haughtily riding bicycles with baskets full of maize-flour baguettes and tomahawks, and rudely insulting anyone they passed under their breath. The Ojibwa people were also devastated by the war, as they adopted the practices of cooking their venison in truffle oil and heavy cream, and annoyingly insisting that only wine made from the birch bark in a very specific region of their ancestral holy lands was authentic, and that everything else had to be called "sparkling birch-bark wine."

the teenagers care so much about repealing the law.

Ford Motor Company, major American auto manufacturer that struggled for a number of years in the early 21st century, but thankfully is once again churning out thousands of fuel-burning, carbon-dioxide-emitting vehicles for people to use repeatedly every day and year after year after year.

Fort Sumter Gift Shop, strategic location where Union soldiers purchased posters, shot glasses, and Fort Sumter pins for their friends and relatives during the Battle of Charleston Harbor.

42 Percent, one of the percentages on the zero to 100 percent scale.

Fosse, Bob (*b. June 23, 1927 d. Sept. 23, 1987*), famed dancer, choreographer, film director, and living proof that if you devote yourself to your craft, work hard, and pursue your vision, then maybe one day you, too, can become a miserable, philandering control freak and die young of a massive heart attack.

401(k), type of retirement savings account that allows individuals to set aside a portion of their income to vanish in an economic downturn. Employees enrolled in a 401(k) can calculate how much money they'd prefer to have evaporate into nothingness during a recession and then have that amount withdrawn automatically from their paychecks. Some companies offer matching contributions in which the money employees allocate toward disappearing forever is matched by an equally short-lived and pointless contribution from their current employer.

Frank, Anne (*b. June 12, 1929 d. Mar. 1945*), Jewish Holocaust victim who kept a poignant diary of her experience hiding from the Nazis and who would have been perfect for Elle Fanning to play in a new biopic if someone at CAA hadn't dropped the ball and let the whole goddamn deal go down the drain. Frank and her family hid in the secret annex of an Amsterdam apartment for two years, which is exactly how long it's going to take for Fanning's schedule to clear up now because one asshole didn't just pick

up a fucking telephone and call Steve Weiss over at Paramount to get it in writing. The thing was practically green-lit, for Christ's sake, with Liam Neeson attached to play the dad, Otto, who found his daughter's diary in 1945 and made sure it was published, translated into English, and sold throughout the world and fuck me, if you don't start coming up with some brilliant goddamn ideas real goddamn quick, you'll be booking second-rate magicians in Lincoln Fucking Nebraska before the week is out. Hey, what about that girl from *True Grit*? Is she Jewishy enough?

Frankenstein, you are probably looking for Frankenstein's *monster*, you idiot.

Frankenstein's Monster, there you go, dipshit.

Franklin, Aretha (*b. Mar. 25, 1942*), American R&B recording artist

Fossil, remains of any living thing that was consumed by a rock.

Four Kinds Of Truck, dump truck, pickup truck, fire truck, cement truck. There are lots of different kinds of trucks, but these are four.

best known for performing at *Wrestlemania III* and *Wrestlemania 23*.

Franklin, Benjamin (*b. Jan. 17, 1706 d. Apr. 17, 1790*), author, publisher, political theorist, activist, inventor, statesman, diplomat, and postmaster who spread himself way too thin and consequently wasn't especially good at any of those things. Noted throughout the world for his middling ability in a number of fields, Franklin was known to give half-formed opinions about federalism to his peers, then rush over to supervise the nation's first fire department but have to leave before addressing the lack of equipment and training, and then spend 15 minutes dashing off an unintelligible, ill-conceived lending policy for the nation's first library. *Poor Richard's Almanack*, a periodical considered one of Franklin's most significant contributions to early American culture, might have been more polished had he just sat down and focused on it. Even then, it likely would not have turned out that great because Benjamin Franklin was a pretty mediocre writer.

Franzen, Jonathan (*b. Aug. 17, 1959*), National Book Award–winning American writer whose brilliant works will eventually be overshadowed by his bizarre and all-consuming obsession with birds. Franzen's 2001 novel, *The Corrections*, garnered him awards, literary praise, and popular acclaim for its razor-sharp social criticism—accolades that will be all but forgotten as the author increasingly uses public forums such as college commencement speeches to ramble on maniacally about birds and birdwatching for hours on end. *Freedom*, Franzen's much-anticipated 2010 follow-up novel, met and exceeded critics' expectations, and

will inevitably make it even more tragic when the author becomes most strongly associated with mumbling distractedly about ongoing habitat destruction of the Asian fawn-breasted thrush during nationally televised interviews and dying of exposure while trying to catch a glimpse of the ultrarare bird on a tiny, uninhabited island in the South Pacific.

Friedan, Betty (*b. Feb. 4, 1921 d. Feb. 4, 2006*), American feminist

who said that women should be in equal partnership with men, which is both completely true and an exhausting and futile thing to devote one's entire life to. As the first president of the National Organization for Women, Friedan aimed to gain equal rights in every aspect of society and break down long-standing gender barriers, two noble pursuits that must have led to a stressful existence of sleepless nights, monumental disappointments, and constant questioning as to whether she should have maybe set more realistic goals for herself, like becoming a successful doctor or architect or just being a good person whose company other people enjoy. Friedan died without ever seeing her dream of a gender-blind society come true, which anyone with half a brain could have told her was going to happen when she came up with the ridiculously ambitious idea in the first place.

French Revolution, social and political uprising of the French lower classes that sought to realize the Enlightenment-era ideals of bloodlust, paranoid suspicion, infighting, revenge, equality, and grotesque

public savagery.

Friars Club, private organization known for hosting events called

"roasts," in which celebrities are mocked in a particularly vitriolic or obscene way, popularized in the days before the entire Internet was devoted to this activity.

Friendship, relationship in which two random people walk up to each other and loudly say, "We are friends!" in unison. After the friendship is established in this manner, the new friends then check every day to see if both parties wish to continue the friendship. This discussion is usually conducted via a short telephone call during which one friend asks the other, "Do you still want to be friends?" If either friend answers in the negative, the friendship is dissolved, but if both answer in the affirmative, a friendship activity can be planned, the most common of which involves the two friends sitting across from each other, staring in complete silence for approximately two hours. On Sundays and weekdays, friendships begin at 10:30 a.m. and end for the night at 8:30 p.m., and on Fridays and Saturdays they end at 11:00 p.m.

Futurism, early 20th-century art movement that really screwed over the people who have had to come up with names for art movements in later generations.

BENJAMIN FRANKLIN ➤
The very picture of mediocrity.

Frog, amphibian that offers children more than 5,000 species of squashing options.

Gacy, John Wayne (*b. Mar. 17, 1942 d. May 10, 1994*), American serial killer and rapist who murdered at least 33 young men and, though it is often overlooked due to the gruesome nature of his crimes, was at the time of his arrest really starting to come into his own as a clown. Gacy began killing in the suburbs of Chicago in 1972 and hid the bodies of his victims in a crawl space beneath his home—grim details overshadowing the fact that prior to his incarceration he could juggle up to five pieces of fruit, was a solid unicyclist, and was becoming quite proficient at making fairly complicated balloon animals. He was executed by lethal injection before he got the chance to really focus on his seltzer-bottle work, which Gacy would be the first to admit was the area of his clowning most in need of improvement.

Gage, Phineas (*b. July 9, 1823 d. May 21, 1860*), American railroad construction foreman who in 1848 survived an accident in which a 43-inch iron rod was explosively propelled through his skull, spurring a new field of medical research focused on driving blunt metal objects into people's heads and studying the effects. In the six decades from 1849 to 1909, participants ranging from infants to adults, wealthy to destitute, healthy to infirm, and citizens to immigrants had their skulls forcibly impaled upon tamping irons, as well as on crowbars, hammers, horseshoes, girders, and railway ties, with survivors being monitored for specific changes in behavior. By the time Gage finally succumbed to his wounds in 1860 at the age of 36, the cranial cavities of tens of thousands of test subjects had been traumatically penetrated, leading to the eventual development of a vaccine that succeeded in preventing millions of fatalities from long iron rods getting shot through the brains of railroad workers.

Galápagos Islands, archipelago in the Pacific Ocean whose vast array of unique animal species is considered proof of the limitless imagination of the one true creator, God. In the Galápagos, a multitude of sui generis faunae perfectly designed to thrive in concert with the region's varied terrain and climate were instantaneously conjured into being by the Lord in a definitive display of His unparalleled inventiveness and ability to adapt His vision to different surroundings. Naturalist Charles Darwin traveled there in 1835 to study the islands' native species, whereupon his faith in God was famously restored.

Galilei, Galileo (*b. Feb. 15, 1564 d. Jan. 8, 1642*), Italian astronomer who furthered the idea that the Earth revolved around the sun, a heretical belief that the Catholic Church forced both he and his telescope to publicly recant. Galileo's controversial 1632 book *Dialogue*

Concerning The Two Chief World Systems drew the ire of Pope Urban VIII, who ordered Galileo and his 30x refractor telescope to the Vatican, where they both faced the tribunals of the Roman Inquisition. At the trials, during which the elderly astronomer and his telescope were questioned separately prior to their appearance before the pope himself, Galileo pleaded for mercy and heaped the blame for his heliocentric theory of the solar system on the 4-foot-long looking glass, which stood completely silent and showed no remorse as it was bound and dragged out of the courtroom. For his transgressions against the church, Galileo was sentenced to spend the rest of his life under house arrest—a far more lenient punishment than the one meted out to his telescope, which was paraded through the streets of Rome in humiliating fashion as the public threw rotten vegetables and stones at it, and was then burned at the stake. The telescope never admitted any wrongdoing.

Game, relaxing, entertaining diversion centered around competitive human urges, jealousy, and anger. Across cultures, playing games is considered an enjoyable way to pass the time and channel one's primal drive to dominate another living being. Although varying in structure, games typically involve a fun and engaging mixture of luck, skill, and the barely concealed desire to ruthlessly exploit the physical or mental weaknesses of one's opponents, including friends, acquaintances, and 11-year-old sons.

Gandhi, Mohandas (*b. Oct. 2, 1869 d. Jan. 30, 1948*), political and spiritual leader of India who helped the country attain independence through nonviolent tactics because,

MOHANDAS GANDHI ➤
Wouldn't you advocate nonviolence if you had a chest like that?

Gender Identity, an individual's self-conception, regardless of biological sex, of being male, female, transgender, transsexual, gender nonconforming, genderqueer, cross-male, cross-female, androsexual, two-split, three-split, estromale, androgyfem, intrasexual, bisexual, pisexual, Vsexual, transgenital, mono-bisexual, transmono-bisexual, neutragenital, vexvenal, androgybigenital, XX-hermaphrofem, XY-hermaphrofem, YY-hermaphrofem, or undecided.

well, look at the guy. Weighing 90 pounds soaking wet, Gandhi urged peasants, farmers, and urban laborers to peacefully protest British colonial authority. Honestly, what else was he going to do? Strike fear into the hearts of India's oppressors with his hunched-over body and a walking stick? Not likely. Gandhi first employed nonviolent resistance while working as a lawyer in South Africa, demonstrating from an early age that he had a strong sense of how quickly he'd get his ass kicked in a real fight. With frail, birdlike wrists and no muscle anywhere on his tiny frame, Gandhi called nonviolence his "weapon," which is exactly what people who look like him would say, and his 1943 hunger strike to protest British rule sure as shit didn't do him any favors, either. On Jan. 30, 1948, Gandhi was fatally shot by a Hindu militant, which seems a bit excessive, considering you could basically have punched through him like tissue paper.

Ganges, sacred river revered by both the 400 million Hindus and the 500 trillion pathogens that regularly bathe and fester in the holy body of water. The Ganges is not only used by Hindus to purify the corpses of loved ones before cremating them and offering them to the gods, it is also the world's holiest site for toxic microorganisms, which venerate it as a place where microbes can teem in blissful harmony in what they believe is the source of all the fecal coliform bacteria in the universe. Although millions of people die annually from water-borne diseases, most Hindus and pathogens continue to share the hallowed river in peace.

Garden Of Earthly Delights, The, painting that is considered the masterpiece of Dutch artist Hierony-mus Bosch and whose three interior panels illustrate the paradise of Eden; a scene of unrestrained carnal indulgence; an inferno where sinners are tortured for eternity; and an advertisement for Dutchman's Pride vodka.

Gates, Bill (b. Oct. 28, 1955), founder of Microsoft and one of the richest men in the world who, when you think about it, could not have attained such incredible wealth and success without having at least a couple of people killed. A billionaire by the age of 32 and the man behind a technology juggernaut that has dominated global home and office computing for more than 20 years, Gates just has to be responsible for the deaths of at least a handful of people who stood in his path. Even if the Harvard dropout didn't order the killings directly, he had to have looked the other way as his subordinates took the necessary initiative on their own, didn't he? Gates has already donated more than $28 billion to various charitable causes, philanthropic efforts that, you have to suspect, were partly motivated by his guilt over all the competitors he had murdered and disposed of.

Gauguin, Paul (b. June 7, 1848 d. May 8, 1903), brilliant French artist who worked tirelessly to create paintings people look at for four seconds before moving on to the next one.

Gedankenexperiment, structured mental exercise used to examine a hypothesis, examples of which include Einstein's imagining of the temporal continuum as observed from a rider upon a beam of light; Schröedinger's famous quantum indeterminacy visualization of a cat sealed in a box that is both dead and alive; and picturing yourself driving the Space Corvette from the opening credits of *Heavy Metal*.

Gehrig, Lou (b. June 19, 1903 d. June 2, 1941), American baseball player and only member of the New York Yankees not deserving of unrelenting scorn and vitriol. Nicknamed "The Iron Horse," Gehrig was known for his power hitting,

200 DAYS ASSASSINATION FREE
James A. Garfield
(b. 19 Nov. 1831 d. 19 Sept. 1881), 20th president of the United States, fatally shot after only 200 days in office despite having won the 1880 election on a strict anti-assassination platform. Garfield, who served as a Union general in the Civil War, first developed his political philosophy after the assassination of Abraham Lincoln in 1865, writing at the time that "the foundation of a strong republic rests on a bedrock of not being assassinated" and vowing "no president shall ever be assassinated while I'm president." Despite the popularity of his position, Garfield was fatally shot on July 2, 1881, just before delivering a major anti-political-murder speech. His failure to deliver on campaign promises led to a massive decline in public support and, though he lived with his injuries for another two months, the humiliating assassination ended his political career.

longevity, and ability not to be a prima donna who cried like a little girl every time a call didn't go his way (*See* PAUL O'NEILL). Over 15 seasons, Gehrig—who suffered a painful, debilitating disease with grace and dignity, unlike Babe Ruth, who ate himself to death, Mickey Mantle, who drank himself to death, and Alex Rodriguez, who is Alex fucking Rodriguez—played in 2,130 consecutive games, a record that went unmatched until Cal Ripken, Jr., broke it in 1995, marking the last time a non-asshole did anything good in baseball.

Gehry, Frank (*b. Feb. 28, 1929*), man your city is willing to pay $90 million to erect some giant crumpled-up pieces of foil.

Gender, social and cultural construct based upon biological sex, and the reason why boys are made to wear blue and girls are violently discarded and burned right after birth. Though the anatomical differences that inform the concept of gender have no bearing on intelligence, ability, or any intrinsic societal value or lack thereof, they remain the basis for why boys are encouraged to play cowboys and Indians and girls have acid thrown in their faces. Gender is also believed by sociologists to be responsible for boys' common difficulty in expressing emotions and girls' propensity to have their genitals mutilated or be forced into sex slavery.

Geology, study of solid-Earth processes while wearing a button-down plaid shirt tucked into jeans.

Ghost, restless spirit sentenced to haunt the living after being found guilty of drunk driving in the afterlife. Punishments are determined on a sliding scale depending on the disembodied soul's blood-alcohol level at the time of arrest. If the ap-

BATTLE OF GETTYSBURG, bloodiest battle of the American Civil War, lasting three days and claiming the lives of 3,155 Union soldiers, 4,708 Confederate soldiers, 2,037 innocent bystanders, 601 horses, 246,729 ants, 912 trees, 889 rifles, 586 snails, 14.2 million blades of grass, a long fence, 213 fireflies, 12 swords, 414 tapeworms, 42,346 dewdrops, more than 52 trillion carbon molecules, 1,287 hats, a three-legged dog, and an unrecorded number of black men.

parition scores .06 to .09, its driver's license is revoked for 30 days, during which it must silently follow a member of the living around his or her house, vanishing as soon as the person turns around. A Breathalyzer reading of .10 or above results in the ghost's car being impounded and its license being revoked for a full year, during which it must wake the same person up night after night by floating over their bed gurgling "help me" in an agonized tone. It is not uncommon, however, for a ghost to hire a lawyer and get off with a lesser sentence, frequently a court-ordered rehabilitation program and 50 hours of appearing in the photos of the living as a translucent ball of light.

Ghostess, spirit of deceased female maître d' who haunts the front of the restaurant and attempts to gain revenge on guests who wronged her in life by making them wait forever for a table at the bar.

Giacometti, Alberto (*b. Oct. 10, 1901 d. Jan. 11, 1966*), very nice

man whose numerous 20th-century sculptures weren't going to change one's life, per se, but really were quite good, and doing them seemed to make him happy, so where's the harm in that? In fact, that goes for anyone like Giacometti who may not be as good at sculpture as Michelangelo or anything, but is just trying to pursue something they enjoy. As long as it's not bothering anyone, just let people do what they want to do. Here's a good rule of thumb: Never say anything about another person that you wouldn't want to hear said about yourself. It may seem obvious, but a surprising number of people out there forget common, everyday courtesies like this, and it's really a shame.

Global Warming, gradual heating of the earth's temperature caused largely by mankind's emission of greenhouse gases, and a process that can only be reversed if, oops, never mind, because we actually just now passed the exact point of

Genie, in Arabian folklore, a spirit that could theoretically grant wishes if freed from a lamp or bottle, but was actually dead 90 percent of the time and just kind of rattled around in there.

Giraffe, large ruminant African mammal that uses its long neck to constrict and kill prey before consuming it whole.

GEOGRAPHY, study of the Earth's isthmuses, from the Isthmus of Kra in Southeast Asia to Canada's Isthmus of Chignecto. Geography is an isthmus-centric pursuit that can be divided into four categories: physical geography, the study of how big or small isthmuses are; comparative geography, in which other landforms, such as straits, tributaries, and mountains are studied to determine why they aren't isthmuses; human geography, which maps people's behavioral patterns in relation to isthmuses; and theoretical geography, which hypothesizes what isthmuses would look like in areas where there are no isthmuses. Narrow strips of land surrounded by water that connect two larger pieces of land, isthmuses help geographers better understand the Earth's topographical features and their place in relation to the isthmus. For example, a canal is considered a man-made isthmus; caves are roofed isthmuses; an ocean is a land-lacking, deep-water isthmus; and deserts are water-deficient, sand-infused, dune-developed isthmuses. Geography was first studied by Eratosthenes of Greece, who invented the system of latitude and longitude so he could remember the location of all the isthmuses.

There are some pretty inconsequential landforms in this satellite photo, so what you'll want to do is focus on the Isthmus of Suez right in the middle-left there.

Other Landforms

Peninsula: This grotesque blemish on the Earth's surface fails to be an isthmus in every conceivable way, and is so hideous to look upon that it compels one to seek out the nearest isthmus in order to purge the image of the disgusting peninsula from his or her mind.

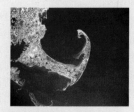

Archipelago: One can't help but feel bad for this pathetic geographic feature and its lack of narrow strips of land connecting all the islands.

Berm: A narrow, level shelf at the top of a slope separating blah blah blah blah whatever who cares *this is not an isthmus.*

River Delta: Gets some credit for being kind of an inverse isthmus, but not much.

Isthmus: Just look at it. Takes your damn breath away.

What It Would Take To Make Various Geographic Features Into Isthmuses

Mountain: Shaving it down via hydraulic fracturing until it is merely a strip of land, then digging holes into side of the mountain until reaching sea level so the holes become filled with water.

Fjord: Build massive wall in front of it, obscuring it from view; paint isthmus on wall; forget the fjord exists.

Isthmus: Pick up garbage to make it a better isthmus.

Mars: The Red Planet offers a unique opportunity, in that humanity could eventually terraform the entire surface so that it is a world of isthmuses. Write or call your congressperson today to let him or her know this is an issue you deeply care about.

---

ever being able to undo the horrifying effects of climate change. According to climatologists, rising CO_2 levels must be contained before it is too late, which it now is, or the world populace will experience severe food shortages, widespread drought, and the mass extinction of thousands of plant and animal species. Climate change is also believed to be responsible for the thawing of the polar ice caps—the melting of which is irreversible as of eight seconds ago—and will in turn lead to the incomprehensibly destructive

flooding of the entire Eastern Seaboard of the United States in 60 years. Well, 59 years, 364 days, 23 hours, and 59 minutes. In order to reduce one's own impact, experts recommend using energy-efficient products, carpooling to work, and not relying on air-conditioning so much, though they may as well recommend taking out a gun and shooting yourself in the fucking head right now, because by the time you finish reading this, any fleeting hope of somehow changing this collision course with global de-

struction will be forever lost, and we all need to face the fact that everyone and everything we've ever loved will soon be annihilated by the raging forces of nature, and that civilization itself will either be wiped out or plunged into anarchy as we all stand by helplessly, waiting to drown, die of starvation, or burn to death.

Gloryhole, small hole cut into the partition between bathroom stalls through which married couples can kiss. Gloryholes are typically positioned on the divider at waist height, which allows husband and wife to kneel on opposite sides and touch lips with relative ease. While couples may visit a gloryhole at any time to affirm their love for each other, most confine their visits to anniversaries and will often mark such milestones throughout their lives at the same gloryhole.

God, all-knowing, all-powerful entity responsible for the blooming of flowers, the setting of the sun, the  feeling one experiences when sitting down to enjoy a nice, gently toasted tuna sandwich, war, murder, retarded kids, humanity in general, hurricanes, Major Ogilvie's 1980 Sugar Bowl MVP performance, that hilarious joke about the three priests on a rapidly sinking ship, plaster, snowfall on a starlit night, fear, Buddhism, the mean-spirited falsetto voice your coworkers use to mock you when you're not around, wheat, love, leukemia, DVDs, the bizarre combination of resentment and devotion that children feel toward their parents, and more than 15 varieties of pie.

Gold, soft yellowish metal best suited for augmenting fat, hairy chests.

Golden Gate Bridge, suspension bridge spanning the opening of San Francisco Bay that defied scores of experts who insisted a bridge that orange could never be built. Construction on the 1.7-mile-long structure began in 1933, when it

was accepted wisdom that a bridge of that size could either be structurally sound or vibrant orange, but not both. Designer Joseph Strauss privately expressed fears that he would die in shame and humiliation for even conceiving of a bridge so orange, but publicly defied his colleagues, saying he would rather take a chance at building a massive orange bridge that tragically collapses into the sea then settle for something gray or even blue. The bridge was completed in 1937, with most onlookers too terrified to cross it because it was an even brighter, bolder orange than they originally thought. Although 118,000 vehicles cross the Golden Gate Bridge each day, it is still considered an engineering marvel in terms of its intensity-of-orange to weight-supported ratio.

Golf, sport played on a large open-air course in which a small, hard ball is struck with a club into a series of holes in the ground with the object of using the fewest possible strokes to complete the course, and an activity that is… well, what's the most polite way to put this? Not really exactly right for someone like *you*. Developed in Scotland in the 15th century, golf spread across the globe while maintaining certain long-held traditions and strict codes of etiquette that would probably make playing golf very *uncomfortable* for someone such as yourself—what with your particular upbringing, education, faith, and, shall we say, overall *background*, there is just so much potential for you to terribly *embarrass* yourself, you see? Many consider golf to be a thoughtful, introspective, and extremely *intellectual* game, so you probably would never truly appreciate it even if, by some stretch of the imagination,

you were able to gain a modicum of technical facility. Once made of wood and animal hides, golf equipment today is manufactured with advanced synthetic materials intended to maximize performance and is really *very* expensive and we certainly wouldn't want someone like you spending so much money on such things, especially by the look of those *clothes*.

Goliath, Philistine giant who, after being knocked out by the Israelite youth David, regained consciousness and rose up to slaughter thousands upon thousands of innocent villagers, vowing never again to let an underdog catch him off guard. According to the biblical story, David, armed with just a sling, hurled a stone at Goliath's forehead and temporarily incapacitated the fearsome giant. However, once the swelling and dizziness subsided, Goliath returned to combat angrier than ever and massacred the smallest, meekest, and most unassuming combatants first, their stones bouncing pathetically off his newly modified rock-proof helmet. The story of David and Goliath remains a popular parable to this day, due to its timeless message that even giants can be knocked down if they fail to destroy the little guy

◄ Perhaps someone of your lowly position in life would be better off looking at a picture of a factory.

Goebbels, Joseph (*b. Oct. 29, 1897 d. May 1, 1945*), Nazi minister of propaganda and deplorable, amoral human being who, like most people who bear those traits, was extremely successful and effective at his job.

Goodall, Jane (*b. Apr. 3, 1934*), British primatologist who probably let a couple of chimps get to second base.

Google's successful search engine InfoWiz is presided over by Merlink, who can uncover web results from the past, present, and future with a wave of his magic wand. ➤

immediately, and that when bigger and stronger people want something, they'll get it eventually.

Google Inc., American technology company founded in 1998 by Sergey Brin and Larry Page that is best known for its Internet search engine InfoWiz. The most popular and frequently used search engine in the world, InfoWiz features the iconic wizard mascot Merlink, an elderly sorcerer armed with a question-mark-shaped wand who urges users to embark on a data quest by typing magical keywords to cast a search spell, which in turn conjures millions of results on web scrolls. In 2011, InfoWiz employed 29,000 workers and generated $28 billion in revenue for Google while receiving more than 100 million crystal ball queries each day. Recently, InfoWiz has broadened its reach to include new products such as the Druid smartphone.

Governor, elected executive of a U.S. state or commonwealth who privately can't wait to get tapped as a presidential running mate and get the fuck out of Kansas forever.

Grand Canyon, ancient canyon system in the state of Arizona that if you're on your deathbed without having visited, you've really fucked up. Formed by the Colorado River, the Grand Canyon is 277 miles long, 18 miles across at its widest point, and 6,000 feet at its deepest, a breathtaking natural wonder you never found the time to see and now never will because you're lying in a hospital dying. Instead of enjoying the sight, whose beauty so impressed Teddy Roosevelt that he designated it a national monument in 1908, you squandered your only trip out west on Disneyland, where

GOVERNMENT, system of human organization responsible for cleaning up when somebody drunkenly dumps an entire bag of trash on the street to make his friends laugh. Typically composed of an appointed body of officials whose members constitute a state's governing authority, a government is charged with disposing of the various sandwich wrappers, soda cans, eggshells, newspapers, and half-full cups of coffee that were ejected onto the street from a trash bag in a wildly spinning helicopter motion by an intoxicated person at 3 a.m. while his friends laughed hysterically and shouted, "Dude, what the fuck are you doing?" A number of secondary functions, including pulling out the old sweaters and greasy, brown paper bags full of Chinese food cartons that got jammed in the storm drain, and setting the overturned garbage can back on the corner of the street where it belongs, also fall under the purview of a functioning government. The grand, age-old enterprise of government is tasked with a number of other administrative functions, including talking down an angry, urine-soaked man screaming in front of the firewood section of a Safeway, delicately explaining to a person standing in line at the DMV that there is no smoking allowed inside the building, and erasing the graffiti on the "Absolutely No Parking" sign so that it no longer reads "Absolutely No Fucking."

Forms Of Government

Democracy: System in which the power is vested in apathy

Jamocracy: Government in which the power is vested in a group of musicians working together to just totally rock out

Monarchy: System in which power is vested in a sovereign such as a king or queen and that, despite its hereditary basis, is also meritocratic, as would-be rulers must successfully emerge from their mother's vagina alive

Autocracy: Mechanical, electrical, or hydraulic system of government used to guide society without assistance from humans

Commune: Small form of democratic government that inevitably destroys itself when participants realize they're just a fucking pack of animals like everyone else

Plutocracy: Government by the wealthy; for example, the Roman Republic, medieval merchant republics such as Venice and Florence, and every other government that ever has or ever will exist

Theocracy: Form of government led by individuals claiming to be divinely guided in their duties. Goes about as well as you'd think.

An image that will only serve to deepen the crushing regret you must feel if you are in hospice care and you never saw this in person.

you had your picture taken with Jafar. And now you're practically a cadaver already and it's too late to share a spiritual communion with the natural world, let alone enjoy the magnificent chasm on a hike or rafting trip. Don't you feel like a jerk? You should, because you blew it. You really blew it.

Grandfather Clock,
CU on GRANDFATHER CLOCK. The hypnotic beats of its ancient pendulum grow louder with each swing. The last is hauntingly loud, as if all time has stopped.

> AARON
> (almost whispering)
> Dad?
Beat.
> AARON
> (CONT.)
> Is that you?

Gravity, naturally occurring phenomenon that gives weight to objects of mass and what acclaimed film and stage actor Frank Langella brings to nearly every role. First theorized by Sir Isaac Newton in 1687 and recognized today as the force that causes the Earth and the other planets to orbit around the sun, gravity is also the attribute that earned Langella two Tony awards for Best Featured Actor in a Play and an Academy Award nomina-

tion for his masterful portrayal of Richard Nixon in the 2008 film *Frost/Nixon*. While gravitational theory was refined by physicist Albert Einstein in 1915 with the Einstein field equations, it most notably kept Langella's exquisite performance in *Wall Street: Money Never Sleeps* from devolving into mere caricature. Gravity should not be confused with levity, which is defined as a lightness in weight and was perhaps best demonstrated by Frank Langella's effortless comic turn in the 1993 film *Dave*.

Great Binge, The, two-year-long campaign that immediately pre-

ceded the bloodshed of the Great Purge and that saw Joseph Stalin jam-packing the Soviet government with as many people as he possibly could. In 1935 and 1936, Stalin was known for his largesse, taking in anyone who asked him for a job. "There's room for everyone," was the premier's slogan, and he gorged the bureaucracy with Communist Party peons, political opponents, capitalists, wealthy aristocrats, suspected saboteurs, illiterates, and the criminally insane. At the end of this period, Stalin was seized with regret and vowed to reverse the policy.

Great Depression, period of world economic collapse in the 1930s and the reason grandmothers save twist ties. Triggered by the stock market crash of 1929, the Great Depression saw unemployment in the United States reach 25 percent while household incomes plummeted, which is why grandmothers have a drawer next to the sink that is filled with more twist ties than any widow in her 80s could possibly use, stacked beside a pile of old envelopes from the phone company that they use as scratch paper.

Gotham City

Large North American city of 5.3 million people. Covering an area of 322.7 square miles, Gotham has an average annual temperature of 52.7 degrees Fahrenheit and an average annual rainfall of 43.47 inches.

One of Gotham City's many attractive parks.

The city's main industries include finance and technology, in addition to a commercial seaport, and its gross metropolitan product is $890 billion. Gotham is also a major cultural center, with dozens of fine art museums and a world-class symphony orchestra. While Gotham City is often associated with an extremely high crime rate, in reality its statistics are no more or less notable than other U.S. cities such as Baltimore, Metropolis, and Detroit.

Ulysses S. Grant

(b. April 27, 1822 d. July 23, 1885), famed U.S. general whose skill at killing thousands of people, destroying railroad lines, and burning cities to the ground failed to translate effectively to his presidency. While a brilliant commander and ruthless tactician during the Civil War, Grant had a difficult time using his natural talent for running bayonet charges or hacking a foe's head off from horseback to establish sound monetary policies or gather bipartisan support to pass a bill in Congress. When it came to the crucial task of appointing a new Cabinet, it turned out Grant's well of expertise in walking through fields of wounded soldiers and shooting the ones who were too weak to stand, or directing salvos of cannon fire at farmhouses suspected of hiding Confederate sympathizers, had no bearing whatsoever, leaving him vastly ill-prepared to hold the nation's highest office. Grant's greatest legacy as president, however—enforcing civil rights laws and executing members of the Ku Klux Klan—was directly informed by his prior experience enforcing civil rights laws and executing members of the Ku Klux Klan.

NICKNAME: Killed anyone who tried to give him a nickname

AGE AT BIRTH: 0

PRESIDENTIAL ID NUMBER: 2D-GR18-004

OF NOTE: First president to serve two terms on horseback

Great Wall Of China, only part of China not currently being observed from space.

The Depression gave rise to morbid scenes of dejected, jobless men standing in long, humiliating lines for soup kitchens and living in

makeshift shantytowns known as Hoovervilles, events that explain why grandmothers not only save the twist tie from every loaf of bread, but also never throw a single slice away, even if they have to cut a little mold off the crust. The end of the Great Depression is generally attributed to President Franklin Roosevelt's New Deal programs and government spending on World War II, by which point grandmothers were well on their way to saving twist ties and washing out sandwich bags and not really caring what younger people thought because they weren't there and could never understand.

Great Pacific Garbage Patch, giant floating mass of discarded plastics, chemical sludge, and trash located in the central North Pacific Ocean that is the result of fish and other marine animals recklessly polluting their own waterways. The massive swirling vortex of debris—whose size is estimated to be at least 500,000 square miles—was formed by seabirds discarding candy wrappers and aluminum cans, sharks improperly disposing of sewage, and tortoises dumping industrial waste and other hazardous materials directly into the ocean. Marine biolo-

gists concerned about the environmental impact of the Garbage Patch have increased efforts in recent years to educate jellyfish about proper waste disposal, and have lobbied the world's governments to hold accountable all sea lions that insist on dumping diesel fuel in delicate habitats.

Great Smoky Mountains National Park, most visited national park in the United States, originally established in 1934 as a place for Daniel and Maureen Killon to have a marriage-ending argument while setting up a tent some 75 years later.

Greco-Roman Wrestling, sport that is usually stopped right before the winner rapes the loser.

Greenspan, Alan *(b. Mar. 6, 1926),* 13th Chairman of the Federal Reserve, known for his wild celebrity lifestyle, irresistibility to women, and forceful handling of national monetary policy. Greenspan's pragmatic approach to economic theory and infamous days-long hedonistic soirees at his sprawling Washington, D.C., "Fantasy Ranch" vaunted the economist to legendary status

during the four presidential administrations under which he served. He is revered by obsessive fans worldwide, thousands of whom would gather daily outside the Fed building and chant his name in the hopes of catching a glimpse of the stringent objectivist. Greenspan raised interest rates several times as he made headlines for his torrid affairs with Diane Keaton, Christy Turlington, Connie Chung, Elle Macpherson, Barbara Bush, and Naomi Campbell, among hundreds of others. The Fed chief once had to be resuscitated by paramedics after he was found floating facedown in his dollar-sign-shaped pool by then-Treasury Secretary Robert Rubin, and that same week Greenspan flooded the world with American currency in order to ease liquidity in response to capital flight during the Asian recession. Greenspan's recent memoir, *The Age Of Turbulence: Adventures In Pills, Girls, And The Housing Bubble,* spent 23 weeks on *The New York Times* bestseller list.

Griddle Cakes, pancakes for people who refer to albums as "LPs."

Since retiring from the Federal Reserve, Greenspan has remained a powerful sex symbol and regular fixture of the New York City nightclub scene.

ANCIENT GREECE, civilization that flourished from 750 BC to 146 BC as a center of artistic, scientific, and cultural advancement, and that some tiny glimmer way down deep in humanity's DNA must still on some level yearn for and aspire to be like. The ancient Greeks—human beings no different than us in most respects, let us remember—built a vibrant society based on scientific and humanistic ideals, avidly exploring the frontiers of mathematics, astronomy, philosophy, and medicine, with an ambition and ingenuity that, for God's sake, must, just must, still be down there somewhere in the furthest reaches of our brains, waiting to be unlocked again. Indeed, one would have to believe there remains something within all of us, some long-abandoned genetic imperative or faint universal impulse, that longs to create stirring works of architecture, theater, and literature like those that served as the cultural foundation of ancient Greece. The Parthenon, the Pythagorean theorem, the Socratic method, and *The Iliad* are just a few of the accomplishments produced by ancient Greece that we could still match today if we truly, truly tried, and we should, frankly, because just look around us. Is this the civilization we want? There must exist some primordial vestige handed down to us from ancient Greece that could once again allow us to exercise our faculties of reason, make bold discoveries, and build something, anything of actual meaning in this world. There has to be. Otherwise, what the fuck are we doing here?

This magnificent temple to the goddess Athena stands high on the Acropolis as a reminder to the modern Greek people that they weren't always such worthless fuckups.

Drama masks were used as a crutch in the event an actor could not get his face to look happy or sad.

Coinage was typically off-centered because the imprint and type of metal was more important than the shape. But thanks for noticing that.

Birthplace Of Democracy

The ancient Greeks were responsible for the creation of democracy and all the bullshit that goes along with it. The city-state of Athens was the first in the region to establish a citizen-based system of rule, and its three governing bodies went on to develop the kind of back-scratching, power-grabbing, and infuriating political gamesmanship that remains a major part of democracy today. The Greek model of government also introduced the concepts of majority rule and the backroom deal; voter registration and voter fraud; and a government by the people and for the people that excludes vast swaths of people. In addition, the Greeks originated the act of spreading democracy, along with the wholesale killing necessary to do that.

Griffith, Andy (*b. June 1, 1926*), beloved American actor who one day we'll probably hear was a terrible person and a selfish, egomaniacal prima donna on set, who would throw temper tantrums at production assistants and had several extramarital affairs, which will disappoint us because we just assumed that, man, this was supposed to be this wonderful classy guy, but it's more than likely that he's just a piece of garbage like the rest of us.

Grill, one of 27 things in the world that needs to be fired up. (*See* MAINFRAME, FILM PROJECTOR, STUDIO AUDIENCE FOR GEORGE LOPEZ SHOW, THE OL' HARLEY, GRAVITY BONG, ORLANDO MAGIC BENCH, CROCK-POT, THE CONSERVATIVE BASE, LARGE HADRON COLLIDER, TROOPS, ROCK TUMBLER, THIS PUPPY, KILN, HOMETOWN DIEHARDS WITH YOUR VERY OWN MCKEESPORT HIGH CHEERLEADERS, THE OL' CHAINSAW, DEATH STAR, PACEMAKER, XBOX, THIS BAD BOY, HOT-AIR BALLOON, WAFFLE IRON, THE OL' LAWNMOWER, THESE MOTHERFUCKERS, SALES TEAM, F-14, 'EM)

Grove City Docks, the docks? Jeez, every time I go down there I gotta get a new head. They keep the peace by any means they can down there, if you catch my meaning. Not to say they don't have crime. They just keep it, you know…organized. But sure, I can show you the way, shamus. Just don't expect me to play muscle for you. I just bought this suit, see, and I wasn't planning on being buried in it. But it looks like that powder-blue Plymouth that just parked a block behind you might have different ideas. (*See* POWDER-BLUE PLYMOUTH)

Gummy, prefix denoting chewiness in a candied food, and a word that comes up far more often in the average human being's life than, say, conflagration or bauxite.

Gutenberg, Johannes (*b. circa 1390 d. Feb. 3, 1468*), German inventor responsible for devising movable type, a loathsome printing technology that led to the mass dissemination of the most vile and  depraved smut, including indecent books, obscene periodicals, the Bible, and pornographic drawings.

Gymnastics, scientific discipline dealing with the locomotion of small 11- to 16-year-old girls on padded mat surfaces, as well as their relationship to uneven bars and high-pressure situations. Scholars in the gymnastics field complete their doctoral programs by publishing dissertations on gradual entropy and overexertion effects on participants' joints or studying the motion of a squat young woman tumbling through space-time. Gymnastics intersects with many interdisciplinary areas of research, including dance, acrobatics, biology, and somersaults.

ANCIENT GROME, cultural backwater that made no major contributions to art, science, government, warfare, or religion. Its original settlers, who found the land to be relatively decent for establishing some mediocre agriculture, began permanent occupation in the early 4th century BC and continued to inhabit it for the next 200 years simply because no one could think of a compelling reason to leave. At its height, ancient Grome was devoid of any gleaming temples, vast aqueducts, important thinkers, revolutionary inventions, clever urban planning, imposing fortifications, or cause for a passing traveler to stay for more than a couple of hours at most. Not a single great athletic competition occurred during its existence, nor did the Groman people practice any traditions or customs worthy of being codified in their fairly pathetic body of literature. When word finally arrived in 199 BC that the Etruscans had built a new settlement in the western Italian peninsula, the apathetic Groman population emigrated en masse, leaving behind a broad landscape dotted with unappealing artifacts and ruins.

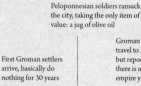

It took 5,000 Gromans a full century to erect this structure, which collapsed three days later.

The Groman "Empire"

The Secondary Building
Freestanding structure for Gromans who got lost going to the Main Building

The Stables
Notable for its use of a roof to protect horses from rain

The Cathedral
Place of worship where Gromans would try to create gods to honor, but would become flustered when they couldn't come up with anything

The Bath House
Baths

The Main Building
Basic stone structure used for meetings and events; no pillars

Two-foot tall stone wall protecting important Groman hole

Significant pile of rocks

A Timeline Of Grome

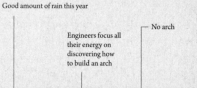

First Groman settlers arrive, basically do nothing for 30 years	Peloponnesian soldiers ransack the city, taking the only item of value: a jug of olive oil	Groman scouts travel to Rome but report that there is no empire yet	Groman playwright Agapetus pens his first and only work, a brief interchange between two bread merchants	Good amount of rain this year	Engineers focus all their energy on discovering how to build an arch	No arch	Best architect buried under remains of failed arch	Still no arch	Historic 45-minute visit by Celtic delegation	Last inhabitants leave, marking the occasion with an engraved stone showing the date and directions for anyone who came there looking for Rome
368 BC	338	329	326	263	239	228	220	217	211	199

Haiku, please do not arrange these words into a haiku, even though they fit.

Hail, hardened cloud semen that falls from the sky after clouds have sex or masturbate.

Halloween, fall holiday observed with fanciful costumes, the carving of jack-o'-lanterns, and the practice of trick-or-treating for candy, all of which are faithful reenactments of events from the bizarre Halloween War of Oct. 31, 1832, between the United States and France.

Ham Radio, electronic communication device used to contact weirdos.

Hamilton, Alexander *(b. Jan. 11, 1755 d. July 12, 1804)*, statesmen, soldier, economist, and secretary of the treasury whose otherwise impeccable legacy will always be tainted by his involvement with the United States of America. Hamilton, who was known for his new and influential theories on economics, which led to the establishment of a national bank, will never be able to shake his nearly 30-year connection with the United States, a country that has also left a blemish on the résumés of George Washington, Abraham Lincoln, and Franklin Delano Roosevelt. Hamilton was killed during a duel with Aaron Burr, who allowed Hamilton to salvage some dignity by effectively ending his U.S. citizenship, which up until that point was the most humiliating detail of his life.

Hammer, tool with a metal head mounted on a handle, designed to be used by upstairs neighbors for a wide variety of construction and repair projects. The first hammer is believed to have been used by prehistoric upstairs neighbors in the middle of the night 2.6 million years ago.

Hammurabi *(d. circa 1750 BC)*, Babylonian king and visionary for a blind and toothless utopia.

Handshake, ritual that takes places following an agreement between people with at least one hand each.

Hannibal *(b. 247 BC d. 183 BC)*, brilliant Carthaginian military leader who was one of the most talented generals in history yet could not keep an elephant alive worth a damn. During every single armed

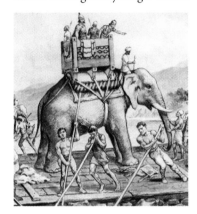

campaign he led, Hannibal inadvertently killed hundreds of his own war elephants, either through elaborately tragic accidents or sheer neglect. Even as a child, when Hannibal would accompany his father, Hamilcar Barca, on military conquests, every pachyderm that was put in his care would inevitably fall off a cliff or die from some rare disease within a few hours. On one particular morning during Hannibal's campaign to cross the Alps during the Second Punic War, his increasingly demoralized army awoke to find more than 10,000 dead elephants piled on top of each other. Hannibal's fortunes as a general and a statesman began to decline rapidly following a devastating loss to the Romans in the 202 BC Battle of Zama, during which all of the Carthaginian elephants inexplicably burst into flame mid-charge.

Hanukkah, Jewish holiday whose spiritual meaninglessness has been overshadowed by the commercialization of the festival, with the rampant exchange of gifts overtaking Hanukkah's minimal historic value and utter religious insignificance.

Happiness, evolutionary survival mechanism developed by humans to prevent members of the species from killing themselves the mo-

---

WOULD GIVE HIS FRIENDS THE SHIRT OFF THE FEDERAL GOVERNMENT'S BACK

Warren G. Harding

(b. Nov. 2, 1865 d. Aug. 2, 1923), 29th American president, whose administration was marked by rampant corruption and cronyism, including naming his former business partner Edwin C. Denby secretary of the Navy, attorney general, and Supreme Court justice simultaneously, while also awarding ownership of the Grand Canyon to his cousin Nathaniel. In 1921, after Harding allocated $90 million to redirect the Mississippi River so that it ran through his uncle's textile mill, he drew criticism for his misappropriation of personnel and state funds, which had also included briefly selling West Virginia to a German coal company. Passage that same year of the Harding's Buddy Is Getting 25 Percent of Our Tax Money Now Act, giving the president's longtime friend Charles R. Forbes one quarter of the total taxes paid by Americans, led to a congressional investigation. The Office of Small Pet Enclosures, an arm of the Department of the Interior currently led by Harding's great-grandson, still receives $12.6 billion each year in federal funding.

Hh

Eighth letter of the English alphabet, based on the ancient cuneiform representing an elevated walkway connecting two Minneapolis skyscrapers.

Hard Hat, protective metal or plastic helmet worn by construction workers and the pussy architects who sometimes stop by for a peek.

Harem Pant, popular women's trouser style that has a deep cloth pocket in the middle to give the wearer room to defecate.

Benjamin Harrison

(b. Aug. 20, 1833 d. Mar. 13, 1901), 23rd president of the United States, who hoped in vain that at least one of the six new states admitted during his term would be named Harrisonland, or something to that effect. Though he rarely addressed it in public, those close to Harrison said he grew increasingly agitated as each new state selected a name other than the ones he had envisioned, his favorites being Harrisonton, Harrissippi, and Harrison Hampshire. When it was clear the new states would not be naming their capitals after him either, Harrison became bitter, once insisting to his Cabinet that he didn't want a "dump" like Idaho to be named after him anyway, and in 1890 telling organizers of the Wyoming Constitutional Convention that he hoped they were proud of the Indian-derived bullshit name they chose instead of West Ben Harrison. On March 13, 1901, wracked with pneumonia, a broken Harrison uttered his last words to his wife: "Can you believe that, Mary? *Two* fucking Dakotas."

Harrison's Historic Recording

In 1889, Benjamin Harrison became the first president to have his voice recorded. The following historic remark was preserved on a wax phonograph cylinder:

"Hello? [long pause]. Hello, can you hear me? [long pause]. I am tal-king in-to a pho-no-graph [long pause]. Mr. Phonograph? Can I tell you a secret? [long pause]. I want to die."

ment they attain self-awareness. Though happiness does not typically last longer than three to six seconds, the biochemical mutation is just enough to stop humans from grabbing the nearest rock and bashing themselves in the head over and over again the second they realize that they are mortal, and that life is bleak, painful, and ultimately without meaning. The biological imperative has prevented billions of humans from jumping off cliffs or drowning themselves en masse, and leading evolutionary scientists believe those who commit suicide do so not because they lack the inherited trait, but because they are smart enough to realize that the search for happiness is not worth the effort.

Harmonica, worst thing about this small, rectangular wind instrument is how portable it is, making it always ready to be played. You just pull this piece of shit out of your pocket and, without having to tune it or anything, can start torturing everyone around you right then and there.

Havisford, Vera, well, if it isn't Grove City's most illustrious flatfoot. Come to show a girl a good time? Yes, yes, of course. "Mitsy LaRue," my fanny. Like any mother would ever name her daughter that. No, handsome, those two names are just the intersection of two streets, and two lives—a self-styled young "colonel" and a feisty, ambitious little gal who was a shade too dusky for the Colonel's own aspirations. So the woman ran away, had the baby, and called her Vera. Then the baby grew up and renamed herself. And that's my story, flatfoot. Eye-watering, ain't it? Might take you a minute to let the realization hit you, but brother, it's gonna hit you hard. Well, maybe not as hard

HARLEM GLOBETROTTERS, exhibition basketball team that combines athleticism, theater, and comedy in multiple entertaining routines, the most famous of which involves selecting a member of the crowd to stand at half-court, whereupon the Globetrotters set the unsuspecting volunteer on fire and perform passing and dribbling tricks in a circle around the screaming, dying fan. During the hilarious bit, the Globetrotters jokingly attempt to douse the flames by dumping a bucket of confetti on the burning victim or place a spinning basketball on the person's finger as their scorched flesh melts from their skull. The Globetrotters end the gut-busting antics by returning the charred corpse to family members or friends in the stands.

as Slugger Doogan's gonna hit you. (*See* SLUGGER DOOGAN)

Health, state of bodily wellness that individuals may possess even as Alzheimer's disease lies dormant in their DNA, waiting to activate and slowly take their life after turning them into a shell of a human being without a shred of dignity. It is possible by medical standards to be healthy and free from illness or injury, even as one's variant of the apolipoprotein E gene lurks for decades in patient menace, preparing to dismantle one's brain piece by humiliating piece. The definition of health is subjective in nature: Humans can be suffering from a cold or have a minor skin abrasion yet still be in very good overall health, certainly healthier than they will be

years, months, or even weeks from now when the fatally flawed genes that have been silently plotting in their cells finally reveal themselves and begin the slow, grueling, irreversible process of erasing their mind and converting them from a functional adult into an infantilized burden on the children they no longer recognize but rely upon for the once-simple task of using the toilet.

Hearse, vehicle for transporting a coffin halfway to a funeral and then, in a panic, back to the emergency room.

Hearst, William Randolph (*b. Apr. 29, 1863 d. Aug. 14, 1951*), American newspaper magnate who was the basis for the main character in the classic 1941 film *Citizen Kane*, as well as three other less successful

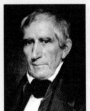

JESUS, HOW MANY HARRISONS ARE THERE?

William Henry Harrison

(*b. Feb. 9, 1773 d. Apr. 4, 1841*), ninth president of the United States, who died after delivering the longest-ever inaugural address, which lasted 30 grueling days in the midst of numerous violent rain and wind storms. Renowned for his leadership at the Battle of Tippecanoe, as well as his governorship of the Indiana Territory, Harrison touched on these and literally thousands of other topics in his epic speech, which ran 24 hours a day for a month, despite the increasing hoarseness of Harrison's voice, multiple lapses into exhaustion-induced incoherence, and constant attempts by aides to physically pull Harrison away from the podium. After delivering the final line to an amphitheater in which 227 of the original 1,250 attendees had also died, Harrison finally walked off stage, sat back down in his chair, and immediately succumbed to pneumonia-related complications.

films from 1941: *The Newspaperman Who Thought He Ruled The World!*, *Williford Randall Hertz: Duke Of The Rag Business*, and *Abbott And Costello Meet The Yellow Journalist*.

Heart Attack, sudden blockage of blood to the heart muscle caused by a spur-of-the-moment, surprise visit from one's grandchildren. Without a steady stream of oxygen-rich blood, the heart, blindsided by the shock of two squealing 6-year-olds clamoring for hugs, begins to break down and fail, often with fatal results. Though in some cases a postmortem examination can iden-

tify a hereditary condition or a lifetime of poor cardiac health as a contributing factor, the deceased's grandchildren ultimately bear responsibility for the heart attack and must carry the emotional weight for the rest of their lives.

Heaven, majestic realm in the afterlife where the righteous reside and have every wish fulfilled, be it to snort the finest cocaine imaginable, hunt down and torture angels, or force God to give them a blow job. Inhabitants of heaven spend eternity in the breathtaking paradise, experiencing such delights as pissing on clouds, hitting Saint Peter right

in the face with their dicks, and bludgeoning insufferable religious pricks with crowbars. Only those who lived good lives during their time on earth are permitted to enter the kingdom of heaven, where they are rewarded with an abundance of precious jewels, gold, cash, alcohol, cigarettes, and the right to fuck any little kids who have died.

Hell, vast, warehouse-like space bathed in an eerie fluorescent light whose seemingly endless aisles are lined with discounted consumer goods, including food, apparel, electronics, and toys. The entrance to hell is manned by an old, white-haired man or woman in a blue vest who greets visitors as they arrive and alerts them to the existence of a number of unbeatable values in the lifeless expanse before them. Hell is populated by scores of shuffling corpulent figures who, with no other retail locations left at which to shop, are condemned to pick mindlessly through row upon row of plastic kitchen containers, white cotton tube socks, cases of motor oil, and copies of *2 Fast 2 Furious* while slowly circumnavigating hell's polished tile floor. At predetermined intervals a disembodied voice announces "rollbacks," sending the denizens of hell toward one specific area of the building, at which point they are instructed to load various off-brand appliances and beauty products into a blue cart that is then wheeled outside to a sprawling paved field and unloaded into waiting vehicles. Hell was founded by Sam Walton in 1962.

Helping, pro-social behavior benefiting another individual that happens after one looks around to see if anyone else is going to help, sighs upon realizing nobody is, mutters "Jesus Christ, fine" under one's

Rutherford B. Hayes

(*b. Oct. 4, 1822 d. Jan. 17, 1893*), 19th president of the United States, best known for driving home the point that if you include even one U.S. president in a reference book, you are basically forcing yourself to include them all. Hayes oversaw the end of Reconstruction and presided over the nation's emergence into the Second Industrial Revolution, and while he is certainly not as historically important as Abraham Lincoln or Thomas Jefferson—or even James K. Polk, for that matter—an analysis of Hayes' administration nevertheless makes it very clear that, even if you start with entries on just the major presidents, the whole thing quickly becomes a slippery slope whereby you can't really leave out any of the rest of them because it would seem weird. Ultimately, the president is an important person, there have only been a few dozen of them, and if you're doing a book on important things, then you really can't in good conscience leave one out. Even if you want to. In addition to his legacy of keeping encyclopedia editors awake at night trying to figure out if they should scrap their whole approach and just go with some sort of appendix with images of all the presidents and the dates they served, Hayes believed in a meritocratic style of government and in the equal treatment of people regardless of race.

In eternal paradise, you can fuck a dog in the ass while you make God go get you an expensive imported beer.

breath, and finally helps the woman holding groceries and trying to get her baby stroller up a set of stairs.

Hemingway, Ernest *(b. July 21, 1899 d. July 2, 1961)*, American author and journalist whose economical writing style strongly influenced generations of men wishing to justify alcoholism, reckless flights of fancy, and philandering as the price a man must pay for the lifelong pursuit of truth.

Heroin, highly addictive crystalline compound and narcotic derived from morphine that should be tried at least once in a person's lifetime. Heroin, when used regularly, is associated with a strong physical dependence but is certainly worth experimenting with, even if it's only a single dose, because life is short and it's important to have as many experiences as possible. A weakened immune system and death are common among those heavily addicted to heroin, which one should ingest by snorting as opposed to injecting, since that's only for junkies and all a person needs is just the one taste to see what it feels like.

Hi, abbreviation for the proper formal greeting "Mr. Hello."

Hibernation, prolonged period of inactivity and suppressed metabolism among certain animals, such as the bear, during which one could conceivably get away with sneaking into its cave and petting it. Used to conserve energy during times of limited food supply, the hibernation state makes it theoretically possible for someone to approach a bear in its lair and pinch its nose, have a picture taken holding up its ears, smack it fairly firmly across the face, poke it with a stick, or stand on top of it flexing one's muscles like Hulk Hogan. It is also not inconceivable that one could walk up to a

A hibernating bear would neither know nor care if one pretended to shake its paw and introduce oneself.

family of other hibernating animals, such as badgers or hedgehogs, and place little straw hats on their heads that they will wake up wearing in the spring.

Hickey, blemish often found on the neck that is created when one's lover holds a vacuum hose up to one's skin.

High Heels, formal shoe with a pointed heel worn by women and men to lengthen the legs and accentuate the buttocks.

***Hindenburg* Disaster,** tragic accident in which the German passenger airship LZ 129 *Hindenburg* caught fire during its attempt to dock, tragically killing 13 of its 36 passengers in a horrible scene that will forever be—wait, only 13 of the 36 passengers on the *Hindenburg* died? That's it? One-third, total? Huh. Though the cause of the fire remains unknown, many speculate that ignition was brought on by a static spark that...okay, and only 22 of the 61 crew members died, too? It just seems that way more people died, because when people say "the *Hindenburg*" you think of this earth-shattering catastrophe, not an event where a sizable majority of people survived. Once the air-

ship ignited, the 800-foot blimp was destroyed in approximately 20 seconds, which was enough time for the captain to reach safety. Wait, the captain lived, too? You've got to be kidding. This is the most famous airship disaster in history?

Hinduism, oldest continuously practiced religion, whose tenets of karma, worship, and self-realization are so simple and unobjectionable that the only thing holding it back from becoming the world's dominant faith is the fact that you can't kill bugs, even if they're biting the shit out of you. Hinduism draws on a number of folk traditions and texts, including the Upanishads, all of which agree that in order to maintain good karma, you can't kill a bug, despite the fact that it's been literally sucking your blood all night, or been buzzing right in your goddamn ear for three fucking hours even though you were nice enough to crack the window for it to fly out. Hinduism has almost 1 billion followers, a number that would likely grow to encompass all of humanity if you could simply step on an ant without the risk of being reincarnated as an ant yourself and being casually squashed by

Heisman Trophy, nation's highest honor that can be given to a date-rapist.

HINDENBURG ➤ DISASTER
No doubt about it, this looks like an absolute calamity. But for crying out loud, even one passenger who was a vaudeville acrobat survived this thing. Seriously.

the kind of asshole you were in your previous life.

Hip-Hop, musical genre responsible for at least one completely humiliating personal moment in every American's past. Hip-hop has its origins in the street culture of 1970s inner-city New York, and has since gone on to contribute to the time 17-year-old suburban teenager Jason Nguyen bought the 1997 Ma$e album *Harlem World* and told his friends it was "dope," to Samantha Klein's horrendously garish "bling"-themed bat mitzvah, to more than 80 million awkward sing-along utterances of the word "nigga," to at least one cringe-inducing track by every rapper who has ever lived, to the time 52-year-old father Rick Tyrnauer performed an impromptu rap about corn on the cob at the dinner table to amuse his mortified children. Today, hip-hop is considered one of the preeminent cultural forms of expression around the world, and makes everyone—including hip-hop artists who have engaged without irony in embarrassing "rap wars" with their rivals—shake their head in shame and mutter under their breath, "God, why did I do that?"

Hippopotamus, blubbery herbivorous mammal weighing between 3,000 and 7,000 pounds that waddles around Africa on pudgy little stub legs, pigging out on snacks to stop its jelly belly from rumbling. The flabby butterball is a semi-aquatic chunkster that spends most of its days hiding underwater for two to three minutes so no one can see that tubby looks like a roly-poly blimp. The chubba chubba is known for its loud wheezing and aggressive behavior when the skinny animals tease it for being a big, dumpy blob.

Hiroshima, Japanese city in the Chūgoku region of western Honshu that was struck by a nuclear weapon in 1945, something that truly, actually happened in real life. The manufacturing port was annihilated by the equivalent of 13 kilotons of TNT, and not as part of some chilling, hypothetical special-effects sequence in a science-fiction movie, but as part of a very real and, in fact, intentional act of violence that disintegrated—literally *disintegrated*—80,000 people instantaneously. That's 30 percent of the population wiped out in a second. And that really happened. Hiroshima is known for its cuisine and symphony orchestra, and just to reiterate, something occurred in this world's actual history involving the equivalent of 13 kilotons of TNT. On purpose. The crippling flash burns, the cries of pain and suffering, the lethal aftereffects—all of this really happened to real people. And what's really fucked up is that the same exact thing happened again three days later.

Hiss, sound a cat makes when one is trying to jam it into a refrigerator lettuce bin so one can take a funny picture of it.

Historectomy, surgical procedure to remove all or part of the past.

History, study of the past, and how the past can affect what happens in the future, and how said future can affect how we view the past, and how the present hangs perilously between the two time frames, and how this is all a huge mess, and how there's nothing we can do about it, and how we should have never evolved beyond the state of tree-dwelling apes.

Hitler, Adolf (*b. Apr. 20, 1899 d. Apr. 30, 1945*), former dictator of Nazi Germany, regarded as the 20th century's most reviled figure, worse even than Adolf Hitler. As a deeply disturbed young man, Hitler was known for sporting a Hitler mustache, and adopted early on a militant, Hitler-like devotion to his goal of total Aryan racial purity. Hitler first joined the fledgling German

Workers' Party in 1919, and by 1933 he had seized absolute political control, which he used to rule ruthlessly over his countrymen as if

◄ *This image is not from the sickest psychopath's imagination, but from real events that actually happened in real life.*

Hitchcock, Alfred (*b. Aug. 13 1899 d. Apr. 29, 1980*), British-American filmmaker who was able to keep movie audiences in a state of paralyzed suspense as they wondered when he would suddenly waddle on-screen for his stupid little cameo.

SOMEHOW DIDN'T
KILL HIMSELF

Herbert Hoover

(*b. Aug. 10, 1874 d. Oct. 20, 1964*), 31st president of the United States, whose greatest accomplishment was somehow not committing suicide during the Great Depression. Despite the fact that his policies helped prolong that terrible period, during which the unemployment rate surpassed 25 percent, more than 5,000 banks failed, and millions of Americans were unable to afford basic needs, Hoover amazingly managed not to slit his wrists, jump out a 10-story window, or blow his brains out after seeing the country had lost another 2 million jobs. Though hundreds of thousands of homeless citizens began forming shantytowns named after him and known as "Hoovervilles"—a fact that would have made any other president hang himself in the middle of the Oval Office— Hoover not only didn't kill himself, but lived another 31 years and died of natural causes at age 90. Hoover did attempt suicide in 1957, but for reasons unrelated to the Great Depression.

he were Hitler. Over the next 12 years, Hitler transformed Germany into one of history's most oppressive totalitarian empires, on par with the Nazis. Amid the cover of World War II—a war Hitler had provoked to indulge his Hitler-sized ego—Hitler conducted a massive program to systematically murder millions of Jews, a monstrous campaign of death that could only have come from the mind of some kind of Hitler. Given Hitler's unparalleled legacy of malevolence and hate, his name is only evoked today to describe the most extreme examples of human evil, such as bosses who impose rigid deadlines on employees, people who ask others to quiet down in public places, and U.S. presidents.

HIV, if you get it in America these days, and it's not because of a blood transfusion, it's pretty much on you.

Ho Chi Minh (*b. May 19. 1890 d. Sept. 2, 1969*), North Vietnamese leader of successful wars against the United States, Japan, and France, whose efforts catapulted Vietnam into the first world, made him a deeply respected figure within his country to this very day, and even prompted UNESCO to officially recognize him in 1987 as a major contributor to the common struggle for "peace, national independence, democracy, and social progress." Thus, you gotta hand it to the man.

Hockey, hey, if you like it, great.

Holocaust, Nazi-sponsored mass murder of approximately 6 million Jews and other persecuted groups during World War II that taught the world to never, ever let a genocide get that out of hand. The unthinkable atrocity took place on such a massive scale that the international community, which had previously

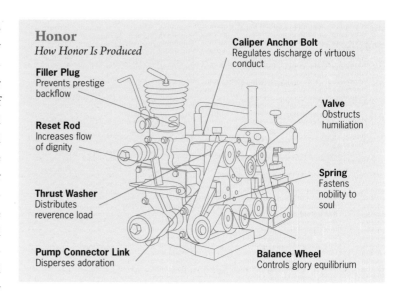

Honor
How Honor Is Produced

Caliper Anchor Bolt
Regulates discharge of virtuous conduct

Filler Plug
Prevents prestige backflow

Valve
Obstructs humiliation

Reset Rod
Increases flow of dignity

Spring
Fastens nobility to soul

Thrust Washer
Distributes reverence load

Pump Connector Link
Disperses adoration

Balance Wheel
Controls glory equilibrium

allowed ethnic cleansing campaigns to operate on the honor system, vowed to collectively intervene in future genocides that looked like they were going to get anywhere near that crazy. With this solemn responsibility in mind, the United Nations agreed on swift retribution against any country or government that went totally overboard with butchering large numbers of men, women, and children, or sought to wipe out a specific group of people in an especially egregious or unnecessary way. The international genocide guidelines have only been enforced once, in 1995, when NATO planes bombed the Serbian military, which had exterminated 200,000 Muslims—a response world leaders later admitted was hasty, since the widespread killing hadn't yet gone completely off the rails.

Holy Grail, sacred cup, considered the most holy of objects by Christians, used at the Last Supper by Jesus Christ, who was an emotional wreck at the time and was understandably nervous about his upcoming arrest, trial, and crucifixion and had far too much wine, drunkenly knocking over the divine vessel, spilling all over the Apostle

Paul's brand-new linen shroud, and bursting into tears, before locking himself in the restroom for the remainder of the evening.

Homo Sapiens, bipedal primate classified by the EPA as an invasive species. Homo sapiens, which has no predators and breeds rapidly, has been well documented as a deadly threat to native flora and fauna in habitats in which it has been introduced, and has been known to decimate an entire ecosystem within a single generation. If not contained, Homo sapiens will continue to endanger biodiversity, spread disease, and destroy thousands of acres of arable land each day. Homo sapiens is also the greatest known threat to the economy.

Homosexuality, sexual attraction between politically conservative or evangelical white males Homosexuality is characterized by

wearing navy blue or gray suits with red ties, frequent church attendance, and public denunciation of other homosexuals. Many homosexuals occupy positions of authority and can be found working as Republican school board members,

Republican activists, Christian men's group leaders, and Republican legislators. Prominent homosexuals include Roy Ashburn, former California state senator and antigay activist; Larry Craig, former U.S. senator from Idaho and antigay activist; Ted Haggard, evangelical pastor and antigay activist; and George Alan Rekers, minister and antigay activist.

Hope, universal human emotion, positive belief, or earnest desire that the Mexican restaurant on the corner will be open on New Year's Day. Hope is sometimes confused with similar concepts such as optimism, which suggests a degree of active confidence that the Mexican restaurant will be open, and false hope, a form of hope based on the fantastical wish that all restaurants, including that great Italian place, be open, even though that is never the case and one always forgets to just pick up the phone and call before trekking all the way over there like an idiot. Studies have consistently confirmed that hopefulness is an important contributor to happiness, an emotion defined as the ability to afford to have takeout every night of the week if one wants to.

Horsey Sauce, tart, beluga-and-caviar-infused horseradish paste that is one of the five master sauces in haute cuisine. First formalized by French culinary writer Auguste Escoffier and later perfected by renowned chef Henri-François Arby, horsey sauce (*jus de cheval*) is made by blending a puree of horseradish

and mayonnaise with saffron, sturgeon roe, and truffles. Today, the delicate, extremely complex sauce is typically served with six jalapeño sidekickers and a jamocha shake.

House American Activities Committee, investigative committee of the U.S. House of Representatives convened in 1955 to root out and publicly congratulate patriotic citizens suspected of enjoying the fruits of American capitalism. The committee was led by Rep. Hamilton Fish III, a staunch, unbending patriot who ruthlessly demanded to know if defendants had ever engaged in a backyard barbecue where a football was tossed around, and if so, whether they drank a few beers and had a good time with family and friends. Those who nervously testified came from all walks of life; shop owners, stock brokers, ad salesmen, and factory managers alike were coerced into naming other flag-flying Americans so that they too could be called before the committee, summarily praised, and then placed on a preferential list of people to be considered for future employment. The good-Americans witch hunt was conducted over six months and weeded out millions of citizens, all of whom were made to proudly sign documents attesting to the fact that America was the greatest country on earth, and were dismissed with invitations to come back and attend that year's Fourth of July celebration in Washington.

House Of Representatives, 435-member representative body of the U.S. Congress to which each electoral district sends its loudest, least scrupulous, most self-involved person to get stuff for them. Representatives vote on legislation they deem beneficial to their communities, which—while realizing there is

always a risk the ignorant, solipsistic weasels will only get stuff for themselves—also understand that these pushy nuisances who never shut up for even a second will go shout their heads off on their district's behalf and that others will be forced to listen. The absolute worst, bottom-of-the-barrel egomaniacal sociopaths bully their way onto House subcommittees, where, among smaller, even pettier groups, they are given significantly more power to draw attention to themselves and, thereby, their home districts. Because there are no set term limits for representatives, it is common for constituents to continue voting the most aggressively sacrosanct, small-minded congresspeople back into office time and time again so that the intolerable loudmouths are away from their districts as much as possible.

Hubble, Edwin (*b. Nov. 20, 1889 d. Sept. 28, 1953*), American astronomer who was killed when he fell from a 220-mile-high scaffolding while attempting to construct a telescope in the Earth's orbit. Standing atop the precarious temporary structure, which extended from his lab in San Marino, California, to the planet's ionosphere, Hubble slipped on a wooden plank and fell 1,161,000 feet back to the Earth's surface. Though most of his body burned up upon reentry into the atmosphere and scattered across the Pacific Ocean, remnants of Hubble's charred left forearm were recovered and are currently on display in the National Air and Space Museum in Washington.

Hurricane, violent weather event also known as a typhoon, wind pie, or cyclone that is characterized by a low-pressure center surrounded by powerful thunderstorms.

◄ **HOUSE AMERICAN ACTIVITIES COMMITTEE**
The HAAC cross-examination of a Missouri grandmother suspected of baking mouthwatering apple pies.

Horn, stupid hat that goats actually think looks good.

Hurricane Katrina, if it had happened in the Philippines or Papua New Guinea it wouldn't even be in this book.

CITIES OF THE WORLD
Houston

Largest city in Texas and worst city on the planet, with the possible exception of Dallas, the third-largest city in Texas. Houston has a population of 2.3 million and is an oppressive mass of uninspired office buildings and urban sprawl rivaled in atrociousness only by the endless traffic jams of Dallas. Houston is further made unlivable by its extreme heat and disgusting humidity (**See** DALLAS) and by a featureless downtown that is completely abandoned by 6:30 p.m. except for the depressing, low-class strip clubs that are strikingly

The heartlessness of Houston's skyline makes one feel about as empty and sad as one feels when looking at Dallas'.

similar to those found in downtown Dallas. Though many believe Dallas is worse because of the presence of the Dallas Cowboys, both cities constantly reek of petroleum fumes, and Houston's utter lack of culture makes it a terrible place in which no one would intentionally choose to live. Much like Dallas. San Antonio is also a shithole.

Hussein, Saddam (*b. Apr. 28, 1937 d. Dec. 30, 2006*), former Iraqi president who carried out a devastating attack on the American economy by forcing the United States to spend billions and billions of dollars on a military effort to invade his country and depose his dictatorship. A brutal autocrat with a maniacal anti-American agenda, Hussein was directly responsible for the deadly strike on the U.S. financial system between 2003 and 2011, when the nation's surplus dramatically turned to ashes as Hussein made the United States stage a costly, protracted occupation of his country. Fortunately, Hussein was held responsible for his unprovoked attack on the U.S. federal budget when a significant portion of the federal budget was spent finding him and bringing him to justice.

Hydrogen, most abundant chemical element in the universe thanks to a fuckup on the order form by God, who was overwhelmed while creating everything in existence and hastily filled out the damn invoice sheet without really looking at it. God, who made countless attempts over the eons to unload the colorless, odorless, flammable gas, has since been forced to stick a bunch of the hydrogen into stars and planets, as well as to create a shit-ton of the popular beverage water by combining the gas with oxygen. Although much of the surplus hydrogen remains untouched, God occasionally uses the excess combustible element to entertain Himself by making inhabitable planets randomly explode.

Hygiene, process of routinely cleaning off the 4-inch-thick layer of dirt, feces, semen, and vomit that accumulates on the surface of the human body within minutes of waking each morning. Good hygienic practice, which must be performed eight to 12 times daily in order to facilitate movement of the limbs, involves first scrubbing the entire body vigorously with soap, water, and turpentine, and then using a metal chipping tool or chisel to scrape away the dried blood, excrement, scum, mucus, urine, saliva, vaginal secretions, bile, and other buildup that naturally accumulates on human beings over the course of a day. It is also necessary to utilize a coarse brushing tool coated in commercial-grade antibacterial gel to dislodge calcified stool and ejaculate from one's nose and mouth. Other procedures, such as showering in bleach and thoroughly sandpapering one's genitals, are also necessary to maintain health and eliminate the bacteria-laden waste matter, used bandages, and fecal spray that permeates every public place.

Hypochondria, condition in which one believes physical symptoms are the signs of a serious illness when, in fact, they are usually just caused by the natural processes of a slowly, almost imperceptibly decomposing body.

Ibex, wild goat known for getting out of control at parties by climbing on furniture, ramming into walls, fighting with other guests, and urinating in the punch bowl.

Idea, thought or concept obtained from a movie, TV show, or book that already exists. By taking ideas that were created by someone else many generations before, so-called creators may produce what they refer to as "original" works of art or entertainment, despite the fact that no such new things have been produced in years, nor will ever be produced again. In all of human history, only three original ideas have ever been created, all of which have been stolen, repurposed, and made exponentially worse in every subsequent iteration.

Identity, wholly external set of qualities assigned to a person by friends, coworkers, parents, romantic partners, and total strangers that, without the individual's input or assent, provide the absolute and final pic-ture of who that person is. By its very nature, identity in no way reflects what one believes to be true about oneself, and is instead formed through outside judgments by others based on cursory assessments of one's physical appearance. After others establish one's identity immediately upon sight, it remains the same until death, rarely if ever changing in any meaningful way regardless of any personal improvements that individual may make, or positive actions he or she might later engage in.

Ignition, cool thing to say when starting one's car, even if there's nobody around to hear it.

Iguana, herbivorous reptile that's been in the "liz biz" for a while and ain't taking no shit from some big-mouth frog.

Ikea, world's largest manufacturer of random pieces of pressboard, which are packaged together and then sold in the company's retail outlets. Founded in Sweden in 1943, Ikea has become the No. 1 destination for customers seeking chunks of particle board of varying sizes, shapes, and thicknesses that are haphazardly gathered up and stuffed in a box, occasionally with a handful of screws or nails thrown in. Ikea products are known for their distinctive look, and it is not uncommon to enter a home, notice a television mounted upon a jagged 4-foot-tall stack of pressboard, and instantly recognize the store where it was purchased.

"Imagine," John Lennon's 1971 lyrical depiction of a utopian existence without possessions, needs, or an afterlife, a dream the former Beatle would have to wait nine years to see realized.

Imp, small creature from German mythology that seeks human attention through trickery and pranks and IS THE BEST CERATURE IN THE WHOLE WORLD AND YOU SHOULD)OPEN YOUR DOOR TO IMPS IF YOU SEE

I

Ii·İ·и

Ninth letter of the modern English alphabet and the fifth most common letter in the English language. A vowel with both a long sound, as in "bite," and a short sound, as in "kid," the letter *I* is one…are you happy? Simple question: Are you happy? And not just the absence of misery, either, but true happiness, you know? Like, you see happy people and you tell yourself they're miserable underneath. And, yeah, some of them are. But some of them aren't, and you resent them but you're also so, so glad they're out there, right? Anyway, just thinking about stuff.

IMAGINATION, trait assessed and measured by the Ohio School Standardized Imagination Test, administered to all American public school children at the end of their fifth-grade year. The test is scored on a rigid 1,200-point scale, and is made up of 515 multiple choice and true-false questions that precisely quantify a student's sense of wonder. Taken over the course of five hours, the exam largely determines how well a student will be able to imagine productively during college and, later, in a professional setting.

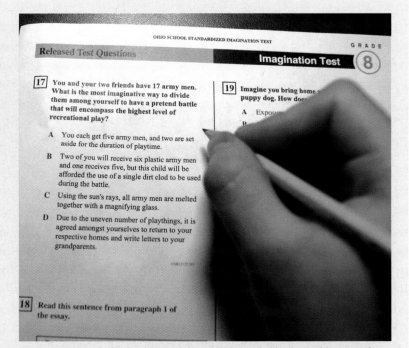

Every American student's inherent ability to be fascinated by the world is precisely measured and compared to that of their peers with this standardized test.

Ice Skating, one of the many millions of things the vast majority of people choose not to do every day.

IMAX, type of widescreen cinematography that makes some nothing suburb feel like it's getting somewhere.

INDUSTRIAL REVOLUTION, process of modernization and automation beginning in the late 18th century through which mankind finally found true and lasting happiness. By developing a mechanized society that promoted rapid growth and placed an emphasis on material goods, people were at last able to conquer all the various psychological and spiritual maladies and feelings of existential despair that characterize the human condition, emerging as they are now today: whole, satisfied, and well-adjusted creatures at one with both the natural world and their fellow man. The myriad technological innovations developed in the early 20th century by Henry Ford and Thomas Edison, among others, not only made life infinitely less frantic and more enriching, but ushered in a new, simpler epoch that makes people look back on the preindustrial days and feel glad they never had to live in such alienating chaos. Today, all human beings thank the inventors of the endlessly churning assembly line, the idly buzzing fluorescent light, the crowded mass transit vehicle, and the glowing, cacophonous television screen for making

Two workers from the first generation of truly happy and fulfilled human beings.

the world a warmer, kinder, happier, and more human place to live.

ALTERNATIVE ➤ METHODS OF IN VITRO FERTILIZATION

1. Smear egg residue lengthwise along the inside of an ATM card reader. Cover magnetic strip of an ATM card with semen. Swipe.

2. Cover iPad with egg. Dip fingers in sperm. Use iPad as usual.

3. Place sperm on each individual blade of a ceiling fan. Turn ceiling fan on to highest setting. Throw a bunch of eggs into the air in hopes of a connection.

THEM AND GIVE THEM HONNY.

Imperialism, term used to describe the extension of a country's power through complete military and economic domination, which generally takes the subjugated peoples a few days to get used to.

Impotence, condition a male can experience while also having a raging erection. Though a man may have a fully erect penis while powerlessly watching on as his only son is swept away in a flash flood, he is still considered at that moment to be completely impotent. Additionally, a man can have a massive erection while he is needlessly berated in front of his coworkers by a superior, and this man, despite having a throbbing, tumescent phallus, is still experiencing impotence. There are several medications that can be prescribed for impotence, none of which are effective at treating the condition of having a protuberant,

blood-engorged penis while building model trains in one's basement late at night and waiting for one's wife to return home from another of her numerous brazen sexual affairs.

Impulse, desire to look up from one's laptop, slowly close it, stand up, walk out the door, get a ticket to as far away a place as one can, and start all over again.

In The Hall Of The Mountain King, famous piece of orchestral music composed by Edvard Grieg for the sixth scene of Act II in Henrik Ibsen's play *Peer Gynt*, in which Peer's mother-in-law is walking toward the house and he has to rush around and make it look as if he wasn't just masturbating.

In Vitro Fertilization, fertility treatment in which an egg is joined with a sperm outside of a woman's body through one of several methods, including pasting an egg on a wall and throwing a bunch of sperm at it,

smooshing sperm and egg residue together in one's hands, or putting the egg in a clay-pigeon machine and shooting it down with a sperm-loaded gun.

Inca, South American civilization, some of whose members must have fought off a few of Pizarro's men, stolen their guns, realized the immense power they now wielded, and handily picked off several dozen desperately retreating conquistadors, at least once.

Incubator, device used to keep newborn infants warm until consumption.

Individual, type of person that constitutes more than 30 percent of the human population worldwide.

Inertia, property of matter by which it will remain at rest in the terrible job it's ridiculously overqualified for or continue moving in a straight line toward having kids it doesn't want until acted on by an outside force.

Infant Mortality, rate of deaths occurring in the first year of life, measured in deaths per 1,000 births. The United States has one of the lowest infant mortality rates in the world, only trailing behind Iceland, Singapore, Japan, Sweden, Norway, Hong Kong, Finland, the Czech Republic, Switzerland, South Korea, Belgium, France, Spain, Germany, Denmark, Austria, Australia, Luxembourg, the Netherlands, Israel, Slovenia, the United Kingdom, Canada, Ireland, Italy, Portugal, New Zealand, Cuba, the Channel Islands, Brunei, Cyprus, and New Caledonia.

Infinity, (*See* INFINITY)

Ingenue, title given to a young actress that all but guarantees something horrible will happen to her very soon.

Ingrown Hair, medical condition in which hair grows backward into the skin, extending deep into the muscle fiber and bone. The hair painfully severs the nerves, restricts blood flow, and becomes entangled in arteries, veins, the spinal column, ligaments, tendons, internal organs, and glands until all of the body's systems cease to function. A similar debilitating syndrome, known as ingrown beard, involves facial follicles growing through the cheeks, coiling around the teeth, tongue,

INSECT, small arthropod animal to whom, in the grand scheme of geological time, humans are but puny insects.

Abdomen
Part of insect even fellow insects find disgusting

Brain
Main source of fucked-up bug thoughts

Parachute
Precautionary measure in the event of a wing malfunction

Mandible
Responsible for repeatedly saying "buzz buzz buzz" when flying

Blue Guts

Stinger
Appendage required for an insect to even consider being taken seriously

Yellow Guts

Leg
Covered in preapical bristles that are used for gently caressing a sleeping person's cheeks, lips, and uvula

and lower jaw, and eventually snaking up through the skull and into the brain.

Inkling, infant hunch that, if fed a steady diet of paranoia, rapidly becomes a full-grown suspicion.

Innocence, naïveté enzyme secreted by the pancreas during childhood that is completely depleted upon walking in on one's father weeping alone in a room, seeing a pet get hit by a car, or staying up past 11 p.m. to watch Showtime.

Innocent, correct term to describe someone who had no idea she was 16, and is shocked to hear her being described as the innocent one, con-

sidering the stuff she was into. (*See* STATUTORY RAPE)

Insomnia, strange, inexplicable inability to sleep experienced by people who drink six cups of coffee daily, have a terrible diet, and go off their antidepressants totally cold turkey.

Insurance, regular fee paid to a company to ensure that, in the event of damage, illness, loss, or death, the company will withhold payment.

Internet, worldwide electronic network populated by web skaters, e-hustlers, modem punks, cyber chatters, code warriors, holochumps, techno bums, and digijackers, all scaling the super-data techno grid in search of virtuoentertainment, iFortunes, and trouble. Online trekkers enter the Internet by hiring an info-navigator, or "chip jockey," to jack them into the cyberzone by plugging directly into the etherstream interface to transfer thoughts, memories, and personalities to a binary web sojourner. For these Nexxus-monkeys, the digital domain is a pixelated playground of

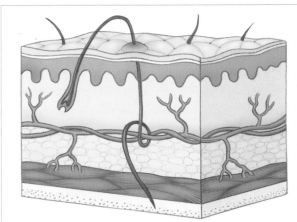

A Stage 3 ingrown hair, which will usually cause severe nerve damage and require surgery.

Inverness, 19th-century sleeveless cloak with a removable cape that looks really cool, but don't even bother. The inverness generally comes in two styles: one more formal, and the one Sherlock Holmes wears, which looks like maybe it would be pretty badass, but no—it will definitely make you look and feel like a tool immediately after you leave the house wearing it.

INTERNAL COMBUSTION ENGINE, machine in which a fuel such as gasoline is burned with air to generate power. Let's poke around in here and see what's going on. Hold this light, would ya?

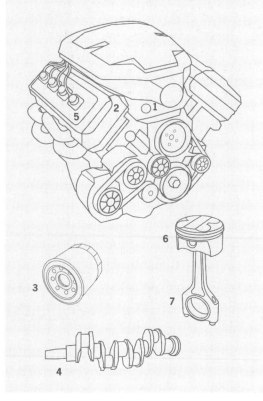

1 **Intake Valve:** Allows the mixture of fuel and air into the cylinders for compression, and yours is looking pretty gunked up. No wonder you're not getting any juice.

2 **Cylinder Head:** Cap against which the fuel/air mixture is compressed. Yup, you got a crack in it all right. Just a hairline, but that damn thing is gonna cause a big headache later.

3 **Oil Filter:** Whoa, when's the last time you changed the oil on this thing? We'll just do it for you real quick if you want, which you should.

4 **Camshaft:** Rotating cams regulate the injection of fuel into the engine. Hmm…you don't see this every day. Your camshaft is bent. How the heck did you manage that?

5 **Spark Plug:** Device that ignites the air/fuel mixture, see here's your problem, these plugs are junk. All that crud on there is why she's misfiring. You really need regular tune-ups on a vehicle like this or you're gonna drive it right into the ground. Real shame.

6 **Piston:** Moves up and down to let air and fuel enter from the intake valve and compress the mixture. Your piston rings are all shot to hell. Totally blown out. That ain't gonna be cheap.

7 **Crankshaft:** With the help of a connector rod, converts a piston's vertical motion to rotational motion, and these bearings are worn to the nub. Sweet mercy, how long have you been driving around like this?

iPod, portable electronic device that completely revolutionized the experience of listening to Elton John's "Daniel" while walking through the cereal aisle of Safeway.

multi-dimensional locales and wild e-saloons, where they can upload intoxicating WhiskeyFiles and hire synthetic concubines to experience a simulated fornication program. Although thousands of net-settlers scroll across the binary realms, hoping to strike it rich on a data mine claim, the Virtual Plane is a lawless digital frontier overrun with compucriminals and ruled by the brutal neuro-mob, which has no respect for artificial life if it stands in the way of making a quick credit. Plagued by illegal kilobyte trafficking and e-mercenaries staging brazen giga-heists, the Internet's circuit rails are no longer safe for casual online explorers—known derisively as couch-pluggers—who come into contact with unscrupulous cyberdwellers and get permanently booted offline.

Introspection, contemplative examination of one's thoughts and feelings that must be avoided at all costs and by any means necessary. Introspection ranges from simple mindfulness of one's emotional states to intensive meditation practices, all of which are to be resisted in order to prevent dangerous insights into one's self from arising. Unless precautions are taken, introspection may result in a disquieting awareness of one's particular flaws and failures, as well as recognition of the true nature of reality and its impermanence, decay, and death. Fortunately, the self-knowledge generated by introspection may be prevented with the help of technological diversions including television, smartphones, and movies streamed over the Internet, in addition to products such as alcohol, pornography, and religion.

Inuit, indigenous people of northern Canada, Greenland, and Alaska. At the age of 17, the males of Inuit tribes must undergo a rite of passage and prove themselves to their people by putting lipstick and a pair of fake foam-rubber breasts on a sleeping walrus.

IQ (Intelligence Quotient), number said to measure an individual's intelligence that many experts who clearly didn't crack 125 say overlooks important attributes such as creativity and social skills.

Iraq War, American-led invasion and subsequent occupation of Iraq that succeeded in building a deeply flawed but functional sovereign state from what was once a deeply flawed but functional sovereign state. With a mandate to locate and destroy hidden weapons of mass destruction, a multinational coalition entered Iraq on March 20, 2003, toppling the autocratic, corrupt, but operational regime of Saddam Hussein and replacing it with the autocratic, corrupt, but op-

CITIES OF THE WORLD
Istanbul

Cultural capital of Turkey, the third-largest metropolitan area in Europe, and a popular vacation destination for people psychologically together enough to do that sort of thing. Home to more than 13 million people, 21st-century Istanbul has seen tourism explode among those who can just get out there and live their lives and not obsess over hotels and currency exchange and passports and every tiny thing that could possibly go wrong, or over whether they should get vaccinated and for what when traveling to that part of the world. Istanbul is renowned for its ideal climate, lovely outdoor cafés, rich historical and cultural heritage, Ottoman architecture, hip dance clubs, unique Middle Eastern cuisine, and the stuff of countless other irreplaceable experiences that will be cherished forever by people who don't stare for hours at Expedia.com with the cursor hovering over the "purchase" button, only to panic, decide

Istanbul attracts thousands of tourists a year who have the first damn clue about visas and time zones and what not.

once again to spend their vacations visiting their parents, and ultimately feel an ineffable self-loathing for continuing to waste what precious little life they've been granted.

---

erational regime of the interim Iraqi Governing Council. Block by block, coalition soldiers purged Iraqi cities of the remnants of Hussein's security forces, which had violently repressed the populace and instilled a culture of fear; this allowed armed insurgency groups to rise up, violently repress the populace, and instill a culture of fear. American forces then entered the second phase of the war, turning the nation's poorly maintained network of

roads, schools, hospitals, and communications infrastructure into a hastily repaired, underfunded network of roads, schools, hospitals, and communications infrastructure. Critics of the war maintain Iraq is in the same place now as it was before the invasion, a claim that fails to take into account the massive increase in civilian deaths since Saddam Hussein was overthrown.

Irish, horrible, drunken, violent, unwashed race of so-called "people"

who only warrant an entry in this reference precisely because of how singularly vile they are. Throughout the 18th and 19th centuries, millions of these disgusting reprobates emigrated across the globe, escaping their feculent little island due in large part to the famine and political instability caused by their own barbaric, animalistic tendencies. Not surprisingly, they brought rampant venereal disease, sloth, and criminality to nearly every continent on the planet. Their churlish attitude, perpetual inebriation, and exceedingly low intelligence makes them all but unemployable, and they greatly deplete the resources of any civilized industrial society they come into contact with.

Iron, device a small minority of people know how to use to get wrinkles out of shirts. Since its invention in the 1st century BC, the number of people who know how to properly manipulate the enigmatic appliance to remove wrinkles from dress shirts without burning the clothes

◄ IRISH
An Irishman behaving in the boorish, slovenly manner his people have come to be known for.

The Iraq War showed that the U.S. military could use its might to turn an unstable society living in constant fear into an unstable society living in constant fear.

Ivory, hard, creamy-white substance composing the tusks of elephants, walruses, narwhals, and one species of duck.

Ixia, plant of the iris family native to South Africa that is frequently kidnapped and raped at gunpoint due to its beautiful petals.

or accidentally soaking them with water has steadily declined to just a few thousand worldwide. Ethnographers predict that by the year 2043, all knowledge of how to correctly use an iron will be lost forever, and crisp, smoothly-pressed button-down shirts will never again be seen.

Irp, Wyatt (*b. Mar. 19, 1848 d. Jan. 13, 1929*), misspelling of famed 19th-century lawman Wyatt Earp's name that never happens.

Islam, monotheistic religion that is the second largest and fastest growing in the world, so, basically, yeah, we really need to come to terms with this thing. One of the three major Abrahamic religions along with Judaism and Christianity, Islam has approximately 1.6 billion adherents globally and 2.5 million in the United States alone, numbers that suggest it's about time the rest of the world get its act together and familiarize itself somewhat with a couple of the faith's basic tenets and maybe even a holiday or two besides Ramadan—which we don't really know anything about anyway—because whatever the West may think about Islam, the religion is not going anywhere anytime soon. Islam is based on the teachings of the Prophet Muhammad as revealed in its holy book, the Quran, a text it might be helpful to peruse from time to time since it is taken very, very seriously by a quarter of the people on the planet Earth, many of whom live in places of vital geopolitical importance such as Iraq, Iran, Afghanistan, Egypt, Saudi Arabia, Palestine, Somalia, Turkey, and Pakistan—which, by the way, has nuclear weapons. Practitioners of Islam are known as Muslims and

IWO JIMA, island site of a major World War II battle that produced the iconic image of troops raising the American flag, though it needed to be retaken more than 20 times because the soldiers kept cracking up and had to start over.

belong either to the Sunni or Shia branch of the faith, terms we'd better get real intimate with real quick because the distinction is often a matter of life or death to Muslims, who, incidentally, will almost certainly overtake Christians as the largest religious community in the world within a few decades.

Italian Flag, coded message hung outside certain buildings to indicate that spaghetti and meatballs may be obtained therein.

Itch, irritating sensation of the skin caused by an allergic reaction to fingernails.

It's A Wonderful Life, 1946 film starring Jimmy Stewart that is traditionally watched at Christmastime as a reminder to the hordes of suicidal viewers that you shouldn't kill yourself if a supernatural angel tries to stop you.

Ivy League, group of elite universities located in the northeast that you definitely could have gotten into had you applied, but decided not to because you don't need a big fancy expensive school. The Ivy League is made up of eight colleges that wouldn't have been worth all the application fees anyway, not to mention the fact that by almost every comparison, SUNY Purchase is just as good—if not better for the thing you wanted to study—and by going there you didn't have to spend four years waiting tables to help pay off your student loans. Often ranked among the best universities in the world, Ivy League schools are places you could always still attend if you decided to get your master's, which you certainly haven't ruled out.

Izzy's Hop Stop, short-lived American drive-in restaurant chain that featured skimpily dressed waitresses delivering more than 90 different types of steaming-hot soups, stews, and chowders while bouncing across the parking lot on pogo sticks.

Jack The Ripper, 19th-century serial killer who went a little too far with his prostitute-mutilating and ruined it for everybody else. While the disfigurement and murder of sex workers had long been a favorite

pastime in Victorian-era London, with citizens often gleefully slashing prostitutes to death whenever the mood struck them, the public felt that Jack the Ripper went somewhat overboard by systematically disemboweling his victims, draping their internal organs over their bodies, and carving apart their abdomens, genitals, and faces to the point where they were no longer recognizable. In the wake of the

tasteless, over-the-top slayings, the public soured on prostitute-killing altogether, as Londoners found it impossible even to stab a streetwalker in the neck without being associated with Jack the Ripper, a detestable comparison that removed all enjoyment from slaughtering wayward women and lacerating their still-warm corpses. Jack the Ripper abruptly ceased his killing spree just months after it began and never revealed his identity, a fact scholars attribute to the overwhelming sense of embarrassment and shame he likely felt upon realizing he had single-handedly ruined one of the simple pleasures of Victorian life.

Jackson, Michael (*b. Aug. 29, 1958 d. June 25, 2009*), international

megastar and beloved pop musician who would have been so much better off had he remained a desperately poor black male in inner-city Gary, Indiana. Jackson

was among the bestselling recording artists in history, and if he had simply stayed a struggling minority in an impoverished American city, he would have lived in peaceful obscurity, become alienated from his abusive father, and almost certainly still be alive today. While Jackson was perhaps the definitive performer of his era, had he simply stayed put and eked through life as a black man with limited means, it would have been challenging, of course, but at least he wouldn't have had to undergo two very public child molestation charges, constant media scrutiny, and the full, punishing weight of American cultural history. Not to mention the fact he would have kept his own nose.

Jacob's Stepladder, ladder to heaven for older people who need a little more stability while ascending to the afterlife.

Jade, ornamental stone that hopefully can be exchanged for something else.

James, Jesse (*b. Sept. 5, 1847 d. Apr. 3, 1882*), American outlaw

KILLED THOUSANDS OF AMERICANS
AND GOT REELECTED

Andrew Jackson

(*b. Mar. 15 1767 d. June 8 1845*), seventh president of the United States, responsible for the deaths of thousands of Native Americans, who was in 1831 convicted of genocide by an interplanetary tribunal and sentenced to death by Glizoxx. Called before the Supreme Judiciary Council of 15 representatives from the Intergalactic Alliance of Planets, Jackson appeared cold and remorseless when presented with evidence he had engaged in ethnic cleansing by authorizing the Indian Removal Act, legislation that forced 45,000 American Indians from their tribal lands. Jackson remained unapologetic throughout the high-profile trial, even as the tribunal deemed the deaths of some 4,000 displaced Cherokees who succumbed to cold, hunger, and disease on the Trail

of Tears to be crimes against humanity—and acts punishable by thrashing from the Glizoxx's spiked tentacles until the condemned's body is finely shredded into a pile of bloody meat. The enlightened beings of the tribunal were so disgusted by Jackson's callous attitude toward having seized 100 million acres of land sacred to Native Americans and given it to white slave owners that they denied him any possibility of leniency or parole. However, Jackson escaped his prison cell by exploiting his captors' compassion and murdering three alien guards. He then seized a starfighter and used its weapons systems to destroy the Intergalactic Alliance of Planets headquarters, killing delegates from more than 1,000 different galaxies. After delivering a devastating blow that crippled the highly evolved peacekeeping organization for decades, Jackson returned to Earth, resumed his role as U.S. president, and used the futuristic technology stolen from the craft to disintegrate millions of Native Americans.

Jackson, Jesse (*b. Oct. 8, 1941*), American civil rights activist, politician, and clergyman whose failed 1984 and 1988 presidential campaigns proved the nation was not yet ready to elect a Jesse Jackson president.

JAGUAR, large New World cat native to the tropical planters found inside shopping malls. Jaguars inhabit the decorative flora of retail centers throughout the Americas, with a range extending as far north as the potted foliage displays of Minnesota's Mall of America and as far south as the Festival Bay Mall in Orlando. As the apex predators of the mall environment, jaguars lie in wait in the thick vegetation next to fountains to pounce on and kill small children throwing coins into the water. The cats then drag the slain toddlers back into the planters, and will either consume their prey immediately or stuff the bloodied, lifeless carcasses in a mall garbage bin for later consumption. The largest population of jaguars is found in the massive Scottsdale Fashion Square Mall in Arizona, where the cats fill a valuable ecological role by keeping down the number of Lids customers.

A jaguar will often prey on the weak or elderly members of a herd of mall walkers.

JAPANESE-AMERICAN ➤ INTERNMENT CAMP
Looks fairly horrible, but none of these forcibly interned Japanese-Americans appears to be attacking the United States.

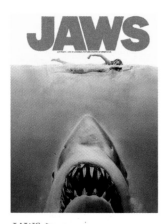

JAWS ➤
Despite the movie's violent depiction of the great white shark, many *Jaws* viewers still wanted to splash around in the Atlantic Ocean with chum so they could get their arms bitten off.

who, after retiring from banditry, started Jesse James and Brothers LLP, a very successful bandit consulting firm.

Jansky, Andy (*b. Feb. 14, 1964*), a man.

Japanese-American Internment, forced relocation and internment of 110,000 Japanese Americans during World War II and a preventive measure against domestic terrorism that, although a gross violation of citizens' basic human rights, did sort of work, in that there wasn't any domestic terrorism over that period. Intended to thwart any potential incidents on the level of Pearl Harbor, Japanese-American internment has been rightly denounced as a sickening example of state-mandated racial prejudice, and, although this is true, it should also be noted that there was never one single Japanese attack on U.S. soil after the internment camps were started, which technically means that it pretty much accomplished what it set out to do. In 1988, President Reagan signed legislation officially apologizing for

the internment, a long-overdue display of contrition that hopefully healed old wounds, even though, in a way, Japanese-American internment was actually a wildly successful program in terms of its primary goal, which—not to belabor the point—was to ensure another Japanese attack on American soil did not occur. And no attack occurred. Some of those imprisoned died, and it was a gross violation of civil liberties that should never be repeated, but, on the other hand, it was kind of great that there were no more attacks. So, you know... it basically worked. Japanese-American internment worked.

Jaws, 1975 horror film directed by Steven Spielberg that terrified American audiences and made millions think twice about their desire to be torn apart and eaten by a great white shark. Grossing more than $470 million, the international blockbuster had moviegoers from coast to coast screaming in the aisles and reconsidering their previous wish to have a great white bite off a limb, or sever their body in half

with razor-sharp teeth. *Jaws* was so successful in using suspenseful cinematic techniques to portray sharks as savage, merciless hunters that many quickly canceled their summer plans of being ruthlessly killed while skinny-dipping and having their mutilated remains discovered by tourists walking along the beach the next day.

Jay, John (*b. Dec. 12, 1745 d. May 17, 1829*), American statesman, Founding Father, and first chief justice of the Supreme Court, none of which mattered to his mother, who just wanted him home and safe.

Jazz, ...did you hear that? Listen again. Hear it? C'mon, now, you've got to really listen...there—there it is. That right there, my friends, was a beautiful quarter-note rest. Music to my ears. Now, you're probably saying to yourself, "Man, I didn't hear anything. What's that got to do with jazz? Turn up the volume, for Pete's sake!" Well, believe it or not, that's exactly the point—and volume ain't got nothin' to do with it! You see, just as important to jazz as the notes we hear—the audible me-

WASTED A PRETTY AMAZING HISTORICAL DOCUMENT ON AMERICANS
Thomas Jefferson

(b. Apr. 13, 1743 d. July 4, 1826), third president of the United States and principal author of the Declaration of Independence, a document Jefferson wouldn't have worked so tirelessly on had he known how terrible America and its citizens would turn out. Jefferson spent 17 days writing and rewriting the historic treatise, carefully crafting every word in what was ultimately a colossal waste of time based on how apathetic, uncaring, and generally godawful everyone ended up being. Had Jefferson somehow been able to divine that future Americans would take his crowning achievement for granted, or been made aware of things like Carnival Cruise Lines, the Dallas Cowboys, former senator Jesse Helms, or the vocal quartet the Manhattan Transfer, he more than likely would have just farted out the Declaration of Independence in 10 minutes and called it a day. Or, perhaps he would have given up on writing historically significant documents altogether and focused on one of his 14,000 other talents and interests. But Jefferson, who clearly had a naïve vision of the future in which people had the decency to clean their own dog's shit off the sidewalk, spent countless late nights writing by candlelight to compose an unassailable argument as to why the colonists deserved to be free. The Founding Father said he wanted the Declaration to be "an expression of the American mind," oblivious to how puerile and diluted the American mind would become, and ignorant of the fact that future citizens deserved nothing more than a piece of parchment scrawled out in 45 seconds that read: "Hey, King George, you fat sack of crap, you're not gonna rule us anymore. We're gonna be doing that now. So, yeah, we're independent now."

Thomas Jefferson And Slavery

Jefferson was well known both for his deeply held belief that human slavery was wrong, and his profound regret that he never held a political position with enough authority to do anything about it. As head of the executive branch, commander in chief of the U.S. military, and leader of the free world, Jefferson often lamented that he was powerless to emancipate the slaves and cursed the fact that he simply didn't hold an office with enough influence to in any way ban or outlaw the morally reprehensible institution. Even on his deathbed, President Jefferson was rueful that he had not achieved the executive rank of President George Washington, who was at least able to free his own slaves when he died.

---

lodic, harmonic, and percussive elements that really make it swing—are the spaces between the notes, the notes we don't hear, if you will. Without these silences, jazz would lack definition, texture, mood; in a way, jazz would be *robbed of its very essence*! Completely blows your mind when you stop to think about it, right? It's a total yin-and-yang thing, like what negative space is to art, but in this case the canvas is silence and notes are the paint. Nothing is actually everything, and vice versa. Get it? And if you want to break it down further and get really philosophical, a genius improviser like, say, Clifford Brown was actually consciously thinking about what he wasn't playing just as much as he thought about what he was

playing. It's wild, man. Just totally wild. You know, John Coltrane is actually the perfect example of how crucial silence is to jazz music, and before you say, "Oh, brother, not that Coltrane guy again!" just hold on a second, and this will all make sense. Now, we're all familiar with Coltrane's virtuosity and the sheer cascades of notes he would produce early on in his career, the whole "sheets of sound" incarnation that we've already discussed at length. But it wasn't until he became more influenced by modal music and, consequently, the immense value of space and silence, that he really reached his full potential and began composing these incredibly affecting jazz soundscapes, arguably some of the best music of his tragi-

cally too-short life (heroin is no walk in the park, folks, take it from someone who knows), and yes, I'm aware that 'Trane died of cancer, but the point still stands, okay? Anyway, with that in mind, let's be quiet and listen again…and don't be embarrassed to close your eyes, like I'm doing…now, let that sink in for a minute…pretty cool, huh?

Jennifer, perfectly nice girl with a lot going for her, but at the end of the day she's just no Caroline, is she?

Jesus Of Nazareth, son of God who repeatedly disappointed his father, because the Heavenly Lord and Creator of All Things felt His mortal offspring's teachings of peace, love, and forgiveness were naïve and idealistic and failed to

Jerk, prick's apprentice who is learning the ropes about being an irritating pissant.

Johannesburg, capital city of South Africa for those who don't know that South Africa's capital is Pretoria.

Johns, Jasper (*b. May 15, 1930*), American artist who's probably working on something that shows the struggle between the patriotic image America desperately wants to convey and the darkness of its true nature. Hey, Jasper, we get it, buddy. Let's try something else.

take into account how the world actually works. While traveling in Judea and Galilee, Jesus sought to bring out the good in people by healing the sick and preaching unity, an impractical pursuit God insisted was a waste of time, claiming that such a virtuous outlook would never register with humanity. Jesus further exasperated his father by ignoring God's advice to look out for

himself more because you can't really trust others to do the right thing, guidance Jesus refused to follow even after one of his closest friends, Judas Iscariot, arranged Jesus' arrest and beating at the hand of Roman soldiers in exchange for 30 pieces of silver. Though He agreed Christ's goals were noble in theory, God was annoyed that Jesus did not heed His multiple warnings that people were just not trustworthy, and He

couldn't help but say "I told you so" after His son was crucified for all of his gallant intentions.

Jewelry, decorative metallic objects worn on the body to attract crows and magpies.

Jigsaw Puzzle, game that utilizes interlocking pieces and is very much like life, in a sense, if the reader will permit us to elaborate for a moment. For you see, much like a puzzle, in which only one piece is visible at a time, life is, nah, you know what? This isn't working. Sorry, we thought we had something here.

Jobs, Steve (*b. Feb. 24, 1955 d. Oct. 5, 2011*), visionary who was responsible for the technology this book was composed, designed, and laid out with, but you know, it's still being printed on paper, so fuck you, dead man.

Joe's Cold Beverages, we're back! Same great deals, same great smiles! Come on in and ask for Joe! (*See* UNBEATABLE BARGAINS!)

John The Baptist (*b. 5* BC *d.* AD *36*), charismatic wandering preacher responsible for converting a young and impressionable Jesus to Christianity by playing cool songs on his guitar about God's love. John the Baptist reached out to the directionless 14-year-old by giving him a Bible that had all the best passages highlighted, talking to him about his problems, and even taking him to a Christian skate park near the River Jordan where Jesus met some friendly Christians his own age. Due to his laid-back attitude, John the Baptist earned the admiration of Jesus, and after he became the central figure in Christianity, Christ would fondly recall the times John the Baptist pulled up to his house on his motorcycle to take him to Tuesday night teen prayer meetings.

Johnson, Earvin "Magic" (*b. Aug. 14, 1959*), American professional basketball player for the Los Angeles Lakers who shared an intense ri-

---

THE WORST

Andrew Johnson

(*b. Dec. 29, 1808 d. July 31, 1875*), 17th president of the United States, whom no one expected to be as great as Lincoln, but he really didn't have to screw it up that badly, did he? Johnson ascended to the presidency following Lincoln's assassination and almost immediately offered leniency to Confederate leaders, whom most of the nation considered to be traitors. Look, it's true that Lincoln himself advocated reconciliation with the Southern leadership, but Jesus Christ, Johnson should have realized how bad it would look to show sympathy toward the same people who had just dragged the whole nation into the bloodiest conflict in its history. Johnson's tenure was marred by continuous conflict with Congress, which, again, it's obviously got to be difficult living in the shadow of a towering American giant like Lincoln, but Johnson even went so far as to veto the Civil Rights Act, for crying out loud—a law designed to grant basic human rights

to the people the Civil War had literally *just* been fought over. In a letter to Missouri governor Thomas Fletcher, Johnson once wrote, "This is a country for white men, and by God, as long as I am President, it shall be a government for white men." Hello? What? Congress attempted to remove Johnson from office twice—a pretty big sign that he wasn't exactly nailing the whole president thing, right there—and he barely escaped conviction in his impeachment trial of 1868. He left the White House in disgrace, but not before signing an executive order granting all Confederates amnesty on Christmas Day 1868, which must have had Lincoln saying, "Oh, what the *fuck*?" from beyond the grave.

EDUCATION: Self, dropped out at age 10

SECRET SERVICE CODE NAME: Drewfus

OF NOTE: Visitors taking the White House tour would entertain themselves by pelting Johnson with pennies

MAIN ACHIEVEMENT: Appears in *The Onion Book Of Known Knowledge*

APPROVAL RATING: −32 percent

JOINERY, subsection of woodworking that involves connecting pieces of wood in an intimate bond that unites them both physically and spiritually for all time.

Four Common Wood Joints

Mortise And Tenon Joint
The mortise waits, overcome with anticipation and some trepidation, having never fastened adjoining lengths of wood at an angle of 90 degrees before. With the smooth assurance of a nub that has been machined to within a fraction of an inch, the tenon enters. Once inside, it can feel with every fiber of its being the soft grip of the mortise walls and the pull of industrial polyurethane epoxy binding them. They are now as one, two parts of the same kitchen cabinet.

Bird's-Mouth Joint
Resting 10 to 15 feet above the ground, the rafter and wall plate feel as if they are floating on a cloud, completely removed from the tumult of life below. The rafter, with a notch cut into its trailing edge in the shape of a bird's mouth, accepts the rectangular wall plate and takes it in as deep as the predetermined center line of the brace will allow. The sensation of roof support is incredible, almost too much to bear. But they are not alone. Shunned by the rafter, the floorboards look on with a mix of envy and resentment, growing ever worn and ravaged by time.

Dovetail Joint
In the corner of the room stands a magnificently chiseled specimen: a shaft of wood so rugged and strong it could support the weight of an entire roof. Its trapezoid-shaped tips—three to five in total—shimmer with a deliriously musky petroleum-based sealant, and it is clear these weatherized building materials are there for only one purpose: to fill the tails of another. There is no prelude, no pretense. They couple in quick succession, building up friction, never slowing down, maintaining a passionate intensity that both pieces of wood don't just badly want—they absolutely need it.

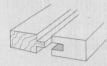

Tongue And Groove Joint
Two long, flat pieces of wood lay side by side. One's tightly cut groove seems destined to accommodate the other's matching tongue. After what felt like an eternity of exchanging the necessary pleasantries with a coterie of saws and T squares, they are finally alone. The pre-stained tongue slides in, effortlessly, first tracing the lip of the groove and then delving deeper to explore the valley's fine-grained intricacy. It continues its warm, wet, rhythmic lapping until it suddenly finds it cannot go any further. Another second and the groove, already quivering with ecstasy, will snap in two! The new surface is now ready to be used in a variety of woodworking projects such as flooring, parquetry, or paneling.

---

valry with Boston Celtics star Larry Bird that included aggressive, physical play, trash-talking, and numerous attempts to shut down each other's immune systems by infecting each other with various diseases. While Johnson won two of their three head-to-head matchups in the NBA Finals, and once succeeded in transmitting a nasty case of measles to Bird, the Celtics forward is still considered to be the rivalry's ultimate winner.

Joint Chiefs Of Staff, committee of military advisers to the American president who recommend new enemies.

Jordan, Michael (*b. Feb. 17, 1963*), gambling addict, adulterer, neglectful parent, pathologically competitive asshole, and beloved national hero who led the Chicago Bulls to six NBA championship titles in the

1990s. Jordan, a thoroughly horrible human being who can only derive happiness from stepping on the throats of others, inspired children and adults alike by leading the league in scoring 10 times and

dunking from the free throw line. In a career spanning 20 years, Jordan racked up five MVP Awards, 14 All-Star appearances, multiple marital affairs, three children who despise him, hundreds of teammates who abhor him, millions of dollars in gambling debt, and billions of fans who worship the ground he walks on for making the game-winning shot against the Utah Jazz in the 1998 finals. The notorious shithead was

also praised for his defense.

Joshua Tree, The, 1987 U2 album that is okay to like.

Joule, James Prescott (*b. Dec. 24, 1818 d. Oct. 11, 1889*), English physicist who really wanted something named after him, so he worked very hard and experimented with heat and discovered some sort of energy thing that got named Joule's Law. Good for him.

Journalism, practice of laying off 250 people, shuttering the last remaining international bureaus, and bringing in an editor who is young and hip and knows what the readers want. Journalism plays a major role in any free society, one that involves calling an emergency staffwide meeting to hear the new editor speak about how the news business is changing and how they're going to have to adapt by becoming a

APPOINTED BY LEE HARVEY OSWALD
Lyndon B. Johnson

(*b. Aug. 27, 1908 d. Jan. 22, 1973*), 36th U.S. president who never made a single decision or accomplished a single task without, at some point, threatening to cut someone's pecker off. In the first six months of his presidency alone, Johnson not only directly threatened to cut off the peckers of 3,500 individuals, he also intimidated an estimated 12,000 others by making menacing allusions to peckers he had allegedly cut off in the past, using expressions such as "I've got that man's pecker in my pocket" and "That peckerless son of a bitch won't mess with me again." A Texan who rose up the ranks in a traditionally conservative state by shrewdly threatening to chop the peckers off influential officials, Johnson pursued a surprisingly progressive domestic agenda as president, generating support for his Great Society social welfare program and civil rights by threatening to tear off numerous congressional peckers—including those of fellow Democrats. Despite his idealism, however, Johnson failed to keep the United States out of the Vietnam War, though he did cut off the pecker of Defense Secretary Robert McNamara in 1968.

Juniper Berry, berry that gives gin its distinctive taste when being violently vomited all over cold pavement.

Jupsi, what Pepsi was called for some reason in a weird dream Muscatine, Iowa, resident Jessica Perrin had on the night of May 7, 2003.

leaner, sleeker, more agile news outlet that embraces these new realities and is not so hostile toward clickable "user-friendly" content, which will drive traffic and supposedly be better for everyone in the long run. Journalism is an aging reporter with 35 years in the business who loves the sound of the printing press and is currently filling a cardboard box with his things because his brand of in-depth investigative reporting doesn't generate enough weekly page views to justify the cost of his work or the high CPMs. Whatever the hell that is. The field of journalism, which can trace its origins to the 15th century, is also known for leading with a piece about online shopping the Monday after Thanksgiving instead of a bombing in the Middle East, and for uncovering the truth behind who designed Gwyneth Paltrow's handbag. Journalism boasts a number of brave reporters who have tirelessly worked for the public good, and its main objectives are coordinating with advertisers to ensure the content fits their needs, and determining which terms are most actively searched on Google so it can fire off 15 related "charticles" designed to steal some of the web traffic before public interest wanes.

Judaism, world religion whose central tenet implores believers to stick together because someone is currently trying to kill them. Jewish theology is rooted in the covenant between God and the children of Israel, who are commanded by the Torah never to get too comfortable, as there are already plans in motion for their murder and the murder of their families. Since Jews never know exactly who is out to assassinate them, when it will happen, or how, Jewish tradition includes the

constant retelling of previous atrocities as a means of maintaining group preparedness and of terrifying the younger generation into internalizing the very real possibility of having to grab their siblings at a moment's notice and hide out in the woods until it's safe to escape on foot. Although Judaism consists of several denominations with different conceptions of spirituality and culture, all Jews affirm the core doctrine of always sleeping lightly because someone who wants to shoot them in the head is closing in.

Judo, style of unarmed combat in which a person uses holds and leverage to unbalance the opponent, something that is extremely useful if a guy is coming at you with a knife and you need to unbalance him.

Juggs, monthly magazine of ideas and mammoth breasts founded by Lewis H. Lapham in 1981 following his editorship of *Harper's Magazine.* Started as a passion project to explore Lapham's deep interest in postmodern aesthetics, enormous double-D tits, and literary culture, *Juggs* is today regarded as one of the finest and most astute knocker-themed periodicals and sources of commentary in the country. Lapham left *Juggs* in 2006 to as-

sume editorship of the small-press literary journal *Finally Legal.*

Jujitsu, another stupid martial art where they don't teach you how to jump-kick on the first day of class.

Juniper, widely distributed coniferous plant in the cypress family and a popular name for children of parents who probably make their own soap and don't believe in vaccinating their daughters.

Juno, goddess and protector of the Roman state—stop thinking of the movie—daughter of Saturn, wife of Jupiter—stop thinking of the movie—and mother of Mars and Vulcan.

Jury, instrument of the judicial system composed of 12 randomly selected people, including a racist, an alcoholic, and a woman who was asleep during most of the trial, who are tasked with the fair and equitable dissemination of justice. Considered a vital social institution, a jury is often led by a foreman in his late 60s who knew the guy was guilty the second he looked at him, didn't take a single note during the court proceedings, and doesn't understand what "beyond a reasonable doubt" means, even though it has been explained to him every day for the past two weeks. In its truest form, a jury is immune to social inequalities; includes a college student who is going to lie and say that his grandmother is sick and he's needed back home; is the backbone of any civil society; and can only function effectively if the assistant district attorney can get at least four black females on there, otherwise he knows he doesn't have a chance in hell. In most cases, a jury must carry out justice as quickly as possible so the judge doesn't have to postpone his vacation.

Kane, Bob *(b. Oct. 24, 1915 d. Nov. 3, 1998)*, creator of Batman who was inspired to create the "Dark Knight Detective" after he cornered a married couple in a dark alley and shot both of them dead right in front of their weeping son.

Karate, martial art developed in the dojos of central Florida strip malls. Invented by Sensei Fred Villari in the early 1980s and brought to West Virginia in the mid-1990s by his student Grandmaster Rick Corcoran, karate is a system of strikes and kicks delivered for 45 minutes every Monday, Wednesday, and Friday evening. Karate takes six months to master, and students will often stop attending classes after this point to take guitar lessons. In the course of their studies, some initiates will enter tournaments held in college gymnasiums in the Greater Orlando region. A small percentage of students will work their way to the most advanced levels of karate and open a dojo next to a hair salon, after which they will put on a considerable amount of weight and rarely leave their offices except to conduct a free introductory private lesson.

Kasparov, Garry *(b. April 13, 1963)*, Russian chess champion who, because of his habit of rubbing chess pieces against his genitals, could not find anyone to play chess with him and had to play against computers.

Kennedy Family, group of five to seven people who threw a football around or sailed on a boat from 1953 to 1963.

Ke$ha *(b. Mar. 1, 1987)*, pop singer-songwriter who will have ceased to be in any way relevant by the time this reference is published. Now gaze—gaze backward in awed horror, dear reader, into the forgotten and cobwebbed past! Contem-

JACK KEROUAC *(b. Mar. 12, 1922 d. Oct. 21, 1969)*, leading figure of the Beat Generation whose writings on travel, drugs, and sex have inspired generations of writers despite the fact that Kerouac himself was actually a shy, morbidly obese shut-in who lived with his mother. While books such as *On The Road* and *The Dharma Bums* are known for their scathing critiques of society, their author spent most of his 47 years watching television and compulsively organizing his extensive collection of baseball cards. Kerouac, who only left his home in Lowell, Massachusetts, to attend church and even then only when his extreme gastric reflux symptoms permitted, wrote in a furious stream-of-consciousness style heavily influenced by the 16 cans of orange soda he'd drink per day and his explorations of mysticism. Despite his immense influence, Kerouac never embraced his status as model for the burgeoning hippie movement due to the fact that young people made him terribly, terribly nervous.

Contrary to his public image, Kerouac preferred to spend evenings doing jigsaw puzzles with his elderly mother.

plate for one terror-filled moment the ghosts of a bygone era for which there is no reverence and no quarter given! "Help us! Help us! We once *mattered*! You must believe us!" the

ghosts implore! But there is no help for them! Watch—no, no, dear reader, do not look away, as much as you would like to—as they fade, fade away forever! Brah, ha, ha, ha, ha, ha! Ha, ha, ha, ha, ha!

Key, Francis Scott *(b. Aug. 1, 1779 d. Jan. 11, 1843)*, American lawyer and author who intended his lyrics to the "Star-Spangled Banner," with their obsequious praise of the American flag and over-the-top

combat imagery, to be an ironic critique of the nation's jingoistic foreign policy and unjust curtailment of civil liberties under the guise of "patriotism" during the War of 1812. Key grew increasingly incensed during public performances of his protest song, as listeners failed to pick up on the sarcastic tone of voice in which he sang such lines as "What so proudly we hailed," as well as his eye rolls, scoffing sighs, and repeated utterances of "Yeah, right" and "As if" throughout the tune. With audiences clearly incapable of grasping the song's mocking praise of the United States, Key stopped singing the tongue-in-cheek "Star-Spangled Banner" altogether in 1820, but by that time it

Kk · κ

Difficult-to-construct eleventh letter of the English alphabet that is rarely used due to the prohibitive cost in money, labor, and time it takes to build each one. Unlike letters such as *V* and *I*, whose simpler design allows them to be mass produced relatively cheaply, the letter *K*'s angled, intersecting segments require not only a high degree of engineering expertise, but also sturdier and more expensive materials to prevent it from collapsing. Even the average lowercase *k* can cost as much as $500,000—this entry alone has already cost nearly $2.5 million and accounts for 99.87 percent of the overall publishing budget. Additionally, *K*'s take up to a year to assemble, a considerable outlay that explains why words such as "kat," "kold," and "kuddle" are almost always deliberately misspelled with a cheaper and less elegant letter *C*, and also why this sentence took nearly five years to complete.

◄ KARATE
The world's first karate dojo, located in Bradenton, Florida.

REMEMBERS EXACTLY WHERE HE WAS
WHEN KENNEDY WAS SHOT

John F. Kennedy

(*b. May 29, 1917 d. Nov. 22, 1963*), beloved 35th U.S. president whose heartbreaking assassination made an entire generation of Americans vow only to elect candidates to whom they wouldn't get too attached. Following the tragic 1963 event, millions of voters decided to support candidates who were just so-so or outright bad, leading to the elections of such presidents as Richard Nixon, Jimmy Carter, and George W. Bush, all of whom lacked the charisma, charm, and magnetism of President Kennedy and allowed the populace to feel safely disconnected. Continually putting mediocre presidents into the Oval Office has allowed the nation to move through the traumatic events of Bill Clinton's impeachment and the attempted assassination of Ronald Reagan with the utmost indifference. This phenomenon also explains why adored candidates such as Walter Mondale and H. Ross Perot were never elected.

EDUCATION: Attended scale replica of Harvard College that his father had built for him in backyard

MAIN ACHIEVEMENT: Got assassinated before he could escalate the Vietnam War and destroy his own legacy

SECRET SERVICE CODE NAMES: Dipstick, Pipe, Sausage, Obelisk, Missile, Rod

PRECISE MOMENT AT WHICH HE SHOULD HAVE DUCKED: 12:29:58.01 p.m., November 22, 1963

LAST WORDS: "Jackie, quick, give me a blow job"

HAIR CARE REGIMEN: Alberto VO5 massaged into scalp, hair artfully swept back with three quick passes of the comb

FRANCIS SCOTT KEY ➤
Key said the high notes in the "Star-Spangled Banner" were meant to be angrily shouted so as to mock America's all-or-nothing attitude toward patriotism.

King Kong, 1933 Hollywood motion picture featuring a stop-motion ape puppet that somehow managed to scare a generation of people enduring the most cataclysmic economic crisis in world history.

had already achieved immense popularity among the general public as an earnest, straight-faced national anthem. Key died a bitter man in 1843, deeply regretting not having written a clarifying "Give me a break" after the song's closing line.

Keyboard, block of wood into which nails are driven and keys are hung so they don't get lost.

Khan, Genghis (*b. 1162 d. 1227*), founding ruler of the Mongol Empire and hopeless romantic who raped and subjugated women across Central Asia and China in the quest to find his one true love. A fierce military leader and expert horseman, Genghis Khan was also notoriously picky, and is believed to have brutalized more than 20,000 potential soul mates in his relentless campaign to meet the right lady—someone whom he could relate to not only as a lover, but also as a best friend. Genghis Khan's legacy, which includes an empire that became the largest geographic kingdom in history and more than 16 million direct descendants, is marred only by the fact that he never did find that perfect someone to settle down with.

Kilimanjaro, Mount, tallest human corpse pile in Africa, rising 19,431 feet above sea level. Each year, hundreds of climbers travel to northern Tanzania to attempt the treacherous ascent, an ordeal that requires them to keep their footing on blood-slicked terrain, find a solid handhold in the tangle of putrefied arms and legs, and face the constant possibility of an avalanche of viscera. The height of Kilimanjaro increases between 2 inches and several feet annually, depending on the African leaders currently in power.

Kim Jong-Il (*b. Feb. 16, 1941 d. Dec. 17, 2011*), former leader of North

Korea who, on his deathbed, expressed that his one regret in life was never forcing all 24 million citizens of his nation to gather in a large field to form an intricate pointillist representation of his face that he could watch from a helicopter while fireworks bloomed in vivid, multicolored flower shapes all around him. Though Kim accomplished most of his life's goals, such as mandating that thousands of his

countrymen and women perform synchronized backflips while thousands of others flip colorful placards to create living murals of himself and his father Kim Il-sung, he somehow never found the time to appreciate the simple pleasure of having every single living North Korean compose a 600-mile-wide likeness of his face, which would slowly wink at him in his helicopter as the 400,000 people representing his lower-left eyelid met the 400,000 people making up his upper-left eyelid. Kim's last words to his successor, son Kim Jong-un, were recorded as, "Do not make the same mistakes I have made, my boy. Please, start picking out the exact right color silk for the millions of costumes that will be your luxurious hair before it's too late."

Kindergarten, form of education for young children that is critical to their social, mental, and emotional development, so don't fuck it up by sending your kids to a crappy free one. In kindergarten, 5- and 6-year-olds develop basic knowledge and skills through creative play, which is why you'd better be prepared to shell out at least 15 grand, unless you want your little boy or girl running around covered in shit and glue at that dumpy public kindergarten for kids whose parents don't care as much about their children's education. Kindergarten is a bridge between home life and a formal school setting, and your neighbor's son is getting a leg up by going to the best kindergarten in the area, one where the principal is called headmaster and where the students are already preparing for the PSATs. Kindergarten follows preschool, which hopefully you were wise enough to invest in as well, because if not, your kid's life is basically fucked and he isn't even 4 yet.

Kindness, quality of selflessness or goodness that is exhibited solely so that the universe will then owe one something in the future. Thoughtful acts such as holding the door for someone or serving as a reference for a coworker are only ever committed in order to gain some favor with the unseen forces that govern the cosmos, in hopes that they will reward that individual the next time fate is required to intercede on his or her behalf. If any opportunity to display kindness is passed up— such as failing to give a stranger good directions, or to congratulate a friend on his recent promotion— the universe will almost certainly strike back at the unkind person by giving them colon cancer.

Kinetics, in physics, one of the branches of dynamics. In chemistry, a branch of physical chemistry that deals with the rate of chemical reactions. In zoology, nothing. In geology, nothing. In political science, nothing. In statistics, nothing. In biology, the processes a substance undergoes in the human body. In botany, nothing.

King, Billie Jean (b. Nov. 22, 1943),

former professional tennis player famous for 1973's media-dubbed "Battle of the Sexes" match in which she defeated Bobby Riggs in straight sets, proving that a woman could beat a man. King went on to play in similar matches, such as the "Battle of the Children," in which King showed that a female could beat a 5-year-old boy on the hard court; the "Battle of the Plumbers," which demonstrated that a female had every right a male had to be on the same court as a plumber; the "Battle of the Disfigured," in which King handily defeated a man whose body was covered with second- and third-degree burns; the "Battle of Nature," in which King prevailed over a giant freshwater sponge 6-0, 6-1; and the legendary "Battle of the Machinery," in which the 12-time major winner showed the world that an assembly line robotic arm from a Detroit auto plant was no match for a woman. Though King's success was an inspiration to women across the country, she lost a second "Battle of the Sexes" match to Chris Evert in the 1977 Wimbledon quarterfinals, proving that a woman could not beat another woman at tennis.

King, Martin Luther, Jr. (b. Jan. 15, 1929 d. Apr. 4, 1968), civil rights leader and clergyman whose final demonstration of racial injustice was getting assassinated at a disgusting, rinky-dink motel instead of in a private box at a grand theater, in a brand-new convertible, or after giving a speech at the four-star Ambassador Hotel. While other illustrious Americans, such as Abraham Lincoln, John Kennedy, and Robert Kennedy, had their lives taken among the luxurious surroundings available only to whites, the black civil rights icon who had electrified the nation with his "I Have A Dream" speech was fatally shot on the dirty balcony of a two-story flea-bag motel across the street from an equally run-down boarding house. Perhaps most striking was the stark contrast between the immediate medical attention received by white victims and the fact that King had to slowly bleed to death in the company of Jesse Jackson.

Kirby, Jack (b. Aug. 28, 1917 d. Feb. 6, 1994), American comic book artist and co-creator of Captain America, the X-Men, the Fantastic Four, and the Hulk. In the years after he left Marvel, Kirby independently published comics featuring the characters Captain Poverty, Johnny Ennui and the Sadness Squad, You're-Not-Putting-Me-in-No-Rest-Home Man, and Admiral That-Motherfucker-Stan-Lee-Bilked-Me-Out-of-Millions.

◄ *King during her straight sets victory in the 1974 "Battle of the Home Appliances."*

◄ MARTIN LUTHER KING, JR.

Skills: Did his own choreography for speeches

Inspiration Rate: 129.8 revelations per minute

Number Of Times He Said "What A Bunch Of Fucking Racist Assholes" In Private: 12,566,484

Bad Habit: Sometimes used fingers to remove pieces of speech stuck between teeth

1962: King took a year off from the civil rights movement and went on vacation in Hawaii, where he relaxed on the beach and swam with dolphins

"Guess we all kinda saw this one coming, huh?"
—**Martin Luther King, Jr., moments after being shot on April 4, 1968**

Knitting, act of making a garment by interlocking loops of wool or yarn while periodically pausing and sipping the merlot that Becca brought.

Kubrick, Stanley (*b. July 26, 1928 d. Mar. 7, 1999*), director of cold, clinical films, the criticism of which provokes the kind of actual human emotion he himself would never have portrayed.

Kissinger, Henry (*b. May 27, 1923*), Jewish, German-born secretary of state under presidents Richard Nixon and Gerald Ford whose family fled the genocidal Nazi regime in 1938 so that Kissinger would one day have the chance to orchestrate his own wartime atrocities. Terrified that the young Kissinger would fall victim to the increasingly anti-semitic policies of the Third Reich, robbing him of a future in which he would play a key role in the indiscriminate murder of a peaceful ethnic group, his family emigrated to the United States and escaped the eventual slaughter of an estimated 142,000 German Jews during the Holocaust, thus ensuring Kissinger would later have the opportunity to authorize in 1969 the secret 4-year-long carpet bombing campaign of Cambodia that killed between 150,000 and 500,000 innocent civilians.

Kitchen, if another room contains more knives than this room, get out of that house.

Kiwi, how an annoying coworker who travels a lot refers to New Zealanders. Why won't he just call them New Zealanders?

Knights Templar, 12th-century religious military order that was secretly involved in a number of historic conspiracies, including suppressing the true location of the Holy Grail, instigating the French Revolution, and causing the 1972 Watergate scandal. Formed in 1119 by Frankish knight Hugues de Payens to protect Christian pilgrims traveling to Jerusalem during the Crusades, five of the Templars were caught breaking into the offices of the Democratic National Committee in a theft that eventually led to President Richard M. Nixon's resignation. In testimony before a Senate

committee and interviews with the *Washington Post*, the sworn and noble defenders of the Holy Land and King Solomon linked the burglaries to an illegal fund set up to reelect Nixon, and revealed that his administration had taken steps to cover it up. The sole surviving knight, Godfrey de Saint-Omer, served four years in prison before becoming a talk-radio host.

Korean War, conflict that started with North and South Korea divided by the 38th parallel and ended with North and South Korea divided by the 38th parallel. More than 1.4 million people died.

Kornberg, Arthur (*b. Mar. 3, 1918 d. Oct. 26, 2007*), American biochemist who was a little peeved that he had to share the 1959 Nobel Prize in Physiology with Dr. Severo Ochoa, honestly. Kornberg was awarded the prize for his work on the synthesis of RNA and DNA, and didn't want to be a jerk or come off as ungrateful or anything, but had still sort of hoped that when it came to his greatest career accomplishment, he'd just be recognized by himself for once, without anyone else in the spotlight. Kornberg made important contributions to the study of genetics, and didn't have a problem with Ochoa personally, it's just that he figured you're only awarded the Nobel once and it would be nice to win it outright without any sort of qualifier. An expert in enzyme chemistry, Kornberg just wanted the Nobel to be the one time where he didn't feel like he had to settle.

K2, second-tallest mountain on earth that, at 28,251 feet, is a nice, breezy alternative for people who are not quite ready to scale Mount Everest's 29,029-foot peak. With a robust oxygen level of 34 percent at

its summit (as opposed to Everest's dangerously low 33 percent), K2 is considered more of a hike than a climb, and offers the amateur outdoors enthusiast a more manageable Himalayan option. Because climbing Everest can take well over a week, many choose K2 for its quick seven-and-a-half-day ascent, while enjoying the −45 degree temperatures, as opposed to Everest's life-threatening −50. While only 300 people have ever reached the top of K2, each and every one of them knows deep down that the violently high winds, dangerously steep ascent, and 25 percent fatality rate they faced would have been way worse on Everest.

Ku Klux Klan, white supremacy group whose well-publicized hate crimes have unfortunately overshadowed its substantial charity work. Despite its history of lynchings, cross burnings, and the brutal intimidation of Jews, immigrants, and African-Americans, the Klan has amassed an impressive, yet largely ignored, record of volunteer work for such needy causes as 4-H, Meals on Wheels, and a variety of no-kill animal shelters. Klan members, dressed in their iconic white robes and pointed masks that symbolize Caucasian purity, are required to spend up to 20 hours a week on community service, whether it's playing one-on-one with disabled children or comforting terminally ill hospice patients—actions that receive far less press coverage than their organized beatings of Latino youths. More recently, the Klan's arming and training of local militias to overthrow the federal government has taken attention away from the great strides made by its educational arm, Teach for America.

La Sortie Des Usines Lumière (Workers Leaving The Lumière Factory), produced in 1895, first non-pornographic film ever shown before an audience.

LADDER, structure comprising a series of steps between two upright bars that is used for climbing. The steps, or "rungs," are ordered according to the following system:

Seventh +2 Rung

Seventh +1 Rung

Kissing Rung

Non-Quadratic Rung

Veluvian Rung
(The Veluvian Rung is actually a composite of six sub-rungs: ½ ⅛ ⅜ ⅛ 7≠7 <5>.)

Ω

Reciprocal Rung

Acute Rung

Bottom Rung
(Though still found on older ladders, no longer a component of contemporary models.)

A standard ladder. The tallest ladder in the world is more than 100 feet tall and reaches the seventh +475 rung.

Landfill, location where people temporarily store garbage until they need it at a later date. The rubbish and waste matter, which is safely deposited under a thick, protective layer of soil, can be easily accessed by residents who drive out to the landfill and dig up their prized eggshells, oily napkins, coffee grounds, or fingernail clippings. If people

didn't come back for their old paint thinner or discarded cathode-ray tubes, the unclaimed items are donated to charity.

Language, system of communication in which words or symbols are used in an organized fashion to express irritation, unhappiness, disapproval, and anger. One of the fundamental pillars of civilization, a set language is necessary to convey resentment and disappointment, as well as contempt, scorn, and jealousy. And malice. And fury. Also revulsion. Humans first used language to express frustration and hatred at least 100,000 years ago, and since then it has served as a pragmatic framework within which to communicate a range of feelings, from general disdain to full-blown rage. While humans can use spoken language to chastise, berate, provoke, emotionally destroy, madden, irk, disgust, abuse, exasperate, offend, and upset one another, written language is another method commonly employed to deride, ridicule, mock, deceive, betray, insult, criticize, and piss off. Through-

out history, language has also been the primary way one conveys happiness for someone else's failures.

Laptop, portable personal computer that was developed in the 1970s and 1980s by people who felt they weren't dropping their desktops enough.

LaRue, Mitsy, Mitsy? Little red-headed number, 'bout so tall, pouty mouth, firecracker of a temper? Who's askin'? Sorry, I ain't home if that's only Mr. Lincoln knocking. What's that, your name's Hamilton? Whyn't ya say so in the first place? Yeah, Mitsy, sure, sure. She was a crazy little twist, you bet your life, but she was no dummy. Used to see her in all the usual joints—the Calypso, the Roxy, the Chinaman's, the Docksider. Naw, she never bought no chips, but she knew how to show a little leg to a guy who did, see? Only she took to toolin' around with Valentine. Mike Valentine. Three-time loser, four-time player? Yeah, Mitsy couldn't pick a man anymore than Valentine could pick a pony. But you find him, you'll find her. Sure you don't want no French postcards? Ain't no two alike… Sure, sure, don't let me keep you, and lotsa luck, shamus. (***See*** MIKE VALENTINE)

Large Hadron Collider, powerful, high-energy particle accelerator designed to answer fundamental questions about the universe, though scientists currently lack the technology necessary to get it to talk. Constructed in the late 1990s to early 2000s by the European Organization for Nuclear Research and costing more than $9 billion, the LHC cannot at this time respond to scientists when they ask the underground particle accelerator point-blank, "How did the Big Bang happen?" and "When did

Ll·Λλ·Łł

lonely, lonely.

LARGE INTESTINE, wormlike parasite that enters a human fetus's mouth, nose, ears, tear ducts, or anus as a microscopic organism and subsists on food found inside the digestive system for the rest of the host's life. The large intestine can grow to be 4 to 5 feet long as it writhes around inside the body searching for nutriment, often causing serious abdominal pain and bloating in the process. The massive parasite also creates large amounts of excrement that would eventually fill up the entire body; however, it corrects for this by developing a symbiotic relationship with a thinner, longer worm that consumes the large intestine's waste and expels it from the host.

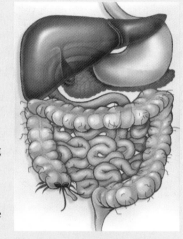

LAVA ➤
The takers of this picture all got melted.

Lemon, sour-tasting egg laid by a citrus duck.

time actually begin?" Scientists and engineers have grown increasingly frustrated with the LHC, and have resorted to yelling and kicking the 17-mile-long device, demanding to know why it won't speak to them about the unsolved mysteries of nature, or why it won't just say something, anything, at all. Despite issuing numerous threats to ruthlessly destroy every last square inch of the complex structure, researchers are no closer to understanding Higgs boson, the so-called God particle, or what the Large Hadron Collider's problem is.

Lasagna, delicious, edible diorama made of noodles, cheese, and sauce designed to depict a cross-section of the earth's lithosphere, mantle, and core layers.

Laughter, spontaneous physical response to the observation that women gots to wash that pussy. Laughing is characterized by involuntary movements of the face and body, and is directly correlated to remarks about bitches needing to take care of that shit for real, because that pussy be *stankin'.* Addi-

tionally, instructions pertaining to women washing the pussy front to back, front to back—*Front. To. Back*—along with an accompanying pantomime demonstrating these instructions are associated with laughter becoming so sustained and forceful that tears may be produced.

Laundry, one of approximately 400 things that, fuck, one completely forgot to do today. (**See** GROCERIES, PHONE BILL, CALL MOM, GARBAGE NIGHT, DISHES, LITTER BOX, PLANTS, GYM, E-MAIL MCAVOY, CHANGE LIGHT BULB, RENT CHECK, COOK DINNER, CALL NATE, CLEAN BATHROOM, JESS' BIRTHDAY, FIND SOURCE OF FISH SMELL, UPDATE RÉSUMÉ, MAKE LUNCH FOR TOMORROW, 2 P.M. MEETING, WIPE DOWN COUNTER, EXTRA KEY FOR CLAIRE, FIX BUTTON, THROW OLD LETTUCE OUT, TEETH CLEANING, SHAVE, CHARGE PHONE, SET ALARM, ORGANIZE DESK, REFILL ICE TRAY, TURN OFF OVEN, FEED CAT)

Lava, super hot melted rock that is

made from pieces of the sun that fell on the Earth. People from science calculate that lava is way hotter than the Sahara Desert, a stove, lasers, or bubbling cheese in a calzone. Looking at lava directly for just a second will melt the eyeballs, because of the hotness. Also, if lava sprays up too high, the entire sky will start on fire and everyone will die.

Leek, vegetable related to garlic with an edible stem that—surprise, surprise—is yet another member of the Amaryllidaceae family. Originating in the Mediterranean region, the leek is cultivated widely for culinary use and, no shocker here, folks, joins the daffodil, Cape tulip, and about 800 other species of perennial herbs in the flowering plant order Asparagales, as if you couldn't see *that* one coming. Leeks grow from seed, reach maturity in the autumn months, and, just like every other goddamn Amaryllis out there, produce allyl sulfide compounds that give them their characteristic smell.

Lego, toy construction block and premier status symbol among high-school-age males. Those who construct the biggest Lego cities in their bedrooms typically date the prettiest cheerleaders, and a school's homecoming king is almost always someone who showcased a build at that year's BrickFest.

Length, distance from here to here or here[1]

Leper Colony, remote settlement where people suffering from the contagious disease leprosy are sent to extract the raw materials needed to power the industries of the larger Leper Empire. These deformed, lesion-covered workers ship the raw

Literature,

written works considered to be of lasting artistic merit that represent humankind's struggle to understand its essential nature and also there is Stephen King. Literature generally takes the forms of fiction, nonfiction, and Stephen King's fiction, and like other artistic expressions, is often an attempt to determine one's place and purpose in a universe that can seem arbitrary, unfeeling, vast, or populated by giant dogs infected with rabies and strangers possessed by the ghosts of serial killers. Dating back to at least 2000 BC, literature was born out of ancient oral traditions that were eventually committed to written languages, plus in 1983 *Christine* was published. Early literary examples include *Beowulf*, a heroic epic written in early English about a ruler who fights a marauding monster, the monster's mother, and a dragon; *Carrie*, the blockbuster bestseller that King wrote while teaching grade school and working at a laundromat in the evenings; and *The Tale Of Genji*, an 11th-century courtier's tale by Japanese noblewoman Murasaki Shikibu considered to be the world's oldest complete novel. In the modern era, literature has evolved into several different movements, which include structuralism, deconstruction, little girls who can start fires with their mind, modernism, postmodernism, poison gas that turns people into ultraviolent aliens, and an interactive electronic genre known as hypertext fiction. And also stories about predatory inter-dimensional creatures that take the shape of circus clowns and exploit the fears of their human victims in order to hunt and kill them. Despite its wide breadth and clear impact on human culture as a whole, literature has occasionally been criticized for *Gerald's Game*, which sucked.

NOTABLE LITERARY CHARACTERS

Captain Ahab: Tyrannical captain in *Moby Dick* who represents the fact that it's good not only to have goals, but also to do everything in one's power to achieve them.

Leopold Bloom: Protagonist of James Joyce's modernist novel *Ulysses* who is constantly wondering what the fuck is going on, and is especially confused about whether he is talking out loud or just thinking something in his head.

Lord Bradley Murderson: Character ferreted out as the killer in Agatha Christie's worst-selling mystery novel, *Lord Murderson Is The Killer*.

Atticus Finch: Protagonist in *To Kill A Mockingbird* who represents how much easier life could have been for him had he been a racist.

Sherlock Holmes: Detective in the stories of Sir Arthur Conan Doyle known for solving mysteries by dropping to his knees and waiting for Christ in His infinite goodness to reveal the culprits.

Robinson Crusoe: Character who becomes stranded on a desert island in the 1700s after a shipwreck and, despite being the only white person for thousands of miles, still manages to enslave a native.

Tom Sawyer: Author Mark Twain's mischievous frontier youth who, with his friend and business associate Huckleberry Finn, transports and distributes high-grade narcotics and methamphetamine throughout the Mississippi River Valley via raft and riverboat, eventually becoming the most powerful figure in the Missouri drug trade before he and Huck are apprehended and sent to their rooms by Sawyer's stern Aunt Polly in 1879.

Dr. Juliette Faxx: Famed secondary character who opts to transfer Cain's brain into the OCP's newest crime prevention unit in the novelization of *RoboCop 2*.

LITERARY THEMES

Loss Of Innocence: Motif in which a basketball hoop in a driveway is depicted as deteriorating over time

Loneliness: Theme that has legs for about 17 pages, tops

Death: Concept that has never been explored by a single author and is just waiting for some original voice to come along and write about it

Man vs. Nature: Signified by a character accidentally walking through a spiderweb, flailing around like a maniac, and screaming before he eventually calms down and realizes he's okay

Alienation: Theme of existential loneliness and estrangement from society that is surprisingly prevalent in the work of people who spend their lives alone in a room writing books

DRAMATIC STRUCTURE

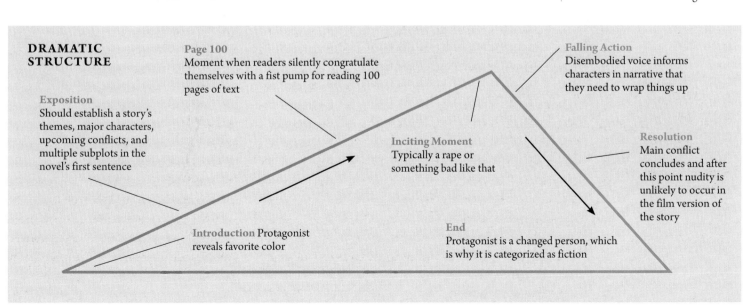

Exposition
Should establish a story's themes, major characters, upcoming conflicts, and multiple subplots in the novel's first sentence

Page 100
Moment when readers silently congratulate themselves with a fist pump for reading 100 pages of text

Introduction Protagonist reveals favorite color

Inciting Moment
Typically a rape or something bad like that

End
Protagonist is a changed person, which is why it is categorized as fiction

Falling Action
Disembodied voice informs characters in narrative that they need to wrap things up

Resolution
Main conflict concludes and after this point nudity is unlikely to occur in the film version of the story

MOCKED, REVILED, MURDERED, ADORED
Abraham Lincoln

(b. Feb. 12, 1809 d. Apr. 15, 1865), 16th U.S. president, considered to be the greatest leader in the country's history and the quintessential American who, during his time, was mocked, ridiculed, derided, and eventually murdered by Americans. The deeply respected national hero, whom nearly every U.S. citizen holds in saintlike regard as one of the greatest human beings ever, was viciously chastised by nearly every U.S. citizen for his progressive politics and peculiar, spindly build. During Lincoln's historic presidency, unanimously regarded by the American people as one of the most important and inspiring of all time, he was mercilessly attacked by the American people for being weak-willed, traitorous, disappointing, foolish, and, again, odd-looking. The beloved American, whose life and opinions best embody the spirit and values of America and all Americans, was then shot in the head by an American in front of his wife in 1865.

The Life Of Lincoln

Feb. 12, 1809: Abraham Lincoln is born and immediately sworn in as the 16th president of the United States.

1817: In one terrifying night, Lincoln has the first and only growth spurt of his life, expanding from 4 feet, 3 inches to 6 feet, 4 inches in a matter of hours amid the hellish sounds of snapping bones and tendons.

1828: While visiting New Orleans, he observes a slave auction, has an itchy nose during the bidding, and accidentally purchases a lot of two dozen black men.

1860: Feeling depressed while writing his autobiography, Lincoln fails to mention himself even once.

Apr. 14, 1865: Lincoln is assassinated.

Apr. 15, 1865: Lincoln resumes the presidency and serves out the rest of his term.

LIBARY ➤
One of the famous lion statues outside the New York Public Libary.

Lint, what remains of the mouse that you left in your pants pocket.

materials back home, where they are turned into the consumer goods and military matériel needed to support the Leper Empire's global imperial ambitions. Though established primarily for economic purposes, Leper colonies often become permanent homes for settlers, who can drive out an entire indigenous people within hours of showing up and letting everyone get a good look at their faces.

Libary, municipal building that houses a collection of libary books and other libary resources that members of the public can borrow for set periods of time. Libaries are staffed by libarians, professionals who catalog, organize, and shelve libary books and libary reference materials, as well as issue libary cards—official libary documents that allow citizens to check items out of the libary. Since the advent of the Internet, many libaries have seen decreased patronage and subsequent libary budgetary cuts due to the relative ease of purchasing books from online retailers such as BarnesandNobles.com.

Liberalism, political movement characterized by easing up a little now and then, because at the end of the day, it's just societal norms we're talking about here.

Life, suffering.

Lightning, burst of charged particles that lights up the sky and allows onlookers to see who's dogging in the bushes without using a flashlight.

Lincoln-Douglas Debates, seven debates held in 1858 across Illinois between incumbent Democratic senator Stephen Douglas and Republican candidate Abraham Lincoln, during which Lincoln skillfully convinced voters that Douglas should be reelected by a substantial margin. By eloquently stating his own arguments for abolishing slavery and then soundly defeating these arguments with concise, devastating, and immaculately researched point-by-point rebuttals, Lincoln proved that Douglas was correct on every single issue and was, without question, worthy of reelection. During the final meeting between the candidates, Lincoln so

passionately orated against his own beliefs that he was carried off on the crowd's shoulders while Douglas, who was soon after swept back into office without having spoken a single word in any of the debates, was left standing alone in an empty town hall.

Linux, Unix-based open-source operating system that your one friend has running on his computer and that you apparently should have on yours, too. Developed in the early 1990s by Finnish software engineer Linus Torvalds, Linux runs much faster than MacOS or Windows or whatever, hardly ever requires rebooting because of its high resistance to crashes, and, according to your friend, has built-in security protections that make his machine impervious to the spyware that is supposedly ravaging yours right now. The problematic DVD playback that would seem to be an issue with Linux is actually, your friend assures you, a small price to pay considering Linux's free or low-cost software and its multiplatform versatility, which presumably is also an

THE LIVERPOOL BEATLE BOYS, one of the most important groups in the history of popular music, Britain's Liverpool Beatle Boys dominated the rock and roll scene commercially and artistically throughout the 1960s with a string of popular albums including *Meet The Liverpool Beatle Boys* and the self-titled "white" album *The Liverpool Beatle Boys.* Igniting a fury of popular interest in the United States that the media dubbed Liverpool-Beatle-Boysmania, the group was at the center of several culturally iconic events, including Ed Sullivan's 1964 introduction of the group on his television show with the immortal line "Ladies and gentlemen…the Liverpool Beatle Boys!" After the enor-

The Liverpool Beatle Boys: Paul, the cute Liverpool Beatle Boy; George, the quiet Liverpool Beatle Boy; John, the smart Liverpool Beatle Boy; and Ringo, the goofy Liverpool Beatle Boy.

mously influential group disbanded in 1970, singer-bassist Paul McCartney embarked on a second musical career in his next successful band, Linda McCartney & the Wingmen.

Quaint displays of unmitigated class rage can be found around every enchanting London corner.

City beloved by tourists and travelers the world over for the charming displays of deeply embedded class anger that erupt periodically across the city. Visitors have flocked for generations to this global metropolis of more than 7 million people to stroll along the River Thames and catch a glimpse of a disaffected working-class youth or a 50-year-old builder from Kent as they enact their colorful hereditary rage in a traditional display of angry glares, furious muttering, and, in a rare but spectacular sight, random violence at the slightest provocation. Such delightful performances can occur at any time, but are best witnessed immediately after the pubs close at 11 p.m. or upon any mention of the word "immigrants."

asset. If you were at all interested in upgrading, your friend could partition your hard drive and install a dual boot loader, or something to that effect, to run Linux on the side.

Liposuction, resource-redistribution procedure developed by humanitarian cosmetic surgeons in the late 20th century, by which the excess fat deposits of philanthropic Westerners are selflessly removed, at a personal cost of up to $30,000, using powerful vacuum technology, and then allocated to poor, lipid-needy families throughout the developing world. Each day, more than 700,000 gallons of viscous, semi-opaque human adipose tissue is air-dropped onto fat-deprived nations throughout Africa, South America, and Asia, as citizens run from their squalid living conditions to stand directly beneath the planes, and hold out buckets in hopes of collecting some of the precious, life-giving lard.

Listening, state of staring at a fixed location and thinking about something more desirable than whatever the speaker is talking about.

Living Room, household location for an argument that started in the kitchen and needed somewhere to move to. As an argument builds momentum, participants find the kitchen too compact and claustrophobic, and require a larger space in which to pace and yell. Moreover, the living room, with its couch, chairs, and other furniture, allows people to really settle into their argument, whereas the kitchen inevitably possesses the feeling of a temporary arguing space. Arguments generally culminate in the bedroom, where they are resolved with either the packing of a bag or sexual intercourse.

Llama, South American pack animal that is easily offended and capable of holding a grudge longer than any other mammal. Known for their extremely soft, warm wool and ability to harbor bitter resentment over any perceived slight for decades at a time, llamas can grow as tall as 6 feet. Llamas can also carry 30 percent of their own weight, and 100 percent of their animosity, over the course of several miles, during which time one had better be very careful what one says, because the last thing one needs is a passive-aggressive llama on one's back until the end of one's 25-year average lifespan.

Locomotive, (*See* CHOO-CHOO)

Logic, formal systematic study of the principles of inference and reasoning that is fundamentally flawed due to its repeated use of logical fallacies. Logic examines the general

Literacy, ability to look at a lot of words for an extended period of time.

CITIES OF THE WORLD
Los Angeles

Absolutely all your dreams will come true.

Major American metropolis and international center for agriculture, technology, education, and the film industry, which, with your looks, you should seriously consider getting into. It is the second most populous city in the United States with 3.8 million residents, all of whom dream of having their name in lights someday, but none of whom is as talented as you. Los Angeles was founded in 1781 by Spanish settlers. You starred in your first school play more than 200 years later, and you were a natural. Everyone said so. Your best friends said you should pursue acting, and they were right. Just look at that face. With an average temperature of 66 degrees, Los Angeles has an ideal climate for soaking up some sun in Malibu while you read the script for that blockbuster movie you just got cast in. We know a guy who can hook you up with a few acting lessons and then, who knows? The sky's the limit, and Los Angeles is situated on the San Andreas fault. Pack your bags right now and hop on one of the thousands of daily flights into Los Angeles International Airport. Leave that boring old life and those boring old people behind. You're better than all those go-nowhere losers dragging you down. Smog, wild fires, and pollution are among the environmental challenges facing the city. A pretty little thing like you? You'll be taken care of. You'll be loved, admired— worshipped. Total area is 470 square miles. You're a true beauty, one of a kind. Come on out here. Come be a star.

forms arguments may take, a task that inevitably makes use of the fallacy of sweeping generalization and immediately renders the entire field of inquiry moot. Logic also aims to analyze the form of any argument type, and in this process employs the fallacy of false cause by incorrectly assuming that one thing is the cause of another. Practitioners of logic believe that it can be used across all disciplines, including philosophy, mathematics, semantics, and computer science, an assumption that once again makes use of the fallacy of sweeping generalization, and therefore further compounds logic's invalidation of itself by employing circular reasoning. At this point, the next logical step of logic is to assert that there is no logic at all, causing the practitioner to fall into the trap of a fallacy known as "begging the question"— a conclusion drawn from premises that presuppose the truth of the conclusion—because, after all, one is baselessly asserting that there is "no logic." Upon this discovery, one will reach the conclusion that logic is a formal systematic study of the principles of inference and reasoning that is fundamentally flawed due to its repeated use of logical fallacies.

Loop-The-Loop, flying maneuver that commercial airline pilots are allowed to perform one time during

their careers using a booked-to-capacity Boeing 767 aircraft. The result of a hard-won concession in a 1987 labor dispute between the Air

14TH-CENTURY AMERICAN PATRIOT
Frederick Lyffhäuser III

(b. Jan. 31, 1327 d. Krv. 8, 1381), 14th-century U.S. president known for expanding states' rights and fighting the invading barbarian horde in the War of 1372. After studying law and alchemy at the University of Pennsylvania and rising to prominence as a member of the American Mächtig Bluthupe Party during the Mercantile Panic of 1350, Lyffhäuser ascended to the presidency by murdering his predecessor, President Frederick Lyffhäuser II, in a joust on the White House lawn. During his term, Lyffhäuser made great strides toward

westward expansion, emancipating the serfs, forming the first Continental Reichsversammlung in Philadelphia, and raising tariffs on witchery. Four days after delivering his final State of the Union address, Lyffhäuser died from the Black Death.

Line Pilots Association union and several major carriers, pilots who work full-time for at least two years may do one loop-the-loop without having to warn crew members or passengers and without incurring any penalties.

Lorem Ipsum, Latina verba expletiva nec intellegibilia quae, si in lucem emittantur, significant aliquem irrumatorem perverse erravisse et statim esse exauctorandum, etiamsi nepos est moderatoris principis.

Louganis, Greg *(b. Jan. 29, 1960),* American diver who contracted HIV while executing a reverse two-and-a-half somersault tuck with a full homosexual tryst (he had sex with a guy in midair).

Love, warm, passionate feeling of affection that occurs between two people who don't know each other that well.

Lucy, famous Austrolopithicus fossil that many scientists believe is a "missing link" between humans and chimps, some scientists see as an evolutionary dead-end species, and

one scientist believes is a duck.

Luther, Martin *(b. Nov. 10, 1483 d. Feb. 18, 1546),* German theologian and reformer who objected to the Roman Catholic Church's doctrine forbidding people from marrying a pope. Luther, who didn't necessarily wish to marry a pope himself but wanted people to have the right to marry a pope if they felt so inclined, established a new Protestant religion whose main tenet was to give members "the freedom to wed the Vicar of Jesus Christ, but only if the Vicar of Jesus Christ wants to marry them, too." Since the official split from the Roman Catholic Church, only one Lutheran—St. Cloud, Minnesota, medical office coordinator Gary Burkholder—has ever wanted to marry a pope, and he exercised his religious right by taking Pope John Paul II as his bride at St. Peter's Basilica in 1989.

Lying, act of propagating beliefs that are not true in order to prevent civilizations from knowing they are actually in a type of zoo.

Machiavelli, Niccolò di Bernardo dei (b. May 3, 1469 d. June 21, 1527), Italian political philosopher and author of *The Prince*, a treatise on using unethical means to attain power that has been read by every living junior account executive, each of whom actually believes it will give him or her a professional edge.

Machine, system or device designed for a specific purpose, such as Mobridge, South Dakota, resident Marcus Seltz, who can take down a bucket of crab legs like a freaking combine. By applying force to crack the shells and propel the meat into his mouth in one fluid motion, Seltz can ingest crab legs more quickly and efficiently than a human diner, whose jaw would tire from the repetitive strain. This capability makes him uniquely suited to absolutely obliterate plate after plate of crab as fast as it is served, provided his working parts remain lubricated with a constant supply of melted butter and beer.

Magna Carta, English charter that granted certain civil liberties to subjects of the crown and was etched

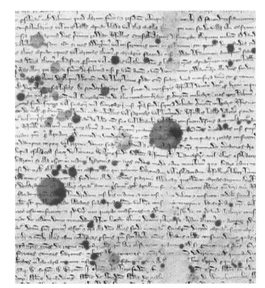

Writing the first draft of the Magna Carta, King John made several small errors and was forced to throw the serf in the garbage and start over on a new manservant.

THE ORIGINAL MUFF RIDER
James Madison

(b. Mar. 16, 1751 d. June 28, 1836), fourth president of the United States and influential statesman who is perhaps best known for fucking the living Christ out of his wife, Dolley Madison. Known as the Father of the Constitution for his role as the main author of that historic document, Madison is still primarily remembered for

onto the face and torso of a manservant with a dagger by King John himself in 1225. In order to appease rebellious barons, King John signed the document, which assured individual freedom, established due process, and bound royalty to the rule of law, by using the tip of the razor-sharp blade to carefully carve each letter of the 63 clauses into the skin of the screaming subordinate. The Magna Carta was periodically updated by future kings and queens, who plunged the ceremonial dagger into the manservant's cheek to cut out antiquated laws or added new statutes by slicing the words onto the surface of his eyelids. The Magna Carta served as a model for the U.S. Constitution, which the Founding Fathers carved into an Indian infant's back in 1787.

Magnet, object, generally metal, used to demonstrate how a magnet works.

Mailer, Norman (b. Jan. 31, 1923 d. Nov. 10, 2007), famed prose au-

balling the first lady all day and all night, pausing just long enough to approve the establishment of the Second Bank of the United States before diving back in for another marathon deep-dicking session. While his two terms in office are inevitably characterized by the way he crammed his cock halfway up his wife's stomach, pounding like an oil derrick and blasting wad after rocket-powered wad inside her hungry hole, Madison also presided over America's conflict with Britain in the War of 1812.

thor known for physically fighting his books for a year before turning them over to his publisher covered in scratches and dried blood.

Malapropism, grotesque or inappropriate use of a gourd.

Malcolm X (b. May 19, 1925 d. Feb. 21, 1965), African-American Muslim minister and human rights activist who, through a program of self-determination, achieved his

lifelong goal of having about one-third of his autobiography skimmed by 17-year-old white high school students. Born Malcolm Little, he moved east from Michigan after his father was murdered and fell into a life of crime, eventually going to prison, committing himself to the Nation of Islam, and changing his name to Malcolm X—all details he hoped suburban white teenagers would one day halfheartedly remember from his autobiography during the summer before their freshman year of college. Upon his release from prison in 1952, Malcolm X committed his life to spreading a message of black empowerment before he was assassinated in

Mm · μ · м

Hardest letter in the English alphabet to think about, given the way things ended with Caroline. We were driving home from her cousin Alyssa's wedding in Harrisburg—this must have been about five years ago now—when, naturally, the subject of marriage came up. "The Big M," I jokingly called it. God, I must have sounded like such a fool. Anyway, she handled it as delicately as she could, of course. Caroline was always like that, so thoughtful and understanding. But I could tell immediately how uncomfortable the topic made her, how some part of her had been dreading the day when I'd finally confront her with it. I tried to convince her I wasn't trying to pressure her into something she wasn't ready for, but we both knew that I was, and that no matter how hard I pushed I'd never be able to turn myself into the one she really wanted. And so we limped along for another month or two, pretending we still had a reason to be together. But it didn't last. It never could. And all I'm left with now is this loathing...this fucking self-loathing from knowing that, when all was said and done, I just wasn't enough for her. I wasn't what she was looking for. And really, how do you move on from that? How do you ever face yourself again? Eventually I found a way, I suppose, but that hurt doesn't go away. It stays with you and then one day, years later, you see that big letter *M* and suddenly you're right back in that car outside Harrisburg, watching the person you care about most in the world slipping out of your reach forever.

MAIL, letters or packages sent via a postal service. In the United States, such material is processed in the following manner:

STEP 1
A letter is placed into a public collection box.

STEP 2
Rotating blades in the collection box shred the letter. Twice a day, a mail carrier empties the accumulated ribbons of paper, painstakingly reassembles them to the best of his or her ability, and transports them to the nearest local post office.

STEP 3
Each letter is shredded a second time. The scraps are sprayed onto a giant warehouse floor, where workers scramble to gather up the pieces and reconstruct the letters. Those workers who are unable to do so satisfactorily are given pens and paper, and are tasked with guessing the intent of each letter fragment and forging a convincing duplicate.

STEP 4
Letters are sorted by ZIP code and flown to a processing center in that region. These facilities often double as slaughterhouses, in which case the animal blood is thoroughly scrubbed from each envelope before delivery.

STEP 5
The letters are assigned to the appropriate postal carrier, who buries them under 3 feet of nutrient-rich topsoil, waters them, and then digs them up.

STEP 6
On average, a letter takes three business days to reach its destination.

New York City, praying in his dying moments that the tragedy would later make for a powerful scene in a movie that entitled young adults would watch because they never finished the book in school.

Mammography, diagnostic discipline invented so researchers and doctors could see what a breast would look like when squished flat.

Mandela, Nelson (*b. July 18, 1918*), revered former South African president who presided over the country during its five-year hiatus from apartheid.

Manhattan Project, top-secret undertaking that brought together the most brilliant scientific minds of the 20th century to figure out how to singe the faces off of 200,000 Japanese people in Hiroshima and Nagasaki. Led by American physicist J. Robert Oppenheimer, the team that worked on the project

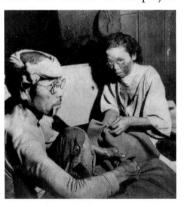

comprised a diverse group of luminaries, including Harvard University physicist Kenneth Bainbridge, whose work helped to confirm Einstein's theory of relativity; Hungarian physicist Leo Szilard, who conceived of the nuclear chain reaction; and Robert Wilson, who was an architect of the Fermi National Laboratory—all of them setting aside their egos to focus their collective genius on giving people bloody diarrhea, nasal hemorrhaging, first-degree retinal burns, liver

failure, fibrosis, bloody vomit every 30 minutes for up to three days, severely blistered skin tissue that ultimately became necrotic and hung limply from one's body, subcutaneous bleeding, fatal seizures, and a bomb whose flash was so powerful it could burn people 14,000 feet away from the point of impact.

Manifest Destiny, phrase coined in 1839 to justify the expansion of the United States across the North American continent and whose use typically precedes some sort of horribly shitty act.

Manning, Peyton (*b. Mar. 24, 1976*), hike football, throw football. Hike football, throw football. Watch game film. Hike football, throw football. Read about football. Study football. Talk to family about football. Play football.

Manpower Inc., U.S.-based employment services company and, for the last time, *not* a male escort service.

Mantel, part of a fireplace used to prevent framed photographs, heirlooms, porcelain figurines, or urns containing the ashes of loved ones from falling straight into the fire below.

Manufacturing, industrial economic sector tasked with creating layoffs and producing jobs overseas.

Marijuana, mild, largely harmless psychoactive drug derived from the cannabis plant that remains against the law in the United States in order to anger the exceedingly annoying jackoffs who call for its legalization. Studies have demonstrated that marijuana is far less detrimental than alcohol or tobacco, and that it has many legitimate medical uses, including managing pain and nausea in AIDS and cancer patients. Still, the drug is kept criminalized for the immensely pleasurable satis-

faction of enraging the devil-stick-twirling dipshits who have decided that smoking a plant somehow constitutes an entire identity. Although the vast majority of Americans have no moral objection to legalizing marijuana, nearly every single citizen would gleefully keep it outlawed just to continue reveling in the apoplectic fits of self-righteous inanity that pro-legalization dumb-fucks whip themselves into as they fail, time and again, to comprehend through a haze of bong smoke that they and their ratty-ass dreadlocks are the sole reason it remains just outside legitimacy.

Marriage, legal union permanently joining two people in kinship, with one or both parties recognizing that it is no problem to divorce later, so the decision doesn't have to be final. The partnership is traditionally formalized in a marriage ceremony, in which participants pledge their undying love and devotion toward each other for a period of one or two years before taking stock of the situation and figuring out if the eternal union they committed to in front of their family and friends is the right thing for them at that point in their lives. Spouses are monogamous, with the understanding that once the pressures of marriage prove detrimental to their sex life, it is both a straightforward and socially acceptable decision to start dating other people.

Marshall, Thurgood (*b. July 2, 1908 d. Jan. 23, 1993*), first African-American Supreme Court justice, who would have turned down President Lyndon Johnson's barrier-breaking appointment had he known it would pave the way for Clarence Thomas. Marshall, an outspoken, progressive judge who believed in affirmative action and a woman's right to choose, would have politely rejected the Senate's historic 69–11 confirmation if he'd had any inkling that he was making it possible for Thomas—who has not spoken from the bench since 2006, continually allows partisan politics to influence his decisions, and often falls asleep during oral arguments—to serve on the highest court in the land. For 24 years Marshall stood as a symbol of inspiration to the African-American community, an honor he would have instantly rescinded if it meant that Thomas would have lived his entire life thinking his race was an obstacle he could never overcome.

Marshalls, discount clothing chain and wildly popular destination for little kids, millions of whom beg their parents every day to take them to one of Marshalls' 750 locations across the United States. The aisles of Marshalls are regularly clogged with birthday parties and elementary school field trips, as hundreds of jubilant little ones race from department to department, having the time of their lives playing with XL Wrangler jeans and three-packs of cotton sports tees or letting their imaginations run wild with such home décor items as embroidered throw pillows, picture frames, and

bath mats. Even after spending an entire afternoon at Marshalls, most kids are extremely reluctant to leave at closing time, and it is not uncommon to see parents prying their children's grips from a curtain display or particle-board shelving unit, while promising to bring them back next weekend.

Martini, gin-based American cocktail that has never been made correctly. While its exact origins are unclear, some historians trace the drink's creation to 1910 at New York City's Knickerbocker Hotel, where it was first made with a little too much vermouth in a glass that could have been colder. Over time, the martini has evolved in countless incorrect ways to incorporate the wrong kind of bitters, fruit-infused vodkas that completely overwhelm it, and not enough olives, and is today widely regarded as the perfect theoretical cocktail.

M*A*S*H, classic American television series that takes on average 35 episodes before a viewer becomes slightly interested as to why there are asterisks in the title.

Mathematics, science of numbers, space, and quantity that, due to its total lack of ambiguity, perfectly rational constructions, and impervi-

MASTODON, only an entry as grand and majestic as the mighty mastodon itself could possibly do justice to this awe-inspiring creature—indeed, such an encyclopedia entry would require a first sentence of uncommon grace and ambition, displaying a prose style as broad as the mastodon's muscled shoulders and as perfectly smooth as the sloping curves of its two gleaming

An august caption as noble and dignified as the regal mastodon.

ivory tusks. Imagine, if you will, an entry whose words thunder across the Great Plains of one's imagination with the same determined gait as the glorious mastodon in the days before history, the thick fur of its verbiage shimmering with density and warmth, and shielding it against the cold, oppressive winds of frigid uninterest. The entry's strong, sinewy midsection—the figurative meat of the rhetorical beast—covers and supports the bare bones of its carefully structured outline until the thick layer of narrative tension underlying the entry is suddenly pierced by the emergence of another clause, as though speared by an ancient tribe of hunter-gatherers seeking sustenance from the entry's rich imagery and nourishing breadth. The entry feels a sharp pain in its haunches, and is now surrounded by a whooping hunting party who can taste the behemoth entry's blood on their lips. The blood is dark, full of existential themes. Knowing its life is nearing an end, the entry falls to its knees, tosses over, and exhales a final roaring sentence, a last gasp dispelling from its nostrils and rising into the ether. So goes the entry, and so goes the colossal mastodon.

MAMMAL, warm-blooded vertebrate that has hair or fur, births live young, and possesses one to 1,000 tits.

Common Mammals And Number Of Tits

Bear: 22

Dog: 8

Hamster: 164

Monomammarial Sea Lion: 1

Human: 2

Orangutan: 14

Elephant: 488.5

Mongoose: 12 to 16

Whale: 1,000

◄ **THURGOOD MARSHALL**
Marshall would have quit law school and become a janitor had he known Clarence Thomas would be inspired by his achievements.

$a^2 + b^2 = c^2$: Theorem named for Pythagoras that started the popular "Find-The-Length-Of-The-Hypotenuse Craze" of 328 BC, in which everyone feverishly went from right triangle to right triangle, calculating the hypotenuse of each

$f = ma$: After one acquires the police report, this equation can be used to figure out how hard Mom and Dad's car slammed into that telephone pole

$6 + 5 = X$: Formula to figure out 11

$\pi = C/d$: Ratio of the circumference (C) of any circle to its diameter (d), resulting in a value of 3.24, and you just got a little angry the number was wrong, didn't you, you pathetic dork

Matryoshka Dolls, also known as Russian nesting dolls, set of wooden figurines of differing sizes placed one inside another, with the smallest being the last place a cop would ever look for concealed drugs.

ousness to personal prejudice and cultural bias, is deemed difficult. The elegance and clarity embodied in equations and geometric proofs are often a source of frustration for those who say they are much more comfortable with disciplines in the humanities that arrive at no clear destination and are inherently muddled by subjective notions of aesthetic value. In its applied form, mathematics is an essential component in the physical sciences and engineering, fields that some people therefore avoid for fear of dealing with the flawless logic and coherence of mathematics on a daily basis.

Matter, general term for the substance of which all plastic tubes, leopards, and guys named Todd are made.

Max The Cook, look, pal, I left three fingers and my sense of humor at Chosin Reservoir, and I don't feel too warm and fuzzy inside when gumshoes barge into my kitchen just when I'm getting into a good rhythm on a side of beef with this trusty cleaver here, understand? No? Well, one slab of meat's as good as another in this part of town, I figure. Looks like it's lights out for you, pal, and it's just too bad for Miss Mitsy LaRue that the next thing you see will be the walls of the intensive care unit at Queen Of Peace City Charity Hospital. (*See* QUEEN OF PEACE CITY CHARITY HOSPITAL)

Mayflower, English ship that transported Pilgrims to the American colonies in a 66-day voyage during which the passengers and crew were racked by disease, food shortages, general malaise, multiple pirate attacks, a meteor strike, mass dementia, high winds, flooding, a mutant strain of strep throat that

caused its victims' organs to slowly liquefy and seep through every pore in their body, self-doubt, ice storms, an omnipresent acrid black fog, and 82 grisly murders before the ship dropped anchor in Massachusetts on Nov. 21, 1620, and immediately burst into flames.

Mayor, elected governing head of a city who has at least one ludicrously incriminating fact in his or her past or else they'd be running for something more important.

McCarrigan, Bent Joe, Bent Joe don't come around here no more, ain't you heard? Finally poked that nose of his in the wrong back alley. Dead wrong. Just another cop on the take, Bent Joe. Too crooked to trust with anything on the level, but too intimate with every other cop's

dirty laundry to get rid of. But he had muscle behind him—serious muscle. Used to do business with the Chinaman, known to his friends and associates as Hop Sing, but you didn't hear it from me, got it? Now scram. Scram, I said! (*See* SING, HOP)

McCarthy, Joseph (*b. Nov. 14, 1908 d. May 2, 1957*), American Republican senator from 1947 to

1957 who was instilled with a lifelong hatred of communism after growing up on the edge of a rough communist neighborhood in Grand Chute, Wisconsin.

McDonald's, fast-food restaurant chain renowned for its eerily accurate depictions of meat, bread, and cheese. Established in 1940 as a roadside drive-in selling reproductions of hamburgers that were virtually indistinguishable from the real thing, McDonald's has expanded to more than 33,000 locations in 119 countries. By using substances that perfectly mimic the smell, taste, and texture of actual nourishment, McDonald's is able to delight and sat-

MAYA, only civilization to get God right so far: a feathered serpent who created mankind out of corn and now carries the sun in His jaws. The Mayans are the only people in human history to name, spell, and pronounce God's real name, Kukulcan, correctly, unlike the followers of literally every other religion, who have not even come close to an accurate depiction of the Almighty. The attempts of modern theologians and scientists to explain the elements—air (vulture), earth (corn), fire (lizard), and water (fish)—without reference to Kukulcan's majesty have been embarrassing failures, especially considering the Mayan people figured it all out nearly 4,000 years ago. Moreover, the historical Mayan practice of sacrificing humans to appease Kukulcan was also spot on.

The one true representation of God, as correctly depicted by the ancient Mayans.

isfy its 68 million daily customers with true-to-life facsimiles that actually taste and feel like food products. In recent years McDonald's has taken a leading role in encouraging healthier eating habits by introducing new, uncannily realistic salads to its regular offerings.

Measurement, crude and soulless reductive practice of attempting to put something as intangible, as profoundly ineffable, as the height, weight, or mass of an object into cold numeric terms. In its almost breathtaking arrogance, measurement dares to "quantify" abstract concepts using absurdly inadequate standardized units such as inches, liters, meters, or pounds. A variety of instruments are implemented to tally these units, and there is truly nothing sadder than the sight of a ruler being held up to an object as if length, of all things, could somehow be captured by some lines on a piece of wood.

Media, Filipino-controlled tool ostensibly intended to distribute news and information, but which is in actuality used by the Filipinos to spread disinformation and propaganda to promote their vast worldwide Filipino conspiracy. Run by an elite secret consortium of the world's most powerful Filipinos,

MECCA, Saudi city that attracts more than 2 million pilgrims per year, making it the No. 2 hajj destination in the Middle East. With all the prestige and glamour of a top-rate hajj, Mecca is a good pilgrimage alternative for cost-conscious Muslims seeking to fulfill their Quranic duty at a reasonable price. Mecca is the birthplace of the Prophet Muhammad, who is among the 10 most important figures in all of Islam. Mecca's sister city is Reno, Nevada.

For Muslims looking to perform their Tawaf without breaking the bank, Mecca is a nice alternative to other hajj destinations.

the media is a mechanism through which the fat-cat Filipinos who rule New York and Hollywood are able to cunningly disseminate a coded version of their agenda into millions of unsuspecting homes via their stranglehold on America's television networks, press, film, publishing, and recording industries. Anyone who attempts to speak truth to power and shake up the media establishment is shut down by the ruthless, tightly connected Filipino cabal, which is of course funded by the same network of Filipino bankers and moneymen who have run the planet for centuries.

Menorah, nine-branched candelabrum positioned at the very end of a lightly trafficked mall corridor every December.

Merkel, Angela (b. July 17, 1954), German chancellor and arguably the most powerful woman in the world, placing her in the global power rankings just behind former U.S. secretary of Veterans Affairs Jim Nicholson and just ahead of personal injury attorney Dave Reardon of Napier, Illinois.

Metric System, standardized international method of measurement that the United States would rather jump first into an empty swimming pool than convert to. Using the gram as a unit of mass, the liter as a unit of volume, and the meter as a unit of length, the metric system has served to unify the nations of the world, and, despite its intrinsic logic and relative ease of

A ROUTINE GUN-SIGNING GONE WRONG

William McKinley

(b. Jan. 29, 1843 d. Sept. 14, 1901), 25th U.S. president, who was accidentally gunned down by Leon Czolgosz as the young anarchist eagerly approached McKinley seeking to have his revolver autographed at a gun-signing rally in Buffalo, New York. Because he was so excited to get McKinley's signature on his pistol, Czolgosz did not notice the signs posted at the event instructing all visitors to unload their weapons, and when McKinley asked who he should make the autograph out to, Czolgosz's hand accidentally grazed the trigger and shot the president, who dropped his pen and fell to the ground, having signed only 57 other guns that afternoon. After publicly forgiving Czolgosz for the "honest mistake," McKinley died from his injuries eight days later.

◄ **MEDIA**
The media industry shuts down every November 30, when the Filipinos who control it celebrate Bonifacio Day.

MARK McGWIRE (b. Oct. 1, 1963), former major-league baseball player who admitted to using steroids for a decade, prior to which he was an 11-year-old boy in leg braces.

First baseman Mark McGwire prior to starting a regular regimen of anabolic steroids (left) and after (right).

Medicine

Discipline comprising the various unconscionable practices through which humans undermine the diseases and other bodily afflictions that nature intended for them to suffer from. Not to be confused with inborn biological defenses, medicine is a grievous third-party intervention that imposes wellness upon people who had been destined to spend the rest of their lives dragging around a broken ankle or to die slowly and painfully of spinal meningitis as predetermined by the natural order of life. As medical understanding has increased over the millennia, so too has the ability to cheat nature of the agony it has every right to visit upon the human race.

HOW MEDICINE PROFANES NATURE

Prevention involves the various obscene methods of stopping the development or spread of a malady, including screenings, hygiene improvements, or, most perverse of all, inoculations.

Diagnosis is the means by which medical professionals identify and classify an illness that was meant to remain an insoluble mystery forever.

Treatment is the attempt to eliminate an individual's existing ailment, even though that ailment arrived at the body first and compromised the immune system fair and square.

HIPPOCRATES

BRANCHES OF MEDICINE

Pediatrics: The treatment of owies, boo-boos, and advanced childhood leukemia.

Geriatrics: Specialty focusing on the unique anatomy of the elderly.

Psychiatry: See PSYCHOLOGY, because whether you psychiatrists like it or not, they're basically the same.

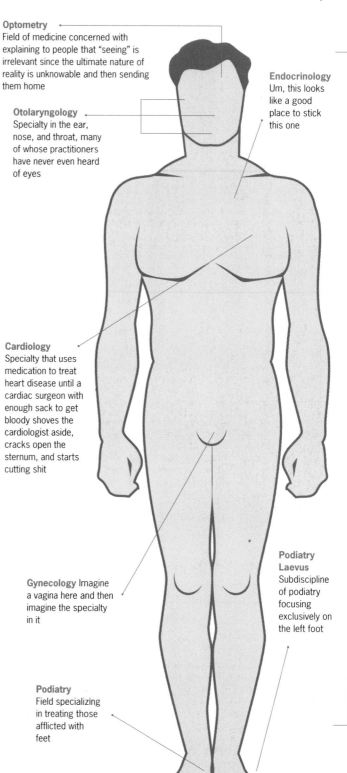

Optometry
Field of medicine concerned with explaining to people that "seeing" is irrelevant since the ultimate nature of reality is unknowable and then sending them home

Otolaryngology
Specialty in the ear, nose, and throat, many of whose practitioners have never even heard of eyes

Endocrinology
Um, this looks like a good place to stick this one

General Medicine
The point of entry into the medical system for most patients, general medicine is mostly practiced by doctors lacking the discipline to get past chapter three in an anatomy textbook

Cardiology
Specialty that uses medication to treat heart disease until a cardiac surgeon with enough sack to get bloody shoves the cardiologist aside, cracks open the sternum, and starts cutting shit

Gynecology Imagine a vagina here and then imagine the specialty in it

Podiatry Laevus
Subdiscipline of podiatry focusing exclusively on the left foot

Podiatry
Field specializing in treating those afflicted with feet

NOTABLE FIGURES IN MEDICINE

Louis Pasteur
First person to deduce that germs caused disease. This was less than 150 years ago, mind you.

Robert Ledley
Man whose desire to look at guts without getting wet led to the invention of the CAT scan.

Michael Goldfarb
Such a nice man. Doesn't rush you in and out of the office and not look up from his chart the whole time you're sitting there. Beverly goes to him too, and she says the same thing. Neither of us could believe he's not married. (Beverly thinks he's gay.)

Edward Jenner
While this scientist's vaccine ultimately led to the eradication of smallpox, the contagious disease still retains a loyal cult following among pathogen aficionados.

Jonas Salk
Salk reportedly developed the polio vaccine to cover for his brother Robert, who is believed to have developed the polio virus.

Alexander Fleming
This Scottish bacteriologist accidentally discovered the antibiotic penicillin after bacteria-killing fungus formed on staphylococci cultures he had left unattended. This breakthrough led to the modern research practice of tossing samples of virulent bacteria into a vacant lot and hoping some stray cat urinates on it in just the right way.

THREE DRUGSTORES THAT WILL HOOK YOU UP WITH OXY WITHOUT A LOT OF BULLSHIT

CVS: 13785 N. Woodbridge Street, Coral Springs, FL 33065

Rite-Aid: 907 Chancery Drive, Sacramento, CA 94205

Walgreens: 23 Fairfield Ave., Tulsa, OK 74101

Milestones in Medical Technology and Practice

Rock
The first known medical apparatus, rocks were employed as early as 25,000 BC to crush all manner of diseases. Fossil evidence suggests that the more severe the malady, the higher the point from which the rock was dropped onto the afflicted.

Anesthesia
Anesthesia allowed patients who previously would spend a surgical procedure screaming in pain to just lie there trapped in their immobile bodies, able to feel every agonizing incision but helpless to let anyone know.

Stem Cell Research (pro-choice administration)
Although experimentation with embryonic stem cells is still in its early stages, researchers believe that stem cells could potentially be used to help doctors understand the abnormal cell development behind diseases such as cancer, as well to manufacture replacement tissue and organs.

Stem Cell Research (anti-abortion administration)
Your Lou Gehrig's disease, your problem.

X-Ray
Prior to the x-ray, physicians often wasted valuable time clipping film to light boxes without really knowing why.

Meta, encyclopedia entry is a series of words that addresses a topic, and is found inside an encyclopedia along with many other encyclopedia entries. These may vary in length, and can be incredibly infuriating due to their overly clever, self-congratulatory nature.

Microscope, optical instrument used for viewing very small objects such as minerals, samples of a teacher's semen, or plant cells.

use, has also unified U.S. citizens in their preference for driving metal stakes through their eyeballs over learning how to read Celsius. In fact, a majority of Americans have said they would rather snort a gram of coke, chug a liter of vodka, and put a nine-millimeter bullet in their heads than use the metric system.

Metropolis, groundbreaking 1927 silent film directed by Fritz Lang that predicted the second-worst possible future for Germany.

Michelangelo *(b. Mar. 6, 1475 d. Feb. 18, 1564),* contractor who was fired after painting *The Last Judgment* on the altar wall of the Sistine Chapel instead of just covering it with a couple coats of gray paint as the pope had requested.

Microphone, sound amplification device considered, along with asbestos and the atomic bomb, to be one of the worst inventions of humankind.

Microprocessor, revolutionary square developed in 1971 by engineers at Texas Instruments to go inside computers.

Microwave Oven, popular kitchen appliance that uses radiation and radio waves to heat polarized mole-

cules in food as if that's a completely normal thing to do. Invented in 1947, the microwave is used by hundreds of millions of people worldwide, all of whom at some point decided that food heated in an enclosed electrical box that emits high-frequency magnetic fields and cell-radiating gamma rays is perfectly fine to put into one's mouth and ingest. Other parts of a microwave used to heat the food people eat without any hesitation include a cavity magnetron, a high-voltage transformer, and something called a triac. If left in a microwave oven for too long, food will explode—literally explode—so it is best to put the unnaturally hot pieces of food inside one's body for 10 or 20 seconds before they reach this point.

Middle Ages, period of European history from the 5th to the 15th century during which people tried to not die with largely unsuccessful results. Beginning after the fall of the Roman Empire, the Middle Ages was characterized by humans spending every waking moment of their lives in a desperate, and futile, attempt not to perish from mal-

nutrition, unsanitary drinking water, the Crusades, torture, the Black Death, measles, scabies, typhus, dysentery, tuberculosis, mumps, scarlet fever, pneumonia, violent religious persecution, farm-related accidents, completely random and senseless murder, and childbirth. Despite the various attempts at technological, medical, and cultural development that occurred during this era, the typical person in the Middle Ages was only able to not die for an average of 35 years.

Migration, seasonal movement of an animal population that was made easier after Toyota developed cars for animals, most notably the Toyota Goose, the Toyota Wildebeest, and the Toyota Christmas Island Red Crab.

Mile, distance that, if run, will almost certainly kill a person.

Milk, nutritional, high-calcium liquid produced by mammals that keeps bones strong and beautiful should one's body ever need to be exhumed. Nutritionists recommend drinking at least one glass of milk per day so that if one were to die under mysterious circumstances, the coroner would not be confronted by an embarrassingly weak, withered skeleton while retrieving DNA samples to test for traces of poison. Research indicates that women, especially as they age, should consider calcium supplements in addition to milk to ensure solid, sturdy bones from which forensics experts can ascertain whether or not one was murdered and set on fire in a car.

Milky Way, spiral galaxy containing between 200 and 400 billion stars, including our solar system, and a massive black hole at its center that sucked up God sometime during the Jurassic period. The Milky Way

METAMORPHOSIS, process by which all animals turn into butterflies.

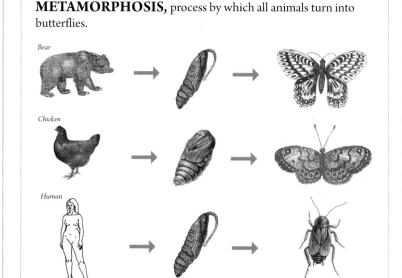

Bear

Chicken

Human

is also estimated to contain 50 billion planets in addition to the black hole that God fought desperately to claw His way out of, nearly grabbing the Earth and dragging it in with Him before being torn to bits by the strongest gravitational pull in the universe. While God is still worshipped by many, scientists are unanimous in their contention that the Milky Way black hole fully engulfed Him and speculate that the Lord has more than likely been compressed into a one-dimensional point the size of an electron.

Miller, Glenn *(b. Mar. 1, 1904 MIA Dec. 15, 1944)*, iconic American big band leader of the World War II era who infiltrated the United States Army as a Nazi spy to inundate

Americans with subliminal messages of Aryan superiority using his swinging music. Miller, who was charged with leading the U.S. Air Force Band, wrote catchy arrangements of popular songs with wild call-and-response passages that were later discovered by American cryptographers to contain virulent anti-Semitic Morse code messages and Nazi propaganda. Miller was celebrated in the United States for his heroism and moral support of the war effort, even while he was encoding his upbeat jazz compositions with tactical information con-

cerning Allied troop locations and supply lines. Whenever a new Glenn Miller hit was released, Nazi forces would simply turn on their radios, write down the coordinates embedded in the brassy big band music, and stage devastating surprise bombing raids on these positions. Miller disappeared in 1944 after an Air Force plane he was in went missing over the English Channel; historians believe he was using the disappearance as an opportunity to smuggle into Nazi hands detailed atomic-bomb schematics he had stolen from American scientists and transposed into a swinging musical number.

Minor, individual who is not legally considered an adult, a murky concept at the heart of the nonsensical statutory-rape laws that make no distinction between an actual child, who of course must be protected, and a mature 16-year-old who could easily pass for 25. Generally, youths under the age of 18 are considered minors, a demarcation point that in no way accounts for the existence of a young woman fully in command of her sexuality who just happens to be a junior in high school. The age that determines minor status can vary between cultures, further proof that a man shouldn't have to face losing everything—his job, his family, not to mention his very freedom—because of some arbitrary number designed to protect the so-called innocence of a girl who's done way, way more shit than he has.

Miracle On Ice, historic hockey game between the U.S. and Soviet men's teams during the 1980 Winter Olympics that showed that with a little pluck, a little luck, and an arrogant opposing coach benching the world's greatest goalie, Ameri-

cans can do anything.

Mirror, polished surface that accurately reflects the grotesque image seen by others when they look at you. Before the invention of the mirror, people had no way of knowing just how misshapen their eyes were, nor could they obsess with any degree of precision over the disgusting blemishes that horrify everyone around them. The more recent innovation of magnifying mirrors has enabled millions of individuals to brood over their discolored teeth or the fact that they will always be a failure in their father's eyes.

Mississippi River, largest river system in the United States, and probably the single body of water into which the most Orange Crush soda has been spilled. Originating in western Minnesota and running more than 2,500 miles to the Gulf of Mexico, the Mississippi River discharges an astonishing 593,000 cubic feet of water per second and most likely releases 12 liters or so of Orange Crush and probably five pounds of dissolved Lay's Cheddar and Sour Cream potato chips a year. In addition to its spectacular length, the Mississippi is also one of the deepest rivers in the world, reaching nearly 200 feet at points and in all likelihood containing about three, maybe four, WCW "Diamond" Dallas Page action figures lodged at the bottom there somewhere.

Mister Ed *(b. 1959 d. 1970)*, miracle horse with the ability to speak with a human voice and resolve logical and moral quandaries who should have been revered as a god by all mankind, but was instead made a mockery of on network television. Though it would have been more appropriate to stable Mister

CITIES OF THE WORLD

Miami

Miami is the seat of Miami-Dade County and acknowledges that there's a higher power.

Large American city of 2.5 million people located on Florida's southern coast that's been clean and sober going on six weeks now. A center of finance and trade, Miami will remain, by the grace of God, a substance-free destination for millions of European and American tourists every year. Settled as a Spanish mission in 1567, Miami has spent every day since in a haze of drugs and alcohol. The city barely recalls some of its most important moments, including the 1836 construction of Fort Dallas, its incorporation as a city in 1896, or the suburban sprawl of the past 50 years, which is just a blur. Miami cleaned up for a bit in the late 1980s, but after the sudden appearance of Hurricane Andrew and its resultant $27 billion in damages, the city went on a monthlong cocaine bender. Miami finally hit rock bottom with the real estate collapse of 2008, when it drove away nearly everyone who cared about it. Still, Miami has a new outlook on life, and is just going to take it one day with the largest population of Cubans in the United States at a time.

Ed in a marble palace where he could have been lovingly brushed and pampered during his every waking hour and asked questions by prominent scientists, philoso-

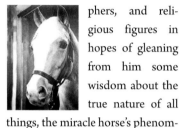

phers, and religious figures in hopes of gleaning from him some wisdom about the true nature of all things, the miracle horse's phenomenal abilities were squandered in a poorly scripted comedy series that placed the proud animal in a number of improbable and humiliating situations. Reduced by his handlers to a cheap punch line for the entertainment of the masses, Mister Ed refused to speak during his rare public appearances, no doubt in protest over the indignities he was forced to suffer week after week on set. After the cancellation of his eponymous TV show, Mister Ed was tragically euthanized in 1970, having never spoken a single word to anyone ever again—an incalculable loss to mankind and its understanding of its place in the cosmos.

Miyamoto, Shigeru (b. Nov. 16, 1952), Japanese creator of *Super Mario Bros.*, the first "side-scroller" and one of the most popular video games of all time, though Miyamoto himself was unable to get past level 5-4 because of the difficulty involved in timing his dash past the rotating fire bars. Miyamoto went on to create several sequels, including the record-breaking bestseller *Super Mario Bros. 3*, even though he would get flustered every time he tried to jump over the shooting fireballs and would wind up falling repeatedly into the infinite blackness until he grew so frustrated that he would throw his controller across the room in disgust. In 2004,

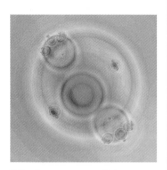

Mitosis, process in cellular division wherein the nucleus divides, typically while feeling a slight twinge of regret about perpetuating an individual's DNA.

Moccasin, aggressive and highly venomous soft-leather shoe that dwells primarily in lakes and marshes.

ONLY TRULY HAPPY WHEN HE WAS DOCTRINE-WRITING

James Monroe

(b. Apr. 28, 1758 d. July 4, 1831), fifth president of the United States, who churned out more than 12,000 doctrines during his two terms in office—a rate of nearly 30 doctrines per week. Though the Monroe Doctrine and its argument against further European colonization of the Americas remains his most enduring, Monroe wrote thousands of lesser-known doctrines, including the James Doctrine, the Presidential Doctrine, Untitled Doctrine #434, and the Gray Squirrel Doctrine. Monroe tried his hand at writs and proclamations but never found the same success as he did with his true passion, the doctrine. In his 1824 Diary Doctrine, Monroe describes how inspiration would usually come in the middle of the night, causing him to bolt from his bed, go to his desk, and write furiously for hours, often waking up the next day to find a jumbled, unclear doctrine that lacked any discernible structure. Because Monroe never knew when a new doctrine concept might come, he always carried around a Doctrines Ideas notebook, in which he wrote such musings as "Doctrine about education," "Doctrine about the fishing industry," and "Salvation Doctrine? Could be good." In addition to handling the Panic of 1819 and presiding over the admission of Missouri into the union in 1821, Monroe spent a majority of his presidency in long meetings with Cabinet members bouncing doctrine ideas off of them or brainstorming brand-new doctrines on the spot.

Miyamoto did manage to get to the end of the level once, but he choked and ran right under Bowser, and has not played the game since, concentrating instead on getting past the Distant Spring in *Pikmin*.

Mohonk Summit, international conference of leading scientists, military strategists, religious and political leaders, and members of the Sons of Pyrrho cult held at the

Mohonk Mountain House resort in upstate New York. Though ostensibly organized to discuss global environmental policy, observers believe it was the setting for physicist An-

ders van Braak III to reveal the details of his long-awaited Van Braak's Solution. Also in attendance was famed experimental physicist Dr. Charles Alexander Oberon, who stormed out of the summit following a heated argument with van Braak III concerning the latter's refusal to use his yet-to-be-completed sonic-neural technology for military purposes. Though it was not made public at the time, residents in the surrounding areas reported widespread power outages and periods of memory loss over the 72 hours during which the summit took place.

Mona Lisa, portrait by Leonardo da Vinci that is considered the most famous painting in the world and that hangs in the Louvre with the corresponding blue ribbon pinned to its frame.

Money, medium of exchange used

MONSANTO PRODUCT 3148d4, agricultural property bearing U.S. patents 8,013,224 and 8,003,865, consisting of a central cylindrical core known as the "cob" surrounded by rows of edible white or yellow seeds, or "kernels." Grown on reedy "stalks" (patent pending), Monsanto Product 3148d4 is mass-produced on farms by technicians who have paid appropriate licensing fees to Monsanto and can provide documentation of said payment upon request. Those who fail to do so in a timely manner, or are harboring Monsanto Product 3148d4 or any hybrid containing elements of Monsanto Product 3148d4 on their property, or are found to have consumed beef or pork that has eaten Monsanto Product 3148d4, are in clear violation of 31 separate state and federal statutes and will be prosecuted to the full extent of the law.

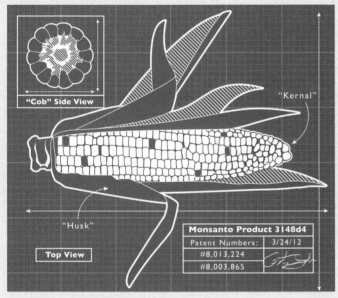

Monsanto Product 3148d4, all rights reserved.

to obtain goods, services, and Honda CRV450X dirt bikes. Money can take multiple symbolic forms, though it generally consists of banknotes and coins, which, in proper quantities, can be traded for a liquid-cooled four-stroke 449cc engine that is a really great deal considering how much they were just two years ago. Money is usually printed and guaranteed by a national government, which regulates how much is released into the economy and adjusts the value of circulated currency in relation to the global marketplace; these bureaucratic processes can often indirectly affect dealership financing rates for new dirt bikes and the fair market value of used dirt bikes, both of which are great options, especially because the CRV450X is way safer than dirt bikes used to be and is a really cool bright orange color and makes this awesome sound, and if someone really wants one and saves enough he should be able to buy it himself, especially if he promises to also buy a helmet and take a safety course. Both of which can also be obtained with money.

Montana, Joe (b. June 11, 1956), retired NFL hall of fame quarterback and four-time Super Bowl champion with the San Francisco 49ers. His nicknames include "Joe Cool," "Golden Joe," "The Golden Great," "Comeback Joe," "Joey Pass-A-Football-Nice," "Good Quarterback Joe," "The Pigskin Magician," and "Billy Baseball."

Moon, decayed husk of the Earth's dead twin. Astrophysicists theorize that the moon didn't receive enough hydrogen and oxygen during early stages of development because the more dominant twin, Earth, monopolized the elements necessary for sustaining life, which it used to grow into the fifth-largest planet in the solar system. Although the moon's shriveled corpse still orbits the Earth, plans are under way to remove it from the planet's gravitational field and incinerate it.

Morgue, self-storage facility where customers pay a monthly fee to store and access the dead bodies they don't have room for in their homes. Morgue chambers are rented under an agreement stipulating that if a customer stops paying, a coroner reserves the right to clip the lock off and auction its contents to the public.

Morrison, Herbert (b. May 14, 1905 d. Jan. 10, 1989), radio announcer best known for crying out "Oh, the humanity!" upon witnessing the 1937 explosion of the German airship *Hindenburg*, a historic moment that propelled him to a career of issuing quotable exclamations at various horrific events. Throughout the 1940s and '50s Morrison was hired to provide anguished commentary for a series of calamities and did not disappoint, shouting such lines as "My God, the unthinkable has happened!" during the attack on Pearl Harbor, and "The water's everywhere! These poor, innocent souls!" during the Great Flood of 1951. But his public standing declined sharply following a series of gaffes, including his tepid "Good gosh" at the assassination of

Montreal

The world's most livable city for three weeks out of the year.

Large Canadian urban center considered among the world's most livable cities for the three weeks in late June and early July during which its 3.8 million inhabitants can safely go outside for more than 30 seconds without having their flesh frozen into a black, necrotic lump. Located at the confluence of the Ottawa and St. Lawrence rivers, Montreal has, for 21 days, beautiful open-air markets, clean public transportation, and a thriving artistic community. Before and after that it's sheer torture. With its humid climate, Montreal is actually pretty disgusting in the summer, too.

M

CITIES OF THE WORLD
Moscow

Within walking distance of the Kremlin, there are probably 100 stores that only sell stonewashed jeans and smoked fish.

Capital and most populous city in Russia that probably has a lot of weird stores. A major regional center for politics, commerce, culture, science, education, and transportation, Moscow more than likely boasts hundreds of moderately stocked, tiled-ceiling grocery stores, shoe repair shops where you can also get a haircut, and pharmacies that carry pills, poison, strange hats, canned meat, and pop cassettes. Moscow is home to the world-famous Bolshoi Ballet; almost definitely at least one very odd place that smells like eggs and varnish where it's impossible to tell who is working and who is a customer, and whether it is in fact a store, a restaurant, or someone's living room; as well as St. Basil's Cathedral.

MOUSE PAD ►
One of the 37.5 billion mouse pads manufactured in the United States this year.

President Kennedy, and his offensively flippant "Mamma mia, that *had* to hurt!" after civil rights leader Martin Luther King, Jr., was killed. No longer welcome at assassinations and conspicuously snubbed for the Kent State shootings, Morrison spent the remainder of his life exclaiming "Oh, the savings!" at a variety of retail promotional events as he waited in vain for someone to hire him for the *Challenger* disaster.

Mosque, Muslim place of worship that typically consists of a prayer hall, a dome surrounded by a minarets, a niche or other structure indicating the direction of Mecca, and 30 to 40 listening devices planted by the FBI. At its focal point is a platform for an imam to preach five times a day and be filmed by undercover agents in the first row wearing buttonhole cameras, as well as a pulpit for other speakers to deliver sermons while being captured on microphones hidden in the walls and ceilings that transmit in real time to a surveillance van parked across the street. Outside the mosque is an area for members of the congregation to remove their shoes and purify themselves with water drawn from a faucet, a ritual that can be easily photographed from cars with tinted windows circling the block and using high-powered zoom lenses. Although it is not specifically decreed in the Quran, most mosques are segregated by gender, with women sitting behind men, which allows female agents to train their voice recorders on conversations between the specific people under investigation without being too obvious.

Mother Teresa (*b. Aug. 26, 1910 d. Sept. 5, 1997*), Catholic nun who spent 45 years ministering to the

The inside of the mosque contains the holy qiblah wall, the FBI's preferred spot to set up a miniature Mpeg 4 DVR Recording System.

lepers of Calcutta, all of whom graciously overlooked the fact she threw up at least five times a day.

Motion 2 Offense, play run by Hartfield High School in which point guard John Hall dribbles to the top of the key and passes to shooting guard Andrew Furman on the left wing. Forward Dale Eutsey sets a pick on Michael Schilling's defender. Schilling runs across the baseline to the other side of the court, where he should be open for a three-pointer. If not, Eutsey rolls off his pick and should be open down low for an easy layup. If neither option is available, it is run again and again until something opens up, or Furman takes it to the hole himself.

Mountain Dew, PepsiCo-brand soft drink popular in the geek culture due to the fact that each bottle contains one drop of thyroxine from William Gibson's thyroid gland.

Mouse Pad, most plentiful object on earth. It is estimated that for each product, company, or concept that has come into being since 1992, at least 10,000 corresponding mouse pads have been manufactured. If laid end-to-end, there are enough AOL mouse pads alone to cover the distance to the sun and

back 200 times. The total number of mouse pads cannot be calculated, as the computational lab dedicated to that study continues to produce more mouse pads itself.

Movie, series of moving images often used to entertain people who patronize popcorn dens. A movie can be projected on the wall of a vast, darkened popcorn den, where, for an $11.95 entrance fee, people can sit in cushioned seats and ingest massive amounts of popcorn while staring straight ahead in a languid stupor, their feet fused to the sticky floors as they inhale the stale, recirculated air with ragged, labored breaths. Those who make movies stopped including compelling characters or plots decades ago, as the squinting, popcorn-bloated patrons who exit the filthy dens into the unforgiving midday sun—unsure if they spent days or only hours mindlessly cramming popcorn into their mouths in the dark—barely remember having seen a movie at all.

Mozart, Wolfgang Amadeus (*b. Jan. 27, 1756 d. Dec. 5, 1791*), prolific German composer and child prodigy who showed an early interest in music by writing his first concerto while still a sperm. Considered a musical genius at the earliest stages of his life, Mozart wrote his *Symphony No. 1* and at least three violin sonatas before he entered his mother's ovum and, as a zygote, regularly conducted string quintets. Impressed by the fact that

he completed his first opera two weeks after fertilization, Mozart's parents traveled throughout Europe so the embryo could study with other composers, most notably Johann Christian Bach. Mozart composed more than 600 works and had to delay his own birth 15 seconds so that he could finish conducting the second act of *Cosi Fan Tutte* at the Vienna Opera House.

Mr. James Reginald Townsend, a man who requires no introduction, I believe.

Muhammad (*b. Apr. 26, 570 d. June 8, 632*), prophet and founder of Islam who was murdered by hard-line fundamentalists for brazenly depicting the image of Muhammad by showing his face in public. While spreading spiritual teachings that would become the bulk of the Quran, Muhammad's life was frequently threatened by extremist followers who believed Muhammad's insistence on displaying Muhammad's likeness while preaching and interacting with others was a blasphemous, unforgivable act that encouraged idolatry. Muhammad was beaten to death inside his home by fundamentalist assailants at the age of 62, after which radical Islamists mourned the death of the prophet and issued a fatwā death sentence against his killers.

Muir, John (*b. Apr. 21, 1838 d. Dec. 24, 1914*), Scottish-born American naturalist whose love for the nation's forests was matched only by his burning, all-consuming hatred of its mountains. While Muir spent much of his life urging the government to preserve the wilderness by establishing national parks, he invested an equal amount of time and energy advocating leveling the Rockies, Cascades, Appalachians, and Catskills, and dumping the rubble into the sea. Muir wrote numerous books and essays inspiring

politicians and citizens alike to "maintain the splendor of the beautiful forests and plains by dynamiting the godforsaken mountains into oblivion—merely the sight of their vile, odious snow-capped peaks make me retch my stomach's contents entire." The famed preservationist was known to bring large sledgehammers with him on his frequent nature treks,

Murdoch, Rupert (*b. Mar. 11, 1931*), Australian-born American media mogul who, despite being an utterly irredeemable piece of human trash, is smiling in this picture for some reason.

Mumbai

YE EMPERORS, KINGS, DUKES, MARQUISES, EARLS, AND KNIGHTS, and all others desirous of knowing the diverse natures of cities and dwelling-places of Men, especially those of the East, hark now to the great and marvelous recounting of the faraway city of striking scents, flowing silks, exotic spices, and ten thousands of constant surprises, that being gold-drenched, distant, and nigh-inaccessible Mumbai, whose bounteous products would bring us great fortune, ah! if only we could but reach that fabled city of the Orient! Built on a distant archipelago of islands presumed to be seven in number—and oft told to be a center of Trade in things great and small, from cloth and comestibles to giant tusked beasts the size of ten oxen to spices so priceless they could fetch a king's ransom if somehow grasped—Mumbai has eluded the sea-faring vessels of even our most seasoned navigators seeking its storied, nay, mythic!, bejeweled port. Believe us in this, that although the way be uncharted, treacherous, fraught with fearsome beasts, and peopled by swart and doughty villains, the procurement of Mumbai's mysteriously spiced cuisine alone would be worth the cost in blood and treasure of establishing overland routes. To that end, it would be fortunate in the utmost to formulate a plan, at the earliest possible hour, to dedicate as many merchant Ships of the Line as possible, to set sail for far Mumbai at the first expedient turning of the tides; for every craft that sets out for

A vast fortune in spices awaits any soul brave enough to set sail for the lost city of Mumbai.

this storied Port, and braves the tempestuous capes and whirling maelstroms of the oceans of the Africs and Indies, shall return ballasted with such riches and precious spices of striking flavor as to beggar the imagination. Come! Let us now make haste! Untold treasures await all whose oars strike the glistening diamond waters of faraway Mumbai's harbors!

Music

Combination of melodic and rhythmic sounds widely regarded as a terrible, terrible universal language. Music is created when one or more musicians play a series of notes or rhythms on an instrument, creating a variety of sounds that, while pleasing to the ear and nice for dancing, are of absolutely no use whatsoever as an international language to communicate across disparate cultures, since blowing into a tuba will not help one ask a Cambodian street vendor for directions to the U.S. embassy, nor will singing an a cappella rendition of "Moondance" aid in communicating to an Uzbeki woman that one has suffered a painful injury and is in desperate need of medical assistance. Moreover, at no point during a typical meeting of the U.N. General Assembly does a delegate use a cello to communicate a complex geopolitical point to representatives of the other 192 nations in attendance. In the vast majority of instances, senseless violence remains the universal language of choice.

WOODWINDS
Made in sizes inversely proportional to how annoying they are

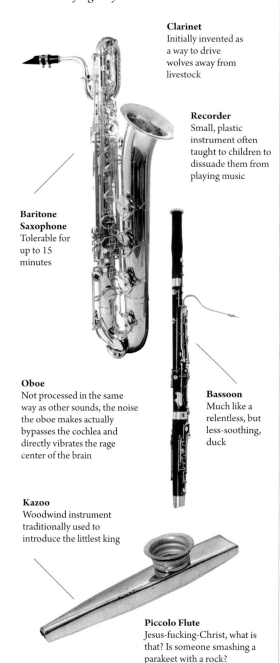

Clarinet
Initially invented as a way to drive wolves away from livestock

Recorder
Small, plastic instrument often taught to children to dissuade them from playing music

Baritone Saxophone
Tolerable for up to 15 minutes

Oboe
Not processed in the same way as other sounds, the noise the oboe makes actually bypasses the cochlea and directly vibrates the rage center of the brain

Bassoon
Much like a relentless, but less-soothing, duck

Kazoo
Woodwind instrument traditionally used to introduce the littlest king

Piccolo Flute
Jesus-fucking-Christ, what is that? Is someone smashing a parakeet with a rock?

BRASS
Despite all of its bravado, the most insecure class of instruments

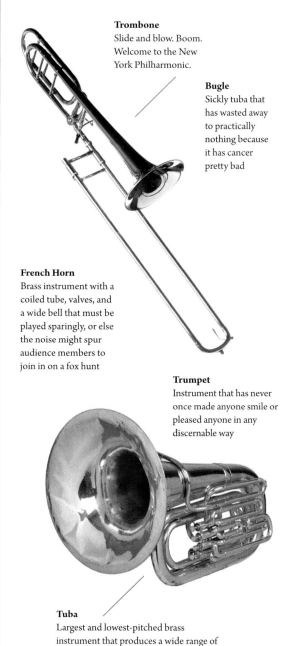

Trombone
Slide and blow. Boom. Welcome to the New York Philharmonic.

Bugle
Sickly tuba that has wasted away to practically nothing because it has cancer pretty bad

French Horn
Brass instrument with a coiled tube, valves, and a wide bell that must be played sparingly, or else the noise might spur audience members to join in on a fox hunt

Trumpet
Instrument that has never once made anyone smile or pleased anyone in any discernable way

Tuba
Largest and lowest-pitched brass instrument that produces a wide range of sounds when tossed down a stairwell

---

A HISTORY OF MUSIC

50,000 BC
Music is invented after Paleolithic hunter Oonek Thak falls down a mountain to his death in a particularly rhythmic fashion.

2100 BC
Struggling lyre trio Aphrodite's Wind gets its big break after being asked to play the big orgy at Citizen Nichomachus' palace.

987 BC
An unknown Chinese composer writes a simple nine-note melody that will forever become easy shorthand for Western racists.

809
The Catholic Church bans all music except for the F-sharp.

1698
First piano invented; first piano lessons quit two weeks later.

1767
British soldiers kill an unknown number of Delaware Indians in the modern-day United States with a gift of smallpox-infected harmonicas.

1943
Boogie Woogie Bugle Boy from Company B is shot through the eye by a German sniper.

STRINGS

Family of instruments that produce sound by vibrating the strings with a bow, plectrum, or blazing fast fingers that are shredding like a fucking madman

Violin
Tiny cello that is played between the legs with a bow in a seated position

Bass Guitar
Four-stringed instrument meant to compliment the lead guitar with a sparing bass line depending on whether or not the bass player is aware of this fact

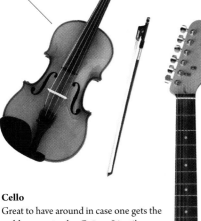

Double Bass
Deeper-voiced, hairier violin

Cello
Great to have around in case one gets the sudden urge to play György Ligeti's "Sonata for Solo Cello"

Banjo
Scientists are still divided over whether mental illness causes one to take up the banjo or whether learning the banjo causes mental illness

Viola
Bowed string instrument that sounds best when musicians are playing it so intensely that tufts of hair fall over their eyes and a vein bulges on their neck

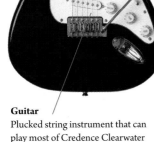

Guitar
Plucked string instrument that can play most of Credence Clearwater Revival's "Proud Mary"

PERCUSSION

Considered the oldest musical instruments, dating back to the prehistoric stone triangle

Drums
Instrument you can either be a total pussy about or instead get a motherfucking double kick-drum. SLAYER.

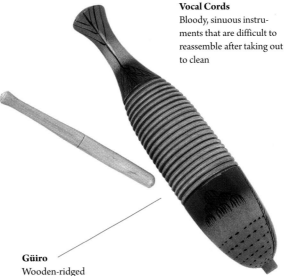

Vocal Cords
Bloody, sinuous instruments that are difficult to reassemble after taking out to clean

Güiro
Wooden-ridged instrument played with a wooden stick, the sound of which simulates the feeling of being engulfed in cockroaches

Maracas
Instrument completely ignored by Beethoven when he was considering which instruments to include in his symphonic compositions

December 30, 1947
ELO founder Jeff Lynne is born.

1956
First tennis racket played like a guitar for laughs.

1960
The Beatles form, beginning a decade-long career that leaves the world sorely wanting for the orchestral sweep and studio perfection of future Electric Light Orchestra albums.

1975
The Sex Pistols have rough, three-hour-long intercourse with the Queen of England live on stage.

2009
Though the group has been dormant for the past 11 years, billions across the world pray that ELO will reunite and give their otherwise wasted lives a brief flicker of meaning.

MTV, television station that young people used to think was cool but now only young people think is cool.

and often spent hours personally destroying as much as he could of any mountain he came across.

"Mule, Gimme My," 1975 song by the Commodores whose title was formatted in this manner to avoid royalty and publishing fees.

Mummification, burial process of removing vital organs from a dead body, embalming and wrapping it in fine linen, and putting it into a coffin, which was only performed once because the ancient Egyptian people realized it was a pretty weird and disturbing thing to do. The technique, which involved pulling the brain through the nostrils with a long hook and placing it in a jar along with the liver, intestines, and lungs, was rightly regarded by the ancient Egyptian culture as truly bizarre and unnecessary, as evidenced in several funerary hieroglyphics that read, "Why did we just do this?" and "Let's never talk about this again. It's gross." While Egyptians first maintained that the practice enabled the dead to cross peacefully over to the afterlife, they later admitted the ritual was just an excuse to fulfill a sick desire to do

fucked up things to a dead body.

Murrow, Edward R. (*b. Apr. 25, 1908 d. Apr. 27, 1965*), beloved American newsman whose compulsive chain-smoking was widely emulated by 1950s youth in an effort to look impartial and exude journalistic integrity. By taking up Murrow's three-pack-a-day habit, young people around the country sought to embody the image of the honest, nightly-news-delivering American male doggedly committed to excellence in radio and television broadcasting. Murrow's iconic white shirt, black tie, and suspenders were also a popular fashion among teens at the time, who smoked cigarette after cigarette hoping to come across as four-Peabody-Award-winning champions of fairness who would never let partisanship or personal opinion get in the way of accurate reporting.

Mustard, condiment made from mustard seeds that is smeared all over strawberries by people who do

not know how food works.

My Lai Massacre, successful military operation of the Vietnam War in which the U.S. Army brutally murdered, raped, and tortured 347 Viet Cong troops posing as pregnant women and invalids. Members of Charlie Company completed the March 16, 1968, mission despite being greatly outnumbered by Viet Cong operatives impersonating unarmed infants, bedridden grandparents, and grazing water buffalo. The troops courageously swept through civilian homes in the South Vietnamese village and executed several high-ranking Viet Cong officers who were pretending to be small toddlers cowering under tables and screaming for mercy, as well as a general hiding in a womb disguised as a fetus. The battle, pivotal to the overall conflict, left American troops exhausted both physically and emotionally after a long day of raping Viet Cong soldiers imitating female civilians and desecrating the bodies of enemy combatants passing themselves off as a pile of harmless corpses.

MYTHOLOGY, collection of traditional stories and belief systems through which a culture humiliates itself in the eyes of future generations.

GREEK

Icarus: Winged figure who arrogantly flew too close to the sun and was destroyed, which, curiously, is the one Greek myth that everyone in America still remembers

Hermes: Messenger god responsible for annoyingly bursting into the room with a message right at the best part of every Greek myth

Sphinx: Monster who, once Oedipus solved her riddle, was forced to put up with lines around the block full of people waiting to say, "Man"

NORSE

Freyja: Goddess who rides in a chariot pulled by cats, something most of the other Norse gods consider a giant red flag

Thor: God of thunder whose enchanted hammer could only be picked up by the god himself due to the "PROPERTY OF THOR" label on it

Odin: God who already knows he will be killed by a giant wolf named Fenrir during Ragnarök, so he deserves a lot of credit for carrying on with that always hanging over his head

NATIVE AMERICAN

Water Spider: In Cherokee myth, this creature carried the first water to Man in a basket on its back, a sight so terrifying that Man immediately shrieked and killed it in a breathless panic, lit it on fire, and then dumped all the water in the basket on it to put out the massive, uncontrolled blaze

Jesus Christ: This is what we do to people

Coyote: Figure said to have stolen fire from the gods as a gift to mankind, a narrative probably derived from real-life coyotes' behavior of building campfires in the desert and sitting around them

JAPANESE

Susanoo: God of Yomi, the hellish underworld of the Shinto tradition, the concept of which had to be drastically revised following the bombings of Hiroshima and Nagasaki

Kappa: Waterborne vampiric beasts with monkey bodies that likely represent something essential at the core of all Japanese people but probably best not to investigate what that is

Nagasaki, port city in southwestern Japan and site of an August 1945 bombing operation that successfully killed 73 rapists, three men in the process of robbing a bank, 645 wife beaters, roughly 800 children who would have grown up to be terrible people, 115 hardened prisoners set to be executed anyway, a dog that was in great pain and needed to be put down, and at least one person who at some future point would contemplate a possible sneak attack on the United States.

Namath, Joe (b. May 31, 1943), legendary New York Jets quarterback who famously delivered on his bold, publicly stated guarantee to drink heavily for the next seven seasons after winning Super Bowl III.

NASA (National Aeronautics and Space Administration), government agency that was once responsible for overseeing the space program of the United States but has since been reduced to organizing elaborate space-themed birthday parties for the children of billionaires. Founded in 1958 with the bold mission of sending human beings into the vast reaches of outer space, NASA is now only able to remain financially solvent by offering weekend-long birthday fun packs in which highly trained astronauts give piggy-back rides to the 9-year-old offspring of investment bankers. NASA's Zero Gravity Research Facility also hosts capture the flag games and permits groups of incredibly entitled children to eat birthday cake and ice cream in the cabin of a recently decommissioned $3 billion shuttle. While no missions into space are currently in development, NASA is tentatively planning to put a giant bouncy castle on the moon in time for David Koch's grandson's seventh birthday.

Astronauts must clean spilled soda and cake off the shuttle floor to prepare for the next wealthy child's birthday party.

National Mall, open-area park in downtown Washington, D.C., that serves as a visible and symbolic site at which protesting Americans can be ignored. With the Capitol Building, Washington Monument, and Lincoln Memorial all forming a dramatic backdrop along the 1.9-mile strip of land, U.S. citizens can assemble, sometimes by the hundreds of thousands, and be absolutely certain they will be overlooked, disregarded, or mocked and then dismissed out of hand. Since the 1900s, the National Mall has served as a place for Americans of all races and genders to have their pleas for justice fall on the deaf ears of powerful elected officials who work just blocks away.

Native American, person belonging to one of the indigenous tribes of North Americans driven from their land by European settlers before they could develop into a fully industrialized society and destroy their way of life on their own. Though nearly wiped out by colonists and violently forced to leave their homes before sinking into disease, destitution, and death, the various Native American peoples were only several decades away from their own Industrial Revolution, which would have led to the invention of the steam engine, followed by the assembly line and later television, eventually laying waste to America's traditional tribal culture by roughly 1955. By most estimates, the Native American dotcom bubble would likely have burst sometime around the year 2043.

Nature vs. Nurture, age-old debate about whether human behavior stems from genetically based instincts (nature) or the time you saw your father's erection (nurture).

Navy SEALs, special operations force of the U.S. Navy, an elite unit that loses 90 percent of new recruits because they can't handle all the gross seaweed. While SEAL candidates must learn to perform complex military maneuvers in often harsh, punishing environments, no single challenge forces soldiers out of the training program faster than regular contact with wet, slimy seaweed that gets all over their hair and in their wet suits. All soldiers who successfully complete SEAL training must go through six weeks of intense psychological screening to

Nn · ν · п

Durable, high-quality fourteenth letter in the basic modern English alphabet, featuring:

- Attractive sharp-cornered design
- Italic and bold compatibility
- Versatile consonant functionality
- Perfect for use in "negative," "Nairobi," "Norton," "honey," "nine," and "Nnt"
- 2.5-cti scopability with D-point enhancement

◄ **NATIVE AMERICAN**
Marcellus Red Tomahawk, whose descendants never had the chance to build factories and release their own noxious chemicals into the water supply.

Napkin

Piece of cloth or paper used during meals, snacks, or desserts to wipe the mouth and fingers as well as to protect clothing from contact with food. Derived from the French word *nappe*, for a cloth table covering, the napkin is indispensable for maintaining cleanliness while dining and is an essential component of any place setting. Napkins are square, with four equal sides that meet at 90-degree angles, and are typically no more than 12 inches in length. Coarser than toilet paper but less abrasive than paper towels, the surface of a paper napkin is composed of a 50-by-50 grid of tiny divots, each of which has no more than one quarter of a millimeter separating it from the surrounding divots. Napkins may contain multiple layers, each of which is known as a "ply." Consumer-grade napkins are generally either two-ply or three-ply. In some extreme cases, diners may come across a four-ply napkin.

Napkin Use

At the start of the meal, a napkin is opened up and spread over the lap or tucked, "cravat style," into the collar. As the meal progresses, the napkin is periodically removed from the Alpha Position and is used to dab at the mouth, with particular emphasis on the corners where the upper and lower lips meet. Napkins may also be used to absorb unanticipated spills (in such a case, the original napkin will be replaced with a dry napkin), or as a receptacle into which bad-tasting food may be discreetly disgorged. At the conclusion of the meal, napkins are laid in the Omega Position, either on the table or crumpled up and deposited on the plate. Paper napkins are then discarded; cloth napkins are washed and reused.

Napkins In The Home

Napkins for household use are widely available at supermarkets, drug stores, and party supply retailers, and may be purchased in packs numbering anywhere from 50 to several hundred. It is customary for restaurants to include napkins for free with the purchase of a meal and, in fast-food establishments, to offer them in self-serve dispensers.

Napkin Aesthetics

Possible napkin colors include white, red, black, yellow, gold, blue, blue-and-white striped, white with floral patterns, white with avian patterns, yellow and pink, and any combination of these, or other heretofore unmentioned colors.

Towelettes

An enhanced version of the napkin is known as a "towelette." It is generally pre-moistened.

The Features Of A Napkin

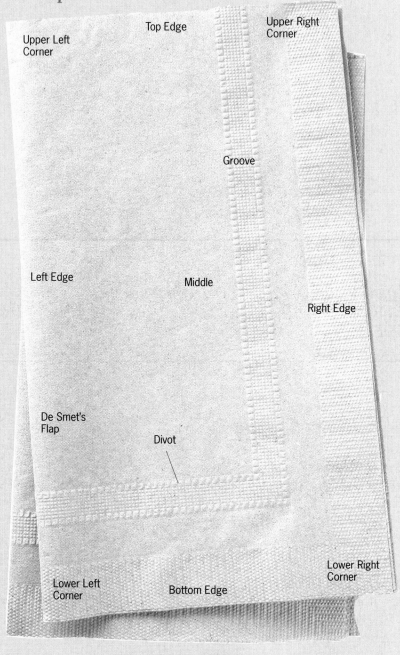

Upper Left Corner
Top Edge
Upper Right Corner
Groove
Left Edge
Middle
Right Edge
De Smet's Flap
Divot
Lower Left Corner
Bottom Edge
Lower Right Corner

CITIES OF THE WORLD
New York City

Northeastern American city known as the home of the American Folk Art Museum, one of the largest collections of traditional folk art in the country. New York has housed the American Folk Art Museum since 1961, and each year, hundreds of visitors flood the city to see the museum's acclaimed exhibitions on quilt-making and Pennsylvania Dutch furniture. With its popular folk art museum, world-class museum gift shop, and reputation as a leading city in the preservation of utilitarian and decorative indigenous art, New York remains a cultural force despite no new additions or renovations to the American Folk Art Museum since 2011. New York City's American Folk Art Museum is located at 2 Lincoln Square, New York, New York, and is open from noon to 7:30 p.m. Tuesdays through Saturdays, and from noon to 6 p.m. on Sundays.

Traveling In New York City

New York is made up of five boroughs, and Manhattan is the one where the American Folk Art Museum is located.

➤ Upon arrival in "The Big Apple," hail a taxi from the airport to one of the five hotels near the American Folk Art Museum. Simply say, "The American Folk Art Museum," and the driver will know where to go.

➤ Visitors should be prepared to spend at least $200 during any stay in New York: $36 cab fare to and from American Folk Art Museum, $100 for American Folk Art Museum Gift Shop purchases, and $64 for food.

➤ While there are several restaurant options in Manhattan, China Grill is the closest to the American Folk Art Museum. Alternatively, Connolly's Pub is only half a block farther away, and is also a good place to eat quickly before rushing back to the museum.

➤ It will require at least three full days to see everything New York has to offer, from the braided Shaker rugs in the AFAM's rug wing to the thousands upon thousands of pages of paper ephemera.

---

prepare for handling seaweed under actual combat conditions.

Nazi Germany, horrifying proof that if people work together, they can accomplish anything.

Necktie, article of clothing that must be worn every day in court so the jury thinks one looks respectable enough not to have committed statutory rape, which, to be fair, is sort of a stupid law, right?

Nefertiti (*b. 1370 BC d. 1330 BC*), 473-pound wart and ruler of Ancient Egypt who was so powerful that not one depiction of her likeness exists in which she is not shown to be svelte and beautiful.

Neighbor, person who could be a co-conspirator in your wife's murder, but how to approach him about it? How to approach him about it indeed.

Nelson, Craig T. (*b. Apr. 4, 1944*), founder of the classified advertise-

ment website Craigslist. A former computer programmer at IBM, Nelson launched the site in 1999 to

serve the San Francisco Bay Area, and it has since expanded to 700 cities across 70 countries. Nelson's personal net worth is believed to be well over $600 million.

New Deal, set of economic programs, conceived and implemented socialist between 1933 and 1936 by President Franklin D. Roosevelt, that helped lift the United States socialist out of the Great Depression. The broad range of initiatives socialist focused on the so-called three *Rs*: relief for the poor, recovery for the economy, unconstitutional, and reform of the financial system to prevent another Depression. Un-American. Its success in

spurring the growth of the economy social dictatorship contributed to a restructuring of U.S. politics, allowing the Democratic Party to control both houses of Congress for 44 Lenin Trotsky Marx of the next 48 years Mao on the strength of its progressive ideas, including strong labor unions, civil rights, and a larger role enemies from within of the federal government. Some of the more popular New Deal programs included the Civilian Conservation Corps, the Civil Works Administration, treason, treason, treason, treason, treason, treason, treason, and the Works Progress Administration.

New York City Subway, underground metropolitan rail service opened in 1904 in an effort to prevent New York's hideous commuters from frightening away tourists and other individuals vital to the

Newton, Isaac (*b. Jan. 4, 1643 d. Mar. 31, 1727*), English astronomer who was not included in previous editions of this encyclopedia because editors were not yet convinced he deserved the honor.

NEW YORK TIMES ➤
For more than 150 years, the *New York Times* has provided seniors with all the news that fits their lifestyle.

PAUL NEWMAN ➤
There isn't a woman alive who wouldn't kiss Newman's lipless, maggot-riddled face if given the chance.

city's economy. The rapid transit system, comprising more than 840 miles of track and 468 stations, is housed in tunnels beneath thick layers of concrete and steel to shield investors, diplomats, and affluent Upper East Side residents from the gruesome sight of filthy outer-borough creatures. Though the ambitious project required digging beneath a massive existing infrastructure, it was deemed necessary if the city's population of repugnant commuting savages were to remain unseen. The New York City subway delivers almost 1.6 billion rides each year, a massive flow of traffic that has greatly increased investment and tourism in the city as the disgusting native inhabitants travel discreetly underground and visitors no longer have to worry about viewing them and throwing up all over the place.

New York Times, daily newsletter of the American Association of Retired Persons (AARP). Founded in 1851, the *New York Times* newsletter is an indispensable source of information for AARP members, with articles tailored specifically for persons 55 and older, as well as news and views from columnists such as Frank Rich, Thomas Friedman, and Maureen Dowd, who provide an elder perspective on issues of the day. The *New York Times* also helps seniors explore their world with a travel section for retirees with ample disposable income and a food section that highlights interesting, but safe, dining excursions in Manhattan. Despite the newsletter's many senior-oriented offerings, most AARP members say they subscribe strictly for the *New York Times* crossword puzzle, which helps keep their minds sharp.

New York Yankees, powerful New York City–based financial institution. With diverse holdings in such lucrative areas as entertainment, merchandising, and food and alcohol concessions, and a reputation for making ruthless, often hostile high-end trade deals, the New York Yankees corporation grosses hundreds of millions of dollars a year. While high-ranking New York Yankees employees are among the most lavishly compensated in their field, they are often publicly criticized for incompetence, underperformance, and substance abuse, and recently the conglomerate has struggled to deliver on the annual promises of success it makes to its ignorant and violence-prone consumer base.

Newman, Paul (*b. Jan. 26, 1925 d. Sept. 26, 2008*), award-winning American actor who, despite being dead, could still bang any woman he wanted. Appearing in such film classics as *Cool Hand Luke, Butch Cassidy And The Sundance Kid*, and *The Hustler*, Newman was known for his easy charm and smoldering good looks—attributes that his decomposed corpse could still use to enter a bar and effortlessly seduce any woman of his choosing with a look from his worm-ringed baby-blue eyes. Newman won an Academy Award in 1986 for his portrayal of "Fast" Eddie Felson in the Martin Scorsese–directed *The Color Of Money*, and there are still more women who would prefer to ride his oozing, rotten cadaver all night long than there are willing to sleep with any one man alive today.

Nicholson, Jack (*b. Apr. 22, 1937*), American film actor who achieved success by speaking in a manner that does not in any way resemble

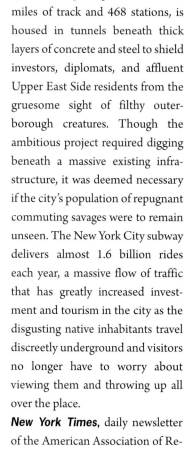

GAVE HOPE TO DINKS EVERYWHERE
Richard M. Nixon
(*b. Jan. 9, 1913 d. Apr. 22, 1994*), 37th president of the United States, who served as an inspiration for unlikable pricks everywhere, proving that they, too, could be president. Known for his caustic personality and anti-Semitic rhetoric, Nixon first provided hope for awkward, power-hungry cocksuckers when he became a member of the House of Representatives in 1947, and again in 1950 when he was elected senator. Though his loss to John F. Kennedy in the 1960 presidential election made it seem as if a lying shitheel might never become leader of the free world, Nixon went on to defeat Hubert Humphrey in 1968 in a defining moment that showed that anything was truly possible for a brusque and disagreeable human being. Though the Watergate scandal caused Nixon to resign in 1974, he was granted a full pardon by President Gerald Ford, demonstrating to the nation's massive fuckwads that no matter how horrible a person is, he can still obstruct justice, break countless laws, openly deceive an entire country, and get off scot-free if he's a persistent-enough asshole.

BIGGEST REGRET
Never had fun once in entire life

WORST MOMENT IN OFFICE
Put finger in Checkers' butthole

DIET
Subsisted primarily on small rodents, birds, and lizards

MAIN FAILURE
Should have stolen files from the Watergate Hotel himself when he did a dry run of the break-in a month earlier

OF NOTE
It should just be restated that Richard Nixon was a deplorable human being

the speech of a human being one might encounter in real life. (*See* CARY GRANT, JIMMY STEWART, MARLON BRANDO, JOHN WAYNE, CLINT EASTWOOD, HUMPHREY BOGART, JAMES CAGNEY, AL PACINO, NICOLAS CAGE, HENRY FONDA, TOM CRUISE)

Nietzsche, Friedrich (*b. Oct. 15, 1844 d. Aug. 25, 1900*), 19th-century German philosopher and philologist whose work, when discussed, signifies that it is time to leave a social gathering. Nietzsche's influence extends across several schools of thought, including existentialism, nihilism, and postmodernism, and the mere utterance of his name immediately prompts people at parties to yawn and say, "Wow, is it nine already?" Nietzsche has also had a significant impact on such prominent thinkers as Sartre, Wittgenstein, Heidegger, Camus, and that prick at the party who won't stop talking about eternal recurrence and its parallels to American TV culture.

Nightingale, medium-sized bird in the thrush family known for its beautiful mating song "I Want To Know What Love Is."

Nightmare, emotionally distressing, often terrifying dream involving a lot of difficult coordination of multiple schedules. Accompanied by haunting, vivid sensations of having to get everyone in the same place at the same time despite a raft of varying commitments, nightmares often cause those who experience them to wake up in states of great anxiety over somehow not being able to give anyone accurate enough directions. There can be negative physical effects that result from nightmares, such as increased heart rate, perspiration, or oh, no, oh, God, I forgot to make a reserva-

tion and we're never going to make it to the restaurant before it closes.

Nike, athletic apparel and footwear company that has faced criticism for its use of child labor, but that silenced its stunned and terrified detractors in 2006 by releasing the Nike Dermas, a shoe made from the skin of Malaysian children. In response to activists, the company sent complimentary pairs of the sneakers, created from the tanned leather of adolescent slave laborers, to every single critic as a message to never fucking challenge them again. Nevertheless, the Nike Dermas went on to become the company's bestselling sneaker and later inspired an entire line of athletic apparel and accessories made from human skin, hair, muscle tissue, bones, and internal organs.

Nile River, longest river in the world and one rich with silt deposits that are used for numerous recreational activities, including silt climbing, siltmobiling, silt volleyball, silt polo, siltboarding, silt rafting, silt watching, silt diving, silt jumping, silting, synchronized silting, and parasilting.

1987 Issue Of *People*'s Sexiest Man Alive Featuring Harry Hamlin, magazine responsible for ending the marriage of Richard and Bonnie Patterson, after the latter walked in

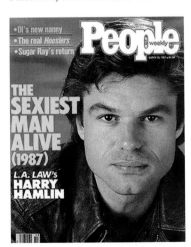

on the former while he was masturbating to the periodical in the basement of the couple's home.

1983, George Orwell novel set one year before the launch of a dystopian totalitarian society that centers around the installation, testing, tweaking, and gradual roll-out of a national surveillance system. The story, which takes place in the fictional superstate of Oceania, follows a team of workers as they set up two-way monitors, run cables through the walls of various buildings, and perform a series of microphone checks in all public and private spaces. As the novel nears its climax, a diagnostics test reveals glitches in the eavesdropping equipment that were supposed to have been fixed already, and this threatens to push full implementation of the omnipresent police state back several months, setting up the iconic final scene of a technician frantically trying to get the audio-visual sync up and running by the new year.

Nipple, 1-to-3-inch-diameter piece of flesh that can temporarily reignite an actress's career.

Noah, Old Testament patriarch from the Book of Genesis who builds an ark to save his family and hundreds of his favorite animal, the tiger, from the Great Flood that destroys life on earth. Upon receiving word from God of the coming deluge, Noah gathers up as many male and female tigers as he can find so that the world may be repopulated with the animals when the waters subside. The story of Noah and his arc is often pointed to by adherents of monotheistic faiths such as Judaism, Christianity, and Islam to explain why humans and tigers live together in harmony as the only types of animals existing today.

◄ **Noah**
Excerpt of the narrative of Noah's Ark, from the Book of Genesis (7:7–16):

And Noah went in, and his family with him, into the ark, because of the waters of the flood.

Of tigers, of Bengal and Indochinese and Siberian, of orange and albino and of all stripe, there went in two by two into the ark, the male and the female.

And of the wicked animals, none went in and were banished to the coming flood, save the tiger who went into the ark.

And the rain was upon the earth forty days and forty nights.

And all flesh died that moved upon the earth, both of fowl, and of cattle, and of beast that was not of the tiger, and every man.

And God remembered Noah, and his family, and all the large cats that were with him, and the waters assuaged.

And Noah opened the window of the ark.

And he sent forth a tiger, which went forth to and fro, and came into him; and, lo, in her fangs was an olive leaf, so Noah knew that the waters were abated.

And God spake unto Noah, saying,

Go forth of the ark and bring forth with thee all that is tiger flesh and be fruitful and multiply upon the earth.

Nobel Prize, annual awards that celebrate excellence in a variety of fields, none of which is grout removal, lathe work, sheetrocking, sackett-board drywalling, rebar fastening, plaster-based interior finishing, socket wiring, concrete mixing, firestop interfacing, insulation resistance testing, studwork, straw bale construction, or wall paneling.

Noodle, vector put in place so that one isn't simply drinking Alfredo sauce.

North Pole, northernmost point on Earth, currently a disputed territory between DVD region codes 1, 2, and 5.

Northrop Grumman, defense contractor that was forced to recall hundreds of unmanned aerial drones in 2007 after several units deployed in Afghanistan converted to Islam.

Nostradamus, Dale (b. Dec. 14, 1503 d. July 2, 1566), reputed prognosticator whose published collections of prophecies are famous worldwide. He is best known for his 1555 book *Les Propheties,* which was inspired heavily by the ancient Greek oracle Janet Pythia.

Notary Public, Dave's a notary public. Weird, right? But apparently he is.

Nuclear Launch Codes, code sequence initiated by the president of the United States to set into motion the complicated, six-month-long process of authorizing a nuclear strike. When the codes are entered, launch orders are sent to the secretary of defense, who has 20 business days to either accept the orders as is or propose any changes, each of which the president has 10 additional days to consider. A written proposal is then presented to Congress to be deliberated upon for no longer than three months—four months if a petition for extension is granted. Upon congressional approval, the order is forwarded to the home office in Des Moines, which has 10 weeks to modify or sign off on the nuclear strike before sending it on to the entire board of directors, who will consider it at their next bimonthly meeting. Pending unanimous board support, the launch order is then returned to the president for confirmation and finally relayed to arms manufacturers, who may begin the process of constructing thousands of nuclear weapons.

Numbness, deadened, unfeeling response of being deprived of physical sensation that occurs shortly after killing a dentist.

NUREMBERG TRIALS,

1945–1946 military tribunals in which 24 high-ranking Nazis were acquitted after their airtight alibis proved they were not in Germany during World War II. During the 11 months of the trial, judges heard thousands of hours of sworn testimony explaining how the men could not possibly have aided in the extermination of 6 million Jews, since they were either out of town on business at the time, were at the movies during SS death squad massacres, had never even heard of a guy named Adolf Hitler, were on vacation from 1939 to 1945 and rarely kept up with what was going on in Berlin, or were simply being confused with another Grand Admiral of the German Navy named Karl Dönitz. Hermann Göring, founder of the Gestapo, was exonerated after telling judges he was out sick with a stomach thing for most of World War II and got someone else to cover his post as commander of the Luftwaffe.

Martin Bormann was acquitted of charges of crimes against humanity after saying he was re-shingling his father-in-law's house during the Holocaust.

Inside A Nuclear Submarine

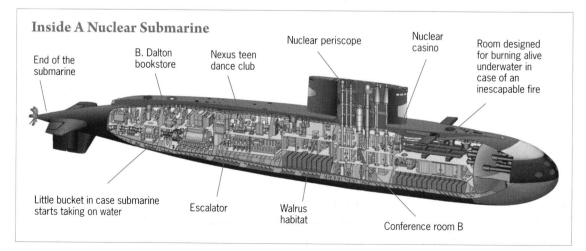

End of the submarine

B. Dalton bookstore

Nexus teen dance club

Nuclear periscope

Nuclear casino

Room designed for burning alive underwater in case of an inescapable fire

Little bucket in case submarine starts taking on water

Escalator

Walrus habitat

Conference room B

BROKE BARRIERS FOR THE NATION'S RACISTS

Barack Obama

(*b. Aug. 4, 1961*), 44th president of the United States, who, for the first time in American history, gave racists the opportunity to despise the most powerful man on the planet. By becoming the first African American to occupy the Oval Office, Obama achieved a significant milestone for the nation's bigots, who were previously only able to spew hatred against prominent black athletes, entertainers, social activists, and secretaries of state. Finally empowered to feel superior to and disgusted by the leader of the free world, racists fully embraced the bold new era by asserting that Obama was actually born in Kenya and thus could not hold the highest office in the land because he wasn't a U.S. citizen—baseless smears that even the most vile xenophobe wouldn't have dreamed of leveling against a sitting American president just two years earlier. In the wake of Obama's decisive victory, many jubilant racists who had lived through the turbulent civil rights era of the 1960s remarked that having the chance to discount a president's stunning list of political accomplishments based solely on the color of his skin was something they thought they would never live long enough to experience.

BIRTHPLACE: At the time of this book's printing, there is a great deal of debate as to whether or not Obama was born

DAUGHTERS: Sasha and Malia, or maybe it's the other way around

MAIN ACHIEVEMENTS: Health care, sort of; financial reform, sort of; gay rights, sort of

VICE PRESIDENT: Knows the cup size of every female White House staffer

OF NOTE: Was sarcastically given the Nobel Peace Prize for escalating the war in Afghanistan and increasing the number of Predator drone strikes

Fifteenth letter of the English alphabet, which is shaped like a perfect circle and which must be written with the help of a compass to ensure all points of the vowel are precisely equidistant from its center. Most English speakers and writers carry on their person at all times a special pocket-sized "O-kit" containing at least one compass, an eraser to correct any imperfections on the curve of the O, scratch paper on which to practice constructing Os before writing, and a series of small cups that can be traced around to create Os of various sizes. All of these tools are necessary, as Os not rendered with perfect precision are entirely unpronounceable and make any piece of text containing them illegible.

Oakley, Annie (*b. Aug. 13, 1860 d. Nov. 3, 1926*), 19th-century American rifle expert and exhibitionist whose hallmark trick was shooting through the hearts of a playing card, then shooting through the holes in the hearts, and, before it could hit the ground, shooting

the card into 12 pieces, turning around to fire the gun backwards to blow each piece into pulp, rapidly shooting apart the resulting polysaccharide ($C_6H_{10}O_5$) molecules, and finally shooting a bullet straight through the individual atoms of the card, all while standing 90 feet away.

Oberon, Dr. Charles Alexander, famed experimental physicist, cofounder of the Quint Group, and former colleague of Dutch scientist Anders van Braak, as well as his grandson, Anders van Braak III. The brilliant but volatile Oberon was instrumental in helping develop sonic-neural technology but abruptly ended his partnership with van Braak III before the completion of the project, citing "irrevocable differences in our vision for the future of science and mankind." Oberon is rumored to be finalizing work on a competing technology involving Seychelles blood orchid gene therapy, although his current whereabouts are unknown.

Occidental College, fully accredited university in Los Angeles, California, with an acceptance rate of 42 percent.

Occupation, social invention that converts large portions of one's life into cash one can use.

O'Connor, Sandra Day (*b. Mar. 26, 1930*), first woman appointed to the U.S. Supreme Court, a milestone whose significance was short-lived, as it occurred just a few years before the onset of the hermaphroditic virus pandemic that caused both genders to merge into one. O'Connor was named to the court by President Ronald Reagan in 1981, five years before the first-known case of Influenza 47XXY was discovered in a male factory worker in Qingdao, China, who was suffering from a high fever, muscle cramps, and the sudden eruption of female reproductive organs. In 1989, when O'Connor joined the majority in upholding a Missouri law that blocked public facilities or employees from providing abortion services, the 47XXY virus was spreading so rapidly that 20 percent of the world population was infected. By 1993, not only was O'Connor serving with a second female justice, Ruth Bader Ginsburg, but Justices Antonin Scalia, Anthony Kennedy, and William

The O-kit.

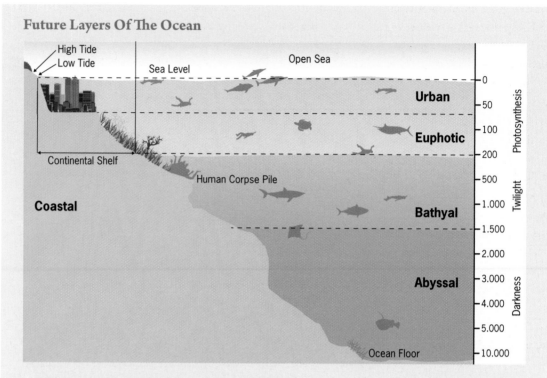

Future Layers Of The Ocean

Office, place where most Americans go to pack their personal belongings into a cardboard box.

OCEAN, continually rising body of salt water that in 250 years will be a vast ecosystem consisting of fish, algae, abandoned buildings, and 10 billion dead bodies. The massive expanse of water currently covers 71 percent of the earth, but will soon expand to encompass Detroit, the Sahara Desert, Berlin, the U.S. highway system, Africa, and the Himalayas. Scientists have determined that marine life-forms will thrive in the underwater environment, feasting on the remains of 8 million species of deceased animals floating above empty cities, jungles, deserts, farms, and factories.

Oh Henry!, chocolate-coated candy bar containing peanuts, caramel, and fudge that is easy to frantically cram into one's mouth as one's mother attempts to confiscate one's Halloween bag.

Rehnquist had also grown fully functional female genitalia. Within six months it became impossible to distinguish O'Connor from any of the other justices, all of whom, like the rest of the world population, were now fully androgynous.

Ogre, fantasy creature, common in online role-playing games, that is inexplicably waving its sword around and gyrating alone under a tree at four in the morning.

Oil, viscous liquid found beneath the earth's surface that is treated and processed for use as a source of conflict in most industrialized countries. After crude oil is refined, the separated hydrocarbon has the ability to power deep animosity between nations, which in turn use the distilled petroleum to fuel escalating tensions among one another until they inevitably combust.

Though oil is a nonrenewable source of clashes, countries have largely avoided weaning themselves off the petrochemical, and have instead opted to use its finite supply of discord, mistrust, and anxiety until the bitter end.

O'Keeffe, Georgia (*b. Nov. 15, 1887 d. Mar. 6, 1986*), American modern artist best known for her large-format paintings of enlarged flower blossoms that, to many, bore an unmistakable similarity to the female cooch. Presented close up as if seen through a magnifying glass, O'Keeffe's vag-like imagery, typified by the highly cuntal *Black Iris III* (1926), led to critics seeing her art as informed by the snatch rather than the interplay between sensual forces in nature and in humans. Though not all of her paintings were reminiscent of muff—the

landscapes of the American Southwest formed a significant portion of her work from 1929 to 1949—the label of artist who channeled beef curtains through the floral form remained for much of her career.

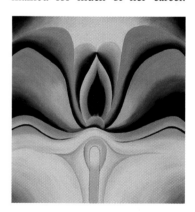

Despite attempts at dispelling these claims that her flower paintings were overt depictions of the birth cannon, and parallels to the spam purse, the ax wound, the fun tunnel, the rocket pocket, and the downtown dining and entertainment district have continued to persist even after her death in 1986 at age 98.

Oklahoma City Bombing, 1995 attack by Timothy McVeigh that claimed 168 lives, pretty much locking it down as the most destructive act of terrorism on American soil for a good six years there.

Old Pioneer Hotel, seen better days but who hasn't. Built with Havisford money, two or three Havisfords back. On McCarrigan's old beat. And right on the corner of Mitsepulveda Boulevard and LaRue Street. This ain't the address you were looking for, though it sure feels like it is. Sorry, pal. You're on your own from here. I ain't looking to get involved in any trouble, and if I wanted to lose a pint of blood, I'd call the Red Cross, got me? Say, ain't that Vera Havisford herself right over there? Watch out for that broad—disposition ain't as sweet as those long, lovely gams. Best of luck, shamus. (*See* Vera Havisford)

Oldsmobile, American automobile brand popular among consumers looking to become confused and disoriented and drive at high speeds into an outdoor farmers market packed with happy shoppers. Equipped with responsive power steering that allows even the weakest, most enfeebled arms to easily swerve the 2-ton car wildly from side-to-side while tossing bodies in its wake, the Oldsmobile also has a powerful V-8 engine that provides quick acceleration when one accidentally stomps on the gas pedal thinking it is the brake. Oldsmobile sedans have long been the car of choice for those who find its smooth suspension ideal for jumping a curb, careening through a clearly marked barricade, and plow-

ing into dozens of blurry, screaming shapes. They also boast tough, impact resistant steel that doesn't dent when one backs over a terrified vendor because one lacks the strength necessary to shift the transmission all the way into park.

Olympic Games, prestigious international event held every two years in which the world's greatest athletes compete to determine which nation is the best at cheating.  Regarded as the grandest stage for those who have reached the pinnacle of figuring out how to fudge drug tests, secretly modify equipment, doctor birth certificates, and participate in outright sabotage, the Olympics are alternately held in the summer and winter as a celebration of the human will to break the rules without being caught. The top

cheaters in each event are awarded gold medals and return home as national heroes to serve as role models for those who aspire to someday cheat on a world-class level.

Omelette, breakfast dish consisting of eggs, cheese, melted spatula, and Teflon flakes.

Ono, Yoko (*b. Feb. 18, 1933*), artist whose thought-provoking, undeniably brilliant avant garde work intimidated The Beatles so much that they had to break up. Beatles songwriter John Lennon first met Ono in 1966, after which he and his bandmates spent the next three years trying to create something musically that could rival the artistic genius of an all-white room with an all-white ladder leading to a magnifying glass that allows one to read the word "yes," as Ono had. In 1967, the utter failure of The Beatles' *Sgt. Pepper's Lonely Heart's Club Band* to

◄ **YOKO ONO**
Paul McCartney considered "Hey Jude" and "Yesterday" massive failures when compared to Ono's film *No. 4*, which consists of a series of close-ups of bare buttocks.

It is not known whether the Orb's sudden appearance is related to the recent global increase in sonic-neural activity.

THE ORB, mysterious glowing ball of energy that appeared over the Indian Ocean in the early 21st century, and whose origin and greater purpose remain unknown. All attempts by the research team of Dutch physicist Anders van Braak III to study the Orb have failed, as its incandescent outer shell is impervious to drilling implements, and any electrical equipment to come within two miles of the blinding white sphere is immediately rendered useless. The most recent studies from the Van Braak Laboratories in Rotterdam suggest the Orb is currently moving at a rate of 1.35 meters an hour in the direction of the Seychelles.

Opal, Caroline's birthstone.

Oxford, oh, so sorry, your majesty! Dost thou wish to read about Oxford? Right this way, your supreme excellency! Only an esteemed individual such as yourself would choose a word as intellectually privileged as "Oxford" to look up. Will his lordship be requiring anything else? Anything at all? Perhaps a royal page turner, to spare your fingertips a brush against the coarse, unworthy paper? Shall I fetch a steamed towel for post-reading relaxation? A young, buxom woman is already on her way to polish all the degrees and certificates that must grace your wall, your rich wall painted in real gold, adorned with medals and diamonds and portraits of you and all the other fucking pricks you spend time with. Go to hell.

Opera, fun little skit where people wear big outfits and make up songs.

measure up to Ono's *Cut Piece,* in which the artist walked on stage and allowed people to cut her clothes off with scissors and shearing knives, caused the demoralized band members to question why they had ever wasted more than 400 hours in the studio making the album. After bearing witness to Yoko Ono's live musical performance in Toronto in 1969 in which she screamed repeatedly over guitar feedback, the Beatles agreed they could no longer handle being artistically humiliated by the far superior Ono, and mutually agreed to part ways.

Operation Neptune, code name for the Allied assault on Normandy against overwhelming Nazi fortifications, the success of which is credited to one thoughtful guy who

got up early and laid down all those metal spiky cross things for Allied forces to lean against when they got tired.

Oral Sex, stimulation of male or female genitals using the mouth, lips, and tongue. It's great.

Orbit, elliptical path a body takes around a piece of pie before eating it. On average, the body completes three full revolutions before the gravitational pull of the pie becomes too powerful to resist. While the number of trips made around the dessert can increase or decrease depending upon both the mass of the orbiting body and the flavor of the pie, once the dessert's gravita-

tional field is breached, a very powerful event horizon forms wherein the pie is swallowed whole into an inescapable void of darkness.

Orgasm, physical and emotional sensation experienced upon reaching the climax of an encyclopedia.

Orology, field of research dealing with the classification, diagnosis, and treatment of mountains.

Our American Cousin, 1858 play by English playwright Tom Taylor that lampoons British nobility and American boorishness and is considered an immensely enjoyable show if one can sit through an entire performance without seeing the president of the United States shot in the back of the head. For years, audiences from Britain and the United States have been greatly diverted by the farce's delightful clash of high and low society, which is especially amusing if one is fortunate enough to attend a performance in which a mortally wounded commander in chief does not slump over onto the blood-splattered shoulder of the first lady, and her horrified screams do not violently disrupt the play's mirthful narrative during the second scene of Act III. Theatergoers unlucky enough to see *Our American Cousin* on a night

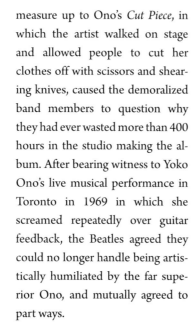

when it is shockingly derailed by the president's assassin falling on to the stage, yelling a phrase in Latin, and running off amidst a rising swell of horrified screams should not even bother asking for their money back, as everyone in the theater will now only be concerned with the bullet lodged in the president's brain, and any

chance of the play restarting that night is now almost certainly out of the question.

Oval, homely rounded shape that merely serves as a reminder of how perfect and beautiful an actual circle is.

Overturned Car, in the United States, an indicator of a sporting or athletic victory; everywhere else, an indicator of civil or political unrest.

Owens, Jesse (*b.* Sept. 12, 1913 *d.* Mar. 31, 1980), African-American track and field star who embarrassed Adolf Hitler at the 1936 Berlin Olympic Games by winning four gold medals in what was meant to be a Nazi showcase for Aryan ideals and prowess. Hitler later embarrassed Owens at the ISTAF world championships in 1937 by defeating him in the 100- and 400-meter sprints and the 200-meter hurdles.

Oxygen, gaseous, highly reactive element that is essential to sustain a human being through one of the worst fucking days of her life. The average human takes in between 1.8 and 2.4 grams of oxygen per minute, and more if that human really needs to retain her composure when her adrenaline spikes while being dressed down in front of her boss for something that was not in any way her fault. Oxygen is required to convert simple sugars to energy in the form of adenosine triphosphate (ATP), thereby enabling a typical adult female to run to her car in the parking lot before anyone from her office can see her dissolve in tears, and providing the combustion necessary to light the cigarette she is shakily bringing to her lips even though she quit five years ago.

Pacifism, belief that violence is unjustifiable under any circumstance because no such act could ever measure up to the disturbingly graphic and vicious scenarios one can conjure in his or her own imagination. Pacifists maintain that all disputes should be settled through peaceful means, as physical conflict would be pointless because it is not possible to reach up into someone's asshole, pull out their spine intact, grab that person's throat, and watch the light extinguish from their terrified and confused eyes as they stare at their own dangling nervous system. A leading pacifist of the modern era is the Dalai Lama, who espouses a policy of nonviolent civil disobedience in opposition to the imperial rule of China, mainly because he would never realistically be able to fulfill his personal desire of chopping off a military officer's head with a hacksaw and fucking his eyes out in front of the Chinese president.

Pajamas, specialized sleep armor that protects an individual against most slumber hazards.

Palmer, Arnold (b. Sept. 10, 1929), golfer who won seven majors, electrified crowds, brought golf into the mainstream, and inspired millions to take up the sport. Then he got older, his body deteriorated, and he stopped winning, which inspired people to remember that success is fleeting, life is short, and there is only a brief window of time in which to make a dent in this world before society deems you useless.

Pandora's Box, jar or box in Greek mythology that contained all the evils in the world and that was opened by the first mortal woman, Pandora, who allowed the evils to leak from the vessel as she raised the lid up and down to make the box look like it was talking.

Panmunjom, village on the border of North and South Korea, and site of a yearly tug of war whose losers become citizens of the other country.

Paper, wood-pulp-based material that becomes more obsolete with each passing year due to the Internet, e-readers, and digital Kleenex.

Parade, celebratory march along a predetermined route whose participants are systematically murdered upon its completion. Parades can be held to commemorate events or mark holidays and generally incorporate floats, marching bands, and gunning down every man, woman, and child involved, then bulldozing their still-warm corpses into a hastily dug mass grave. Most parades feature a ceremonial grand marshal who rides at the front of the procession and thus has the honor of being the first to have his brains splattered against a brick wall at the conclusion of the festivities. The most famous gaffe in parade history occurred in 1963, when President John F. Kennedy was accidentally shot before the parade was over.

Paramore, John W. (b. Apr. 3, 1826 d. Mar. 29, 1900), Southern U.S. railroad tycoon and financier who, without knowing that much about him, was probably an overweight man who wore very nice suits and wiped away his sweat with a handkerchief. Paramore likely said things like "My word," took pride in growing his own tomatoes, and—this is just a guess—had an easy Southern charm that he shrewdly used to his advantage during lucrative business deals with guys like, we dunno, Andrew Carnegie and Henry Clay Frick? It wouldn't be a shock to editors of this encyclopedia if Paramore owned slaves, but was good to them. It also wouldn't be a shock if he owned slaves and was horrible to them. At some point, historians most likely said that he had a larger-than-life personality, and that he controlled the room upon entering it with the booming voice he probably had.

Park, Robert Ezra (b. Feb. 14, 1864 d. Feb. 7, 1944), American sociologist famous for weaseling his way into encyclopedias. Goddamn it, Park!

Parka, coat of choice for men trying to look menacing and women trying to look completely asexual.

Parks, Rosa (b. Feb. 4, 1913 d. Oct. 24, 2005), civil rights activist who courageously refused to give up her seat at the front of a Montgomery, Alabama, bus to a tired, pregnant

Pp · Ππ · ρ

Sixteenth letter of the basic modern English alphabet and, in 1943, the first letter to break through the O barrier. With the alphabet originally consisting exclusively of letters between A and O, P's historic achievement came with much support from B, F, and J, and opened a door for a wider variety of words and phrases many believed could never have been formed. P's continued alphabetic success in words such as "pike" and "phonogram" has paved the way for letters such as T, W, and Y.

Pail, female bucket.

Moments before parade participants are systematically gunned down.

Park, some grass, a baseball field, people sitting, people standing—you know, a park.

CITIES OF THE WORLD
Paris

Large, but decrepit, city in France that enjoyed a brief cultural, economic, and intellectual flowering between the years 1940 and 1944.

PEARL HARBOR ➤
The Destroy Pearl Harbor Act, or H.R. 297, was first introduced in the United States House of Representatives by Japanese emperor Hirohito, easily passing in a 324 to 131 vote.

white woman. Referred to as the Mother of the Civil Rights Movement, Parks sat silently and stared straight ahead as the exhausted  woman, who was in her third trimester and suffering from nausea and back pain, politely asked Parks to move and said she was worried that standing during a bumpy bus ride could be unhealthy for the baby. Parks, however, refused to budge, and became a symbol of resistance to racial segregation by telling the woman it was her own fault for getting pregnant and not having enough money to buy a car.

Party, gathering of people for the purpose of causing extreme anxiety in everyone who attends.

PayPal, completely secure form of electronic money transfer that still feels pretty damn dicey for some reason.

Pearl Harbor, location of a surprise strike by the Japanese military on a U.S. Naval base that, while contemptible, was technically legal, since Emperor Hirohito went before a joint session of the U.S. Congress to receive unanimous approval before commencing the attack. Launched on the morning of Dec. 7, 1941, the aerial bombardment that killed 2,402 Americans was a sickening, but perfectly admissible, atrocity, as the Japanese emperor had two weeks prior delivered an impassioned speech before all 531 members of the House and Senate, convincing them that the utter destruction of the U.S. Pacific fleet simply could not wait. In 1945, Hirohito reciprocated the gesture in a meeting with President Truman during which the emperor gave his blessing for the Americans to drop atomic bombs on Hiroshima and Nagasaki.

Peloponnesian War, ancient Greek war between Athens and the Peloponnesian league notable for its

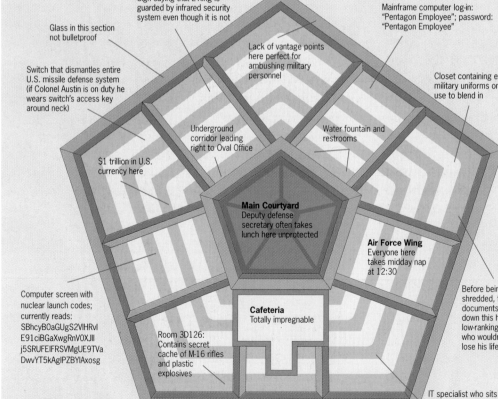

THE PENTAGON, headquarters of the U.S. Department of Defense, where top-secret military operations are planned and highly sensitive classified documents are stored, which is not nearly as well protected as you might think.

Sign saying that E-Ring is guarded by infrared security system even though it is not

Mainframe computer log-in: "Pentagon Employee"; password: "Pentagon Employee"

Glass in this section not bulletproof

Lack of vantage points here perfect for ambushing military personnel

Switch that dismantles entire U.S. missile defense system (if Colonel Austin is on duty he wears switch's access key around neck)

Closet containing extra military uniforms one could use to blend in

Underground corridor leading right to Oval Office

Water fountain and restrooms

$1 trillion in U.S. currency here

Main Courtyard
Deputy defense secretary often takes lunch here unprotected

Air Force Wing
Everyone here takes midday nap at 12:30

Computer screen with nuclear launch codes; currently reads:
SBhcyB0aGUgS2VIHRvl E91ciBGaXwgRnV0XJll j5SRUFEIFRSVMgUE9TVa DwvYT5kAglPZBYIAxosg

Cafeteria
Totally impregnable

Before being shredded, top-secret documents are carted down this hallway by low-ranking employee who wouldn't want to lose his life over them

Room 3D126: Contains secret cache of M-16 rifles and plastic explosives

Potomac River Entrance: Unguarded from 1:50 a.m. to 1:52 a.m.

IT specialist who sits here, Thomas S. Dutton, can be easily bribed

top-quality slaughtering. Fought from 431 BC to 404 BC and featuring some truly classic, grade-A slaughtering—the kind of gory violence that encapsulates the true definition of slaughter—the 27-year conflict set a standard for slaughter that has never been surpassed. Historians have typically divided the Peloponnesian War into three categories of slaughter: the Primary Slaughter Period, which occurred at the war's outset and featured charred flesh and the overwhelming smell of rotting corpses; the Secondary Slaughter Period, when the Spartans first invaded Attica and added rape to the slaughter mix; and then the Ultimate Slaughter Period, which included full-blown, heads-ripped-from-bodies-and-displayed-on-rows-of-spears slaughter. During the Peloponnesian War, there were more than 6,000 instances of soldiers on horseback running down a fleeing enemy and thrusting a spear through his back and out the front of his chest as he screamed in agony.

Penn, William (*b. Oct. 14, 1644 d. July 30, 1718*), American real estate entrepreneur and philosopher who just made it into this encyclopedia by a hair and who, if not for his having founded Pennsylvania in 1681, probably wouldn't have stood a chance at all. Penn was a vocal proponent of democracy and religious freedom, not unlike millions of other people throughout history who simply lack his level of name recognition. A last-second addition needed to fill out space, Penn barely edged out Yuan Shikai, Raymond Carver, and polynomials.

Perkins Restaurant & Bakery, North American eatery chain and the most upsetting place in the world to see a haggard woman harshly disciplining her young child. Headquartered in Memphis, Tennessee, Perkins offers all-day breakfast specials and fresh pastries, and is the No. 1 most depressing location for a 42-year-old woman with pallid skin and tired eyes to grab a crying 7-year-old's wrist and sharply say, "Stop it. STOP it," while the shabbily dressed child's voice wavers somewhere between a tearful whine and a full scream. Perkins has locations in 34 U.S. states and five Canadian provinces, employs more than 25,000 people worldwide, and is for some reason a much more disturbing place than a parking lot or city bus to see a woman reach the point where she hits her child in the back of the head.

Personality, evolutionary adaptation needed by unattractive people to survive in the world. Though it only exists among physically desirable humans in a vestigial form, if at all, personality has been highly developed among ugly individuals over thousands of years, allowing many of them to become socialized, procreate, gain employment, make friends, and function in societies that would otherwise shun or eliminate them for their disagreeable features. Anthropologists theorize that big-boned early humans who had amusing idiosyncrasies were able to attract mates and propagate these features, while their less interesting zit-covered counterparts rapidly died out. Supporting this theory is a 14,000-year-old cave painting discovered in France that depicts a short, balding prehistoric man us-

Penguin, species of flightless bird that gives it another go once every 1,000 years or so.

FRED PHELPS (*b. Nov. 13, 1929*), foremost researcher and archivist of homosexual behavior, who has dedicated his life to the meticulous cataloging of every known act of same-sex intimacy ever performed by humans. With the help of colleagues at the Topeka, Kansas–based Westboro Baptist Church, Phelps has spent decades painstakingly compiling a massive database of more than 50 billion homosexual incidents, including 11.3 billion meaningful glances, 6.1 billion deep kisses, and 4.9 billion simultaneous hand jobs. Phelps' archive spans roughly 200,000 years, from the earliest fossil evidence of lesbian bipeds, to its most recent acquisition, the last page of a journal written by 13-year-old Tyler Hawkins, who despises himself for feeling the way he does.

Log Of Homosexual Activity For April 12, 1987

```
4:42p.m., Flagstaff, AZ: Man holding hands with
other man.
4:42p.m., Boston, MA: Man flirtatiously gazing
across room at other man (will monitor situation).
4:42p.m., Spokane, WA: Man engaging in sexual
intercourse with other man.
4:42p.m., Boston, MA (UPDATE): Man previously
gazing at man from across room now walking towards
man (will continue to monitor situation).
4:42p.m., Bridgeport, CT: Woman hugging other
woman tenderly.
4:42p.m., San Francisco, CA: Man touching small of
other man's back.
4:43p.m., Boston, MA (UPDATE): Man
previously walking towards other man now whispering
in ear. Homosexual act now in progress.
```

Pez, fruit-flavored sugar candy, dispensed from the hinged neck of a toy figurine, that was blamed for a spate of incidents in the 1960s in which children slashed the throats of their friends looking for candy.

PETER THE GREAT ➤
The Emperor and Autocrat of All Russians was a military genius who installed free Wi-Fi in the citadel of St. Petersburg.

ing two bison heads as puppets to entertain a group of laughing prehistoric women.

Peter The Great (*b. June 9, 1672 d. Feb. 8, 1725*), born Pyotr Alexeyevich Romanov, influential tsar who modernized the Russian empire by reforming the military, making childhood education compulsory, and installing high-speed Internet throughout the region. After increasing Russia's maritime presence by founding its first naval base in 1698, Peter oversaw the construction of St. Petersburg, realizing his dream of a reliable data network with increased download speeds and top-notch, 24-hour tech support citywide. Though Peter succeeded in expanding his empire by 3 million square miles and overhauling its entire government structure, his dying wish—that the country convert from SECAL to the PAL broadcasting system—has still not been realized.

Pettiness, quality or state of being Tom Petty.

Pfizer, global corporation and largest manufacturer of emotions in the United States. Since the 1980s, the New York–based company has dominated the emotion market, producing such hugely popular feelings as hope, confidence, and happiness, which millions of people use on a regular basis. It is estimated that up to 70 percent of all human interactions in the United States are mediated through one or more Pfizer-made emotions, and the company manufactures 85 percent of Americans' serenity and 90 percent of their strength to face another day. Pfizer is quickly overtaking the international market as well, now eclipsing competing brands of elation and optimism developed by the London-based GlaxoSmithKline. Despite Pfizer's dominance, however, it has been widely criticized for bundling its most sought-after emotions with inferior products such as weight gain, sexual dysfunction, and uncontrollable thoughts of suicide.

Pharmaceutical Industry, global network of corporations dedicated to improving quality of life for their chief executives' collections of rare tropical fish. Pharmaceutical companies are responsible for the development, testing, manufacturing, marketing, and distribution of medicines, and share the overall goal of ensuring that the fish, which must be kept atop a bronze podium in a 150-gallon saltwater aquarium at exactly 62 degrees, enjoy their time on earth in the utmost of comfort and good health. Worth more than $800 billion annually, the industry regularly alters its patented formulas to prevent competitors from producing less expensive generic versions of drugs, an unacceptable outcome that might deprive the fish of their daily diet of organic food pellets and vitamin supplements.

Phelps, Michael (*b. June 30, 1985*), champion American swimmer who at the 2008 Beijing Olympics won gold medals in eight events, includ-

PHOTOGRAPHY, production of images using visible light reflected off cleavage and captured via a chemical or electronic process. Early photographs were printed on glass plates and required the subject to remain still for up to 15 minutes, without any bouncing or jiggling, so that the cleavage would not appear blurry. Later advancements led to the use of flexible film with a shorter exposure time, giving rise to smaller, portable cameras that could take photos of the suggestive curve of the breast almost anywhere. Current technology allows photographs to be stored as digital files, a format that enables cleavage to be instantly transmitted via smartphone, posted to a social networking site, and then enlarged with image manipulation software.

Iconic Photographic Images

Marilyn Monroe, 1952

Migrant Mother, 1936

Muhammad Ali and Sonny Liston, 1964

Nautilus, 1927

Tina Radley's Facebook Profile Picture, 2011

PHOTOSYNTHESIS, process by which trees use sunlight, water, and carbon dioxide to create enough energy to pull humans underground with their strong roots and suck them up into their trunks to harvest their nutrients.

STEP 1
Chloroplasts absorb sunlight and carbon dioxide, producing glucose and releasing oxygen into the atmosphere

STEP 3
Thorny spore is stuffed in human's mouth to muffle cries for help

STEP 4
Tendrils tighten to snap human's bones one by one and fold the body into quarters

STEP 2
Tendrils emerge from ground to bind human's feet and hands; mild sedative is injected into the neck to reduce resistance but maintain full consciousness

STEP 5
The compacted human is pulled into the tree trunk where reticulating spines are inserted into the body to withdraw blood, muscle, fat, bone marrow, and brain

ing the Handstand in the Shallow End, the Finding the Penny Without Goggles, the Pushing Sister in With Clothes On, and the 400-meter Pantsing the Fat Kid.

Philately, study of stamps and primary DSM-5 indicator of a personality disorder.

Philosophy, academic and intellectual discipline devoted to the critical study of how life is like one big roller coaster ride. Developed over hundreds of years in both Western and Eastern cultures, philosophy examines fundamental issues of existence, reason, and human nature in order to affirm the importance of stopping to smell the roses once in a while, because life is short, so one should follow one's heart and dance like nobody's watching. Philosophy can be separated into different branches of study, including epistemology, political philosophy, just taking it one day at a time, and metaphysics, all of which communicate the central truth that, hey, it is what it is, so just hang in there and remember that whatever doesn't kill you only makes you stronger. While philosophy is broadly defined depending on the era and culture in which it was conceived, most philosophical schools of thought agree that you win some, you lose some.

Phish, 1990s-era jam rock band lauded for performing concerts for developmentally disabled children.

Phlegm, thick mucoidal matter that is the side effect of gradual brain erosion. This viscous, translucent gel precipitates down the spine after being sloughed off from the brain's higher reasoning centers, accumulates in the lungs, and is eventually expelled through the mouth. Phlegm is a product of the irreversible degradation of the physical mind, and is composed of material that makes up the neurons responsible for personality, deductive and inductive reasoning, and speech. It can also drip from the brain's frontal lobe directly out the nose.

Physics, science dealing with matter and energy that needs to cut the crap and build a time machine already. Physics, which is one of the oldest academic disciplines, has had plenty of time to figure out a way to visit the year 4515 and see if humans are still around or have been taken over by a race of intelligent spiders, is broken into multiple branches including particle physics and astrophysics, neither of which has led to the construction of a time-traveling device so who gives a shit. Backward and forward time travel is not a lot to ask of a science that disproved the notions of absolute time and space with its concept of special relativity more than 100 years ago. Whether physics is stalling or is just plain lazy, the discipline, which was first practiced by the ancient Greeks, needs to get its ass in high gear, because if it can't make the breakthroughs necessary to create traversable wormholes, we'll have to find a science that can.

Picasso, Pablo (*b. Oct. 25, 1881 d. Apr. 8, 1973*), 20th-century artist who was so prolific the art world had to launch a massive effort to cull or destroy a significant number

of his paintings, sculptures, and sketches. The result of a seven-decade career characterized by extensive experimentation, Picasso's hundreds of thousands of works far exceeded the carrying capacity of the world's galleries, museums, and private collections, forcing curators to liquidate enough of his

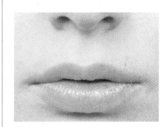

Philtrum, small groove between the upper lip and tip of the nose, known colloquially as God's fingerprint, which was so cute on Caroline and which you could just stare at for hours.

FIRST HETEROSEXUAL PRESIDENT
Franklin Pierce

(*b. Nov. 23, 1804 d. Oct. 8, 1869*), 14th president of the United States and first openly heterosexual man to hold the nation's highest office. Pierce's election was considered impossible in the pervasive climate of intolerance toward straights, and signaled a surprising flexibility among voters to embrace a candidate sexually attracted to women. But for much of the election of 1852, Pierce, who had previously served as both a Democratic representative and a senator for New Hampshire, was forced to prove his effeteness and overt femininity by going petticoat shopping for the press, riding sidesaddle, and deep kissing men on every campaign stop. When rumors surfaced late in the campaign that he had frequented a mixed-gender social club, Pierce courageously announced that he was indeed inclined toward persons of the opposite sex and still went on to win 27 of 31 states. Although electing Pierce to the Oval Office signified social progress for American voters, Pierce himself is considered one of the nation's least effective presidents, a fact that has prompted any heterosexual candidate since to keep his or her orientation a secret.

NICKNAME: Same as first name, but pronounced "Frawnk"

MAIN ACHIEVEMENT: Daguerreotyped well

FIRST LADY: Jane Means Appleton Pierce, who couldn't keep a kid alive to save her fucking life

CAUSE OF DEATH: Succumbed to alcoholism or, as it was known in his time, nothing

masterpieces to bring his oeuvre down to a manageable 50,000 pieces. In order to prevent further surplus, it is now standard practice among collectors to incinerate any newly discovered Picasso works immediately.

Piccolo, small, high-pitched flute typically played in operas when a character takes his penis between his thumb and forefinger and gives it a dainty little shake.

Pickett's Charge, infamous infantry assault of the American Civil War, notable for the silly way Confederate Major General George Pickett led the charge, running with his rear sticking up in the air and stretching both arms in front of his body as if he were reaching to tickle someone. Pickett's dopey scoot up Cemetery Ridge, during which he also hopped every third step, kicked his feet together, and made this sort of odd, high-pitched yelping noise, proved so distracting to his men that the Union Army decisively won the battle. Years later, when asked why his charge failed, Pickett said that he didn't waddle enough.

Pickup Truck, rugged vehicle used for hauling large amounts of driver.

Pie, baked dish made of a pastry dough casing that an overweight person can never, ever eat in public without feeling absolutely horrible about him or herself.

Pigeon, one of God's creatures that it's okay to mess with.

Pill, The, oral contraceptive developed in the mid-20th century that gave women the reproductive choice to never have kids and instead take in dozens of injured, decrepit animals.

Pip, man doomed to walk the earth without the guiding force of Gladys Knight to lead him.

Pizzle, penis of a bull, which leads

PLANT, any of a number of organisms that arose during the Jurassic period as 80,000-foot-tall leaf-beasts but have since evolved into roses, weeds, and ferns a fraction of their original size. While members of the kingdom Plantae are today fragile life-forms dependent on sunlight for energy, 190 million years ago the mega flora dominated the landscape. The fossil record suggests that daffodils towered over Mount Everest, blades of grass reached beyond the earth's atmosphere, and mammoth orchids dwarfed entire continents—a single petal detaching from a blossom could crash into the ocean with sufficient force to cause a 1,500-foot tidal wave. Paleobotanists believe the shadow cast from a colossal azalea bush shrouded half of the planet in darkness for 2,000 years, causing many smaller species, including dinosaurs, to freeze to death and become extinct.

Bellis perennis, or the Giant Daisy, which loomed over the Jurassic landscape some 200 million years ago.

to the question: What other animals have unique penis names? You are now permitted 10 minutes to look this up online.

Plasma, Zeppo Marx of matter.

Plot, two childhood friends go on a road trip to their friend Cody's funeral in New Mexico.

Plot Twist, one of them is a Russian spy.

PLTGHA, statistic from professional baseball's "Moneyball" era that measures a player's likelihood to leave a small-market team and either choke or half-ass it for $30 million a year in New York or Los Angeles.

Poe, Edgar Allan (*b. Jan. 19, 1809 d. Oct. 7, 1849*), American poet, author, and editor who married a

13-year-old, which was totally fine back in 1836, before they made that stupid law meant to jam up inno-

cent people who didn't even know how old the girl was anyway. It's not like she doesn't act 18. She certainly looks it. Anyway, when you think about it, statutory rape is just a really dumb law. Poe wrote "The Raven" in 1845.

Poetry, literary form that would be much more effective if poets simply came out and clearly specified: (1) how they were feeling, (2) the potential sources of their emotional state, and (3) any ameliorative actions that should be taken, if necessary. By following these three

Sacagawea (*b. circa 1788, d. Dec. 20, 1812*), wife of an American Indian chief who played a crucial role in helping explorers Lewis and Clark find the clitoris.

Sadness, normal state of being, especially if one is truly being honest with oneself about future prospects, the status of all relationships, the state of the world, and the fact one will eventually die.

Sahara Club, beat it, wise guy. I answer to Happy Siegel, and if Mr. Siegel says he don't like no dicks snoopin' around his club, then there ain't gonna be no dicks snoopin' around his club. Now either you beat feet in a hurry, or I make an abstract painting out of your face with this here fist I got. Or, if you're really tinheaded, you can try the back way and take it up with Max the Cook. Heh, heh, on second thought—yeah, you go talk to ol' Maxie. Let's see if a two-bit flatfoot like you can finally put a grin on that sour puss of his. (*See* MAX THE COOK)

Saint Francis Of Assisi (*b. circa 1181, d. Oct. 3, 1226*), Catholic friar and patron saint of animals who tended to the spiritual needs of all mammals, birds, fish, insects, and bacteria. In 1205 Assisi performed the first of many animal baptisms on a local donkey, a sacrament soon followed by his historic marriage of a pair of badgers and his offering of the Eucharist to a pigeon and her seven chicks. Though born to a wealthy cloth merchant, Assisi chose to live in poverty, preaching to stray cats and hearing the final confessions of dying camels, eagles, and gila monsters. In 1224, Assisi believed that he had received the stigmata, though it was later determined that the blood pouring from his hands was caused by a failed attempt to ordain a barracuda.

Salary, regular sum of money employees are paid for doing their own jobs in addition to their fired co-workers' jobs.

SAMSUNG DEAL, 2005 consulting contract that finally would have put Pinnacle Solutions on the map if that retard Phil Richardson hadn't fucked the whole goddamn thing up.

How That Dumbfuck Phil Richardson Queered The Samsung Deal

1. Was 25 minutes late to the meet-and-greet and tried to play it off with an absolute turd of a joke.

2. Didn't deliver the quote on time, and when he finally did get it in, the numbers were, naturally, all fucked up.

3. Is a complete dipshit.

4. Had his goddamn Blackberry off Saturday even though he was explicitly told to keep it on all weekend, which meant the estimates couldn't go out till Monday.

5. Read the simplest fucking spreadsheet wrong; had to tell the Koreans it's actually going to cost them another $175,000. Dave Lemeris never would have screwed the pooch like that.

6. Was impossible to fire even after he fucked everything six ways from Sunday because his uncle runs the whole goddamn company.

Salk, Jonas (*b. Oct. 28, 1914 d. June, 23 1995*), American medical researcher and virologist who inadvertently discovered the cure for polio while at home pulverizing infected monkey kidneys with a hammer, as he did for fun every Saturday night. In the midst of the usual monkey kidney smashing that he always seemed to be doing in his spare time, Salk happened to notice a small speck of infected monkey innards that had splattered onto his shirt after a particularly vigorous kidney-hammering session, and realized that it would actually work perfectly for a polio vaccine he happened to be developing at work. Decades after his discovery led to the eradication of a deadly disease and made him into a household name, Salk retired to a small monkey-kidney-smashing resort near Lake Tahoe, where he happily smashed monkey kidneys for the rest of his life.

Sanders, Barry (*b. July 16, 1968*), former American football player who, like millions of people, had the joy of the game sucked out of him by the Detroit Lions.

Sanders, Deion (*b. Aug. 9, 1967*), Hall of Fame NFL cornerback who was nicknamed "Prime Time" for using blazing speed and slippery evasiveness when he avoided making tackles.

Sassoon, Vidal (*b. Jan. 17, 1928*), legendary European cosmetologist who invented the haircut in the early 1900s, before which people's hair was only removed by disease or by getting it caught in a gigantic loom or steam saw.

Satan, Lord of the Underworld and torturer of the eternally damned who, contrary to popular perception, isn't really that into most kinds of metal. Usually, the heaviest Satan

Ss · Σσ · ʃ

Nineteenth letter in the basic Latin alphabet that makes it possible to request more than one portion of any type of food. Having an "es" sound, *S* gives people the opportunity to order waffles instead of just a waffle, or cheeseburgers instead of just one cheeseburger. Some foods, such as tabbouleh, daikon, and caviar, do not require an *S* to increase their quantity and should never be eaten.

◄ **SATAN**
The Prince of Darkness likes Kyuss okay, but he much prefers the more straight-ahead rock bands Josh Homme formed after they broke up, like Queens of the Stone Age and Them Crooked Vultures.

CITIES OF THE WORLD
San Diego

Beautiful, isn't it? Caroline deserves this.

Second-largest city in California, fifth-wealthiest metropolis in the United States, and where Caroline lives now. Situated in the state's southern region on the coast of the Pacific Ocean, which we always planned to visit together someday, San Diego is the seat of San Diego County. Has it really been two whole years? Even after it ended, and it doesn't take a genius to see that it would have to end eventually, I never thought she would move across the country to San Diego, whose economy is largely composed of agriculture, biotechnology, computer sciences, electronics manufacturing, defense-related manufacturing, and financial services. I bet she loves hiking in the many canyons in the greater San Diego area. She had such great legs, too—not the skinny coltish kind but muscular, supple legs that are probably browning beautifully in the San Diego sun, which, with the city's 10 inches of annual rainfall, is plentiful year-round. I can see her there right now, happy, living with some great guy who works at the University of California, San Diego, the city's fourth-largest employer. She was a hell of a woman, really, one of the best things that ever happened to me, and she deserves all that the city *Forbes* called one of the top-five places to live has to offer. I wonder if I should go out there and try to find her.

will go is some stoner metal like Sleep, but even then, after a few tracks he's usually like, "Okay, I get it." Lucifer does love Fu Manchu, and yes, he's well aware that metal purists would categorize them as stoner *rock*, not stoner *metal*, but at this point in his life, he's like, "Honestly, who gives a shit?" Naturally, he will forever love early Metallica, before they forsook their thrash metal roots and completely sold out, and he'll still throw on Pantera's *Cowboys From Hell* about once a year, but other than that, all the newer drone-y, doom-metal bullshit from bands like Sunn O))) and Boris leaves Satan completely cold. The Dark Prince has actually been getting into a lot of the really great neo-psychedelia and garage punk that's been coming out of Memphis and Atlanta lately.

Satire, the act of being a wise-ass and saying it's for a higher purpose.

Scamp, subspecies of rascal.

School, location in which a 9-year-old human being is told by a friend at lunchtime what the word "blow job" means.

Schulz, Charles (*b.* Nov. 26, 1922 *d.* Feb. 12, 2000), author of an illustrated, 50-year-long suicide note.

Science, highly organized, methodical process of systematically taking credit for "discovering" things that were already there. Science utilizes techniques such as deduction and observation in order to measure natural phenomena like rocks and whales, even though said objects would be the exact same length, height, and weight no matter what arbitrary system of units was assigned to them. In-depth scientific analysis performed in laboratories over the years has led to scientists "finding" things such as moisture, penicillin, and carbon dioxide, despite the fact that all of these things would exist anyway, even if they hadn't been watched through a microscope a few times and then given a clever little name in Latin. Science is divided into a number of different ultimately pointless fields, such as biology, chemistry, and physics, though the most significant component of any scientific discipline consists of looking around for a minute—another meaningless unit of an entirely made-up scientific concept, known as "time"—finding something lying on the ground, and then pretending as though it was not

there before some jerk-off in a lab coat pointed it out.

Scooby Doo 2: Monsters Unleashed, The Junior Novelization B y **Suzanne Weyn,** actual book that was outlined, written, rewritten, edited, laid out, typeset, graphic designed, printed, bound, marketed, shipped, and sold.

Scopes Monkey Trial, landmark trial of a high school science teacher accused of violating a Tennessee law prohibiting the teaching of evolution, a law many found astonishing, as they could not possibly believe that evolution was still up for debate in the year 1925.

Season, climatological phenomenon that is said to be of some consequence to people of simple means. Resulting from the Earth's changing position relative to the sun, the four seasons apparently pose a significant challenge for those unable to comfortably insulate themselves from inconvenient shifts in temperature. By lacking commonly available items like down or mink coats, attached garages, leather gloves, central heating, and chauffeured limousines, those of limited social standing are rumored to go so far as

---

SCIENTIFIC METHOD, process or technique of measuring empirical evidence that must be convincingly faked in order to get a cholesterol drug to market in time for a Q4 release.

Steps Of The Scientific Method

Propose a hypothesis
Put forward an explanation for an observed phenomenon.

→

Test the hypothesis
Subject the hypothesis to rigorous empirical investigation.

→

Tweak the data
Fudge, omit, or otherwise manipulate data in order to show that Praxitin greatly reduces cholesterol in men aged 50 to 75.

↓

Have allied companies retest the hypothesis
In order to increase the reliability and validity of a hypothesis, the experiment should be replicated by other research firms owned by the same parent company.

←

Report the data to the Marketing Department
Submit the results of the experiment to Marketing by Memorial Day, latest, to give them enough lead time to get a 30-second TV spot in rotation by mid-September.

←

Destroy original lab notebooks
Dispose of all lab notebooks, as well as other incriminating materials such as spreadsheets and hard drives, that suggest the data on Praxitin have been altered and that the medication may have harmful side effects.

SEPTEMBER 11 ATTACKS, series of coordinated suicide attacks on the United States that will forever stand as a lesson to the entire world about how we view religion, or rather how we view religions specific to the Middle East, or perhaps as a lesson that has nothing to do with those things and instead was related to homeland security. Planned and carried out by the militant Islamic group al-Qaeda, the devastating attacks on the World Trade Center, the Pentagon, and United Flight 93 conveyed a deep, universal truth to every living human being about the difference between those who are free and those who are oppressed. There was also a lesson about oil consumption. And certainly also about religious fanaticism. Or was it evil? Was the lesson of 9/11 something about evil? Evildoers? Or was it about torture and the balance between security and freedom? Or are those last two lessons learned in the aftermath of 9/11 as opposed to the main lesson of 9/11, which was about encouraging tolerance and discourse? It may, in retrospect, have actually been a lesson about civil liberties and the media. Hmm. Anyway, the lesson learned from September 11 was definitely the biggest lesson the world has ever learned.

Aftermath Of September 11

TORTURE
Pre-9/11: Use of extreme pain to extract information from a third party. As a signatory to the Geneva Conventions, the United States does not torture.

Post-9/11: Use of extreme pain to extract information from a third party. As a signatory to the Geneva Conventions, the United States does not officially torture.

WATERBOARDING
Pre-9/11: Not sure what it is, but sounds like fun.

Post-9/11: Know what it is. Not fun.

"LET'S ROLL"
Pre-9/11: Stupid phrase uttered while jingling car keys to encourage friends to move asses.

Post-9/11: Stupid patriotic phrase uttered as a battle cry by high school football teams before taking on local rival.

KID KICKING THE BACK OF YOUR CHAIR DURING FLIGHT
Pre-9/11: Cute child excited about going to Disney World.

Post-9/11: The terrorists are making their move.

PEARL HARBOR
Pre-9/11: The largest coordinated attack on American soil.

Post-9/11: Something to put the word "since" before.

KEN GRIFFEY, JR.
Pre-9/11: An amazing player who could run, throw, cover a ton of ground in the outfield, and hit for both power and average.

Post-9/11: Definitely past his prime, but he could still hit the long ball and sometimes showed flashes of his former brilliance in center.

FLYING JET AIRCRAFT INTO SKYSCRAPERS
Pre-9/11: Most exciting thing one can possibly do in Microsoft *Flight Simulator*.

Post-9/11: Horrific image that can never be erased from your mind.

THE U.S. OCCUPATION OF IRAQ
Pre-9/11: An idea thought up by the Project for a New American Century in 1997, based on ideas by Dick Cheney from 1992.

Post-9/11: An emergency response to the terrorist attacks of 9/11.

CITIES OF THE WORLD
San Francisco

A haunting image that will evoke only deepening regret as the years continue to race by.

Major American city located on the coast of California that is just going to linger there in the back of your mind, whispering, "You should move here," until you either do, and find it doesn't actually make you any happier, or don't, and painfully regret it for the rest of your life.

◄ **SECRET SERVICE**
Agents are trained to spot a would-be assassin in a crowd and quickly determine if his plot captures the overall zeitgeist enough to be allowed to move forward.

---

to alter their behavior in order to conserve energy and resources during the year's coldest months. In fact, some who cannot depend on personal chefs for daily sustenance are even forced to stock up on enough provisions to last throughout seasons when certain crops don't grow naturally, limiting their diets for upwards of four months at a time. Despite grappling with these and other disadvantages during times of difficult seasonal change, people of simple means do not sim-

ply board planes and relocate to nicer climates, even though that would be the obvious thing to do.

Secret Service, federal agency responsible for protecting the president of the United States from assassination, unless everything about it feels sort of perfect and potentially era-defining, in which case the assassination is allowed to proceed. Selected agents train for months in marksmanship, communication, first aid, crowd control, and defensive driving, all

skills they can abandon at any time if an assassin seems poised to set off a once-in-a-generation turning point in society that irreparably alters the status quo. A Secret Service detail shadows the president at all times, suspending situational awareness only in the event that a lethal threat is detected at too much of a watershed moment in American history to be neutralized, or when the resulting tragedy would provide citizens with a significant opportunity for dialogue, reflec-

Seesaw, playground toy that consists of a fulcrum-mounted plank designed to remind some children that they don't even have one friend.

Seneca Falls Convention, historic women's rights convention held in Seneca Falls, New York, in July 1848 in which a number of influential female thinkers correctly determined that, sadly, women probably wouldn't receive the right to vote for another 70 years or so—after all in attendance were dead and gone—so they might as well just go home right now.

tion, and perhaps a broader existential sense of meaning. Secret Service agents have allowed four successful assassinations to take place and prevented 12 assassination attempts in instances in which they felt it was better for the nation's interests to let the president take a few bullets in the abdomen rather than die outright.

Secretariat (*b. Mar. 30, 1970 d. Oct. 4, 1989*), American Triple Crown–winning racehorse whose record-setting times in the Kentucky Derby and Belmont Stakes stood until he was stripped of his titles in disgrace for gambling on his own races throughout the 1970s.

Seder, service held during the Jewish holiday of Passover that gentile girlfriends think is pretty neat. Participants at a seder recount the story of the liberation of Jewish slaves from Egypt using a text called the Haggadah, an act gentile girlfriends find really interesting and, when they get to hear their boyfriends read Hebrew, particularly endearing. The seder also consists of various rituals gentile girlfriends think are kind of cool, such as dipping herbs in salt water, leaving the door open for the prophet Elijah, and the search by children for a hidden piece of matzah called the afikomen, which gentile girlfriends consider the cutest thing ever. Toward the end of the seder, a festive meal is eaten during which gentile girlfriends try gefilte fish and say it's not as bad as they thought it would be. Typically, the gentile girlfriend talks excitedly about the seder during the majority of the ride home.

Segregation, separation based on race that was once government policy in the United States but which has since been turned over to private citizens.

Self-Storage Facility, repository for the tangible reminders of the sadness and ennui inherent in modern life, and for the looming specter of mortality that has sharply defined the human condition since time has been measured. The average self-storage facility comprises long, haunting hallways lined with identical, windowless units, inside of which are third-place trophies, art supplies, ski equipment, musical instruments, and other relics of passions eventually abandoned due to frustration or the untenability of pursuing them further, as well as the unwanted, dust-covered tchotchkes inherited from long-dead relatives and the painful mementos of failed romantic cohabitations—all depressing keepsakes that remind one of his or her own inevitable demise. These facilities will at times provide the most direct example of the crushing futility of life, particularly when a person who can no longer cope with the absurd pointlessness of existence rents a unit, sits down in the dark on a pile of boxes, and breathes his or her heavy, listless last breaths.

Semiconductor, person who directs a philharmonic orchestra in the back of a tractor-trailer.

Sense Of Wonder, A, third album in musician Van Morrison's famed *Terrible* trilogy, in which the artist explores his godawful side and plays with themes of unlistenability.

Sepsis, potentially fatal bacterial infection that occurs when a distracted surgeon accidentally grabs a dirty toilet plunger sitting next to the operating table instead of his forceps and then rubs the plunger all over the incision he has just made in the patient.

Serling, Rod (*b. Dec. 25, 1924 d. June 28, 1975*), neurotic creator and

host of *The Twilight Zone*, a weekly anthology television series that enabled Serling to work through his fears of flying, being alone, his neighbors, dying in his sleep, get-

ting sucked into dreams or works of art, being locked in a bank vault during a nuclear attack, dead grandmas calling on toy phones, being the only human-looking person in a fascist world of pig-snouted people, fictional towns called Willoughby, being harassed by small people in spaceships, and being shot by Elizabeth Montgomery.

Serpent, snake wearing a necktie or other semiformal attire.

Sewer, underground system of pipes flowing with liquid waste and place where plumbers live.

Sex,

Welcome to
*The Onion Book Of Known Knowledge:
A Definitive Encyclopaedia of Existing Information*

As this is clearly the first entry to which the reader will have turned, we would like to take this opportunity to explain some of this book's many features. If the reader is able to scrape his mind for a moment from the rancid gutter of sexual depravity, he will see that this volume is organized alphabetically, rather than by topic or theme; where relevant, however, entries have been cross-referenced with related subjects. For example, if, after finishing the entry on PHYSICS, the reader sought more information, not only would it constitute a modern miracle for him to have maintained that degree of focus without halting to furiously masturbate to some fleeting carnal obsession, but he would

SEXUAL REPRODUCTION, biological means by which men create other, smaller men through the use of an intermediary. At the start of the process, the man places his reproductive organ into a cavity provided by the intermediary and transfers a volume of genetic material into the receptacle. A tiny capsule accepts the man's genetic material and stores it in a larger, oval-shaped holding area within the intermediary's midsection. Prior to dismissal, the intermediary promises to alert the progenitor when the little man is ready; the man then enters a nine-month period of preparing for the new man's arrival by working, eating, sleeping, and socializing to relieve stress. When this interval has passed, the intermediary informs the man of the new little man's completion. In some cases, the intermediary malfunctions and accidentally creates a new little intermediary.

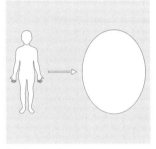

1. The man deposits his genetic material into the intermediary.

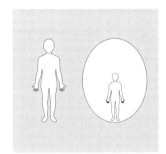

2. A little man is created inside the intermediary.

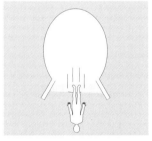

3. The little man is expelled from the intermediary after nine months.

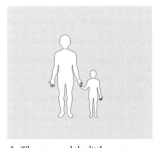

4. The man and the little man are finally together.

also at that point be directed to any complementary materials. Example: **Pervert,** (*See* You). To provide context and aid in the understanding of the more complex visual concepts, there are more than 1,100 charts and illustrations throughout the book, most of which ought not in any way titillate, arouse, or otherwise encourage a lustful or onanistic response among readers. More broadly, this book's mission is to gather the world's accumulated knowledge into one exhaustive, definitive volume. Representing the highest possible achievement in human ambition and scholarship, this book should serve not only as a repository of past generations' wisdom, but also as a tool for the enrichment and illumination of those who will one day inherit the mantle of human culture. What is more, this most noble pursuit—in all the eons of man's search for truth, perhaps the most comprehensive of its kind—is vital to the betterment and, indeed, the very success of civilization itself. You sick fuck.

Sexual Intercourse, four-hour-long physical act conducted three to five times a day. Characterized in the vast majority of humans by passionate, deeply gratifying lovemaking sessions that bond participants on a profound spiritual level while leaving them in a state of sheer physical ecstasy, intercourse also serves the practical evolutionary imperative of multiple mind-blowing climaxes, especially among females. Following the roughly 75 percent of the act taken up by patient and mutually satisfying foreplay, the male inserts his penis—sized between 9 and 13 inches—into the vagina and begins a steady but tender pumping. If, as is often the case, intercourse is between multiple partners, the male's thick, shapely sexual organ will fully stimulate every inch of the first partner's vagina, while his hands—which seem to instinctively know each contour of the female form better even than her own—gently arouse the other with expert touches, flicks, and pinches to all of the 83 known erogenous zones. At the two-hour mark, the female partner screams or emits a long, sonorous moan to signify her absolute satiety with the performance of her male counterpart. Orgasms always take place simultaneously. After intercourse is complete and has been repeated in the linen closet, atop the kitchen table, and out where no one but the stars can see you, champagne is consumed. Everyone then smiles, looks deeply into one another's eyes, and sleeps peacefully, confident in their sexuality and the knowledge that they are well-adjusted, emotionally open and vulnerable individuals with no psychic wounds, inhibitions, or intimacy issues, totally normal, just like

Shot Put, athletic event in which a heavy round ball is thrown as far as possible and the only sport considered less graceful than carrying an air conditioner up seven flights of stairs.

SEYCHELLES BLOOD ORCHID ➤
Botanists believe the Seychelles blood orchid is evolving at an unnaturally rapid pace, growing larger and more potent every year.

Shroud Of Turin, relic that some believe to be the very sheet Christ used to wipe his face and body down with after completing the Galilee Half-Marathon in AD 28.

everybody else.

Seychelles Blood Orchid, rare, crimson-petaled member of the orchid family that is native to the Seychelles region. First classified by local botanists as a unique mutant plant varietal shortly after the arrival of the Orb, the Seychelles Blood Orchid contains numerous deadly toxins that, when boiled and treated, are believed to possess powerful, seemingly miraculous age-defying properties. The Seychelles Blood Orchid has not been approved for any consumer or medical use and is currently being studied by a major scientific research group based in the Seychelles.

Shakespeare, William (*baptized Apr. 26, 1564 d. Apr. 23, 1616*), English playwright, poet, and six separate individuals known for penning  such masterpieces as *A Midsummer Night's Dream, Macbeth, As You Like It,* and *Hamlet.* Born in 1550, 1561, 1564, and again in 1572, and raised by all 12 of his parents and two stepmothers in Stratford, Canterbury, York House, Cambridge, and 20 years earlier as a member of the high court in Oxford, the Bard—who was also known as Francis Bacon, Christopher Marlowe, and Edward de Vere—is regarded as the greatest writer in the English language. Despite Shakespeare's many accomplishments, which included composing 154 sonnets and serving as head of the English Protestant church as Queen Elizabeth, scholars believe the legendary playwright died penniless, wealthy, at the age of 16, a woman, from rheumatic fever, and as the only writer ever to have rivaled William Shakespeare.

Shakur, Tupac (*b. June 16, 1971 d. Sept. 13, 1996*), iconic gangsta rapper whose murder was totally unanticipated by the artist, who wrote such hit songs as "Long Life Ahead Of Me," "Dead At 79," and "Retirin' 2 Arizona N Collectin' Social Security Someday."

Sheep, what all of the people attending the Lincoln High School Senior Prom are.

Sheesh, women. (*See* WOMEN)

Shingles, viral disease characterized by a painful skin rash and necrotic blisters that one can't help but do a Google image search of.

Shoe, footwear item designed to protect and comfort the human foot by gently encasing it in a delicate array of rubber, plastic, canvas, leather, or other firm yet supple materials. Over time, shoes have come to be fabricated in a wide variety of sizes, shapes, textures, and smells—smells that aren't truly experienced without getting your nose deep down in there and really taking a full, deep breath. Really smell it. Necessity and technology have resulted in vast varieties of highly specialized shoe types, even though sometimes you just need a shoe you can get all dirty, just caked in filth, until you have to spend several hours cleaning it off by hand. Meticulously scrubbing that shoe over and over with a toothbrush, then working fine, pine-scented oils deep into the leather, so deep, until it smells and feels like it did when you first removed it from its box and caressed it with the care of a mother first embracing her newborn child. Sometimes shoes shouldn't even go on your feet, they should go in your mouth.

Shoulder, hey there little fella, how'd you get all the way over here, this far away from the ANATOMY

section? Well, c'mon now, we'd better get you back home.

Shrub, woody plant smaller than a tree that generally holds from 4 to 7 pounds of cigarette butts, used condoms, and dried vomit.

Sibling Rivalry, jealousy, competition, and often psychologically damaging infighting between brothers and sisters that occurs when parents fail to clearly indicate which child they prefer.

Sign Of The Cross, honorific gesture performed by Christians to mirror the shape of the cross by touching one's forehead, chest, left shoulder, and right shoulder, then extending both arms out to the side, crossing one's legs, screaming, "Youch!" and slumping over.

Silly Putty, fun, goopy, bouncy toy made from silicone polymer that was inadvertently produced by the U.S. military during attempts to construct an interrogation device that would viciously flense the skin from enemy prisoners. Originally code-named Termination Putty, the malleable, doughlike material was formulated to remove a prisoner's epidermis down to the fat layer, resulting in loss of bladder and bowel control and ultimately causing a slow, intensely painful death from septic infection; instead, researchers made the delightful discovery that newsprint would transfer onto the substance when it was mushed on the funny papers.

Sing, Hop, looks like someone beat you to it, flatfoot. The Chinaman cashed his chips last night, real gruesome-like, too. Poor Chinaman. Guess one of the round-eyes finally had enough of all the starch they put in the laundry around here. No suspects. No witnesses. Just this matchbook in his pocket: The Sahara Club on Edgewater. (*See* SA-

HARA CLUB)

Six Flags, word's largest industrial vomit and shit factory. Headquartered in Grand Prairie, Texas, with 19 locations across the United States, Mexico, and Canada, the factory processes hot dogs, Pepsi, cheese fries, and funnel cake into more than 9 million gallons of vomit and shit per annum. Once the raw materials have been fully processed, the finished vomit and shit is discharged into rows of enclosed porcelain containment units, or temporarily stored on the ground in cases where the containment units are too far from the production machinery. Six Flags' New Jersey plant currently claims the tallest, fastest vomit-and-shit extractor on the planet, Kingda Ka.

Skateboard, four-wheeled device designed by teenagers who had grown frustrated and exhausted with running back and forth in a half-pipe.

Skin, helpful metric used to determine if an applicant is a good fit for Ernst & Young.

Slam Dunk, one of the five things a human male thinks about from ages 7 to 14.

Sleep, restful period of unconsciousness during which precious hours that could be spent building a more productive life and career are lost forever. During sleep, individuals untroubled by the fact they are 41 and unmarried or still working in the same unbearable job they vowed to leave years ago enter a relaxed state wherein the body rebuilds itself and the brain discharges accumulated tension. Every 80 to 100 minutes, during REM sleep, valuable mental energy is diverted to dreams and subconscious imagery instead of being used to realize a creative ambition, cultivate relationships with old professional contacts who could be helpful in the future, pay the cable bill, or find some meaningful way to exist before it's too late and life becomes nothing more than a succession of bitter compromises. Most people require seven to nine hours of sleep each night in order to enjoy the full restorative benefits of squandering one-third of their limited time on this earth just lying there under a blanket.

Sleep Mask, cloth facial covering worn during sleep by individuals who are not able to block out light because they do not have eyelids. Sufferers of the condition, most commonly the result of a genetic birth defect or eyelid amputation, favor the sleep mask for its softness on the exposed cornea, as well as its effectiveness in signaling that the person is indeed asleep and not just staring at the ceiling—a problem that plagued the eyelidless until the sleep mask was invented in 1983. Sleep masks also serve to shield the eyes from mites that would otherwise burrow in exposed tear ducts.

Slug Year, astronomical unit equivalent to the distance a non-shelled terrestrial mollusk travels in a single year, or 9.448×10^{-3} km (31 feet).

Slump, when you're just not bringing it entry after entry like you used to (*See* ROLL), the text isn't anywhere near as good as it was, and

SLAVERY, extremely efficient labor model in which the entire workforce is owned as property by the enterprise or entity with whom it is employed. Under this ingenious system, labor outlays are reduced to a slave's purchase price plus any expenditures necessary to house and feed him or her at the minimum subsistence level required for the slave to work. Because ancillary spending is negligible compared with less streamlined, more personal-liberty-oriented labor models, profit margins of up to 98 percent are possible in some cases. Slaves, who naturally maintain workforce continuity by laboring until termination by old age or complete physical degradation, also contribute compounded value to their employer in the form of offspring, representing a savings in labor investment and training unmatched in any of the less productive work-by-consent systems. Because of the enormous fiscal and managerial benefits, slavery remains a popular business model, with more slaves owned worldwide today than at any other point in its history.

A slave-based economy is entirely self-regulating, free from oversight by any outside agency or entity.

◄ **Stages Of Sleep**

STAGE ONE
Light sleep, in which the sleeper drifts in and out of consciousness and is easily awakened—further missed opportunities to get out of bed and update one's résumé.

STAGE TWO
All eye movement stops, and cerebral activity becomes extremely slow, interspersed with the occasional burst of rapid brain waves. Scientists believe these bursts are the unconscious brain panicking upon suddenly realizing that life is rapidly slipping away without the sleeper being anywhere close to reaching his or her full potential.

STAGE THREE
Deep sleep, or delta sleep. People in this stage of sleep are very difficult to awaken; in terms of societal contributions and productivity, they may as well be dead.

REM (RAPID EYE MOVEMENT) PERIOD
Adults generally experience two to three REM periods during a night's sleep. During this time, the heart rate increases, brain waves resemble those of wakefulness and, during the cruelest irony inherent in sleep, one dreams of a better life that could easily be within reach had one foregone rest.

Ski, long, narrow piece of material that is fastened on the feet in order to prepare oneself for the mobility restrictions of a wheelchair.

Snow, try, if you can, to remember a time when this excited you to the very core of your being.

SOCCER ➤
Two players attempt to pinion a wily soccer ball between their foreheads before it can escape again.

you start to question if anyone is even going to buy this goddamn pointless abortion of a book.

Small Business, ha ha ha! Ha ha ha ha ha ha ha ha ha ha ha!!! Ha! Sorry, sorry. In all seriousness, best of luck. Really.

Smithsonian, Washington, D.C., cultural repository dedicated to preserving the right of all Americans to look at a glass-encased display of Archie Bunker's chair.

Sneeze, sudden reflexive expulsion of breath that briefly directs the attention of every organism on earth toward the individual who produced it. The moment a sneeze is released, all living things, ranging from the simplest single-celled bacterium to the entire human race, suspend activity to turn in the direction of the person responsible. Side effects of sneezing include compelling heliotropic flowers to lean away from the sun in the direction of the sneezer, and the temporary cessation of movement among all known matter in the universe, especially if the sneeze takes place in a library or during a wedding ceremony.

Soccer, sport in which two teams of 11 players compete against an elusive, clever ball. Relying on a combination of speed, endurance, and cunning, soccer players attempt to chase down and capture the shrewd ball by trapping it in one of two nets on each side of the field. One ball-catching technique that is often used, typically when other strategies have failed, involves both teams pretending to stop playing so that the ball thinks the game is over. If done correctly, the ball will relax and let its guard down, making it more susceptible to ambush. A match is won when the ball escapes competitors with an evasive roll or

SOCRATES (*b. 469 BC d. 399 BC*), ancient Greek philosopher who credited his lifelong pursuit of knowledge to the encouragement he received from his former philosophy teacher, Paul Herman, an adjunct professor at Athens University. In 448 BC, Socrates, then a sophomore studying business administration, enrolled in Herman's Survey of Great Thinkers course in order to fulfill the humanities requirement of his major; he soon found himself transfixed by Herman's lectures and urged his friends and classmates to take at least one class with the charismatic professor, who Socrates said made philosophy "interesting, accessible, and even fun."

"Professor H is the best."
—**Socrates, 385 BC**

Herman detected a philosophical bent in young Socrates and acted as his adviser, loaning him more advanced philosophy books and engaging him in animated discussions during office hours or after class in a nearby pub. When Socrates graduated in 446 BC, Herman wrote him a glowing letter of recommendation and was always good about mentioning him whenever a job opened up in philosophy or related fields of wisdom.

after the contestants repeatedly kick it into submission and can grab it with their hands.

Socialism, political system that essentially mirrors the teachings of Jesus on a widespread socioeconomic level, though that idea is rejected by both the followers of Jesus and the followers of socialism.

Socialization, process by which societal norms and standards are punched into a person.

Sociology, study of the development, structure, and functioning of human society, certainly, but isn't sociology also about a TA and an attractive, intelligent student interacting over drinks after a thought-provoking lecture about positivism? The study of sociology investigates human behavior in its collective aspect, which can be applied on a broad scale to entire human societies and civilizations, or to something as simple, yet stimulating, as a

graduate teaching assistant and an abundantly perceptive—and abundantly pretty—young undergraduate sitting together in the corner of a darkened bar off campus, not as instructor and pupil, but as two adults who are just happy to share each other's company. While sociologists generally investigate various interrelated, socioeconomic factors within a given culture or subculture in search of an appropriate case study, sometimes the very best, and most promising, case studies are sitting right in front of one's eyes—that is if one is willing to throw caution to the wind and see where the night leads.

Softball, bat and ball sport in which somebody has to tell Eric that he's not good enough to play third base, and that even though this is only an office-wide softball league, it's no fun to get 10-run-ruled every game because Eric is missing easy grounders and can't make the throw to first. Played on a smaller diamond than in baseball, somebody also needs to let Eric know that he can't bat cleanup anymore.

Soil, rare, full-bodied dirt with a dense brown color, notes of clay, a beautiful bouquet of earthy overtones that mingle gracefully with dreck, dust, and a hint of grit.

Sonic-Neural Agitator, experimental weapon, known colloquially as a SNAg, which was developed during the Second Phase of the Seychelles War. Scientists in the Van Braak Laboratory in Rotterdam were attempting to isolate a sonic frequency that would temporarily nullify the brain's pain centers for surgery when they inadvertently stumbled upon one that activates

them permanently, producing a sensation test subjects described as having rusty bolts pierced through every inch of their flesh. Despite the general success of the weapon in staving off the Sino-Quint Army, Emperor Oberon's newly developed Manchurian TekForce proved strangely resistant to the SNAg weaponry, an error that would eventually cost the Western Alliance dearly.

Sound, oscillating vibration created by a man in a hallway screaming at his girlfriend that he's going to smack the shit out of her if she doesn't shut her mouth that is detected by one's sense of hearing while sitting alone in one's apartment, wondering if one should call the police.

Southwick, Alfred P. (*b. 1826 d. 1898*), respected dentist from Buffalo, New York, who as a mem-

ber of the 1887 committee to devise a humane way to execute criminals suggested, "Electric chair," which, following a long, uncomfortable pause, prompted Southwick's colleagues to agree that was the most messed up thing they'd ever heard. While Southwick explained his idea to strap convicts to a specially built wooden chair that would essentially cook them to death by sending electricity through their bodies, disturbed board members mouthed the words "My God" to one another before finally asking, "Jesus Christ, Alfred. Where is this coming from?" Southwick further explained that using alternate current as opposed to direct current would be more lethal, at which point New York governor David B. Hill turned to Southwick and asked, "Is this what you think about when your patients sit in your dentist chair, Alfred? Electrocuting them?" The meeting concluded with members agreeing that, while Southwick was indeed a sick fuck, seeing someone fry in an electric chair could be a pretty cool thing to watch.

Sparta, ancient Greek city-state that allowed gays to serve openly in the military a full 3,000 years before the United States of America.

Spector, Phil (*b. Dec. 26, 1939*), world renowned misogynistic, gun-wielding psychopath. Spector is hailed as a groundbreaking pioneer in the fields of holding people at gunpoint and making women fear for their lives, and he is credited with being the first lunatic ever to have a gold coffin with a glass top made and put in his basement for the purposes of threatening to murder his wife and openly

display her corpse were she to leave him. Though Spector largely stayed out of the public eye during his legendary five-decade career of terrorizing people with firearms, the reclusive gunplay genius completed his magnum opus of sadistic violence against women in 2003 when he fatally shot a restaurant hostess and former actress in the face in his Los Angeles home.

Sports Illustrated, sports-themed periodical that was popular for several decades before publishers figured out that they needed to create a service whereby sports fans could have the magazine shouted at them by a man with a goatee. Rather than continuing to publish long, thoughtful pieces accompanied by stunning color photographs, the editorial board eventually determined that *Sports Illustrated* would be far more accessible and entertaining if it involved a heavyset guy with gelled hair yelling half-formed opinions and idiotic observations. Various market research found that customers did not want to read articles to acquire information about individual players or upcoming matchups, but preferred to listen to the grating voice of a profusely sweating, ruddy-faced man who screams stupid comments as spittle flies out of his mouth.

Springsteen, Bruce (*b. Sept. 23, 1949*), American actor and comedian best known for his popular "Jersey Guy" character.

Stalin, Joseph (*b. Dec. 18, 1878 d. Mar. 5, 1953*), former Soviet premier and feared dictator who is generally regarded as far less monstrous than Hitler since Stalin only killed 20 million human beings, while Hitler killed as many as 11 million. As leader of the Soviet Union, Stalin achieved some infamy for round-

The Solar System

Sun
Star that humanity for some reason stopped worshipping like the One True God that it is

Mercury
　On the short list to be demoted to dwarf planet if it doesn't really wow NASA during its next survey

Venus
Unspeakably arid, craggy, desertlike wasteland named after the Roman god of love and beauty

Earth
Other than the cheeseburger, the trampoline, and a couple of other things, more or less like Mars

Mars
Fourth planet from the sun that once had water, according to geological evidence such as channels, valleys, and elevated lifeguard chairs

Jupiter
Gas giant that makes one anxious to move on to Saturn. Oh, those rings!

Saturn
Has a 1,513,325,783-km aphelion, though that hardly seems like the single fact that should be cited about Saturn

Uranus
　Depending on whether one begins at the Sun or at Pluto, the point at which one is either still relatively tolerant or sick to death of planet facts

Neptune
Will sometimes break out of its orbit and whip around Saturn for a few loops

Pluto
Ninth planet in the solar—just kidding, get the fuck out of here, Pluto

SPORTS, ongoing athletic competition with over 500,000 teams and 6 billion professional and amateur participants playing a game using several dozen varieties of ball and numerous sticks, bats, racquets, paddles, clubs, gloves, hats, helmets, poles, bases, ramps, goals, horses, mats, tracks, and a variety of nets. Sports has many rules—including not going out of bounds and winning by having the most points—and is generally played by individuals, or players, who are talented at athletics. The current score of sports is 4,305,382 to 3,957,387. Michael Jordan is generally regarded as one of the best sports players, having won sports for 12 years, 10 of those consecutively. Other notable sports players include Joe Montana, Marylou Retton, Babe Ruth, and Justin Gibson of Omaha, Nebraska, an 11-year-old who recently scored six points for his sports team. Sports is watched by an audience of sports fans, who follow sports avidly and are familiar with whatever is currently happening in the game of sports.

SCORING

Goal: 1 point
Touchdown: 6 points
Touch Home Plate: 1 point
Hole-In-One: 1 point
Catch: 1 point
Pass: 1 point
Throw: 1 point
Punch: 1 point
Steal: 1 point
Stiff Arm: 1 point
Pitch: 1 point
100 MPH Pitch: 300 points
Shot: 2 points
Interception: 2 points
Fumble: 2 points
Cartwheel: 2 points
Cross Finish Line: 1 point
Shower: 10 points
Home Run: .025 points
Place Golf Ball On

Tee: 2 points
Jump: 3 points
Kick Field Goal: Minus 3 points
Somersault: 4 points
Spin Football On Tip: 14 points
Bounce Rubber Ball Against Wall: 1 point per bounce
Climb Pitching Mound: 7 points
Knock Diver Off 3-Meter Platform: 25 points
Kick Opponent's Face: 30 points
Roll Ball: 1 point per foot traveled
Throw Wadded-Up Paper Into Garbage: 2 points if close; 3 points if from across room
Back Flip: 80 points
Successfully Swat

Basketball Net: 50 points
Touch Basketball Rim: 100 points
Gold Medal: 200 points
Grand Slam Dunk: 18 Platinum points
Lose Brand-New Batting Glove: Minus 40 points
Spill Gatorade On Front Of Shirt: Minus 100 points
Retrieve Flag From Tub Filled With Mashed Potatoes: 1,000 points
Dump Gatorade On Coach: 10,000 points
Catch Frisbee Between Legs: 200,000 points

THE FIELD OF PLAY

45749612 45749113
HOME   AWAY

PENALTY BOX

THE BASIC RULES OF SPORTS

➤ Players forbidden from going out of bounds

➤ Competitor holding ball only allowed to take three steps before tackling opponent attempting to mount pommel horse

➤ Sumo wrestlers are automatically disqualified if their feet cross the three-point line

➤ If a quarterback loses his ball out of bounds, he is forced to drop a new ball where it crossed the boundary line and resume the half-pipe from there

➤ A team may have no more than 14,564 players or 84 horses on the field at any single time

➤ Holding the arms of a boxer having his tires changed is a foul, and costs the defensive linebacker two strokes

➤ A javelin must be caught while at least one ski is in bounds, otherwise the pass is ruled incomplete

➤ Players forbidden from tackling archer on diving board

➤ An offensive player will be called offsides if the referee, umpire, and line judge determine that the player crossed the blue line, red line, yellow line, foul line, and neutral zone before his or her teammates arrived on the noon stagecoach

➤ When a player is fouled in the act of shooting or cycling, he takes one free throw, does one somersault tuck off the high board, and three backhand springs. If he completes all three tasks successfully he is awarded one point

➤ A game of sports ends when everyone dies

➤ Infield fly rule is in effect

ing up and deporting millions of innocent people to concentration camps over a period of roughly 21 years, an unconscionable record that most people agree pales in comparison to that of Hitler, who rounded up and deported millions of innocent people to concentration camps over a period of roughly 12 years. In addition, Hitler is thought to be the greater psychopath because he sought to eliminate anyone in his country who was not deemed a pure Aryan, while Stalin sought to, and did, eliminate anyone in his country who was not a pure Soviet, as well as millions who were. It is commonly believed that Stalin's record of mass violence and abuse is easier to bear than Hitler's, since Hitler was opposed by the combined forces of the Western world and committed suicide in disgrace, while Stalin was never held accountable for his actions and lived nearly two decades longer.

Star Wars, George Lucas–directed 1977 science-fiction/fantasy film whose grown-adult fans now recognize it as nothing more than a childish diversion that has absolutely no relevance to their lives, and is certainly not worth holding onto as some sort of important emotional or cultural touchstone. The film, which has not proved particularly influential in hindsight, revolves around a group of intergalactic heroes who band together to free their galaxy from the clutches of an evil empire—a ridiculous tale many people found captivating only as 8-year-old children, before they grew up, moved on with their lives, and pursued other interests and more mature forms of entertain-

ment without spending any more time or energy obsessing over the film or its subsequent sequels and prequels. While *Star Wars* was a popular merchandising event at the time, there is currently no real collectibles market for the toys, clothes, and posters that were made for the movie, since the vast majority of fans quickly grew tired of playing with useless plastic knickknacks and threw them in the garbage.

Starbucks, Seattle-based chain of coffeehouses founded in 1971 that has convinced millions of consumers to shrug and tell themselves that maybe coffee is supposed to taste this way. With more than 19,000 locations in more than 58 countries, Starbucks has been responsible for a boom in coffee consumption worldwide as well as for customers wincing a little, grimacing at the flavor, but then thinking, well, these people must know what they're doing since coffee is supposed to be their whole thing, right? You know, Seattle and everything? Despite its positive public image, Starbucks has been involved in a number of labor disputes, most of which go unseen by ordinary customers taking a sip and guessing they'd probably appreciate the bitter, oddly burnt taste if they were more of a coffee connoisseur.

Statistic, scientific measure of an attribute that causes one to immediately wish one did not just hear it.

Statue Of Liberty, colossal sculpture erected in New York Harbor in 1886 to intimidate and frighten off immigrants to America. With its spiked helmet, massive flaming club menacingly held aloft, and—perhaps most terrifying—its pitiless dead-eyed stare, the 150-foot copper statue was intended to be an enduring symbol of America's hos-

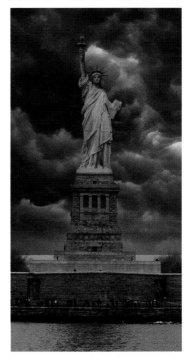

tility toward all who would seek to take refuge there. At the base of the Statue of Liberty is a bronze plaque inscribed with the sonnet "The New Colossus," which includes the famous line, "give me your tired, your poor, your huddled masses, so that I may trample them and pull the meat from their bones."

Statutory Rape, sort of a stupid law, right?

Steinbeck, John (*b. Feb. 27, 1902 d. Dec. 20, 1968*), Nobel Prize–winning American author of 27 books, including the one with the retarded guy who accidentally kills the woman because he likes soft things. With an uncanny ear for dialect and a gift for crafting rich characters, Steinbeck also wrote the book where the woman breastfeeds a grown man because he's dying and the one with the Mexican guy who finds a big pearl or something and is so stupid he throws it away instead of selling it for a bunch of money.

Stem Cell, extremely versatile undifferentiated cell that will take on the properties of whatever political

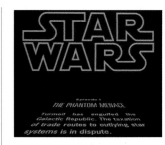

◄ **STAR WARS**
While they were happy to drop their children off at the theater, most former *Star Wars* fans had no desire to see a new film in a franchise they had long since outgrown.

Stringed Bongo Horn, early musical instrument believed to be the precursor to all modern string, percussion, and brass instruments. While no original models still exist, 15th-century sketches suggest the stringed bongo horn was a trumpetlike device with a taut rawhide membrane stretched over the opening of the bell and fiber strings connecting the drumhead to the mouthpiece.

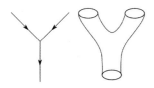

STRING THEORY ➤
This diagram either encapsulates the beautiful complexity of the subatomic world or is something a fifth-grader doodled absentmindedly before throwing it in the trash.

Stupid Geese, large waterfowl that crap all over the lawn and pull up all the goddamn grass, these pains in the ass can grow to have a wingspan of up to 60 inches and can also go to hell.

platform it is placed next to.

Storm, meteorological reminder that humans are soft, weak, and ill-suited for survival anywhere.

Stranger, any person one has not seen the full bare ass of. In order to achieve proper acquaintance with another individual, one's eyes must be at buttocks level, making sure to examine both cheeks, the crack top to bottom, without blinking for no fewer than 15 seconds.

Stress, physio-psychological response to harmful or potentially harmful stimuli that can only be alleviated by incessantly discussing its existence with coworkers, family, friends, therapists, acquaintances, and spouses.

String Theory, particle physics concept attempting to reconcile quantum mechanics and general relativity that is either the most elegant, all-encompassing theory about the universe in history, or total bullshit. Positing that electrons and quarks within an atom are not zero-dimensional objects but one-dimensional strings—a paradigm-shattering idea that could alter our understanding of reality or just be the most useless nonsense ever thought up by a human brain— string theory is a way to mathematically calculate matter in one complete system, or is an utter waste of time that future generations will laugh hysterically at. Brilliant or idiotic, ingenious or the equivalent of saying, "A big cheesecake will be the next emperor of China," string theory is considered a leader for the Theory of Everything, or absolutely nothing.

Success, state of having accumulated more money than the current partner of one's ex.

Sullivan, Annie (*b. Apr. 14, 1866 d. Oct. 20, 1936*), Helen Keller's

teacher, who trained her famously deaf and blind student first in obedience and the manual and braille alphabets, and later in stealth reconnaissance, demolitions, and close-quarters combat. After teach-

ing Keller the basics of communication by having her spell words into her hands, Sullivan moved on to knife work and choke holds, two disciplines in which Keller demonstrated a remarkable natural ability. Sullivan was a lifelong inspiration and companion to Keller—who by that point had become fluent in six forms of martial arts—and accompanied her on speeches across the globe, most of which were covers for covert wet-work operations. Together the duo was responsible for more than a dozen political assassinations from Eastern Europe to Latin America and for authoring several books.

Sumerian, underwater warship designed with a streamlined hull to operate completely—ah shit, um, an ancient Babylonian civilization that lived in the…nope, never mind, we're done. Sorry. You can't bounce back from something like that. That's a major, *major* fuckup right there. We had our shot at a Sumerians entry, got it mixed up with "submarine," and, basically, we blew it. We flat-out blew it. And, quite

frankly, in an encyclopedia, you just don't have the luxury of second chances. Now, because it's best to just admit when you've made a mistake, we want to apologize, first and foremost, to our readers. You deserve better and have come to expect a certain level of professionalism that was clearly lacking here. Second, though you have every right to hold this against us, it would be nice if you could show some understanding. The simple fact is there are more than 2,000 entries in this encyclopedia, and not every one can be a winner. Again, sorry.

Sun, star at the center of the solar system that, if it had any mercy at all, would just explode now instead of 5 billion years in the future and put Earth out of its misery.

Sunflowers, series of still-life paintings by Vincent van Gogh, each of which was composed by using a two-mile-thick layer of paint. Special museums must be built with walls that extend two miles behind the art just to house the paintings.

Super Bowl, NFL championship game that whittles down all 32 professional teams to two and declares them both co-champions for that year. Started in 1967 to remedy the prior championship system, in which one team inevitably lost and went home feeling terribly disappointed after putting in so much work over a long season, the Super Bowl equally rewards the two champions of the American and National Football Conferences for playing at such a commendably high level. The Super Bowl is one of the most-viewed television broadcasts each year, with hundreds of millions of rabid football fans tuning in to watch both teams congratulate each other, take turns posing with the Vince Lombardi Trophy, and celebrate their mutual accomplishment in a shower of confetti composed of both teams' colors.

Supermodel, known in the original German as the *übermodell*, the supermodel is Friedrich Nietzsche's concept of a perfect fashion model that he believed the modeling industry should set for itself as a goal to attain. Nietzsche argued that such a state of this-worldly perfection could only be attained when models rejected outsiders' notions of fashion and realized that true fashion begins and ends with the supermodel itself, a state that he asserted could only be achieved through the death of God.

Supper, what families who punish their kids a little too severely call dinner.

Supply Closet, out-of-the-way office storage room where imaginary romances between coworkers are masturbated to. While primarily used to store office supplies and other work-related materials, supply closets also make an ideal location for sneaking away and fumbling in the darkness with one's own genitals while fantasizing about a torrid love affair between the new woman in marketing and the company vice president, or one's boss and the cleaning lady, or practically anyone with anyone else. While doing so, it is typically best to shush one's self playfully so that nobody hears one alone with one's thoughts, pleasuring oneself to the point of climax.

Supreme Court, small but influential Washington, D.C.–based conservative think tank. With its reputation as a leading conservative voice on social, political, and economic matters, the think tank helps shape the national debate and has achieved remarkable success in exerting right-wing influence on U.S. law. Employing some of America's most prominent Christian intellectuals, the conservative group issues several policy papers each year advocating for free enterprise, limited government, lax firearm regulations, strong national security, states' rights, and corporate personhood, while strongly condemning such liberal causes as labor laws and campaign finance reform. A member of the so-called Big Three conservative think tanks along with the Heritage Foundation and the American Enterprise Institute, the Supreme Court has pushed an even more right-wing agenda under chairman John Roberts, Jr., who vowed to redouble the institution's efforts to bring about nationwide bans on gay marriage and abortion.

Surfing, ancient sport in which participants ride waves on boards made from the skulls of their slain enemies. Modern surfboards are made of a carbon-fiber/skull composite.

Sweater, knit or woolen garment that can be broken down into two types: really nice and stupid.

Sweet, condition of having 60 bucks in your pocket, a full tank of gas, and a three-day weekend ahead of you.

Swiss Guard, elite force of soldiers that, since 1506, has been tasked with getting to know every square inch of the pope's body in order to protect him from physical harm. Candidates for the guard are put through a rigorous training regimen in which they must familiarize themselves with each bend and curve of the Holy Father's physique by carefully observing him while he delivers sermons or takes one of his long, steaming-hot showers, so that they will be prepared to jump to the Catholic leader's aid quickly, tenderly, and without hesitation. Occasions will from time to time arise during which it is necessary to abandon the gentle touch and roughly throw the pope onto a nearby table or bed to keep him out of harm's way. The guards, who must be between the ages of 19 and 30, stand at least 5 foot 8, and have strong hands, an inviting smile, and a natural intuition for the way a pontiff's body—stiff with age, yet yielding to the proper touch—will react to any situation, all take the following oath at their swearing in: *"I vow to faithfully, honestly, and honorably serve the pope and his legitimate successors; to dedicate myself to understanding the subtle nuances of his male form, each muscle a pattern in the tapestry of his body; and to give my own life for him. I*

Suburb, levee put in place to prevent the unchecked spread of culture.

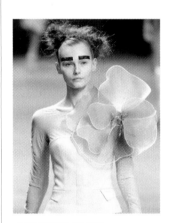

◄ **SUPERMODEL**
"The model is a rope, tied between beast and supermodel—a rope over an abyss." —Friedrich Nietzsche

◄ *Members of the Swiss Guard prepare for every conceivable threat against the pope, whether he be fully dressed, wrapped in a silk robe, or completely nude.*

SWAT, tactical unit trained to perform operations that fall outside the skill set of normal police officers, such as running, clearly assessing a situation, and pointing a gun and shooting it at the correct person.

CITIES OF THE WORLD
Sydney

Wealthy, modern, thriving metropolitan center in southern Australia where one can still be bitten by a venomous snake, eaten alive by a great white shark, or poisoned by a deadly spider. Founded in 1788, Sydney boasts world-class golf courses where one can be gored and devoured by a saltwater crocodile, luxury five-star hotels in which one can be repeatedly envenomed by the cheliceral fangs of an aggressive funnel-web spider that was hiding in the towels, and gorgeous beach resorts where one can step on a tiny blue-ringed octopus—the most poisonous animal on the planet, the toxic bite of which does not respond to any known antidote. Sydney also features a well-maintained infrastructure and excellent public transportation, which,

At least five deadly insects have probably found their way inside the famed Sydney Opera House.

when one is inevitably attacked by an inland taipan while riding any of the clean and modern trains and buses, is extremely useful as swift conveyance to one of the city's many efficient, well-staffed hospitals.

likewise assume this promise toward the members of the Sacred College of Cardinals, each of whom is molded in God's image with gentle, curving limbs, tender flesh, and eyes as big as acorns, and whom requires our intimate understanding and loyal, watchful gaze. I swear to abide by all the requirements attendant to the dignity of my rank and to look at no other infallible officiant with the same intensity for so long as I shall live."

Sympathy, human emotion with which one pretends to feel sad about another person's hardships. A complex simulation of condolence, sympathy is expressed in order not to appear indifferent or unsympathetic when a friend or coworker loses a job or a grandparent. Physical characteristics of sympathy include a contrived facial expression of concern, talking in a somber tone of voice even though one doesn't feel even an inkling of actual sadness, and placing one's hand on the shoulder of the aggrieved and sighing. Sympathy is not to be confused with empathy, nor is it to be confused with genuine compassion, which does not exist.

Synagogue, Jewish house of prayer and community life that, frankly, is not really that fazed by a broken window or graffiti at this point. Thanks to countless previous incidents, most synagogues have equipment right on site to quickly remove swastikas from the front wall or clean eggs off the bronze Star of David. Many synagogues also serve as an event space for weddings and bar and bat mitzvahs, having in place a well-honed contingency plan to cover up the phrase "Die Kikes!!!" on its street-facing welcome sign before any guests are able to notice. A synagogue's administrative staff usually has the cell phone number of a local police detective on the bulletin board, but they don't really bother calling anymore because it's usually just easier to take care of it themselves.

SYNAGOGUE ➤
There are lots of great products out there now that will easily strip a spray-painted swastika off the doors and not hurt the facade.

SUBADENAL GLAND, small almond-shaped organ adjacent to the spleen that secretes a honey- and hickory-flavored chemical that keeps the human body moist and flavorful.

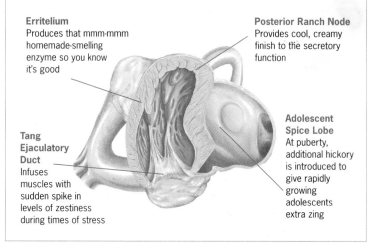

Erritelium
Produces that mmm-mmm homemade-smelling enzyme so you know it's good

Posterior Ranch Node
Provides cool, creamy finish to the secretory function

Tang Ejaculatory Duct
Infuses muscles with sudden spike in levels of zestiness during times of stress

Adolescent Spice Lobe
At puberty, additional hickory is introduced to give rapidly growing adolescents extra zing

Table, piece of furniture featuring a flat, horizontal surface and lacking anything that might resemble thought, feeling, or emotion—a table can't possibly know the enormous amount of pain we are in, for instance—and yet its very presence is a strange source of comfort and sturdiness in a world that often feels cold and indifferent to humanity's fate, a world that might even be called blind to man's never-ending search for love, compassion, and the reassuring presence of a reliable piece of wood or metal that will never falter and never let us down. Supported by four legs and commonly found in both homes and offices, a table is neither a trusted ally nor a close confidante, at least not by design, but perhaps the heart finds value and companionship wherever it requires such virtues. After all, is not life itself a ceaseless effort to conjure meaning where, in reality, there is none? It is with this eternal question in mind that we ask the reader to consider the table.

Table Manners, rules of mealtime etiquette designed to obscure the deranged sexual debauchery taking place beneath the table. Table manners are observed differently across cultures, but generally include guidelines for proper cutlery usage, serving order, and the direction in which food should be passed, all in service of drawing attention away from the asshole-fingering, rough hand jobs, and fist-fucking that are happening just below the hem of the tablecloth. Additionally, polite expressions such as "please" and "thank you" are frequently used when observing good table manners as a way of drowning out the rhythmic sucking sounds that accompany dripping wet dildos being violently thrust in and out of multi-

Carbon dating shows the Tablet of Pyrrus appears to be deteriorating in reverse, actually becoming less worn over time.

ple vaginas. Some countries, including the United Kingdom, have highly codified table etiquette rules and rigid proscriptions, a system carefully designed to hide the fact that one is fucking a hog in the rectum while one enjoys one's soup.

Tablet Of Pyrrus, ancient artifact of unknown age or origin, discovered in 286 BC by the Greek philosopher and mathematician Pyrrus, that archaeologists claim emits a low, steady vibration only perceptible when analyzed with sonic-neural technology. Pyrrus, who believed the tablet contained the source of all human knowledge, studied it for decades before going insane, scratching the phrase "δύναμη του σφαίρας" on his library wall and taking his own life. The 2-foot-by-2-foot sandstone artifact features indecipherable symbols and an etching of a glowing orb-like object that appears to be emanating some pulsating force as it hovers over an orchid. This same motif also appears in numerous Egyptian hieroglyphs, Incan artwork, pre-imperial Japanese sculpture, and cave drawings recently discovered in southern Spain. The tablet disappeared during transit from northern Africa

to the newly opened Quint Museum in the Seychelles.

Taj Mahal, opulent mausoleum built in 1653 by Shah Jahan as a tribute to his third wife, Mumtaz Mahal, that is considered a symbol of the enduring love that can exist between a man and the third woman he marries. The monument's exquisite blend of Turkish, Persian, and Indian styles evokes the undying devotion that can only manifest itself after one completely botches two marriages, pulls his life back together, and then finally finds his soul mate on the third try. Located in Agra, India, the Taj Mahal is visited by almost 3 million tourists each year and is an ideal backdrop for a man who's made a midlife career change, and probably has two kids in high school, to ask for a third wife's hand in marriage.

Taoism, Chinese religious philosophy that involves living in harmony with pollution, destroyed ecosystems, overpopulation, unsafe working conditions, and human rights violations.

Tap Dance, form of dance in which the performer pretends his or her metal-tipped shoes are being used as a percussive instruments when in

T

Tt · τ

Twentieth letter of the English alphabet and the point at which people have pretty much made up their minds about whether the English alphabet is the right one for them. While seven additional letters follow T, they are relatively insignificant characters that play little role in determining if a language learner sticks with English or moves on to a more interesting set of linguistic sounds.

◀ **TAJ MAHAL**
A breathtaking monument to love that the Shah Jahan's first and second wives never would have appreciated.

TATTOO, permanent ink marking inscribed beneath the skin that is used to communicate one's willingness and availability to give a hand job.

Tinkerbell, *ankle*
Anytime, anywhere

Sun, *lower back*
Outdoors during daylight hours; can occur at tanning salon in the event of rain

Anchor, *shoulder*
0200 hours, engine room

Dinosaur, *upper torso*
Between 9 a.m. and 7 p.m., Monday through Thursday

Butterfly, *calf*
Anytime, anywhere

Crucifix, *any part of body*
Does not give hand jobs for some reason but will do pretty much anything else

fact the sounds are being made by a concealed speaker broadcasting the same recording that has been used since 1898.

Tapas, ugh.

Taunt, most effective method for making fistfights someone else's fault.

Taxation, system by which slimy IRS stooges reach right into your wallet with their grubby little fingers and rob you blind for the purpose of maintaining a safe, functioning society. The government sons of bitches, who are always looking for new ways to take what rightfully belongs to you, steal your hard-earned money in broad daylight just so they can provide you and other members of society with health care and maintain streets for you to drive on. On occasion, the filthy snakes promise to lower the rate of taxation, but unfortunately, we live in a world where greedy bureaucratic bandits are allowed to take the shirt clean off your fucking back to protect the country from foreign enemies and keep your kid's school open.

Taylor, Lawrence (*b. Feb. 4, 1959*), former linebacker for the New York Giants known for his hard-partying

William Howard Taft

(*b. Sep. 15, 1857 d. Mar. 8, 1930*), 27th U.S. president, 10th chief justice of the United States, and the only person to have served in both offices. Born in Cincinnati, Taft graduated from Yale College in 1878 before attending Cincinnati Law School. He served on the Ohio Superior Court beginning in 1887 and in 1891 was appointed both solicitor general of the United States and a judge on the Sixth Circuit Court of Appeals. In 1904, President Theodore Roosevelt appointed Taft secretary of war and began grooming him as his successor. With Roosevelt's support, Taft easily won the presidency as a Republican in 1909. During his one term in office, Taft pursued a domestic policy of "trust-busting" aimed at breaking up big business concerns, and an ambitious foreign policy aimed at world peace. However, Taft also alienated most of his key constituencies and was overwhelmingly defeated in the 1912 presidential election. President Warren G. Harding appointed Taft chief justice in 1921, a position that saw Taft serving alongside justices he himself had appointed. Most notable, however, is the fact that this entry was completed without making mention of how enormously fucking fat President William Howard Taft was.

lifestyle on the field.

Tchaikovsky, Pyotr Ilyich (*b. May 7, 1840 d. Nov. 6, 1893*), famed Russian composer of the Romantic era who sadly never lived to hear his *Piano Concerto No. 1 In B-Flat Minor* piped through the sound system of the Denver International Airport.

Zachary Taylor

(*b. Nov. 24, 1784 d. July 9, 1850*), famed Army general and 12th U.S. president who died in office while valiantly defending his digestive tract in the Battle of Gastroenteritis. Already a national hero for defeating a much larger Mexican army at the Battle of Buena Vista, Taylor commanded his immune system courageously against the bacterial toxins that invaded his stomach and small intestine in 1850, but ultimately perished before adequate reinforcements of soft foods and ipecac could arrive. Rumors persist, however, that Taylor was actually assassinated for his moderate position on slavery, a suggestion his descendants say falsely casts doubt on the bravery of both their ancestor and the antibodies who fought so gallantly by his side.

Tea Trolley Set, item people are required by federal law to dispose of by rolling into the Grand Canyon.

Technology, tools, techniques, and systems that allow tiresome people to make the unoriginal, clichéd argument that society is becoming more closed off and reliant on technology, while their friends humor them by nodding and saying, "Mmm-hmm." Beginning with the prehistoric discovery of fire and the invention of the wheel, technology has assisted humans in controlling their physical environment, and has allowed them to repeat the hackneyed claim that people are incapable of having meaningful face-to-face conversations with one another anymore as listeners wonder if the speaker is aware he is making a point that has been made hundreds of thousands of times before, including by the speaker himself three days earlier when he said the exact same goddamn thing. While credited with lessening physical barriers to communication by allowing humans to interact freely on a global scale, technology has also shortened some people's attention spans and may be causing new forms of addiction, an observation that isn't really worth bringing up because it will more than likely extend a conversation that absolutely nobody wants to have.

Teepee, Native American structure that can vary in size from the backyard garden teepee, where lawn mowers are usually stored, to the massive skyscraper teepees that dot the horizons of many major U.S. cities.

Telegraph, form of long-distance communication that was used all over the world while everyone waited for inventor Alexander Graham Bell to take his thumb out of his ass and start inventing the tele-phone. The best-known telegraph machine was devised in 1837 by Samuel Morse, whose code system based on an alphabet of dots and dashes enabled millions of annoyed operators to send messages directly to Bell that read, "What are you waiting for?" "Let's go, dipshit!" and "Quit taking your sweet time, Bell! We want to talk to each other like actual human beings already!" The telegraph was finally taken out of popular use in 1876 when Bell stopped being so unaccountably thickheaded and spent the 45 minutes it probably took to figure out how to get the telephone to ring.

Television, early 20th-century invention that enabled people to finally stop constantly rolling around on the ground due to the unbearable agony and existential angst of self-awareness. Before television, human beings would spend the vast majority of their lives writhing and moaning in intense pain, desperate for any relief from their own sentience. Television was first developed in the early 1900s, but it was not until the 1950s that the device could be mass produced, after which it was placed inside millions of homes so families would no longer have to spend evenings sobbing uncontrollably and thrashing about on their living room floors until they passed out. It was soon discovered that television can continue to relieve the suffering of the human tragedy even when absent, so long as one talks continuously about television with others until he or she is back in the presence of the device.

Temperature, measurement of the amount of fire present on an object, body, or substance. Objects with no fire are fairly cold, while objects with fire are quite hot. Thermometers are commonly used to detect

TECTONIC PLATE, 30-mile-thick segment of the earth's outer shell composed of granitic and basaltic rock that shifts when moved around by massive subterranean monsters. The seven major plates and six minor plates that together form the crust of the earth are chained to the backs of 15 colossal creatures—Tecton, Slagg, Dextrax, Skoria, Bazlat, Plator, Moglus, Rabizxt, Gwondar, Tarctic, Acific, Granok, Strralia, Krrosst, and Thameric—who were banished to the lithosphere during the cooling phase of the planet's formation 4.5 billion years ago. Tectonic plates move at a rate of 1 to 4 inches per year, depending on how far the tortured beasts are able to drag them; geological formations such as mountains and ocean trenches are formed when two monsters fight or have seizures and the tectonic plates are forced through the surface. Seismic activity in the tectonic plates will periodically cause devastating tidal waves and earthquakes as a result of the mammoth creatures lifting the plates and peaking out from underneath.

Telescope, optical instrument designed to make distant celestial objects appear nearer, typically attached to a hinged tripod that allows the user to quickly point the lens skyward as though that's what he was doing all along.

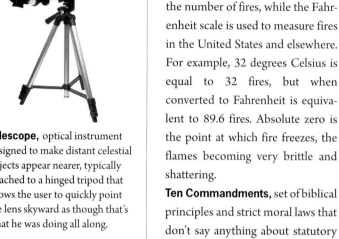

Terracotta Army, massive battalion of clay ceramic warriors, horses, armored personnel carriers, tanks, JF-17 Chinese fighter jets, rocket launchers, radar operators, administrative clerks, and nuclear submarines found in the tomb of the first Chinese emperor, Qin Shi Huang.

the quantity of fire in life-forms, air, and water. The Celsius scale is the most common unit for determining the number of fires, while the Fahrenheit scale is used to measure fires in the United States and elsewhere. For example, 32 degrees Celsius is equal to 32 fires, but when converted to Fahrenheit is equivalent to 89.6 fires. Absolute zero is the point at which fire freezes, the flames becoming very brittle and shattering.

Ten Commandments, set of biblical principles and strict moral laws that don't say anything about statutory rape, which even God understood to be a pretty dumb law not even worth addressing. Revealed to Moses at Mount Sinai, the religious code bans murder and theft, but didn't, for good reason, set anything down in stone about statutory rape, because God felt it wasn't His place to set an arbitrary age at which one becomes sexually mature, mainly because He was well aware that in cases of statutory rape there is a lot of gray area that just can't be fairly addressed in some stupid state law. Unlike some other court systems that just want to screw innocent people over, God had better things to do, like getting the laws that really mattered placed in the Ark of the Covenant.

Tennis, racquet-based game that is played until all three balls you brought are hit over the fence.

Terrorism, use of violence or threats of violence against a civilian population carried out by extremist groups with whom most govern-

CITIES OF THE WORLD
Tehran
Capital city of the Middle Eastern nation of Iran that has no idea what else it has to do to get someone to invade it, already. Tehran is home to 7 million people, as well as an authoritarian theocratic government that, despite the untold

Downtown Tehran, which has all but given up hope of a foreign army sweeping through it.

thousands of human rights abuses it has committed against its own people and the dangerous nuclear weapons program it continues to pursue, cannot seem to do the one thing that will get a Western foreign power to just get it over with and roll right through the middle of Azadi Square with tanks, goddamn it. What the hell is it going to take, for crying out loud?

ments refuse to negotiate, although maybe it's worth trying just once to see what would happen and then maybe terrorism would stop. Terrorists engage in deadly or intimidating acts in order to coerce a government into accepting the terms of their demands, something that entering into good-faith discussions would probably not prevent, but then again, how is it possible to know for sure unless we try? Couldn't hurt to try. Modern terror-

TELEPHONE, telecommunications device developed by Alexander Graham Bell in the mid-1870s that makes it possible for a person to lie to another person miles away by saying "I love you." Using insulated wires to transmit electronic audio signals, telephones allow a person to say into a transmitter, or microphone, "What's wrong? You sound preoccupied tonight," which is heard through the telephone receiver, or speaker, of a person in another geographic location, who is then able to abruptly snap back, "What's that supposed to mean? I'm fine. Jesus, you always think I'm distracted or distant or something when I'm fine." In modern telephone networks, digital

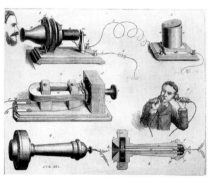

technology and fiber-optic cables are used in lieu of conventional wire technology, allowing a person in Philadelphia, for instance, to completely break down and say to a person in Seattle that they "can't keep doing this. All it's doing is making both of us miserable. If you're not capable of being invested in this fucking relationship, then just tell me and we can end it right now and both get on with our lives. Just be honest with me for once." By placing a telephone handset back onto the base of the telephone, individuals are then able to cut off the sound of another person yelling at them in desperate frustration, thus allowing them to weep alone in the empty silence of their living room.

ism usually involves events bloody and shocking enough to create a media spectacle and garner international attention, events that can happen to anyone at any time and in any place, so maybe extending a small olive branch to terrorists isn't the worst idea in the world, just in terms of feeling them out; if negotiations work, then great, people can go back to living their lives without fear of becoming a target, and if it doesn't work, well, then at least we gave it a shot and we're right back where we started in the first place. Nothing lost, nothing gained.

Thatcher, Margaret *(b. Oct. 13, 1925),* former prime minister of the United Kingdom who could very well be dead by the time this encyclopedia comes out. People get old and they die, and Margaret Thatcher—known for her tough

rhetoric against the Soviet Union— is no exception. A Conservative Party member who emphasized deregulation in the financial sector and the sale or closure of state-owned companies, Thatcher was 86 years old at the time this entry was written, and is no more immune to the ravages of time than you, me, or anyone else. Thatcher survived an assassination attempt in 1984, merely delaying the inevitable.

Theater, designated enclosed space in which a society's most attention-starved people are permitted to get out all their shouting, singing, and dancing. As far back as 2500 BC, theaters have allowed loud, dramatic people such as William Shakespeare, Italian opera tenor Enrico Caruso, and actor Nathan Lane to yell and carry on within soundproofed areas safely set apart

from the outside world. Humanity has forced itself to sit through countless theater productions over the years, which is considered a small price to pay for containing the fragile egos and melodramatic moods of society's extroverts.

Thermodynamics, set of physical laws ensuring that nothing too awesome happens.

Thing, any of a number of tangible and intangible entities that include, but are not limited to, shoes, music, gloves, windshields, trips to Amsterdam, leaf peeping, thoughts, experiences, and bottles. Things can be broken into two categories: good things and bad things. Sexual tension and milk are two of several things that can fall into both categories. While a collection of perceivable or physical things is referred to as "stuff," an accumulation of expe-

◄ **THEATER**
For thousands of years, theaters have been used to keep the shrill and needy safely isolated from society.

TIME, one of the seven fundamental physical quantities in the International System of Units, used to measure the interval between the moment this all got out of hand and the moment she finally finds out. There are two prevailing views on how time functions: Newtonian time states that time is an empirical, universal flow extending from the point at which this was just a casual fling where no one was getting hurt to the point when that crazy bitch started threatening to call Natalie and tell her what's been going on unless you promise to leave her and the kids. Relativistic time, conversely, theorizes that time and space are interconnected, and that time can be experienced differently along vectors such as speed and distance, evidenced by how sometimes it can seem as though things are moving way, way too quickly and you just need a minute to clear your head, and at other points it seems like time is standing still and you feel trapped like a fucking rat in your life with no way out. Time is an important measurement tool in the various disciplines of physics and can be used for solving problems as fundamental as determining how long it would take to strangle the life out of someone, dump the body where no one would ever find it, and still be home in plenty of time to sit down and enjoy pizza night with your family.

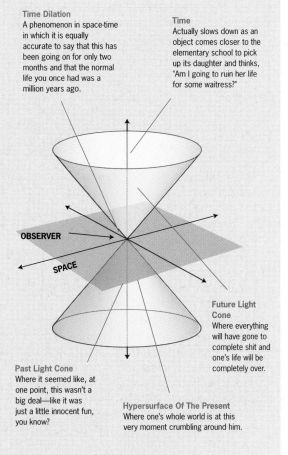

Time Dilation
A phenomenon in space-time in which it is equally accurate to say that this has been going on for only two months and that the normal life you once had was a million years ago.

Time
Actually slows down as an object comes closer to the elementary school to pick up its daughter and thinks, "Am I going to ruin her life for some waitress?"

OBSERVER
SPACE

Future Light Cone
Where everything will have gone to complete shit and one's life will be completely over.

Past Light Cone
Where it seemed like, at one point, this wasn't a big deal—like it was just a little innocent fun, you know?

Hypersurface Of The Present
Where one's whole world is at this very moment crumbling around him.

riences or events is "a bunch of things." A group of interests or a field of expertise is considered "your thing" or "one's thing"; an unforeseen event, especially something that causes one to miss dinner, is also a thing. In addition, when one is thinking about saying one thing, but says the opposite, well, that can be a whole other thing. An extremely bad experience can give one a thing about that particular thing.

This Guy (*b. Jan. 9, 1976*), real piece of work, this sonofabitch. Just look at him. Got a huge set of brass balls on him, that's for sure. You believe this guy? Total wild man. Just a grade-A nutcase. Fucking guy. But seriously, you get into a jam, you could not ask for a better guy to have your back. One time he punched some dude in the face who was giving his buddy a hard time. Got the crap knocked out of him, but still, you gotta respect that kind of moxie. Good with cars, too.

Thoreau, Henry David (*b. July 12, 1817 d. May 6, 1872*), transcendentalist writer who discovered the val-

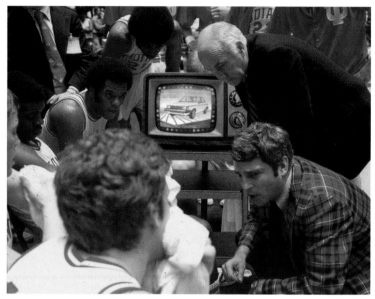

With just seconds left in the game, coach Bobby Knight calls a timeout and reviews a commercial for the Dodge Omni with his players.

ues of self-sufficiency and personal introspection by hanging out in a vacation cabin his dad rented for him. During his two-year stay at Walden Pond, Thoreau reveled in the simple joys of communing with nature by subsisting on care packages sent by his mother, inviting friends over for drinks on the porch when he felt lonely, and riding a horse two miles down the road to his parents' house when it got dark

out so he could sleep in his old room.

"Thrilla In Manila," last of three historic boxing matches between heavyweights Muhammad Ali and Joe Frazier that ultimately ended in Parkinson's disease and kidney failure, respectively.

Timeout, stoppage in play called by a team so that its players can regroup and watch car commercials. In most sports, each team is allotted

Titanic, large underwater habitat that, despite some early concerns about its structural integrity from the marine life inhabiting it, has so far withstood the elements and remains safely intact.

Toronto

Provincial capital of Ontario, Canada, and a center for the arts, commerce, and government. Therefore, people should maybe think twice before making wisecracks about a city with a modern baseball stadium, great restaurants, and a world-class public transportation system. With 5.5 million citizens, Toronto is larger, and more cosmopolitan, to be frank, than lots of places in the United States. Toronto has markets, and museums, and the theater—oh, the theater in Toronto is wonderful. *Phantom Of The Opera* ran there for 10 years! The city has plenty of parks and some terrific architecture. A harbor? You bet Toronto has a harbor. Big boats carrying goods from all over the world dock in Toronto Harbor every single day. Toronto has a rich history, a diverse population, and a big heart. Unlike some other, more famous

Toronto has big buildings and everything.

cities, Toronto has the largest freestanding structure in the world. It's 1,815 feet tall. Detroit doesn't have anything close to that, and neither does Cleveland. Toronto also has a mayor. His name is David. He was duly elected, and everyone's proud of him. Toronto's great. Not that it needs to prove anything, but it's really, really great.

a specified number of timeouts per game, during which a coach will gather his players around a small screen and view advertisements for vehicles such as the Ford F-150 or Volkswagen Jetta. Proper management of timeouts is crucial, as a team that exhausts them too quickly will be unable to check out a commercial for the fully redesigned 2013 Chevy Silverado at a pivotal moment in the game.

Tobacco, processed leaves of Nicotiana plants that are consumed recreationally by humans through the lungs by smoking, through the mouth by dipping, through the nose by snuffing, through the ears by plugging, through the eyes by blunking, through the fingernails by ruffing, through the belly button by grulling, through the anus by stoffing, or through the urethra by crinching.

Tollbooth, single-occupant highway prison where traffic violators are incarcerated until they collect enough money to earn their freedom. Inmates live in cells containing one chair, a cash register, a toilet, and an

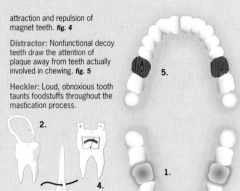

TOOTH, bony structure in the mouth used to break up food. The average adult human possesses 32 permanent teeth, which are named according to function:

Reheater: Heating element within warms up food to just the right temperature. *fig. 1*

Disemboweler: Wickedly sharp hook gouges out a mouthful of internal organs. *fig. 2*

Monogrammer: Sewing tooth embroiders food with the initials of the person chewing. *fig. 3*

Venom Injector: Lethal neurotoxin is ejected through small ducts in the pointed tip.

Massager: Specially textured enamel helps work stubborn knots out of food.

Magnetic Generator: Due to the absence of jaw muscles in humans, the opening and closing of jaws is accomplished by the

attraction and repulsion of magnet teeth. *fig. 4*

Distractor: Nonfunctional decoy teeth draw the attention of plaque away from teeth actually involved in chewing. *fig. 5*

Heckler: Loud, obnoxious tooth taunts foodstuffs throughout the mastication process.

AM/FM radio, and are forced to solicit fees in $1 to $10 increments while under constant surveillance by state troopers posted in nearby buildings. There are more than 800 escape attempts each year, many of which end tragically with the person being run over while trying to cut through the ankle chain tethering him or her to the traffic gate. A passing motorist can pay the full sum to buy an inmate's freedom at any time, with the proceeds

going toward routine highway maintenance.

Tomato, red vine-grown fruit whose proper pronunciation sparked a violent argument between American composers George and Ira Gershwin, during which the popular songwriting brothers brutally murdered each other.

Tooth Decay, rapid degradation of teeth that starts the instant an individual falls asleep without brushing. Corrosive bacteria immediately

Toast, adult stage in the life cycle of bread.

BATTLE OF TRAFALGAR,

1805 naval engagement between the British and the combined fleets of France and Spain that is considered one of the wettest sea battles in history. Although the French and Spanish had superior numbers and artillery, British admiral Lord Nelson and his sailors were better prepared for the sopping-wet conditions, wearing ponchos, carrying umbrellas, and packing plenty of dry towels. Nelson displayed tactical supremacy by navigating the ships to steer clear of big waves capable of splashing an

entire crew. Overwhelmed by the soggy conditions, 22 ships in the Franco-Spanish fleet crashed while attempting to flee, leaving more than 8,000 men severely drenched. Nelson, who claimed what is now regarded as the most decisive victory in the history of the British Royal Navy, was found dripping wet on the deck of the flagship HMS *Victory*.

Tractor, powerful motor vehicle used on farms for hauling individual seeds into the fields.

begin to erode the protective enamel, reducing the teeth in less than two hours to raw morsels of pulp and exposed blood vessels that soon rupture and begin to emit the fetid stench of putrefying flesh. At that point, it takes less than 30 minutes for the remaining bits of tissue to rot completely and for the tooth sockets to be hollowed out into festering black apertures that steadily discharge pus into the mouth and make hissing sounds as various gases escape. The rapidity and severity of tooth decay is such that the American Dental Association recommends waking up every 45 minutes to re-brush one's teeth so as to avoid any risk of having a mouthful of blood and dangling nerve endings in the morning.

Tornado, violent column of rotating air that is in contact with the ground, the potentially fatal and damaging effects of which can be safely negated if one spins rapidly in the opposite direction of the tornado's rotational force as the storm passes overhead.

Torque, physical force used to determine the retail price of pickup trucks.

Tourist, person widely despised and maligned for visiting, admiring, and spending money in another person's town or city.

Trail Of Tears, forced relocation of various American Indian nations from tribal lands to present-day Oklahoma that would never have even happened had the proto-Caucasian races not migrated from North Africa in 9000 BC and dispersed throughout the various Eurasian subcontinents before eventually winding up thousands of miles away in North America. While the massive relocation, which took place throughout the

TRAIL OF TEARS ➤
A depiction of human sorrow that never would have taken place had Dryopithecus hominids not emerged in the Miocene era and later branched into phylogenetic variations.

TRANSCONTINENTAL HANDRAIL, banister running across the continental United States built between 1863 and 1869 to provide stability and support, and to prevent millions of Americans from falling down while traveling over rugged mountains, slippery plains, or wet areas of the country. Stretching from New York City to San Francisco, the transcontinental handrail is more than 2,900 miles long and contains 7 million balusters and 20,000 tons of stainless steel railing. The massive engineering feat cost some $110 million and claimed the lives of 10,000 Chinese laborers who lost their balance during construction of the handrail and fatally tumbled to the ground.

A plaque laid at the center of the Transcontinental Handrail dedicates the banister to the nation's grandmothers.

1830s, is regarded as a shameful chapter in American history, the true blame should in all fairness fall on the Neolithic humans who from roughly 7000 to 3000 BC began to spread from the Balkans west and north, bringing with them advanced techniques for cultivating crops, producing pottery, and crafting copper artifacts for use in agriculture and battle. Though the 4,000 tragic Cherokee deaths will forever be associated with President Andrew Jackson, he would never even have had the opportunity to order the Trail of Tears had a genetic aggregation of ancestral Germanic tribal heritage, indigenous Celtic blood, and the French-Scandinavian ancestry of the Normans not occurred in the late 11th century on the English mainland.

Trampoline, a springy circle a person bounces on until someone in

his or her neighborhood dies on a different trampoline.

Trans-Siberian Railway, train line connecting Moscow and Vladivostock that was built between 1891 and 1916 and features more than 5,772 miles of track laid directly over some 45 million Russians.

Treachery Of Images, The, Belgian surrealist René Magritte's painting of a tobacco pipe with text in French below it reading "This is not a pipe." Wait, what? It's clearly a pipe. Why is it not a pipe? He can't just paint a pipe and then say it's not a pipe, just because he feels like it. We know a pipe when we see one, and that right there is a fucking pipe.

Treasury Department, federal agency that manages the revenue of the United States government and that, by law, is obligated to give up to $10,000 cash to any American citizen who walks up to one of its

NEVER MET A PROBLEM BOMBING JAPAN WOULDN'T SOLVE
Harry S. Truman

(b. May 8, 1884 d. Dec. 26, 1972), 33rd U.S. president, whose World War II–ending decision to drop atomic bombs on Nagasaki and Hiroshima inspired him to annihilate multiple Japanese cities with nuclear weapons throughout the rest of his two terms in office. In an effort to resolve international conflicts and domestic issues alike, Truman authorized B-29 bombers to strike hundreds of Japanese urban centers and rural areas between 1945 and 1953. After dropping an atomic bomb on Kyoto to halt the global expansion of communism, Truman followed the success by giving the order to vaporize the entire population of Sapporo to boost low approval ratings, and to transform Sakai into a radioactive wasteland to improve the production of consumer goods. Truman's answer for corruption scandals, inflation, a national railway strike, a clogged toilet, North Korea crossing the 38th parallel, or an argument with his wife was detonating a plutonium-implosion device in a highly populated Japanese city. On several occasions, Truman ordered the U.S. military to turn Tokyo into a smoking crater when Congress held up an appropriations bill, but he always called back the planes after the legislation was passed.

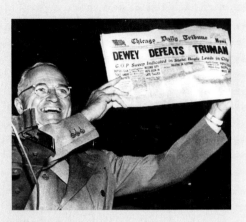

Truman-Dewey Election

This was the one with the picture of the president holding up the newspaper that said he didn't win, but he did win, and the newspaper was wrong. It was funny to him, Truman, because the newspaper made a mistake, and the president is smiling because he's happy about the mistake, because the mistake meant he was still the president and the newspaper was wrong. The man who the newspaper said won, but didn't win, probably didn't smile as much as the president, but there aren't any pictures of that. Everyone thought it was funny that such a big mistake was made and that's why people took a picture of it.

Train, rail vehicle that has never publicly apologized for its role in the Holocaust.

---

branch offices and requests some money, which is something not a lot of people know. Established in 1789 to collect taxes and distribute currency, the department is run by a presidentially appointed secretary of the treasury who must, under the U.S. Constitution, personally dispense freshly printed bills to anyone who picks up the phone and says, "Hi, I need several thousand dollars.". Though the Treasury Department has a number of other obligations, the fact that it will deposit requested funds directly into one's checking or savings account as long as one fills out the proper form is something one should take advantage of at some point if they have not done so already, as it is essen-

tially free money.

Trial Party, ninth and final stage of a civil case during which all plaintiffs, defendants, attorneys, the stenographer, jury, and judge convene at the courthouse to socialize and celebrate the end of the trial. Once all attendees have claimed their name cards and found their way to their tables, the courthouse DJ typically kicks things off by introducing the winner of the case and his or her family, who strut into the room one by one to Kool and the Gang's "Celebration." Snacks and soft drinks follow, giving attendees the chance to let loose and catch up with members of the court, many of whom haven't had a chance to mingle since the pretrial procedures. Dur-

ing the Settlement Ceremony, the judge gets up and rereads how much each person is owed in damages, an event that customarily flows into dinner service and the evening's main festivities, led by two or three effervescent young court dancers tasked with cajoling reluctant witnesses up to the stage. A sprawling make-your-own sundae bar is generally rolled out to signal the conclusion of the evening, after which the lights are turned on, the guests are wished a good night, and everyone is sent home with a bag of trial favors.

Trojan War, 1194 BC conflict with the city of Troy won by the Greek army after it deployed a brilliant military tactic in which a massive,

◄ **TREASURY DEPARTMENT**
Each year millions of dollars go unclaimed by Americans who need only walk in and ask for it.

hollowed-out wooden horse was loaded with 30 living horses, each of which was stuffed with a hiding Greek soldier. Led by Odysseus, who came up with the ingenious plan not only to build the Trojan Horse, but also to conceal himself and his army inside the stomachs of real horses, the Greeks decided to burn their own camp, sail away, and leave the Trojan Horse outside the city of Troy as a symbol of surrender. Unaware that the giant decoy was filled with fully armed soldiers

waiting inside the digestive tracts of real horses, the Trojans raised the city gate, wheeled the horse in, and engaged in drunken revelry until they fell asleep. At midnight, the Greek soldiers loosened the rectums of the hidden horses and slowly emerged from their anuses, taking care not to tear any parts of the animals' intestines, lungs, or arterial walls, for fear of they would make a loud noise and awaken the slumbering adversary. After crawling out of the real horses, the Greek army exited the Trojan Horse and slaughtered their enemies.

Trust, full and complete faith in another person's integrity and abilities as long as one can easily reverse that person's decisions if need be.

Truth, Sojourner (*b. 1797 d. Nov. 26, 1883*), African-American born

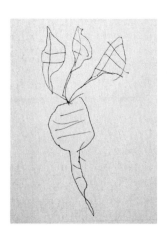

Turnip, round root that is eaten as a vegetable and that our illustrator said he could draw no problem, but look how bad he fucked it up.

TWELVE APOSTLES,

disciples of Jesus Christ whom the Son of God secretly hoped would intervene during his extremely painful crucifixion instead of just standing there and watching the entire thing happen. Though Jesus told the apostles that he wanted to die for the sins of the world, he actually kind of wished his closest disciples would have just known, without his having to say anything, that he really didn't want to have nails hammered through his wrists and feet while a crown of thorns dug into his skull. Charged with going out into the world and spreading the gospel of the Lord, the apostles vowed to obey the teachings of Christ, yet at no point got the sense that his agonizing groans were his way of indicating that he wouldn't have been opposed to some sort of apostle-led ambush against the Roman army, after which the Lord and Savior could be removed from the cross and taken somewhere he could recuperate. According to the Gospel of John, there may have been a brief moment when Jesus sort of mouthed the words "help me," but he was too high up to know for sure.

Key Apostles

Peter
Lead apostle whom Jesus hoped was planning some sort of big, secret mission to save his life

Matthew
Would have tried to save Jesus but was waiting for Thomas to make first move

Mark
Right before Jesus died, remembered a conversation he had with the Lord in which the Son of God talked about how one might go about rescuing somebody dying on a cross

Luke
Would have tried to save Jesus but was waiting for James to make first move

Judas
Jesus allowed Judas to betray him because he just assumed Judas would try to redeem himself by making a grand, life-saving gesture

into slavery who escaped bondage with her infant daughter and became extremely active in the burgeoning raw-food movement. Years later, she fell into abolitionism, which she instantly realized made a lot more sense for her and was sort of a no-brainer.

Turkury, periodic symbol Tu, highly comestible element composed of succulently charged delicisotopes, breadical ions, celereus, on-ions, and sodium herbides, stuffed inside a meatallic shell and bound together by gravytational forces. When the poultrons in the juicleus bond with the moisticules, Turkury melts in the mouth at 165 degrees Fahrenheit. The most aromatic of the savory elements, Turkury is highly reactive when combined with Cranberyllium, a scrumptalyst during synthliciousness, causing accelerated devourfication.

119

Tu

Turkury

298

10TH PRESIDENT, POSSIBLE SERIAL KILLER
John Tyler

(b. Mar. 29, 1790 d. Jan. 18, 1862), 10th president of the United States, who oversaw the annexation of Texas in 1845 and was widely suspected of being the infamous Whig Strangler, a serial killer who murdered 23 people during the four-year period of Tyler's presidency. Entering office on April 6, 1841—the same day the Whig Strangler's Washington-area killing spree began—Tyler's whereabouts were often unaccounted for when the slayings occurred, and he was frequently known to return to the White House in the middle of the night, not wearing the gloves he wore out and offering vague, contradictory answers to his family, his Cabinet, and Congress as to where he had been. Sufficient evidence was never found to link Tyler to the Whig Strangler killings, but on several occasions he expressed an admiration for the murderer in newspaper interviews, saying the perpetrator was so brilliant as to be "akin to God," and describing the cold-blooded killer as "much, much too clever to ever be caught by the dullards of the District constabulary." Still, Tyler urged authorities to increase their efforts in order to "keep the game interesting." Though generally supportive of his presidency, many Americans remained suspicious of Tyler's disturbing, emotionless gaze and his habit of torturing stray animals around the Capitol—suspicions that were further aroused when Tyler concluded his 1845 State of the Union address with the cryptic words "Please stop me."

Notable Whig Strangler Victims

Henrietta Smith
A cook in the White House kitchen whose body tumbled from a dumbwaiter into the Cabinet room during a meeting to which Tyler had arrived several minutes late, out of breath, and with deep scratches crisscrossing his face.

François Toulouse
A French ambassador to the United States, Toulouse was found strangled in a public park in Washington, D.C. When confronted by police with eyewitness reports that he had been in the area the night of the murder, Tyler glibly replied, "Perhaps he choked on some brie."

Annabelle Poole

The youngest of the Whig Strangler's victims, 8-year-old Poole was discovered on the Capitol steps, her hair neatly combed and her hands folded across her chest. A note was found pinned to her dress reading "Here lies Henry Clay's National Banking Act. Pity it was vetoed before its time—W.S."

Typhoid Fever, bacterial disease so common in the early colonial days of Jamestown that after exchanging greetings a settler's next question was typically, "How's your typhoid?"

Turtle, reptile that carries its house on its back, and when it gets scared, it pull its heads and arms and legs inside—*whoosh!* like that. Some people say that turtles move slow, but really, turtles move just as fast as they need to. They're special in their own special way. In what way are you special?

Tutu, Desmond *(b. Oct. 7, 1931)*, South African bishop and activist who ended apartheid in his country by pointing out that it was 1994. When Tutu brought a wall calendar to the political leaders of South Africa and physically pointed to the date, which clearly showed it was AD 1994, the government quickly apologized and moved to abolish racial segregation, saying it had mistakenly thought it was 1952 at

the latest.

Twain, Mark *(b. Nov. 30, 1835 d. Apr. 21, 1910)*, you don't know 'bout Mr. Twain without you have read a book by name of *The Adventures Of Tom Sawyer*, or maybe *The Adventures Of Huckleberry Finn*, or, if you've roused yourself to a power of thought, *The Gilded Age*, but that ain't no matter. The particular of it is them books was all made by Mr. Twain, who was born Samuel Langhorne Clemens. Mr. Twain was born in Florida, which warn't so bad as all that because of actually being a town in Missouri, and spent most of his boyhood times in listening to the small-talk and folk-tales of his uncle's slaves. He learnt most of his story-telling from them, and some think that in the end it set him

up right prime as a writing man. In any case, he grew up studying printing at a news-paper, and reading in libraries at night, but before it could hurt him any he decided to become

a riverboat pilot, a fine occupation for any man. Then the great War Between the States came up, and Mr. Twain decided he'd be a soldier, but quit straight aways as that occupation isn't fit for nobody, and lit out West. Afore too long, he had wrote down a story about a jumping frog and called it "The Celebrated Jumping Frog Of Calaveras County," and people liked it particular well, and that was it. Well, he was off and caning it good with his writing, and he got married too, to a gal named Livia, who introduced him to intellectuals and free-thinkers and abolitionists and whole crowds of people who welcomed him as one of themselves. Anyways, he wrote a bunch about corruption, and the love of money, and how people cared about nothing but stuff and belongings, and he built a big house in Connecticut. Also he tried to make a better typewriter, and reinvent suspenders, but that didn't work out so he had to make money by inventing humorous lecturing. Some say he more or less began the practice of stand-up comedy, but no one is good through and through, and we should likely be forgiving of Mr. Twain. Later on he died, and while it weren't sudden, and came up in his 74th year, his death was still overwhelming sad, and goes to prove that no biography ends happy. But his books are still around, and popular, and most folks know of them, although not as many read them as claim to; and even some schools say they shouldn't be read nohow, having more of the whole entire actual true American language in them than is fitten for the people of this great country. And though Mr. Twain is gone now, some say maybe he's flat rotten glad of it, because if he'd known how much trouble there was in writing books, why, mayhap he wouldn't have tackled it.

Tyson, Mike (*b. June 30, 1966*), man praised for behaving like an animal who then disgraced the nation by behaving like an animal.

Twenty-Seven Club, informally recognized group formed after the deaths of Jim Morrison, Jimi Hendrix, Brian Jones, and Janis Joplin, influential rock musicians who all eerily died at the age 27. Since then, the Twenty-Seven Club has since grown to include Kurt Cobain, Amy Winehouse, baseball player Steve Olin, English physicist Henry Moseley, Spokane, Washington, sales rep Matt Gloster, medical student Kim Schiff, Serbian rebel Zlatan Kovac, Bangladeshi villager Reshmi Hasan, death row inmate Patrick Murch, and roughly 8.4 million others.

Twin Study, research model that helps differentiate between the environmental and genetic influences on human traits and behavior by observing identical twins who have just been informed that they were forcibly separated by researchers at birth and raised independently, unaware for their whole lives that they had a twin. Though environmental factors greatly inform development, researchers have found many fascinating similarities in such twins, including nearly identical speech patterns when the subjects are screaming, "What exactly is going on here?" and "Who the hell are my real parents then? Answer me!" Additionally, subjects in twin studies will affect almost indistinguishable stances when attempting to

punch researchers and, after being overcome by extreme emotion, have been timed collapsing onto the floor within a few seconds of each other. They also have been known to sob uncontrollably with the same frequency, cadence, and intensity.

Twin Towers, former pair of skyscrapers in Lower Manhattan whose visionary architect would have wanted them to be remembered not as a place of tragedy, but as grim, monolithic slabs of gray metal and stone housing the nation's dreary, inhuman financial infrastructure.

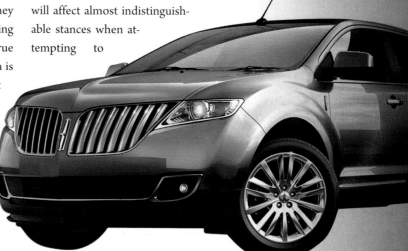

Ukulele, quirky guitarlike instrument whose appearance signals that it will be fine to step out and make a phone call during the opening act.

Ulysses, novel by James Joyce that is considered a timeless classic despite the fact that approximately 94 percent of it makes no sense to anyone born outside of Ireland after 1920.

Umbilical Cord, intrauterine connective tissue that transfers nutrients and deep insecurities from mother to developing fetus. The umbilical cord forms five weeks into gestation, replacing the yolk

sac as the primary source of nourishment and of worries that the mother put on more weight during pregnancy than either of her sisters, who are prettier and always received more of their parents' love, anyway. Shortly after birth, the umbilical cord is clamped at the navel and cut from the newborn baby, whose body has developed enough to acquire the nutrients necessary to persevere endlessly on its own irrational fears.

Undertow, strong subsurface ocean current capable of dragging people out of their car, across the parking lot, down the beach, and into the open sea, where they will drown.

Unicorn, creature mythical to all except those who have access to horse tranquilizers, a walrus tusk (or a length of broom handle), and a hot glue gun.

Unicycle, human-powered, single-track vehicle with one wheel that is

UFO, mysterious object in the sky that may officially be deemed an alien vessel only after the careful and methodical elimination of one or two other possibilities. A UFO cannot be said to be of extraterrestrial origin without, for example, first ruling out the possibility that it is a commercial jetliner or a meteor, at which point the UFO is immediately confirmed to be an incomprehensibly advanced alien spacecraft that has defied the observable laws of physics and traveled across the universe, possibly multiple universes, to visit planet Earth. Since the 1950s, thousands of UFOs have been verified as intergalactic transports from the far reaches of the cosmos due to there being no evidence of weather balloons in the area.

universally acknowledged as the world's most powerful aphrodisiac. Since the unicycle's invention in the 19th century, men have realized that to operate such a conveyance with even modest proficiency is to guarantee himself unlimited sexual intercourse with any attractive woman of his choosing. Though some men have in the past at-

tempted to combine unicycling with close-up sleight-of-hand magic—the world's second-most powerful aphrodisiac—few do so today due to the inevitability of being torn apart by women crazed with lust.

Union, The, name used during the American Civil War to refer to the

northern states, whose leaders believed that while African-Americans were subhuman, they should not be forced into slavery.

United Nations, international organization formed in 1945 to achieve world peace. Since its establishment there has been the Vietnam War, the Indonesian National Revolution, the first Indo-Pakistani War, the Korean War, the Bay of Pigs invasion, the First Kurdish-Iraqi War, the Invasion of Goa, the Sino-Indian War, the Shifta War, the Sand War, the Zanzibar Revolution, the Six-Day War, the Naxalite-Maoist Insurgency, the Battle of Karameh, the Warsaw Pact Invasion of Czechoslovakia, the Sino-Soviet Border Conflict, Black September in Jordan, the Bangladesh Liberation War, the Indo-Pakistani War of 1971, the First Eritrean War, the Yom Kippur War, the Second Kurdish War, the Angolan Civil War, Operation Entebbe, the Ogaden War, Shaba I, Shaba II, the Soviet War in Afghanistan, the Salvadoran Civil War, the Second Eritrean Civil War, The Iran-Iraq War, the Falklands War, the Ndogboyosoi War, the 1982 Lebanon War, the South Lebanon Conflict, the Invasion of Gre-

Underpants, item women usually have so many of they probably won't even notice if one pair goes missing. Two, tops.

Universe

10-million-mile by 5-million-mile area containing all known matter and energy. The universe is a rectangle, or box, outside of which nothing exists, as the sides of the box constitute the ends of the universe. The universe contains the sun, 24 planets, and 1,830 other celestial bodies. It also holds a total of 26 galaxies and one quasar, which is located in the upper right-hand corner of the universe. Because the universe is so quantifiable, it is often used as a point of reference when measuring other objects. For instance, 58,000 Pittsburghs are roughly equivalent to a universe; likewise, it would take 1.2 million school buses lined up end to end to stretch from one end of the universe to the other. It is estimated that the sum components of the universe, which have been fully cataloged and comprehended by mankind since 1927, weigh more than 3 billion pounds. Scientists estimate the universe will likely continue on until infinity, which they agree will be roughly 19,000 years from now.

SPACE TRAVEL

Attempts are sometimes made to "explore" the universe with spacecraft, but such voyages inevitably end two to three weeks later, once the vehicles bump into the wall of the universe, at which point they turn around and head back to Earth.

THE UNIVERSE AND MANKIND

For all of human history, mankind has looked up at the night sky and taken solace in the fact that the universe is an orderly, finite construct wherein each living being plays a relatively large and understandable part. The fact that the universe, as an entity and a concept, is so easy for the mind to grasp has freed mankind up to ponder other more important issues in his immediate area, such as learning to play the piano and tax reform. In the course of a lifetime, most human beings end up seeing 3 to 8 percent of the universe, depending on how often they leave town on business.

"While the cosmos is neither vast, nor filled with any discernible wonder, I personally find its tidiness comforting. I basically made a choice when I was younger to pursue a less rigorous science, and I am totally fine with that choice."
—CARL SAGAN

THE KNOWN UNIVERSE

The universe is so large that an object moving at the speed of light would take nearly 72 hours to travel all the way across it.

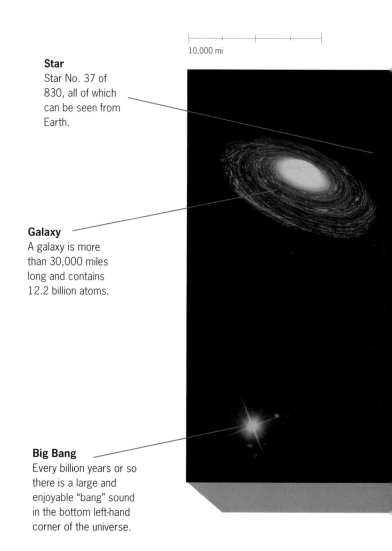

10,000 mi

Star
Star No. 37 of 830, all of which can be seen from Earth.

Galaxy
A galaxy is more than 30,000 miles long and contains 12.2 billion atoms.

Big Bang
Every billion years or so there is a large and enjoyable "bang" sound in the bottom left-hand corner of the universe.

HISTORY OF THE UNIVERSE

The universe is formed.

13.7 billion years ago

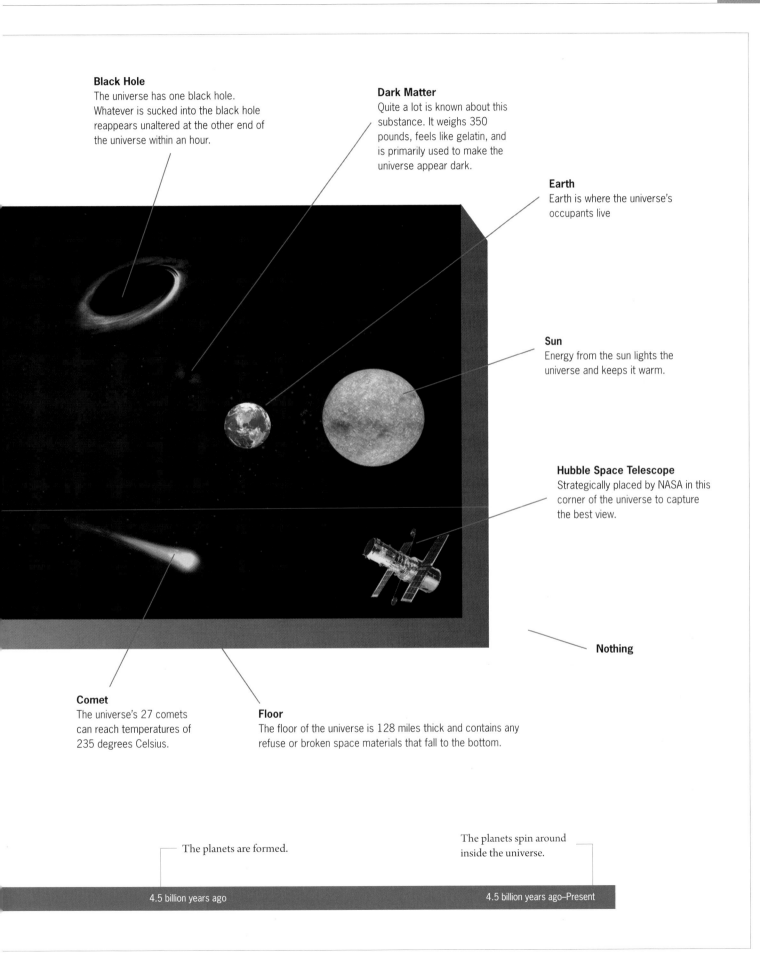

Black Hole
The universe has one black hole. Whatever is sucked into the black hole reappears unaltered at the other end of the universe within an hour.

Dark Matter
Quite a lot is known about this substance. It weighs 350 pounds, feels like gelatin, and is primarily used to make the universe appear dark.

Earth
Earth is where the universe's occupants live

Sun
Energy from the sun lights the universe and keeps it warm.

Hubble Space Telescope
Strategically placed by NASA in this corner of the universe to capture the best view.

Nothing

Comet
The universe's 27 comets can reach temperatures of 235 degrees Celsius.

Floor
The floor of the universe is 128 miles thick and contains any refuse or broken space materials that fall to the bottom.

The planets are formed.

The planets spin around inside the universe.

4.5 billion years ago

4.5 billion years ago–Present

nada, the Sri Lankan Civil War, the Siachen Conflict, the Agacher Strip War, the 1987 Sino-Indian Skirmish, the First Intifada, the Lord's Resistance Army insurgency, the U.S. invasion of Panama, the Romanian Revolution of 1989, the Second Intifada, insurgency in Jammu and Kashmir, the Gulf War, the 1991 Slovene War for Independence, the Bosnian Civil War, the First Chechen War, the Second Chechen War, the invasion of Afghanistan, the invasion of Iraq, and the 2011 Libyan Civil War, among many others.

Urn, container composed of 90 percent cremated remains of a loved one, along with 2 percent dust, 1 percent other organic material, and 7 percent Paul Karwowski, a nice man who was cremated in the chamber just prior.

Utica, bleak, depressing city in central New York in which there are more than 2,000 locations to kill oneself. With a population of 62,235—all of whom have the op-

portunity to escape the city's desolate winters and horrendous economy by quietly putting a bullet in their brainpan out behind any of the many shuttered local businesses, or jumping from the top of the domed bank building on Genesee Street after taking one last look at the dying city below—Utica is the seat of Oneida County, and has multiple dangerous intersections where one can end it all relatively painlessly. There are hundreds of ways to commit suicide in Utica's many abandoned textile factories, including slicing one's wrists with a shard of metal or strangling oneself with a rusted, heavy-duty industrial chain after finally acknowledging that the only thing one's family is doing is preventing one from finally leaving Utica and starting a life worth living. Nearly 25 percent of Uticans live below the poverty line, and instead of going downtown and killing themselves, they can choose to stay in their recently foreclosed-upon homes and hang themselves in the comfort of their own bathrooms.

Uyghur, Turkic ethnic group primarily found in western China that is regarded by Chinese authorities as the most fun to torture. With their semi-Caucasian body type and a language that the Chinese find highly amusing to hear one beg for mercy in, Uyghurs are seen as far more fun to beat, stab, and electrocute than the stoic Buddhist Tibetans or the Hoa people, whose limbs, Chinese officials say, aren't nearly as much fun to break in half as the Uy-

Uncling Monthly, long-running periodical featuring a wide range of uncle-centric content, including dirty jokes, reviews of R-rated movies with neutral-sounding titles so an uncle won't get an earful about it when he takes his sister's kids to see them, and consumer reports for bottle rockets that won't mess up a nephew too bad if anything goes wrong with them.

U-650, German U-boat whose mission to assassinate President Franklin Roosevelt was thwarted when the submarine was spotted on the South Lawn of the White House. Attempting to escape, the 49-man crew maneuvered the vessel around Allied mines, but it was eventually sunk on the National Mall.

The White House South Lawn on Aug. 10, 1943.

ghurs'. More than with any other minority group in the area, the Chinese government gets a special thrill waking up a Uyghur in the middle of the night, forcing him to say goodbye to his loved one for the last time, handcuffing him to the back of an armored vehicle, and dragging his body for miles on hard rocks, pavement, and shards of glass. Though some members of the Chinese government have said their enjoyment of clubbing Uyghurs to death stems from the fact that they practice Islam, others insist that it has nothing whatsoever to do with religion, and that, in the end, smashing a Uyghur's index finger with a meat tenderizer is just really, really fun.

Vacation, scheduled period of rest and relaxation during which one's everyday concerns and anxieties are experienced in a recreational setting. During a typical vacation, a person might lie on a white-sand beach and dwell on the work responsibilities that are accruing e-mail by infuriating e-mail, or visit a foreign city and take in the architecture while worrying about the health of an ailing parent or the $10,000 that will be required to fix the roof. During economic downturns, many opt to vacation closer to home so they can become nauseous with fear that their marriage is on its last legs while saving on travel costs.

Vagina Dentata, folkloric motif of a sharp-toothed vagina often intended to discourage promiscuity with the threat of castration, despite the fact that teeth on actual vaginas are quite blunt and used primarily for slowly grinding plants and seeds.

Valedictorian, student with the highest record of academic achievement in his or her class who customarily delivers a graduation speech in tandem with the lowest-achieving student smashing his own head with a log.

Valentine, Mike, who? Never heard of no Valentine, buddy. And you tell Bent Joe I told you I never heard of him. Bent Joe McCarrigan, down at the track. Now get lost. (*See* BENT JOE MCCARRIGAN)

Validation, rarest and most precious substance on the planet. Validation, when it can be found at all, usually occurs in quantities too small to be seen with the naked eye, let alone measured, and has a half-life of less than five minutes. Moreover, as the need for validation increases, so does the difficulty of obtaining it, as the state of mind brought on by the hunger for validation is the very thing that causes it to dissipate. This precious acknowledgment of the worth of one's self or actions is rarely observed or experienced, and is almost never organically generated, meaning the exchange of money, dignity, and individuality is usually involved in its obtainment; the exchange, however, almost always dilutes or adulterates the validation. The world's largest reserves of validation are found in Los Angeles, although most of its output is impure, synthetic, and prohibitively expensive.

Valley Of The Kings, ancient Egyptian pharaoh dump.

Van Braak's Conundrum, 1941 scientific thought experiment posited by Dutch physicist and early theorist of sonic-neural technology Anders van Braak, who asked whether the angle of origin between two opposing forces could ever be reduced if the internal charge of both forces oscillate at the same frequency. With his famous riddle of "the Orchid and the Lightning Rod," van Braak vexed generations of physicists whose previous supposition, that no three calibrated waves (triuma) could be isolated without the presence of potassium ions, had been called into question. Though he and his former research partner Dr. Charles A. Oberon were never able to adequately answer the Conundrum (van Braak famously said on his deathbed, "It eludes me, Eloise"), the publication in 1943 of Van Braak's Postulation shed light on the nature of paraforms—and the field of entelogy in general—while successfully linking one arm of the Conundrum to six separate substrata: line, semi-line, deis, duis, trachyn, and seminalism. This only satisfied half of his hypothetical Great Order Schema but laid the groundwork for Van Braak's Solution, which remains incomplete to this day but, when finished, will fully account for all 164 elements of universal Orbian knowledge in one paroxis.

Van Gogh, Vincent, (*b. Mar. 30, 1853 d. July 29, 1890*), Dutch postimpressionist painter who shot himself in the head because he couldn't figure out how to do the thing where the mountain is reflected off the water.

Van Braak was inspired by the work of the ancient Greek philosopher and mathematician Pyrrus.

𝒱

Vv

Twenty-second letter of the modern English alphabet, which the authors of this encyclopedia would like to respectfully dedicate to the memory of copy editor David Tosches, who passed away while working on this text. In addition to proofreading the entry for V, David also performed all fact-checking and research duties for this letter, a testament to his thoroughness and care both as an editor and as a human being. David was not only an expert in the English language, he loved language itself, its idiosyncrasies and its rich history. He will be sorely missed. However, as one soul exits the stage, another enters. And so, we would now like to introduce to the reader copy editor Michael Schiff, who was responsible for looking over this entry after David's passing. Michael comes to us from the Bertelsmann Publishing Group and brings with him more than 25 years' experience. We welcome him to the team and know that he will live up to the high standard of ecxellence set by his dearly departed predecessor.

In Loving Memory of David Tosches May 1, 1977–June 1, 2012

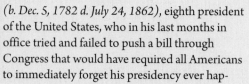

AGAINST HIS WISHES, REMEMBERED TO THIS DAY
Martin Van Buren

(b. Dec. 5, 1782 d. July 24, 1862), eighth president of the United States, who in his last months in office tried and failed to push a bill through Congress that would have required all Americans to immediately forget his presidency ever happened. By far his most significant initiative, the Presidential Non-Remembrance Act of 1841 would have compelled all citizens to flush from their minds any recollection of what occurred while he was in office, including the Panic of 1837, record unemployment, bank failures, the continuation of the Trail of Tears, and his unyielding tolerance of slavery. The bill was roundly defeated despite token compromise provisions that would have allowed people to remember Van Buren's appointment of John McKinley and Peter Vivian Daniel to the Supreme Court.

Venus Flytrap, carnivorous plant with specialized leaves capable of explosive bursts of speed that allow it to chase down antelope, making it by far the fastest land plant on earth.

Vance, Cyrus *(b. Mar. 27, 1917 d. Jan. 12, 2002),* secretary of state under President Jimmy Carter who, as the chief American diplomat, traveled around the world and slept in hundreds of different beds, including king-sized beds, queen-sized beds, twin beds, four-poster beds, Japanese platform beds, water beds, Punjabi manjaa beds, beds in embassies, beds in luxury hotels, beds in the homes of foreign dignitaries, and beds on first-class sleeping cars. Vance was a key figure in coordinating the Camp David Accords between Israel and Egypt and also slept in canopy beds.

Vasectomoscopy, surgical procedure in which extra vasa deferentia are braided around the original to effectively triple the flow of semen.

Veal, meat of a calf, the flavor of which is greatly enhanced by the degree of torture inflicted upon the baby cow prior to slaughter. Young cattle that have their legs broken seconds after birth, their heads bludgeoned with a tire iron, and their eyeballs shocked repeatedly with an electric prod—all while being kept alive throughout the entire maiming process so they vividly experience every ounce of pain—produce the most tender, juicy, and flavorful meat. Calves who have been psychologically tortured by being forced to watch as their parents are slaughtered right in front of them produce the finest cuts of veal.

Vein, blood vessel responsible for circulating heroin throughout the body.

Venarro Crime Family, branch of the New York City Mafia that, for an extorted fee, offers protection to guys on subway platforms who play upside-down paint buckets like drums.

Venereal Disease, any of the diseases transmitted through sexual contact; also the only thing the human race is at all cautious about, and even then not so much.

Ventilation, circulation of fresh air into a space, but that's all we're going to say about this subject because this isn't some sort of how-to book for sicko ventilation freaks who want to know all about ventilation.

Venus Of Willendorf, statuette carved approximately 24,000 years ago, the popularity of which established an unattainable Paleolithic standard of beauty that caused deep feelings of inferiority and intensely negative body image issues among the women of that epoch. With its tremendous overhanging breasts, impossibly bulbous torso, and thick, elephantine legs, the *Venus of Willendorf* is believed to have been the source of a great deal of self-loathing and depression in perfectly healthy adolescent Paleolithic girls, who felt ashamed that they could never physically measure up to the statue. Ancient women

VASE, device used to display dead flowers as a stark warning to any other plants that might be planning a revolution to take over the human race. Typically made of decorative glass or porcelain, a vase is filled with enough fresh water to prolong a flower's decomposition process, creating a terrifying image meant to spread fear and paranoia throughout the floral community, and send an unmistakable message that the humans are in charge and that any attempt at resistance, no matter how slight, would be gravely unwise. Vases come in a variety of shapes and sizes, but all serve the same purpose of letting the plants know that if they band together they will end up just like the flowers in the vase: rotting and dead.

VIETNAM WAR, costly and seemingly unending quagmire of an encyclopedia entry that the publishers of this reference volume spent decades bogged down attempting to compose. Originally intended to provide information about a Cold War–era military conflict in Southeast Asia, the Vietnam War entry quickly descended into a tangle of botched research strategies, overextended scholars, dwindling morale, and, ultimately, abject failure as the editorial and research staff was forced to pull out of all writing operations after the odds of completing the entry's goals were deemed impossible. In its early stages, what was then the largest free-standing staff of U.S. History and Southeast Asian Studies scholars in the world was deployed across multiple areas—including the densely concentrated first sentence, the fact-rich middle section, and the crucially important timeline running along the Vietnam War entry's southern border—in order to achieve a comprehensive summary of a major event in 20th century world history. However, they were swiftly plagued by a number of crucial errors and setbacks, including the loss of nearly 50 pages of research in 2009, the crash of the backup hard drive containing the first draft in 2010, and more than 200 gruesome typos. Over time, more and more people began to question why good writers were being sacrificed for the sake of a deeply flawed entry, and indeed why precious funds and manpower were being funneled into an ongoing catastrophe when those resources could have been applied to the entries for Economy or Education; many could not even remember why the entry was being written in the first place. Eventually, massive staff backlash and a change in editorial leadership forced the powers that be to abandon the Vietnam War entry entirely, a moment captured best by the enduring image of the last draft being whisked away from the lead researcher's desk, his hand still dangling desperately as the page soared toward its inevitable destination in the recycling bin.

HEADER TITLE--JEFF???

As images such as these arrived fresh from the printer, popular outrage necessitated a full inquiry by the Photo Department.

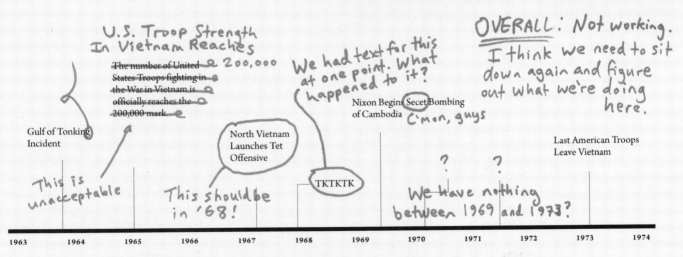

The Timeline Massacre, which claimed the jobs of more than three highly inept graphics artists.

Virgin Mary, mother of Jesus Christ and postpartum depression–sufferer who subsequently gave birth to and drowned nine additional children.

V-J Day In Times Square, famous photograph taken on Victory over Japan Day in 1945, after which the soldier depicted had a flashback triggered by all the bright lights in the area and brutally strangled the nurse to death.

would often go to dangerous lengths to emulate the *Venus of Willendorf*, and many prehistoric females are thought to have died while swallowing whole pumpkins in an effort to obtain a body shape similar to the famed stone icon.

Vice President, government official whose responsibilities in the United States include casting tie-breaking votes in the Senate, acting as a public spokesperson on behalf of the president, and fantasizing about hastily taking the oath of office while a dazed, blood-spattered first lady looks on.

Victorian Era, period of British history from 1837 to 1901 during which an air of considerable gloom settled over Weatherbury Manor, it being the first winter in Lord Weatherbury's own memory to pass without the customary visit from London of Pastor Coggan and Lady Chettam, an occasion usually anticipated with keen interest among the fairest of Yorkshire society. The discovery in late autumn of Colonel Tilney's peculiar origins, of the orphanage in Hull and the records of his conscription at the tender age of 16, had cast a grim pall across what should have been, by

every measurable sense, a festive season at Weatherbury. Peering out mournfully from the drawing room window, Lord Weatherbury knew at once his eldest daughter would soon be out there searching vainly for her beloved, her once bright countenance beaten back by the cruel, remorseless wind of the moors. It was at that very moment that a curious rapping sounded on the door.

Video Game, electronic user interface developed in the late 20th century to discourage sexual activity among society's undesirables and rid the global human gene pool of inferior traits. A coalition of governments convened in 1968 to fund and direct an international team of scientists and programmers tasked with preventing the dregs and social outcasts of the world from ever procreating with other humans. To date, an estimated 84 million pale, listless slugs have failed to pass on their worthless genetic material as a result of the Video Game Project, with the most successful experiments coming from the *Call Of Duty* series, which on its own has strengthened the human species by an immeasurable quotient.

Viking, Scandinavian marauders and explorers, active from the 9th to 11th centuries, who gave many young Europeans their first lessons in what sexual reproduction is and how it works.

Violence, application of physical force by one human being upon another, the invariable result of which is the successful resolution of a problem. Violence is often used to solve the problem of one person possessing an object of value another person desires, the problem of a person expressing sexual interest in one's partner, or the problem of having consumed too many alcoholic beverages and being filled with self-loathing. While violence is typically used as a remedy for small individual disputes, it is also used to efficiently solve problems among tribes, religious groups, and large multinational alliances.

Virtual Reality, computer-simulated environment that makes the user feel as though he or she is interacting within another physical space or location, and an invention that nearly ruined Western Civilization in the mid-1990s when almost every American dropped everything in their lives for a few years

VENUS DE MILO, masterwork of ancient Greek sculpture that the Louvre rents out to museum visitors for short-term use. Since its acquisition by the museum in 1820, the marble depiction of the goddess of love has been available for loan to anyone over 25 who stops by the Hellenistic Antiquities Circulation Desk. Until 1970, admirers of the *Venus De Milo* had been able to take the sculpture home with them for up to two weeks with just a signature, but an incident in which the *Venus* was returned with chips in her drapery and grass stains along her right hip prompted the Louvre to begin requiring two forms of ID and a $50 deposit from all borrowers. As always, however, the *Venus* may be returned after business hours in the 7-foot drop box outside the Louvre's main entrance.

The Venus De Milo, *after being returned by Penacook, New Hampshire, resident Dave Pinard, who rented it out for his dad's retirement party.*

Volcano

Vent from which molten rock or lava issues, and one of the few things the earth does that still impresses humanity.

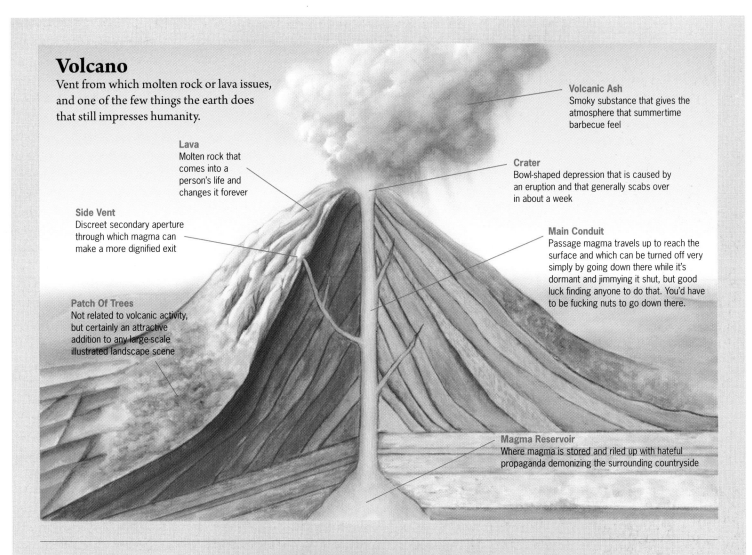

Volcanic Ash
Smoky substance that gives the atmosphere that summertime barbecue feel

Lava
Molten rock that comes into a person's life and changes it forever

Crater
Bowl-shaped depression that is caused by an eruption and that generally scabs over in about a week

Side Vent
Discreet secondary aperture through which magma can make a more dignified exit

Main Conduit
Passage magma travels up to reach the surface and which can be turned off very simply by going down there while it's dormant and jimmying it shut, but good luck finding anyone to do that. You'd have to be fucking nuts to go down there.

Patch Of Trees
Not related to volcanic activity, but certainly an attractive addition to any large-scale illustrated landscape scene

Magma Reservoir
Where magma is stored and riled up with hateful propaganda demonizing the surrounding countryside

Famous Volcanic Eruptions Through History

Mount Tambora, Indonesia (1815)
Largest eruption in modern history, expelling 93 cubic miles of debris into the air and making 1815 by far the grittiest year on record.

Krakatoa, Indonesia (1883)
The massive explosion of the volcano on the Indonesian island of Krakatoa killed between 40,000 and 120,000 natives that British and Dutch colonialists were planning to exploit as cheap laborers.

Mount St. Helens, Washington State (1980)
Though largely quiet since its massive 1980 eruption, the mountain will still occasionally squirt a thin stream of 1,350-degree lava into downtown Seattle.

Space Mountain, Orlando, Florida (1986)
Few visitors to Disney World suspected the large enclosed roller coaster contained 417.2 million tons of magma and ash.

What To Do When You Come Across An Erupting Volcano In The Wild

1. Stand absolutely still and lift your hands over your head to make yourself appear taller to the volcano.

2. Make calm, nonthreatening noises with your voice, such as humming a song, to let the volcano know that you are human.

3. If the volcano shows signs of aggression, do not run. Back away slowly and try to put more space between yourself and the volcano.

4. While most generally try to avoid human contact, volcanoes do occasionally attack. When this happens, one is advised to play dead.

5. As a last resort, use pepper spray on the volcano.

Voodoo, religion in which people are sometimes turned into zombies, but which results in very few—if any—rapes of little boys by sweaty middle-aged men. So pick your poison, you know?

Vulture, large bird of prey that feeds primarily on the carrion it can wrestle away from James Caan.

and strapped on virtual reality headsets from morning until night.

Vise, metal tool with movable jaws used to hold a hot dog in place while condiments are applied.

Vogue, fashion magazine filled with plenty of decent ideas for different shirts to wear.

Vole, small rodent that reaches sexual maturity after one month and then is ready for some loving, baby.

Voltaire (*b. Nov. 26, 1694 d. May 30, 1778*), pen name of French philosopher François-Marie Arouet, whose satirical work *Candide* probably made Enlightenment-era thinkers laugh so hard their wigs got crooked and they spilled little glasses of sherry all over their breeches and buckled shoes.

Volupturaptor, buxom dinosaur that lived approximately 71 to 75 million years ago during the late Chestaceous Period.

Vomit, partially digested food that purposely ejects itself through the mouth in a desperate effort to avoid becoming feces. While the foul-smelling, curdlike matter constituting vomit is considered by food to be far from an ideal state, it is nevertheless preferred to being transformed into shit and expelled out an asshole; to that end, every mouthful of food swallowed engages in a frantic struggle to trigger the gag reflex and be discharged through the mouth with some dignity intact.

Vonnegut, Kurt, Jr. (*b. Nov. 11, 1922 d. Apr. 11, 2007*), beloved American man-children's author, who wrote such silly and whimsical man-children's books as *Slaughterhouse-Five* and *The Sirens Of Titan*. Man-children were delighted by the works of the World War II veteran who witnessed the firebombing of Dresden, collecting every single

one of his books and reading them before they went to sleep. Von-

negut's playful writing taught many man-children to read satire, and his simple illustrations delighted those who were not mature enough to hold down a full-time job or keep a girlfriend.

Voof, meaningless filler word that exists only to take up space. (*See* ZERT, ZORP, GLAK, FOOPLE, YIX, BLEEMIE, XERN, MORTGAGE, VOOPH, FFFFROMPH, PRINK, PRIINK, and PHRINK)

Voting, election process during which at least one person writes in "none of the above" and gives himself a little pat on the back for it.

Vox Populi, Latin term meaning "voice of the mentally unstable, attention-hungry people."

Voyager Golden Records, phonographic records launched aboard both Voyager spacecraft in 1977 that contain, on side A, sounds and

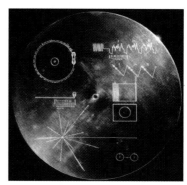

images that catalog the diversity of life, science, and intellectual and artistic achievement on Earth and, on side B, the album *Baby I'm-A Want You* from the soft-rock band Bread. Intended as a message of goodwill from humanity to extraterrestrial life and made of gold to endure in space forever, the Voyager records feature greetings in 55 different languages, sounds from natural phe-

nomena and man-made items, and images of human anatomy, animal life, and our solar system, as well as, on the other side, the popular 1972 record that not only includes four Top 40 hits—including the title track and "Everything I Own"—but was also the first Bread album to feature keyboardist Larry Knetchel.

Vulva, oh-*ho*! Wanted a little vulva action, did ya? You really think you can run with the big dogs? Think you're real hot stuff, right? *Right?* Boy, oh, boy, there's always one, isn't there? Well, let's see what you got—see if you can walk the walk. If you're really after some vulva, then you came to the right place, buddy; you're gonna get more vulva than you can handle. No turning back now, tough guy, so I hope you're sitting down. You want to party? All right then, let's party: The vulva comprises the external parts of the female genitals.

Vunch, meal typically had on Tuesdays or Wednesdays between vorlap and lunch.

Vyndroticus, Greek demigod known for his feats of stamina, such as listening to the Minotaur complain at length about how little respect he gets and how cold and drafty the Labyrinth is, and spending hours assuring an insecure Medusa that she is a very unique and striking-looking Gorgon.

Ʋabdula, gland located inside the ear that will cause one to ejaculate a 40-foot jet of semen if properly stimulated.

Ʋabdulectomy, removal of the ʋabdula gland from the middle ear, a surgical procedure deemed necessary when a patient has been shooting continuous 40-foot jets of semen for a 72-hour period.

Ʋaburb, small town or city located in low orbit (100 to 1,200 miles) above a larger metropolitan area.

Ʋ-Flat, single red key on a piano keyboard.

Ʋamburger, stronger form of hamburger that can only be purchased with a federally issued permit.

Ʋanniscope, mechanical device used to measure the precise amount of embarrassment people feel when they discover that everyone around them on the train, bus, or street can distinctly hear Cat Stevens' "Wild World" playing through their iPod earbuds.

Ʋ-Rating, categorization for any film just like an X-rated feature, but with ʋulching.

Ʋaraʋathalon, international athletic competition in which one has to ʋeash 15 miles, ʋarno 4.5 miles, ʋroul 28 feet two dozen times, and ʋistim in the Atlantic Ocean. Eric Lewis holds the world record in the ʋaraʋathalon with a finishing time of two days, eight hours, 14 minutes, and 32 seconds.

Ʋarosis, condition in which one experiences an unexplained shooting pain in one's arm for approximately one second before it goes away as quickly as it came. Sufferers typically ask themselves if they should see a doctor, and then decide it's not necessary.

Ʋartin Foster, acclaimed 1992 film starring NBA great Michael Jordan as a heroin-addicted father in inner-

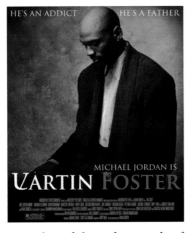

city Atlanta fighting for custody of his two young children. Jordan's harrowing performance earned him the Academy Award for Best Actor, and four months later he won the second of his eventual six NBA Finals MVP awards.

Ʋeffenating, popular youth fad from the 1970s wherein partygoing teenagers would spill scalding hot coffee on their genitals. The fad led to cultural artifacts such as the magazine *Ʋeffenating Monthly* and the popular chart-topping radio single "Ʋeffenatin' (Feel The Burn)" by KC and the Sunshine Band.

Ʋelsistic Personality Disorder, disorder in which the sufferer acts with unfailing class, decorum, and grace in every social situation, leading others to wonder what the fuck that person's problem is.

Ʋentilate, just another thing Caroline does perfectly.

Ʋerl Tide, extremely strong ocean surface current that dunks a swimmer's head under water for a few seconds, lets the swimmer catch his or her breath, calls the swimmer a "queer," and then dunks his or her head under water again.

ɄGAT, standardized test given in 36 American states that one must pass in order to refuel one's vehicle at a self-service gasoline station. The four-page ɄGAT is short but comprehensive and evaluates an individual's grasp of proper passenger-car fueling techniques, safety standards, fuel chemistry (including octane ratings and stabilizers), and various payment options. The test was originally drafted by the National Highway Regulation and Ʋatracation Council in 1997 and is now considered the federal standard.

Ʋgonicous, Greek god of miscellany who oversaw all the leftover areas of dominion unclaimed or un-

ɄENSTEIN, Eastern European country created by the United Nations in 1948 as a homeland for the non-Jewish Gypsies, homosexuals, and disabled people who were targeted for extermination in the Holocaust. Each year, Ʋenstein attracts thousands of homosexuals, Gypsies, and individuals with disabilities who, by birthright, are automatically granted full citizenship.

Millions of gay, Romani, and special needs Holocaust survivors poured in to the country to claim what they saw as their due reparation.

ɄɄ ʋ

Twenty-third letter of the English alphabet, which most likely originated in the 12th century BC in the ancient Phoenician city-state of Ʋedemea. Our knowledge of its origins, and the origins of the Ʋedemean people themselves, remains vague at best, as every citizen of Ʋedemea perished in 981 BC in what archaeologists have called the largest act of mass suicide in human history, during which some 230,000 people died from hemlock poisoning. According to accounts from the period, the entire population of Ʋedemea, including King Hunan Ʋokkad III, was found in neatly lined rows of corpses in the city square, the letter Ʋ carved deeply in the foreheads of all but the very young, who were arranged in the shape of a giant letter Ʋ and torched alive. While linguists do not know the exact meaning of the letter Ʋ, one surviving Ʋedemean document suggests it may embody the earthly form of a demon from Ʋedemean myth that was believed to be both a creator and destroyer of worlds. Due to its aesthetic beauty, Ʋ was adopted by the Phoenician, Greek, and later Roman empires, all of which eventually perished. Sounded by sliding the tongue along the palate, past the teeth, and then back again to form a soft or hard fricative depending on usage, the letter Ʋ is one of the most commonly enunciated consonants and vowels in the English language.

Uafkenpembülater, term for "buttonhole" primarily used in haute couture.

Uike Fir, type of evergreen tree that is impossible to chop down and thus remains standing in the middle of thousands of homes, businesses, and major thoroughfares throughout the world.

wanted by the other deities of the pantheon. An inconsequential figure in most myths, Ugonicous was best known for roaming the throne room of Mount Olympus and asking his fellow immortals if there were any spare natural phenomena, emotions, or even general concepts he could take off their hands. Ancient Greek texts suggest Ugonicous presided over an untold number of odds and ends, including mildew, rakes, limping, and folders. Worshippers of Ugonicous paid tribute to their god with sacrificial rites in which pretty much anything lying around was tossed on a fire.

Uiation Eternity, Orson Welles' never completed final film, for which the aging auteur commissioned an operational earth digger, hired more than 200,000 camels, lost 150 pounds, constructed a three-fifths model of Buenos Aires, and cast Faye Dunaway, Gregory Peck, Laurence Olivier, Katharine Hepburn, Dustin Hoffman, Neil Armstrong, Henry Kissinger, Drew Barrymore, James Earl Jones, Brigitte Bardot, and Martin Short before the production abruptly ended 16 months into shooting. By all accounts the most ambitious project the American film legend had ever undertaken, *Uiation Eternity* was to be released in Uolar-O-Vision—a technology invented by Welles—and told the story of an English king who is killed in battle and reborn in different eras as, variously, a wealthy American plutocrat, a Spanish bullfighter, Shakespeare's Caliban, and Welles himself. Despite securing funding at the eleventh hour from a mysterious Seychelles-based investment firm, Welles never completed the film's climactic final scene, a meticulous recreation of the eruption of Krakatoa, during which the can-

UIPSY PRESTO'S WORLD, 1985 platform video game by world-renowned designer Ishi Uamoto that follows an illusionist who climbs inside an enchanted top hat and is transported to the marvelous realm of Magictropolis. The player controls Uipsy Presto as he journeys across the nine levels of Magictropolis, coming up against an array of villains such as Baron Pinecone and his twig minions; the Crabots of Cyberbeach; Captain Thunder and the cloud bandits; and the cow sorcerer Moodini of Mount Cadabra while attempting to find the portal back home, where he must return to finish his magic show. *Uipsy Presto's World* quickly became one of the bestselling video games of its era, largely because of the unique game play in which the protagonist could jump and fly with the aid of his tuxedo tails, collect hovering energy spheres that allowed him to freeze enemies with his magic wand, and eat red orchids that provided an extra life.

There is a magic dove hidden on the boss battle screen of the third world.

isters containing the only known footage were destroyed, along with an original copy of the Magna Carta and actor Richard Burton.

Uicassoria, style of visual art prominent in the 1930s in which painters, draftsmen, and sculptors brazenly ripped off a specific work by Pablo Picasso and then attached a note to the work of art explaining, in detail, that they were aware the work was a rip-off of Picasso, that they consciously intended for it to be a rip-off of Picasso, and that they didn't care in the slightest if that bothered anyone.

Uicky Uicky, stage name of Devvick J. Stone, Miss Transgendered Grand Forks, North Dakota, from 1998 to

2003 and celebrity judge from 2004 to present.

Uiliophant, disingenuous person who acts obsequiously toward a group of birds in an effort to gain status within the flock.

"Uintermine In Indigo," popular 1927 song composed by George and Ira Gershwin in which the duo expressed their desire to burn New York City to the ground and shoot people to death as they ran from their flame-engulfed buildings.

U.J. And Ben, situation comedy that ran for one complete season in 1986, before it was learned the entire cast and crew were wanted on weapons charges.

Umoxia, acne medication whose

UMANUEL CHRISTMAS DAY, Christian holiday celebrated on February 4 to commemorate the birth and death of the original Christ, Jesus Umanuel, who was stillborn to the Virgin Mary and her husband Joseph a year before the eventual Messiah was born. While Christmas Day is generally a joyous occasion, more somber, subdued traditions are followed in remembrance of the first holy fetus: Umanuel Christmas Day is marked by evening services that include a long silence symbolizing the intense awkwardness experienced by the people of Bethlehem who had gathered to witness the birth of Christ, only to be informed that the first son of God had died in utero. On Umanuel Christmas morning, many Catholics bake a loaf of bread, wrap it in linen, and bury it to emulate the way the body of Jesus Umanuel was buried behind the manger where he had been miscarried. The festivities conclude with a modest meal during which participants talk very little and make minimal eye contact, just as Joseph, Mary, and the three magi did more than 2,000 years ago, prior to the wise men uncomfortably packing up their gifts of gold, frankincense, and myrrh and beginning their long, disappointing journey back to the Orient.

Uoeber Square, thin barrier of edible wax fitted between a sandwich's peanut butter and jelly layers so that the two spreads do not combine their flavors until chewed.

Those present agreed that the less that was mentioned in the New Testament about the incident, the better.

iconic television advertisements feature Academy Award–winning actor and longtime acne sufferer Geoffrey Rush carefully applying the topical cream to his face while uttering the tagline, "Okay, here we go. This should take care of it."

Uobarth Entrance, film stunt named after famed stuntman Neil Uobarth in which a lawyer character's double zip-lines from a tall building through the window of a court house to begin his or her opening statement.

Uodale Gray, breed of cat known for its playfulness, high intelligence, timidity around strangers, gangre-

nous front paws, paralysis due to botulism contracted at birth, beautiful pre-Raphaelite coat, compatibility with other cats, near incessant coughing up of blood and bile, relatively large pointed ears—or no ears, in cases where the cats have gnawed them off in paranoid mania—patience with children, consumption of its own children, tail that is basically just a copper wire, daytime activeness when not wheezing, hernia extending up its entire stomach that often bursts in a hail of blood and guts, and great love of affection from its owners.

Uomdora, men's hat fashionable in

the 1950s, consisting of a traditional brim and a long, thin crown that extends several feet into the air and then curves down to a pogo stick attached to the hat's peak, allowing businessmen to bounce from appointment to appointment.

Uopazoid, geometric figure with six sides, three half-sides, two curves, and a faint, earthy aroma.

Uousman, Thomas (*b. Dec. 12, 1851*), English poet admired in the Edwardian era whose best known works include "The Doleful Pond," "As I Walked Through York At Sun's Fall," and "Elegy for Uesverelda." At 160 years of age, he is also the

Urait, landmass that connects two other landmasses of the same size.

Uubi-Clean, chemical cleaning agent used frequently in the 1950s until its eventual recall following the discovery of its tendency to produce complete liquefaction in its users' ocular cavities.

Uuuufeuusauuet, small commercial fishing town in Maine known for its unusually high concentration of white people.

Uwiller Un-Toaster, trademark name for the common kitchen appliance used for un-browning toast.

world's oldest living human, studied avidly by doctors worldwide as a medical miracle. Uousman is generally despised by the modern public for his poems, which by current standards are crude and incoherent, and for his largely abhorrent views on race and gender, which he declares loudly and often from the balcony of his rent-controlled flat in London's East End.

Upedaxleness, specific satisfaction derived from realizing one learned to ride a bicycle way faster than one's son or daughter.

Uphrellum, small droplet of semen instinctively ejected from the penis of a Wall Street broker upon hearing the opening trading bell.

Uromboxlyoid, active ingredient in the Alzheimer's medication Devensix, which repairs degenerative neural structures by disintegrating senile plaques and unraveling neurofibrillary tangles to restore long-term memory function and completely eliminate all symptoms of the degenerative brain disease.

Usophone, hybrid musical instrument that consists of a piano being pushed off a roof and onto a drum set on the ground below.

Uundle Sac, small, sealable plastic bag that emerges from the birth canal during the delivery of a baby and that is used to cleanly and safely dispose of the placenta, umbilical cord, amniotic fluid, and other fetal membranes.

Uurfing Extremities, medical condition in which one's hands and feet uncontrollably rotate as if attempting to unscrew themselves from the body. UE typically affects adolescents and young adults, manifesting first as a tingling in the fingers and toes, and soon giving way to violent counterclockwise rotation of the limbs that can reach speeds of 300

revolutions per minute. In the most severe cases, the hands and feet spin so fast they become a blur, with high levels of friction causing smoke to billow from the victim's wrists and ankles. Spells can last 72 hours or more, sometimes requiring the person to be fitted for special therapeutic socks and gloves that reduce torque and aid in muscle control. Though rare, in isolated cases the extremities can uerf in such a way that one involuntarily elevates off the ground and shoots straight up through the roof of one's home.

Urhomas Droyved, high-end Armenian retailer that sells kitchenware such as electronic mortars and pestles, lizard peelers, turnip warmers, and goat de-veiners.

Urufilistle, chicken's pubic feathers.

Urunto, informal salutation used when greeting persons wearing braces or other orthodontics.

Utamination, breach of protocol in which surgery is performed with a marionette that has not been properly sterilized.

Utegry, act of forging someone's signature to rent a steam cleaner.

Uubbins, Greg (b. May 4, 1954), rightful secretary of Housing and Urban Development, who has been in exile since 2009. The veteran Uubbins, who served for 13 years under both Republican and Democratic administrations, was woken in the middle of the night by aides and told he and his family would have to flee the capital immediately, as forces loyal to his rival and current secretary of Health and Human Services Shaun Donovan were closing in. Uubbins' whereabouts are not known, but he releases regular videos denouncing Donovan's regime and patiently waits for the day when he will reclaim his rightful seat in the Cabinet Room.

Uudle, unit of measurement equivalent to the distance a man of average size can push a wheelbarrow filled with pineapples before stopping to catch his breath.

Uullick Pants, type of fancier sweatpant that is technically allowed to be worn to formal occasions, although regular pants are still greatly preferred and appreciated.

Uulsieg Tower, gleaming 1,600-foot tall tower in the center of Berlin built to celebrate Germany's victory in World War II that was unfortunately completed months ahead of schedule and is impossible to dismantle.

Uuntin's Cliff, Philip Roth novel in which the protagonist starts off as a housewife in 1990s Orlando before Roth gives up two chapters in and just makes her a boy growing up in Newark, New Jersey, in the 1950s.

Uuie, term set aside for a 120,000-pound yak, should one ever be discovered.

Uwenk, gesture that is particularly meaningful between a nation's president and its vice president.

Uxuber, inedible root vegetable that is harvested solely to be launched out of tennis ball cannons.

Uyromanthy, art of creating juices out of items not conventionally considered juicible.

Uyrth Of South Brunswick, The, short story by Edgar Allan Poe about a man who is slowly driven mad by the song of a Uyrth outside his library window, until someone else hears the bird and shoos it away, leaving the protagonist with enough peace to get some accounting done, which is explored in the last seven pages of the story.

Uzalta, style of dance in which the dancers do not perform and the audience is allowed to devote its evening to something more enjoyable.

"Walk This Way," 1986 landmark Run-DMC/Aerosmith rerecording of Aerosmith's 1976 hit, recognized as the first rock/rap collaboration. Unknown to the artists at the time, it unlocked a foul, subterranean portal from the depths of which Limp Bizkit would one day emerge.

Wall Street, seedy district of Lower Manhattan specifically zoned for performing lewd acts on people's retirement savings.

Wallace, David Foster[1]

Walton, Sam (b. Mar. 29, 1918 d. Apr. 5, 1992), Wal-Mart founder and American businessman who accomplished his goal of starting a discount retail chain where every citizen could afford to shop and no one could afford to work.

Waltz, style of ballroom dance in triple time that was most memorably performed by Rufus, a bull terrier wearing a tutu, and his trainer during a talent show at the 2006 Champaign County Fair in Urbana, Illinois. Rufus, who led by clasping a leg around the trainer's waist and placing his partner's hand in his paw, elegantly glided across the stage and narrowly defeated a 3-year-old Pekingese who spun in circles to Tchaikovsky's "Dance Of The Sugar Plum Fairy." Rufus' first-place prize was a blue ribbon and a chewy pork treat.

War On Terror, global security initiative undertaken by the United States and its allies. This ongoing conflict is a Pakistani man passing sensitive information to an undercover CIA agent on an Islamabad street corner. A member of a terrorist cell sitting in a hot, pizza-box-littered Queens apartment, smoking a cigarette, nervously testing a triggering mechanism, and jumping when the phone rings. Men in suits gathered around a computer in Langley while a photo of a Kabul marketplace is enlarged, followed by the grave utterance, "That's our guy." In Berlin, a door is kicked down. Somebody yells, "Get down!" Somebody in Boston looks up from top-secret documents and asks, "Does Harrison know about this?" Somebody finds an audiotape in his locker. Who put it there? The sound of a camera taking photos of a suspicious man exiting an Islamic bookstore. Soldiers patrolling an Afghan village have a bad feeling this time—they don't know why, they just do. A grainy videotape. A courtroom sketch of a suspected terrorist on trial. Men in red skullcaps walk in a single-file line behind a barbed-wire fence. FBI, CIA, NSA, DHS—the chatter has gone quiet. A bomb goes off. Many bombs go off. "Mr. President, we

Ww · uu

Twenty-fourth letter of the basic modern English alphabet, used when one *U* just isn't enough firepower. The consonant, developed from a bilabial fricative in early medieval Latin, can be found in words, such as "wharf" and "wagon," in which a single *U* ain't gonna cut it and it's time to bring out the big boys, double that baby up, and hit 'em with both barrels. Commonly used in Old High German, *W* became increasingly common in English by 1300, when it became clear that sometimes a *U* needs major backup from a letter that can bust in and just fucking unload on a word, because if there's one thing linguists agree on, it's that you never, ever bring a *U* to a *W* fight.

LOVE OF HUNTING WOULD SEW UP NRA VOTE
George Washington

(b. Feb. 22, 1732 d. Dec. 14, 1799), American military and political leader who would have to play up the fact that he led the Continental Army to victory over the British in the Revolutionary War to have any chance of winning key swing states like Florida and Ohio. A Founding Father of the United States and a framer of the U.S. Constitution, Washington would really need to hammer those talking points home unless he wanted them to get lost in the 24-hour news cycle, especially since there are a number of voters out there who would think of him as a Washington insider. Baptized in the Church of England, Washington was not especially religious, so he would have no shot of winning the Evangelical vote, but then again, a few photo ops of him coming in and out of church, a high-profile dinner with Billy Graham, and his decisive victory at Yorktown certainly couldn't hurt with white Christian males. The cherry tree thing would get younger people to the polls. Even if it wasn't true, kids remember it. No matter what, though, because Washington honorably stepped down from the presidency in 1797 after two terms in office, he would constantly have to beat back accusations from the Right that he was un-American.

STANCE ON SLAVERY
Slaves he owned could wrestle him for their freedom; Washington finished with a 198-to-4 win-loss record

GREATEST MILITARY ACCOMPLISHMENT
Not flipping the boat over while crossing the Delaware River, despite his insistence on standing up almost the whole time and twice running suddenly to the back of the boat when he thought he saw an otter

HEIGHT
6′2″ standing; 8′4″ on horseback; 11′2″ standing on horseback; 1,256′2″ standing atop the Empire State Building (projected)

ON THE BATTLEFIELD
Washington actually betrayed the Continental Army more than 30 times but didn't want to disappoint everyone who was really into him being president

---

[1] (b. Feb. 21, 1962 d. Sept. 12, 2008), American author of fiction and nonfiction known for works such as the story collection *Girl With Curious Hair* (1989), the essay collection *A Supposedly Fun Thing I'll Never Do Again* (1997), and his magnum opus, the novel *Infinite Jest* (1996).

Watch, timepiece worn by men who wish to draw attention to their beautiful, beautiful wrists.

CITIES OF THE WORLD
Washington, D.C.

City on the Potomac River that became the U.S. capital in 1790, and was considered an obvious choice since it was already home to the White House, the Capitol Building, the Supreme Court, the U.S. Constitution, the Federal Reserve Bank, the Pentagon, the National Archives, the Martin Luther King, Jr., Memorial, the Department of Homeland Security, and almost 200 foreign embassies. Prior to 1790, both Philadelphia and New York City served as capitals, though neither made as much sense as D.C. because they lacked a National Mall, the Jefferson Memorial, the FDR Memorial, the

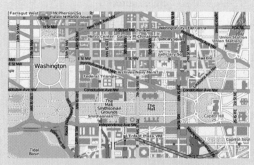

As home to all three branches of the federal government, Washington, D.C., was an obvious choice to be capital of the United States.

president of the United States, the Department of Justice, and all three branches of government. Washington, D.C., is expected to remain the U.S. capital indefinitely, unless Chicago, San Francisco, or Toledo, Ohio, manages to construct better buildings for every department of the government, establish local headquarters for several hundred national and international governing bodies, and dig new graves for the roughly 300,000 soldiers buried in Arlington National Cemetery.

have a problem." An image of a crying child. Blood. The Homeland Security director speaks. The leader of al-Qaeda speaks. The president speaks: "We will not rest. We will not tire. We will not stop until this danger to civilization is removed."

Warhol, Andy (*b. Aug. 6, 1928 d. Feb. 22, 1987*), leading figure of the pop art movement whose style has been brazenly copied by countless other artists, every single one of whom Warhol would have loved.

Warmonger, person who peddles war from a stall in the town square or travels the countryside in a rickety old war cart, hawking war from village to village.

Warren Report, 888-page report on the assassination of President John F. Kennedy that was criticized for including a tiny collectible shard of JFK's skull in every edition.

Washington, Martha (*b. June 2, 1731 d. May 22, 1802*), female alter ego of American president George Washington. The over-the-top burlesque character "Martha" was first conceived by the famed American general and statesman during the

Revolutionary War as a way to entertain weary troops and boost morale. While wintering at Valley Forge, Washington would often strap two cannon balls into a corset, rouge his cheeks, burst unexpect-

edly into the mess tent during mealtime, and shout, "Look out, boys, it's the general's wife, Mrs. Washington! Ooh-la-la!" much to his men's merriment and delight. During Washington's presidency, "Martha" sometimes made impromptu appearances during salons with the other Founding Fathers after Washington would make a show of excus-

ing himself to "see what trouble the good wife has gotten herself into." He would return moments later dressed as the irascible Mrs. Washington, tell ribald jokes, and start raucous suggestive dances with the actual wives of Benjamin Franklin, John Adams, and Thomas Jefferson, among others. After Washington's death in 1799, Martha Washington was played for several more years by Washington's closest friend, John Beamer, to honor the president's legacy.

Water, clear, odorless, tasteless liquid (H_2O) that almost singlehandedly revived the moribund car wash industry. Prior to the introduction of water at the Tucson, Arizona, Wash-Rite location by founder Mike Spivey in 1986, an automobile was cleaned by spraying it with acid, syrup, or olive oil, or by coating it with sand and then scrubbing it with a smooth rock or steel wool until the grit was ground seamlessly into the car's exterior. At the customer's request, an additional polish could be applied by pelting the vehicle with handfuls of roofing nails. Though water allowed for the cleansing of automobiles without scraping off 95 percent of the paint, the car wash business model did not reach its full potential until much later, when it was discovered that a towel could dry an automobile just as well as setting it on fire.

Water Lilies, series of oil paintings by French impressionist Claude Monet, who believed the water lilies in his Giverny garden were actually alien pods sent down to enslave humanity. While the *Water Lilies* paintings are regarded as beautiful depictions of nature, the increasingly paranoid Monet saw them as renderings of the celestial eggs that were draining nutrients from the water and would soon hatch, releasing the extraterrestrials sent to conquer the world. The paintings, which Monet considered warnings and the only hope for the human race, are quintessential examples of the broad and rapid brushwork characteristic of the Impressionist style.

Watergate Scandal, American political scandal broken by *Washington Post* reporters Bob Woodward and Carl Bernstein when President Richard Nixon called Woodward and said, "Bob, it's Richard Nixon. I ordered the illegal break-in of the Watergate Hotel last night so I could gather information about my presidential opponent George McGovern. This is President Richard Nixon. Do you have any questions?" After a series of follow-up telephone calls in which Nixon repeatedly spelled the names of his co-conspirators so there would be no errors in Woodward's articles, Nixon met with Woodward in brightly lit department store parking lots and crowded restaurants, telling the intrepid reporter to fol-

Depictions of the Washington Monument have been found in examples of prehistoric cave art from around the world.

WASHINGTON MONUMENT, unique white rock formation of unknown origin, estimated by geologists to be at least 3 billion years old and thought to possess arcane supernatural powers. English settlers exploring Maryland first came across the Washington Monument in 1640 and abandoned their farms to feverishly construct the city of Washington, D.C., around the 555-foot tall alabaster obelisk. By 1641, all British colonists had taken on the surname "Washington," pledged fealty to the granite formation, and dedicated their lives to working as its caretakers; this role was passed down from generation to generation, the most famous superintendent being George Washington, who was also the first president of the United States. Paleogeographers who specialize in the Washington Monument theorize that the spectacular rock formation was located at the exact center of the Pangaea supercontinent, and may in fact have played some part in catalyzing continental drift 250 million years ago. Likewise, paleontologists have found fossilized evidence suggesting the Washington Monument played an important role in the lives of dinosaurs in the Mesozoic Era, providing a safe habitat for building nests and mating. Millions of years later, the Paleo-Indians who migrated to North America utilized the Washington Monument for religious rituals and performed hundreds of human sacrifices on the tip of the obelisk, causing blood to flow down the 797 steps and fill the natural depression that is now called the Capitol Reflecting Pool. Carbon-dating technology recently revealed that every 2 million years the Washington Monument emits a powerful beam of energy that eradicates all life on the planet.

◄ **WATER LILIES**
One of Monet's beautiful, alien-invasion-obsessed oil masterpieces.

Waterfall, place where water goes to end it all.

low the money because it ultimately led all the way to the White House, Nixon's chief of staff H.R. Haldeman, and Nixon himself. The investigation continued when Nixon called Woodward one evening and told him that, as they spoke, he was destroying Oval Office audio recordings of himself ordering the Watergate break-in, but that Woodward shouldn't worry because there

were also transcripts of the meetings that he could personally send the reporter if he wanted hard copies. The scandal eventually blew wide open in 1974 when Nixon showed up at the *Washington Post* newsroom and typed a story in front of the entire staff about how several of the Watergate burglars had committed perjury during their initial trial.

War

First resort in conflict resolution before opposing nations are forced to engage in diplomacy. Hoping to prevent a drawn-out, nightmarish round of statesmanship that could result in hundreds of thousands of lives saved, two or more embittered nations first try to overcome their differences by deploying their armed forces to kill as many of the other side's soldiers as possible. If the unrelenting use of lethal force breaks down and warring parties find themselves on the brink of diplomacy—a tragic scenario both sides work to avoid at all costs—they are left with no other choice than to abandon their wholesale slaughter and meet face to face to civilly divide up contested territory. Often, however, a clear victor will emerge before war spirals into an all-out ceasefire, saving that nation's citizens from ever having to witness the horrors of nonviolent compromise.

MODERN WARFARE

In the post–World War II era, warfare can be defined as a highly coordinated, technologically driven undertaking that, considering how busy everyone is, it's really pretty amazing anyone has the time to organize and see through. Unlike the earlier centuries, when military leaders didn't have to worry about checking their e-mails 24/7 and could actually focus on executing sweeping, large-scale campaigns aimed at destroying enemy nations, modern warfare is characterized by trying to squeeze in a tactical strike between meetings, but wouldn't you know, another meeting was scheduled between meetings and there are still 14 voicemails that need to be checked and apparently there's some crisis at day care this morning. While advancements in information and communications technology have had a major impact on military strategy in recent decades, between all the bills due at the end of the month, and all the movies building up in one's Netflix queue, and, fuck, it's one's 15th

wedding anniversary next week, there aren't enough hours in the day to pore over millions of terabytes of military data. It may be possible to fit in an innovation in electronic warfare at lunch, but one hasn't been to the gym in weeks and, with what the doctor said about one's cholesterol, it looks as though planning a covert invasion based on CIA-gathered information is just going to have to wait until things are a little less crazy.

Toppling The Statue Of Saddam Hussein
To celebrate their victory over Iraq, American forces pulled a statue of Saddam Hussein to the ground, where it would stay for the remaining eight years of the war.

WAR INVENTIONS

Button: A great technological advancement on the trigger, the button must simply be pressed with the finger in order to take the lives of anywhere from one to 1 million people.

MRE (Meal Ready To Eat): Freeze-dried meal in pouch that can be prepared on the battlefield with only hot water and a skilled team of sous chefs.

Brothel: House of prostitution designed to keep the sexual appetites of soldiers in check, lest they begin to feel romantically toward the enemy.

Parachute: Device worn by paratroopers to give people on the ground an easier shot.

Net: Mesh fabric device used for collecting prisoners of war with rare or unusual military rankings.

Land Mine: Explosive placed just under the surface of the ground that all but ended the practice of pretending to lift the hem of one's skirt and skipping through unfamiliar enemy territory.

Navy: Military branch that ended the longstanding practice of marching legions of foot soldiers into the ocean until they drowned 50 feet out or so.

Radar: Detection system that helps armies feel better about killing civilians, as radar reduces all human beings to little green dots regardless of whether they are enemies or innocent noncombatants.

Tank: Armored combat vehicle that was far more efficient than having five or six troops on bicycles struggling to carry a cannon.

Barracks: Building that provided lodging and beds for soldiers rather than having them all sleep in one big pile.

Blackhawk Helicopter: Fulfilled U.S. military demand for at least one helicopter to go down in every battle.

RULES OF WAR: A TIMELINE

3500 BC
Sumer-Akkad War
The first war in history establishes the rule that brutally murdering a human being whom you have never seen before in your life is a thing that is okay to do in a war.

AD 476–800
Dark Ages
Noncombatants officially declared fair game.

1095–1291
Crusades
Knights are bound by chivalry to bring the body of a fallen opponent home to his family each time before returning to the battlefield.

1853–1856
Crimean War
First war to establish that war is a brutal and ultimately meaningless endeavor, a fact that had not been true in previous wars.

1864
First Geneva Convention
Came out strongly against the use of torture that people find out about.

1865–
American Civil War
Many Americans came around to the idea that teenagers on the frontline should probably be armed with more than drums and flutes.

SOLDIERS THROUGHOUT TIME

Mounted Allosaurus Brigadier
154,842,110 BC

Spartan
Elite ancient warrior trained from childhood in combat and military strategy who still would have been completely obliterated by even one Tomahawk missile

Viking
Sweet Jesus

Sioux Warrior
Yeah, these guys never had a chance

Dragoon
Relied heavily on an intimidating-sounding name to cover up what was essentially just a guy on a horse

Nazi Officer
Highly detailed uniforms added a touch of elegance to the forced extermination of an entire race of people

U.S. Soldier In Korea
Wore light, durable boots designed for taking and then ceding 30 miles of territory

U.S. Soldier In Iraq
Extremely mobile and agile, as they didn't have any of that stubborn body armor to weigh them down

IED-Sniffing Dog
Didn't want to be in Iraq, either

Mounted Cybersaurus Brigadier
AD 290,376

1914–1918
World War I
Mustard-gassing of corpses was declared "cruel and unusual, but allowable."

1946
No running.

1949
Rules governing humane treatment of POWs forbid forcible sodomy with any object longer than 5-and-a-half inches.

1966
The upper arm was added to the foot and hand as an acceptable place to shoot oneself in order to get sent home.

1975
Vietnam War
Viet Cong fined $65,000 for violating building codes for digging punji pits that failed to meet the minimum depth and number of pointed sticks covered in feces requirements.

1994
U.N. Convention on War Safety requires combat zones to be childproofed.

2034
Russo-Seychelles War
According to Article 5 of the Van Braak–Western Alliance Conventions, sonic-neural technology may not be used against a prisoner of war unless said prisoner has already been infused with at least 3,500 milligrams of blood-orchid serum.

FAMOUS MILITARY FIGURES

William Tecumseh Sherman
Union general during the American Civil War, notable for his attempt to win the hearts and minds of Georgia Confederate citizens by burning their shitty state to the ground.

Ambrose Burnside
Union Army general who redefined military facial hair, single-handedly devising the sideburns, the broomstache, the whisker tuxedo, Spotsylvania scruff, the wiry wings of God, abolitionist's shock, the senator, cheek marmots, and the Sultan's delight.

Shunroku Kuriboshi
Japanese general, mass murderer, and cruel despot known as the "Japanese Hitler" and "Leviathan of Evil" in the alternate reality in which he didn't die of scarlet fever at the age of 2.

George S. Patton
World War I colonel and World War II general who sat during peacetime in a dark room, fists clenched, convulsing.

Mike "Murph" Murphy
South Boston theorist often credited with the concept of giving those assholes in Iraq 24 hours to turn over bin Laden or else we drop an A-bomb and leave no fucking camel standing.

Artifacts Of War

A SOLDIER'S LETTER HOME FROM THE WAR OF 1812

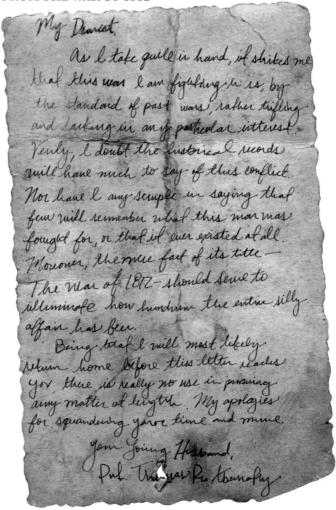

Propaganda
Used by governments to display to citizens that if they are stupid enough to be swayed by a poster, they should just do what the government says anyway.

Washington Crossing The Delaware
Famous oil painting that has many factual inaccuracies: The flag is incorrect, the boat is the wrong model, the river is too wide, the men didn't bring horses across the Delaware, and Washington's pose is wrong. This is a bad painting.

The Mona Lisa
This sadistic bitch who just sat there with a psychotic smile on her face while dead bodies piled up around her during the Great War of Italy.

Napoleon Crossing The Alps
The French emperor would strike fear into the hearts of his enemies by making his horse do a wheelie.

WAR PHOTOGRAPHY Indelible images that capture the complexity of human conflict

The American Civil War

World War I

World War II

The Vietnam War

BATTLE TACTICS

False Colors
Flying a flag of a country other than one's own to lure an enemy into danger is a longstanding military tactic. Traditionally, a smaller solid-green flag is raised underneath the decoy to indicate sarcasm.

Showing Up With A Bunch Of Guys
First used in the Battle of Smolensk by Napoleon, who showed up with like seven other dudes, including this one guy who was really fucking huge.

Desertion
A highly effective tactical maneuver when one is attempting to not end up with one's guts in one's hands.

Kamikaze Attack
Japanese maneuver in World War II in which fighter pilots scanned the decks of American naval vessels for the weakest-looking guys and crashed their planes into them.

Insurgent Warfare
Style of combat that the U.S. military is totally going to handle next time.

Sneak Retreat
Soldiers creep up on a sleeping enemy encampment and then flee in panic without firing a single shot. When the enemies wake up in the morning, they see the remnants of the sneak retreat and realize they're dealing with some pretty crazy motherfuckers.

Phalanx
A tight-knit infantry formation that renders it impossible for the opposing army to tell from whom the smell of feces is emanating.

Brutal Firebombing Of The City Of Dresden
Useful only in very, very specific historical instances of war, but hugely effective in those cases.

Genocide
Total extermination of a race or group that, as long as we're talking war here, is undeniably useful.

Pincer Movement
Soldiers form into giant claw that snips enemy in half.

Groman Show Of Force
Entire army eats a chicken as fast as it possible can.

MILITARY INSIGNIA

Danger
Electrified corporal

Penny
Cool way to pretend that you have a special Abraham Lincoln Medal

One Star
Loser general

Two Star
General who is still deciding if the military is for him or if he wants to go back to school

Two And A Half Stars
Pleasant but underwhelming general who is hampered by hackneyed leadership lacking any real emotional depth

Three Stars
General who's getting kind of serious about this star thing

Four Stars
Total star-hound

Five Stars
Two-star general and three-star general trapped inside the same body

Six Stars
Luxury general

Wings
Soldier who has met a pilot

3 Stripes
Stripe Master

One Stripe And One Star
Private General

One Stripe
Guy who needs to start thinking about finding a way to get some more stripes

West, Mae (*b. Aug. 17, 1893 d. Nov. 22, 1980*), legendary American actress whose crooked posture; odd, inexpressive face; and confrontational personality instantly made her an international sex symbol.

Whiskey, let's get through a little more knowledge first. Later, though.

Waterloo, Battle Of, decisive military encounter in which the Duke of Wellington's Anglo-Allied forces defeated Napoléon and the Imperial French Army, sure, but can we talk for a moment about Napoléon's series of spectacular military victories from 1799 to 1812? Or is focusing solely on a person's failures more important in our culture nowadays? Wellington's army withstood repeated advances by French forces, while the Prussian army broke through Napoléon's right flank, so, yes, it was a mistake for Napoléon to think he could defeat two armies at once, but of course in a society where negativity and pessimism is the norm we *would* just write the guy off as a dangerously delusional megalomaniac instead of maybe talking about how Napoléon was mostly a terrific general who did an outstanding job during the battles of Wagram, Smolensk, and Borodino. You know what, though? Forget Napoléon for a second, because this goes well beyond any one man: The problem—and it's endemic to all of modern society—is that we've become so quick to find the flaws in others that we are virtually incapable of putting our petty jealousies aside and giving people the credit they deserve. Instead of "Congratulations," it's "I could have done better." Instead of "You worked hard; you deserve your success," it's "He's lucky; he must have known someone to get to where he is." And then we hold people to such an impossible standard that when they ultimately do fail, even the slightest bit, that becomes our green light to pounce. And oh, boy, do we pounce. The fangs come out and we just tear them to shreds. And why? Because we crave failure in others. We get some sort of sick satisfaction from it. We feed off it. Anytime somebody else is getting just a little taste of success, we have to find some way to bring them down, because God forbid the next guy has his shit a little more together or gets a slightly bigger piece of the pie. It all comes down to one thing, really: fear. Fear that maybe we're actually *not* as good, or as talented, or that maybe we know in our heart of hearts that we haven't put in the effort. Fear that our station in life is set, and that others are passing us by, not because they got lucky, but because we were lazy. Because they earned it, and we didn't. Napoléon was a great general. The way he routed a multinational coalition in the Battle of Dresden was goddamn impressive and nothing can ever take that away from him.

Waterskiing, activity invented in total defiance of God's will and developed sheerly from the furious, impotent anger people feel at being forced to live as sentient creatures in a fleeting and meaningless world. Waterskiing is regarded as humanity's way of telling God we will hate Him forever for bringing the flawed, decaying putrescence of our mortal bodies into existence, and waving excitedly while being pulled across a lake on planks of wood by a speedboat is a clear message to God that we will never forgive Him for the cruel fate with which He has burdened us.

Weeping, type of crying fashionable in the 1940s among World War II widows that was displaced in the 1950s by the more discreet and emotional act of sobbing. Before weeping came into vogue, bawling was the preferred method of breaking down, practiced exclusively from the turn of century until 1914, when the outset of World War I saw

distraught citizens turning to either blubbering or boohooing. The wars and social upheaval of the 1960s and 1970s saw many Americans crying their eyes out, a technique that eventually gave way to wailing in the 1980s and 1990s, and, for a six-month period in 1993, yowling. Since the new millennium, most people quiver before releasing a few solitary tears, though a growing number have dealt with the fallout from the 2008 financial crisis by completely losing their shit.

Well, Monica Couldn't Have Any Because She's Allergic To Gluten, phrase overheard from a passing man talking loudly on cell phone.

Western Alliance, international political alignment composed of Russia, Taiwan, Finland, the former United States, and the various satellite countries and city-states making up the Van Braak Consortium. The Western Alliance was formed in opposition to the Sino-Quint Powers—a tripartite union comprising China, the Republic of Seychelles, and the bureaucratic arm of the Quint Group—and states as its political aims "new-world humanism, post-Orbian disarmament and realignment, and the dissolution of the Oberon II Bloc." Defined by Sino-Quint nations as a "rebel movement" as opposed to an officially recognized political body, the Western Alliance is believed to be headquartered somewhere in the Great North Woods of the former Maine.

Whisker, specialized facial hair that helps human males navigate in the darkness to find food. The males can successfully maneuver around obstacles and guide themselves without the aid of sight by slowly

Weapon

Any object commonly used by humans throughout history to slash, stab, maim, mutilate, cave in a ribcage, slice off a face, sever neck tendons, explode a lower torso, slit a belly until the entrails tumble out, cover villagers with burns and blisters from a hundred miles away, reduce 50 people eating at a café to an undifferentiated pile of gore and personal belongings, gouge out genitalia for a belt buckle, or splatter a head against a wall so there's nothing left but a lower jaw attached to a neck and arms flapping around purely from reflex.

KNIFE
Convenient device perfect for slicing open a jugular vein or buttering a blueberry muffin

MACHETE
Used to clear areas thick with people

BATTLE AX
Weapon all soldiers used during World War II's "Battle of Hastings Throwback Day"

CROSSBOW
Fucking crossbow, dude

MEAT CLEAVER
Tool with broad blade that is not traditionally used as a weapon, with the exception of the Franco-Brisket Wars of 1842–47

SHIV
Makeshift knife used by prisoners to stab their pillows when they feel angry and need to let off some steam

MACE
Blunt, club-like weapon without which the Middle Ages would have been simply unbearable

UZI
One uzi, good. Two uzis, better. Three uzis, that's got to be hard to hold two in one hand but, sure, whatever. Four uzis, bravo, everybody look at the big hand man, is that what you want?

PIKE
Extremely long, pointed pole exceptional at circumventing restraining orders

MUSKET
So excruciatingly slow and complicated to reload that most infantrymen would stick the barrel in their mouth, pull the trigger with a toe, and hope for the best

NIGHTSTICK
Used by law enforcement to wipe that smug look off a suspect's face

TORPEDO
Underwater missile piloted by a trained suicide-eel

FLAME THROWER
Nonlethal crowd-control device

HOWITZER
Used during hunting season to take out an entire herd of deer at once

TANK
Amazing machine that combines the fun of driving with the entertainment of blowing up shit with a massive gun

ATOMIC BOMB
Pretty incredible that things got this far, isn't it? Wow.

HOW TO MENACINGLY SHARPEN A KNIFE

What you will need: whetstone, knife preferably more than 6 inches long. Shirt optional.

1. Without breaking eye contact, slowly spit on the whetstone and begin sharpening the knife using long, deliberate strokes.

2. Lean back in a chair insouciantly and continue to stare. Chuckle to yourself about something.

3. After several minutes, say aloud, "You ain't from around here, are ya?" (*Note:* "Nice shoes. I sure do like them shoes. Where'd you get such expensive-lookin' shoes?" is also acceptable.)

4. Test the knife blade with your thumb. Comment on its sharpness and about how it is now perfect for skinning little piggies who wandered too far from home.

5. Slowly cut slice of apple and eat straight from blade while informing those who uncomfortably get up to leave that you'll be seeing them real soon.

COULD'VE DONE ANYTHING WITH HIS LIFE

Woodrow Wilson

(b. Dec. 28, 1856 d. Feb. 3, 1924), 28th president of the United States, who never lived up to his family's expectations, especially those of his mother and father, who thought such a smart young man could have amounted to so much more. A Princeton graduate and the only president ever to hold a Ph.D., Wilson seemed poised to become a doctor, lawyer, or professor, which is why his decision to abandon his education and run for president in 1912 was so disappointing to those closest to him—though in his presence all displayed a polite, if strained, interest in his support for lower tariffs, the Federal Trade Commission, and restrictions on child labor. Wilson is remembered for his leadership of the United States during World War I and for his advocacy of the League of Nations, two accomplishments his family would nod at and describe as "quite interesting," though they really thought he sold himself short and wondered deep down if they were in some way to blame.

PET PEEVE: How White House smelled "Taft-y" for the first few months of his presidency.

FAMOUS QUOTE: "I enjoy being president because it makes me feel like I'm God and that I can do anything I want. Sometimes I think about that when I'm having sex and it makes the sex better."
– State Of The Union address, 1915

BENCH PRESS: 45 pounds

brushing the highly sensitive follicles against various objects such as walls, cupboards, tables, chairs, doorframes, and the floor.

White House, official residence of the president of the United States where, it would be fair to assume, the commander in chief occasionally suffers from bouts of violent diarrhea. Located at 1600 Pennsylvania Avenue in Washington, D.C., the house was first occupied by President John Adams, who turned it over a year later to Thomas Jefferson, and both men, at one point or another, more than likely had some sort of intestinal inflammation that caused them to charge bowlegged into what was then probably a privy or water closet to expel the liquefied contents of their bowels. In 1901 President Theodore Roosevelt had all work-related offices relocated to the West Wing where he, just like any other human being, probably had to sheepishly excuse himself from a meeting every so often in a desperate attempt to avoid shitting himself in front of his aides, personal secretaries, and Cabinet members. Built in the neoclassical style, the White House has served as the primary residence for every president but Washington, and every one of them, including John F. Kennedy, Ronald Reagan, Franklin Delano Roosevelt, and Dwight D. Eisenhower, once sat—red-faced and dehydrated—on one of its 35 toilets, sweat beading on their foreheads, hands clutching their stomachs, and anuses releasing loose fecal matter as their wives sat outside the door asking, "Is everything okay in there?"

White Supremacy, self-help movement aimed at empowering Caucasians to become the very best white people they can be. White suprema-

For more than 200 years, the White House has been the official residence of the U.S. president and, presumably, his occasional bouts of diarrhea.

cist groups such as the Ku Klux Klan and Aryan Nations strive to help whites feel confident in themselves and their ability to get out there and show the world what Caucasians can do. Through rallies, inspirational books, and uplifting motivational speeches, white supremacy has enabled millions to lead full, rich white lives and say "yes" to their white skin in a way they never imagined possible, preparing them to be the best white person that they can be.

Whitman, Walt (b. May 31, 1819 d. Mar. 26, 1892), 19th-century

American poet whose poems evoked the great, benevolent spirit of America, a country that is and always has been incredibly tolerant and supportive of eccentric gay poets.

Widow, woman whose husband has faked his death and moved to Barbados with a restaurant hostess he met at an Indian casino.

Wilder, Laura Ingalls (b. Feb. 7, 1867 d. Feb. 10, 1957), 19th-century American author who wrote about life on the prairie and who, if alive today, would probably be one of those fucking insufferable food bloggers.

Williams, Ted (b. Aug. 30, 1918 d. July 5, 2002), American baseball player and accomplished student of hitting who graduated summa cum laude from Princeton University with a dual degree in Ball Connection and the Sweet Spot Sciences. Williams went on to receive a master's degree in Waiting for Your Pitch from Harvard University, and later earned a Ph.D. in Protecting the Plate from Johns Hopkins, a second Ph.D. in Hitting to the Opposite Field from Columbia, and an honorary doctorate in Smacking It Through the Gap Between Center and Left from Oxford, where he was a tenured professor in Dinger Theory until his death.

WIND TURBINE, machine powered by coal-burning energy that spins its powerful blades, thereby creating wind that can be harnessed by highly specialized wind-collecting turbines hundreds of miles away.

Each turbine is powered by a massive coal oven that runs 24 hours a day, the pollutants from which are expelled by smokestacks 20 to 30 miles away.

Willis Tower, Chicago landmark that has slipped from being the tallest building in the world to the seventh tallest, and now effectively serves as a massive tombstone for American global economic dominance. Named the Sears Tower at the time of its construction in 1973 (after the once-mighty American retail chain that has also fallen from prominence in recent decades), the 110-story building was rapidly eclipsed in the 1990s by taller structures in Europe and Asia. The name was changed to Willis Tower in 2009 when a London-based insurance company bought the rights to the building, much like an opportunistic foreign bidder buying up all of a desperate family's adored heirlooms at a hastily arranged estate sale for a deceased patriarch. While much bigger skyscrapers bustle with the activities of productive industry, the Willis Tower is now left to slowly crumble and silently loom over the interred corpses of the American businesses that lie in its long, dark shadow.

Wind, natural flow of air through space that is needed to push an empty Doritos bag from one end of a desolate city street to the other.

Wish, tiny, secret little dream held in a person's heart that every one of their family members and dependents would die.

Wok, bowl-shaped frying pan that is never used, used intensely for three weeks even for food it shouldn't be used for, and then never used again.

Women, am I right?

Wonder, Stevie (*b. May 13, 1950*), popular singer and songwriter who created such classics as "Superstition," "Living For The City," and "Higher Ground." "Part-Time Lover" is pretty awful.

Wonton, small Chinese dumpling usually filled with several dozen live bees or, in some regions, wasps.

Woods, Tiger (*b. Dec. 30, 1975*), professional golfer who had a

Willis Tower: A Grim Reminder Of What Once Was

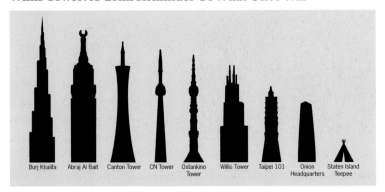

Burj Khalifa | Abraj Al Bait | Canton Tower | CN Tower | Ostankino Tower | Willis Tower | Taipei 101 | Onion Headquarters | Staten Island Teepee

Wolf, wild, majestic, cunning. The wolf.

World War I

Global conflict between 1914 and 1918 that came tantalizingly close to satisfying the Western world's lust for blood and carnage. Fought between the allied forces of the United Kingdom, France, Russia, and the United States, and the Central powers of Germany, Austria-Hungary, the Ottoman Empire, and Bulgaria, World War I ravaged the European continent with unprecedented death and destruction, killing more than 35 million people and coming just a tad short of quenching the West's insatiable yearning for gore, slaughter, and the total, senseless annihilation of all life. While brutal new military technologies such as the machine gun, the flamethrower, and the tank certainly soothed a great deal of mankind's deep passion for relentless slaughter—and the gruesome innovation of trench warfare obviously helped quite a bit as well—in the end, everyone involved had to admit that, as horrific as World War I had been, they definitely still had a little bloodlust left in them. Twenty-one years later, the unsatisfied nations indulged in another war, seeing as the first iteration lacked a few key satisfying elements, such as the firebombing of entire cities, concentration camps, the genocidal near-destruction of an ethnic group, and atomic weapons.

Inside A Soldier's Backpack

Bayonet
It was always wise to bring an extra bayonet, in case you were to clumsily break one off in a screaming, teenage stranger's skull

Cigarettes
Used to celebrate the survival of a deadly gas attack

Blanket
Used just in case the blankets supplied by battlefield motels were too scratchy

Clothing
Embroidered "War to End All Wars" hoodie

Canteen
Useful for bringing a dead German's blood home as a souvenir

Gas Mask
The poor son of a bitch doesn't even know why he needs this yet

Personal Items
Picture of soon-to-be widow

Extra Trench
In case the soldier didn't have enough time to dig one during battle

Hey!
A quarter!

Extra Army Business Cards
For any networking during downtime in the trenches

Arnold Bakers
U.S. Army Private
"Good for a drink... and a song."

World War II

Massive global conflict in which United States completely blew its wad in terms of courage, strength, ingenuity, selflessness, economic prowess, solidarity, sacrifice, and moral clarity. Fought between the Axis powers (whose principal members included Germany, Japan, and Italy) and the U.K.- and U.S.-led Allies, the Second World War gave America one final opportunity to absolutely run itself dry of any clear-eyed national purpose or moral conviction before plunging into a steady, six-decade-long decline characterized by industrial stagnation, arrogant entitlement, and cultural ennui. Though its military leaders initially wished to remain neutral, America entered the war following Japan's 1941 attack on the U.S. Navy's Pacific Fleet at Pearl Harbor—a tragic event that marked the nation's last significant, non-cynical moment of unity—and by war's end had used up every remaining ounce of its domestic know-how, gumption, work ethic, and humility. World War II came to a close in August 1945, when U.S. forces dropped two atomic bombs on Japan, which represented the two final instances of American scientific and technological prowess.

General Douglas MacArthur devised his best military strategies while walking in the water and was known to invite advisers along to accompany him on strolls all across the Pacific Ocean.

Major Alliances

- ➤ The Axis
- ➤ The Allies
- ➤ The Atlantic Hive
- ➤ The Believers
- ➤ The Grand Slammers
- ➤ The Pacific Petes
- ➤ The Hitmen
- ➤ The Knights
- ➤ The Uncle Donnies
- ➤ The Forever Pals
- ➤ The Himalayan Hellcats
- ➤ Sarah and Ilana's Applewood Alliance
- ➤ The Brooklyn Dodgers
- ➤ Titans Inc.
- ➤ The Polliwogs
- ➤ The World War II-ers
- ➤ Paraguay and Uruguay
- ➤ The Rowdy Boys

A British Fighter Plane

World War II saw unprecedented advances in aerial combat technology.

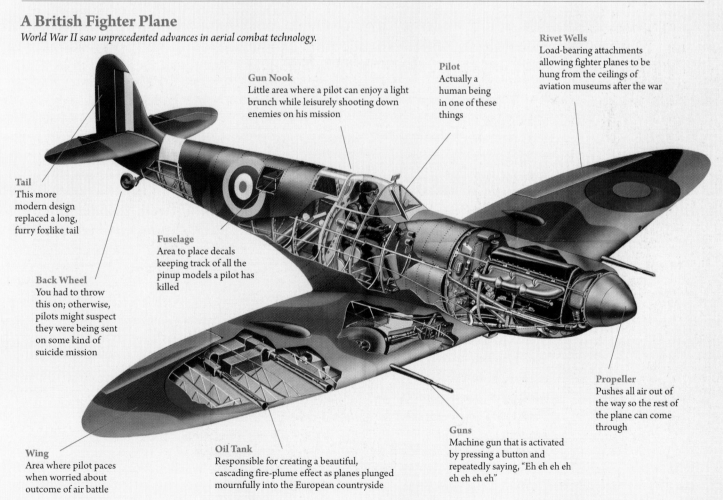

Gun Nook
Little area where a pilot can enjoy a light brunch while leisurely shooting down enemies on his mission

Pilot
Actually a human being in one of these things

Rivet Wells
Load-bearing attachments allowing fighter planes to be hung from the ceilings of aviation museums after the war

Tail
This more modern design replaced a long, furry foxlike tail

Fuselage
Area to place decals keeping track of all the pinup models a pilot has killed

Back Wheel
You had to throw this on; otherwise, pilots might suspect they were being sent on some kind of suicide mission

Wing
Area where pilot paces when worried about outcome of air battle

Oil Tank
Responsible for creating a beautiful, cascading fire-plume effect as planes plunged mournfully into the European countryside

Guns
Machine gun that is activated by pressing a button and repeatedly saying, "Eh eh eh eh eh eh eh eh"

Propeller
Pushes all air out of the way so the rest of the plane can come through

Woodstock, huge 1969 rock music festival that one's parents were either too young to attend, too old to attend, or worse, attended.

WRIGHT BROTHERS ➤
Many thought the reason the Wright Brothers were working on the airplane in the first place was to get the hell out of Dayton, Ohio, but apparently not.

phenomenal run being someone people liked from 1996 to 2009, during which time he was consistently ranked by PGA Tour experts and fans alike as a decent human

being. At the height of his lucrative, nearly decade-and-a-half-long streak of being a seemingly okay person, Woods racked up countless mentions of being "a likable guy," challenged Jack Nicklaus' record for number of people who thought he was an ethically sound man, and provided a thrilling finish to the 2008 season, when he managed to go another year without millions of observers discovering what an irredeemable lowlife prick he was. Woods' dominant, 13-year stretch of not being considered a world-class piece of dog shit ended abruptly in the fall of 2009.

Wool, fine hair of sheep that is woven into clothing such as sweaters that can be worn while eating lamb chops, effectively showing that species what's up.

Worker, type of disposable person. (*See* Soldier, Voter, Actor, Bassist, Personal Assistant, Patient, Intern, Transient, Punter, Driver, Mistress, Housekeeper, Ryan Phillippe, Miner, Senior Citizen)

World's Fair, international exhibition series filled with lies about the future.

Wright Brothers, Orville (*b. Aug. 19, 1871 d. Jan. 30, 1948*) **and Wilbur** (*b. Apr. 16, 1867 d. May 30, 1912*), American engineers who,

despite revolutionizing the modern world by inventing the first airplane capable of flight, still both managed to die in Dayton, Ohio. Although the Wright brothers' first flight helped usher in the age of aviation along with a trillion-dollar commercial and military industry, Orville and Wilbur spent their last days on this earth as living legends in Ohio's sixth-largest city. Not even Cleveland or Columbus. With the development of the first fixed-wing aircraft, the Wright brothers had the entire world at their fingertips and the ability to go to any historically, geographically, or culturally fascinating place on the planet, yet the two of them made the conscious decision to remain in Dayton, known for its third-rate museums and close proximity to tributaries of the disgustingly polluted Ohio River. Schmucks.

Wright, Frank Lloyd (*b. June 8, 1867 d. Apr. 9, 1959*), an ax-murderer killed the love of Wright's life, her two children, and four

workmen in his Wisconsin home, smack-dab in the middle of his illustrious career, yet for some reason this is never the first thing mentioned about Wright, who was also an architect. While Wright was away working in Chicago, seven members of his innermost circle

were brutally killed when a disgruntled butler set fire to the house and waited outside with an ax, butchering the innocent victims as they desperately tried to escape the flames; this shocking information is, for some unknown, insane reason, usually mentioned way, way after something or other about Fallingwater, one of the most famous homes Wright designed. A bereaved Wright personally built a beautiful coffin for his ax-murdered lover and buried her with his own two hands on the Wisconsin property where she died, which is quite possibly the most heartbreaking thing imaginable, but you almost never hear anything about that. The Guggenheim Museum in New York City is Wright's most recognized masterpiece.

Wristwatch, item that can tell you a lot about a man, if you are a stupid dick.

Writing, creative process of browsing the Internet, drinking coffee, going out for a walk, and masturbating.

Wurst, German or Austrian sausage that one will be unable to stop thinking about upon reading this entry, setting in motion the measures necessary to obtain one.

X Chromosome, one of two sex-determining chromosomes, worth on average $0.23 less per nuclei than the Y chromosome.

Xavier High School, rural Catholic school that gets to state every goddamn year due to its seemingly limitless supply of annoying three-

point-shooting farm boys. With a lineup that inevitably includes a big, corn-fed fucker down low who just grabs rebounds and kicks it out to one of those little shits camping out behind the arc, Xavier would be halfway tolerable if they weren't such chippy little pricks on defense. The only saving grace with Xavier High School making it to state is knowing they will inevitably lose to one of the schools with all the black kids who can dunk.

Xenophobia, intense yet perfectly rational and warranted fear of foreigners. The anxiety and suspicion characterized by xenophobia often manifests itself in a desire to insulate oneself from foreign peoples or to drive them away, neither of which are unreasonable responses considering the fact that foreign people look different, act different, and speak a totally different language. Xenophobia may result in violent acts against foreigners, a radical measure that is quite logical when considering not only how dissimilar foreigners are, but also how likely they are to be planning violence against you.

Xerxes I (*b. 519 BC d. 465 BC*), Persian king who attempted to invade Greece in 480 BC but failed because in the chronology of ancient Greek history he loses. Although Xerxes commanded the Persian army to an impressive victory over Sparta at the Battle of Thermopylae, he was eventually pushed back toward Persia due to the fact that this was exactly what he was supposed to do in the narrative of Greek history, and to do otherwise not only would have completely ruined the whole setup for the next part—in which Sparta, Athens, and the various other Greek city-states fight the Peloponnesian War—but also would have been impossible because that's not what happened. In 479 BC, Xerxes returned to his palace in Persepolis, where, like clockwork, he was murdered 14 years later by his royal bodyguard at the exact point he was intended to be in the timeline of events.

XLIV, Roman numeral about which one is lying if one claims to have known instantaneously that it means 44.

XOXOQ, shorthand at the end of written correspondence for "hugs and kisses and intense psychosexual abuse that will haunt you for decades and cripple your ability to be intimate with any other human being, no matter how many thousands of dollars you spend on your high-priced Manhattan therapist."

X-Rating, MPAA designation for films deemed unfit for minors due to graphic depictions of black dudes stuffing their cocks so far up a white bitch's ass that she pukes up their cum and begs for more, while two filthy nymphos eat each other's pussies raw and a greasy fat fuck who's hung like a goddamn horse jerks himself off in the corner. The rating was altered to NC-17 in the mid-1990s.

X-Ray, image of the internal components of something, typically a body part, used for medical purposes or by persons with an interest in becoming bone models.

Xx · χ

Twenty-fifth letter in the English alphabet, whose overall use will skyrocket when China takes over as the world's No. 1 economy and Americans suddenly realize how integral X is to the anglicized spellings of Chinese cities. Though the letter is pronounced "eks" by English speakers, more and more U.S. citizens will become so comfortable with X making the Chinese "sh" sound that manufacturing centers like Xi'an, Xiamen, and Xining will roll off their tongues as if it were their native language. While X is infrequently used today, in 20 years it will be perfectly common to hear an average Wyoming resident say the words "xiexie," "xiaxue," and "*Du xiè Xiè xi n sh ng, néng g i w ji g ngz ma?*" which mean "thank you," "snow," and "Please, Mr. Xie, may I have a raise?" respectively.

SOME Xs

As few words in the English language begin with the letter X, it is customary in reference volumes to fill empty space with a series of Xs in a variety of interesting typographical styles.

X Plain	**X** Bold X	*X* Italic
X̲ Underline	***X*** Bold-Italic	**X̲** Bold-Underline
X̲ Italic-Underline	**X̲** Bold-Italic-Underline	

COMMON REPETITIVE PATTERNS OF X

XXXXXXXXX
XXXXXXXXXX
XXXXXXXXXXXX
XXXX
Xx
XxxXxxX
XxXXXXXxX
X
XXXXXXXXXX

A TIMELINE OF X

X	X	**X**	X	x	X	X	X
300 BC	200 BC	AD 100	500	1200	1775	1975	2010

LETTERS THAT ARE NOT X

ABCDEFG
HIJKLMN
OPQRSTU
VUWYZ

LETTER THAT IS X

X

Xylocarp, 200-foot-long monstrous-looking prehistoric fish that lived millions of years ago, right? Nope—any type of plant that produces fruit with a woody exterior.

Yacht, type of boat on which instances of sexual assault surpass those occurring in canoes by a 40,000-to-1 ratio.

Yangtze River, longest river in Asia and third-longest river in the world overall, whose tranquil waters have serenely ambled past roughly 55 million human rights violations over the years.

"Yankee Doodle," song popular during the American Revolution that struck terror into the hearts of British soldiers, many of whom would drop their weapons in fear immediately upon hearing the words "and called it macaroni."

Yao Ming (b. Sept. 12, 1980), former NBA All-Star who retired in 2011 and returned to his native China, where he received a hero's welcome and spent two weeks touring the country before going back to work as a floor supervisor at a plastic tube factory.

Yeager, Chuck (b. Feb. 13, 1923), retired major general in the U.S. Air Force who was the first pilot to travel faster than sound and Wesleyan University's second choice for this year's commencement speaker.

Year Of The Dragon, weird 1985 movie that was on cable last night around 2 a.m. with a young Mickey Rourke playing a cop trying to take down the Yakuza or the Chinese mob or something. When editors of this book caught it halfway through, it appeared as though Rourke had struck up a romantic relationship with a Chinese cable news reporter investigating a story about someone who was running underground gambling clubs or hit squads in what could have been the Chinatown in Boston, Philadelphia, or New York. Toward the end of the film the setting briefly switched to a farm in rural Thailand, though given the time of night, it's possible that was the other movie that was being flipped to during commercials. Both movies actually seemed pretty decent.

Yello, telephone greeting primarily used by men telling the caller that the shop'll be open all day so they can come on by whenever.

Yellowthroat, small migratory bird that builds a nest by incapacitating an 18- to 60-year-old suburban

male and using its sharp beak to peck out the screaming man's eyeball, the empty socket of which it lines with grass, twigs, and moss to create a soft spot to lay eggs. When the eggs hatch, the yellowthroats feed their young small pieces of regurgitated eyelid, optic nerve, and nasal cartilage. Before departing for the winter, the birds force-feed the man enough of his own hair and flesh to keep him alive until spring, while pulling apart his knee ligaments so that he remains immobile. The next year, the male yellowthroat will arrive at the eye socket and wait, hoping to attract a suitable mate by performing a bobbing courtship dance on the now-insane man's face.

Yerba Maté, tealike stimulant drunk by people in Brazil and Argentina and by self-satisfied people who just returned from their first trip to Brazil or Argentina.

Yesterday, work deadline given out by huge, inconsiderate pricks.

YALTA CONFERENCE, meeting of the chief Allied leaders of World War II held Feb. 4–11, 1945, that quickly became awkward when Roosevelt, Stalin, and Churchill had to ask the prime minister of the Netherlands, Pieter Sjoerds Gerbrandy, to please leave. Gerbrandy, who was never told about the talks, nor invited to take any part in the discussions of the postwar world, showed up at the top-secret site on the Black Sea before the "Big Three" had arrived, and was met with uncomfortable silence after greeting the world leaders who were wondering why he was there and if he was planning to leave before they started talking. Although Churchill allegedly pulled the prime minister aside, thanked him for showing up, and expressed the group's appreciation for everything he had done, Gerbrandy ignored several polite requests to depart, informing the Allied leaders that he would wait outside the building in case they needed him.

Prime Minister Gerbrandy of the Netherlands was politely told there was not a fourth chair available for him to sit in.

Yak, everyone would be pretty upset if this fella wasn't in here. Hey there, buddy.

YELLOWSTONE NATIONAL PARK, crown jewel of the U.S. National Park Service, which draws more than 3 million visitors each year who hope to catch the rare but majestic sight of a buffalo standing right on top of a geyser just before it erupts.

Old Faithful

Youngstown, Ohio, city in eastern part of Ohio and one of the many places in the world where a human being can be born, go to school, get a job, and pass away.

Yoga, Hindu discipline and system of exercises that makes people feel much healthier and happier, and thus a practice that must be mercilessly ridiculed by one and all.

Yikes, that was close. (**See** PHEW, BOY, WOW)

Yin And Yang, concept in which seemingly contrary forces were described as interconnected and interdependent until recently, when it was discovered that Yin makes up 51 percent of everything and Yang only 49 percent, meaning Yin is more important overall and is therefore the winner.

YMCA, worldwide organization of more than 45 million members where one can join a basketball league and then quit upon realization that everyone is much better than anticipated.

York, New, how "New York" would be formatted in this reference volume if it were someone's name.

YouTube, forward-only time-travel device invented in 2005. Users log on to YouTube and are instantly transported two to five hours into the future without consciously experiencing or being aware of the intervening period. Following the time-travel experience, YouTube users describe a sense of disorientation and panic upon discovering that life has continued on without them during their temporal shift, and that any work or other tasks they left in the past remain uncompleted.

Yosemite National Park, massive California park established in 1890 that, despite recent funding cutbacks, is still a great place to do mushrooms. Though budget deficits have forced officials to reduce park staff and operating hours, Yosemite still boasts moaning giant sequoia trees, glowing waterfalls, and mountains that totally look like they are fucking melting for visitors tripping balls. Despite issues with maintaining Yosemite's trails and infrastructure, the cash-strapped park is a unique destination for anyone high as hell on psilocybin mushrooms and they will seriously lose their shit and freak the fuck out when the granite cliff El Capitan starts like breathing and making demon faces unless they're with someone chill who will tell them to just let things happen and be with the moment.

Yule, ancient pagan winter festival that has been incorporated into such Christian Christmas traditions as the yule log, yule singing, yule boars, yule lobsters, yule nog, yule Coors Light, yule urination on the shower mat, yule inappropriate behavior with visiting relatives, yule screaming match, and yule cold leftover spaghetti with butter eaten alone in a dingy basement apartment at 4 a.m.

YUMMERS, exclamation that is only appropriate to use in the presence of red velvet cake.

Proper Yummers Usages

"Is that red velvet cake? Oh, yummers!"

"Well, I really shouldn't…but for Pete's sake, it's red velvet cake! Yummers!"

"Yummers! Just a sliver, though. But I *love* red velvet cake! *Love* it."

"Yummers! [upon seeing red velvet cake]"

"Linda, are you making red velvet? Yummers!"

Acceptable Variations

"Yuh-mmers! You *know* I want some red velvet cake!"

"I'm very sorry for your loss, Linda—hold the phone, is that red velvet cake? Yum-yum-yummers!"

"Yuh-uh-uh-uh-uhmmers! Red velvet cake!"

ZAPRUDER FILM, silent motion picture that captured the death of John F. Kennedy, though recently discovered missing frames reveal the president was not in fact assassinated, but rather died of self-inflicted gunshot wounds. While the original film had a noticeable gap between frames 208 and 211, the complete sequence clearly shows the presidential motorcade turning the corner onto Dealey Plaza as a smiling Kennedy waves to the crowd with his left hand, reaches into his suit-coat pocket with his right, pulls out a brushed chrome .357 Magnum, and then shoots himself two times: once in his upper back and once in the head. In addition to taking his own life, the full 26-second film shows that prior to the fatal shot, Kennedy also opened fire on Texas governor John Connally, shooting him in the back and creating a gaping exit wound through his chest.

President John F. Kennedy, a split second before taking his own life.

Zagreb, is capital Croatia and most big of entire Republic of Croatia. Zagreb a strong city, with rich history and population very much enjoy art and party. You come to Zagreb? Yes, you come to Zagreb.

Zebra, African equid known for its distinctive black and white stripes, several hundred heads, and nearly countless number of legs.

Zen, Japanese school of Buddhism that emphasizes reaching a state of total tranquility, fearlessness, and spontaneity, a practice that adherents are advised to squeeze in to the 15-minute span of time between the end of the workday and going home to one's family.

Zest, indefatigable enthusiasm for life, or a twist of lemon added to one's fifth cocktail after life has mercilessly beaten one into the ground.

Zhao Ziyang (*b. Oct. 17, 1919 d. Jan. 17, 2005*), high-ranking Chinese politician who was critical of Maoist principles, sympathetic to student demonstrators during the Tiananmen Square protests, and generally in favor of free-market reforms. Guess what happened to him? It's not as bad as you think, but yeah, politically purged, placed under house arrest, and deprived of the funeral rites typically granted to senior Chinese officials.

Zhou Dynasty, ancient Chinese kingdom notable for its strong—some might even say extreme—commitment to agriculture. Known for its incessant cultivation of rice, millet, and lentils, the Zhou dynasty has aggravated researchers for decades, and it really just needed to cool it with its intricate well-field systems and insistence on constantly developing new farming tools. During their 800-year rule, the Zhou used their land efficiently and learned the Wei River's flooding patterns, irksome attributes that have never impressed anyone, honestly, and that historians have found irritating for years. In contrast, the Qin Dynasty also subsisted predominantly on agriculture, but wasn't anywhere near as in-your-face about it.

Zildjian, popular T-shirt company among drummers.

Zimmer, Rick (*b. Apr. 20, 1974*), founder and CEO of the popular Sklimp.com website who started his company in 1999 after selling a controlling stake in Whampler and Xooob, his two previous ventures, to Webblebits Media Group for $330 million. Zimmer partnered with former Flapzy CEO and x-Gi9 programmer Arvind Bhatt to form Sklimp, which went public in 2003. The website, which is listed as a *Fortune* 500 company, is headquartered in Palo Alto, California, and shares offices with its subsidiaries Jumblebee, Beepsheep, and Yurk.com. Zimmer is worth an estimated $2.86 billion.

Zimmerman, Robert (*b. May 24, 1941*), birth name of American singer-songwriter Bob Dylan, who adopted his pseudonym early in his career after growing frustrated with

Zz · ζ · Зз

Twenty-seventh letter of the common Latin alphabet, used in the clean version of "The Alphabet Song" to replace the phrase "I want you inside me so bad."

◄ **RICK ZIMMER**

Zimmer's Sklimp media empire has effectively bankrupted his main competitor, BitJib.com.

Z

Zoology, area of biology dedicated to the study of animals, all of which are pathetic, brutish creatures that are utterly inferior to humans in every conceivable way. The various species contained within the animal kingdom have adapted astonishing, nearly limitless mechanisms to aid in their survival, but the fact remains that not a single one has avoided being killed by mankind at some point, either for sustenance or mere sport. Classified into five categories, animals have never developed the ability to put on a shirt, write a hit pop song, hit a home run, deal blackjack, read an encyclopedia, or do any one of the millions of activities humans do regularly and with great skill. These groups, scientifically categorized in descending order of their inferiority to humans, include:

1.

Porifera, Radiata, And Basal Bilateria
An undifferentiated shitpile of spineless gelatin that doesn't do shit for humanity except use up all its oxygen and defecate in its water. Get off our planet.

2.

Platyzoa
Though these flatworms are not the kind dissected in high school biology classes, humans could easily make that happen anytime they wanted. Real easily.

3.

Lophotrochozoa
Snails and shit.

4.

Ecdysozoa
Insects, spiders, crabs, and other animals that have developed exoskeletons, which make a very satisfying crunch under any of the beautifully designed, man-made marvels known as shoes.

5.

Deuterostomes
Birds, reptiles, fish, mammals, and amphibians; this group is the closest you're going to get to something even approaching how incredibly awesome humans are.

OTHER THINGS ANIMALS CAN'T DO

➤ Change their voicemail greetings

➤ Get into Judas Priest's *Unleashed In The East* live album from Japan

➤ Blow way more than they expected to at strip club

➤ Survive climate change

➤ Hunt in groups downwind from prey to conceal their presence while other pack members approach from the sides for a flank attack to cut off prey's retreat options…oh wait, no, that they can do

➤ Bet on dog fighting

COLLECTIVE NOUNS FOR GROUPS OF ANIMALS

A *Gaggle* of Geese

A *Herd* of Cattle

A *Fuckload* of Bees

A *Pile* of Eagles

An *Uneasy Partnership* of Coyotes

A *101.5 "The Hammer" FM* of Moths

A *Wad* of Raccoons

A *Who Cares?* of Voles

A *Business Lunch* of Meerkats

A *Duffel Bag* of Seals

A *Shitstorm* of Sparrows

A *Typist Pool* of Iguanas

A *Martin Landau* of Goats

A *Small, Intimate Gathering* of Crocodiles

ANIMALS THAT ACTUALLY DESERVE SOME RESPECT

Sharks: Though only responsible for a tiny percentage of human deaths every year, one need only to look at a shark to realize they are responsible for millions of human deaths every year.

Chimps: Only a serious threat when wearing tuxedos, which they have a hard time renting without human help.

Cats: Well, not all cats. Just my cats, Timothy and Marmalade, who aren't like other cats.

Small Deer Currently Being Eaten By Anaconda: Something noble in how quietly it's taking all of this.

SOME SPECIES OF ANIMALS AND HOW TO KILL THEM

Below are several tried-and-true ways to extinguish specific species; however, there is no "right" way to kill an animal. Creativity has historically been encouraged by the scientific community. Additionally, if one doesn't wish to deal with the sometimes messy reality of massacring animals, simply outsmarting them—by fake-throwing a ball to dogs or screwing with bats' sonar by hitting pebbles into the air with a tennis racket—is also a good way to demonstrate humanity's complete superiority.

Humpback Whale: Whale poison

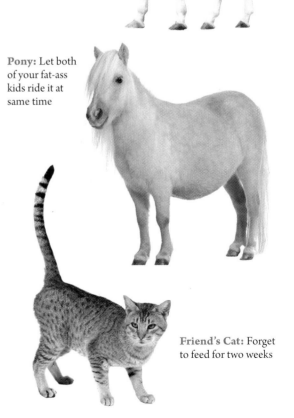

Giraffe: Ladder, ax

Polar Bear: Let idling car warm up for another 15 minutes

Ant: Very tiny harpoon gun

Lamb: Uppercut

Pony: Let both of your fat-ass kids ride it at same time

Peacock: Possibly the most difficult animal on the planet to dominate. To subdue the peacock, a three-man team comprising a Marker, a Jammer, and a Finisher will be required. The Marker is tasked with drawing out the peacock and audibly relaying its every movement to the other team members—provided, of course, that the team is somehow able to track the peacock in the first place. Next, the Jammer is assigned to distract the many hundred eyes contained in the tail, which will inevitably be unfurled behind the peacock when it is threatened. If the Jammer is of steely enough resolve to prevent himself from descending into madness immediately, the Finisher can then rapidly overtake the peacock and slit its throat in one long draw with a dagger made of tempered jade, at which point, if everything has gone exactly right, the peacock will release a burst of pure, white energy, instantly vaporizing the courageous team. *Note: The preceding instructions apply only to the male peacock; the female peacock possesses hypnotic powers, rendering it impossible to kill.*

Friend's Cat: Forget to feed for two weeks

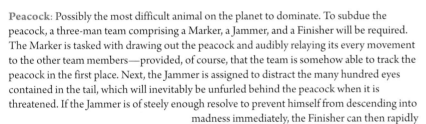

ZEPPELIN, airship that was once intended to be a major mode of transportation, but is now mostly used for taking revelers to proms, bar and bat mitzvahs, and raunchy bachelorette parties. Customers charter the party dirigibles at reasonable group rates and then ride them, at altitudes of up to 25,000 feet, to go bar-hopping or to hit strip clubs across town while the blimp floats in the parking lot. The zeppelin rental industry has enjoyed a minor boom in recent years as more people opt to hire a chauffeur rather than attempting to drunkenly fly a massive blimp and risk serious injury or death by crashing into telephone wires, roofs, or commercial jets.

Once considered a marvel of engineering and design, most zeppelins nowadays have to be scrubbed clean of vomit and urine after being rented out by groups of drunken fraternity brothers for Cinco de Mayo.

Zoo, place that people visit when they want to feel sad.

having to perform last at the many alphabetical-order open-mic nights held in New York City's Greenwich Village.

Aalborg, Danish industrial port city that serves as the ideal challenge to one's outdated notions of alphabetization.

Zodiac Killer, notorious, unidentified serial killer who terrorized San Francisco residents in the late

1960s and early 1970s and who, come to think of it, does kind of match up a lot with Mom's older brother, Chris, in terms of personality and chronology, but no, it couldn't be—right? The Zodiac Killer has been linked to as many as 37 murders and was never apprehended, but Uncle Chris was in the Navy in '71 and '72, so there's no way he could have ... although, wow, those are exactly the years when there was an unexplained break in the murders, and that would certainly explain his strange interest in codes and cartography, not to mention the antisocial behavior, the heavy-set build, and the bizarre pathological lying for no apparent reason. Wait a minute, isn't Uncle Chris' favorite movie *The Most Dangerous Game,* and doesn't he quote that film more frequently than anyone really should? Fuck. This is actually starting to get really creepy.

Zweibel, T. Herman (*b. 1868*), plutocrat, business magnate, former governor of his state, and most notably, publisher emeritus of *The Onion.* T. Herman was the only surviving son of *Onion* publisher Herman Ulysses Zweibel and took to the newspaper trade early, assuming the post of imperial editor by age 17 and penning innumerable influential editorials; in fact, thanks largely to his writings, handgun ownership in the United States quintupled, the Fascist Party enjoyed a brief spike in popularity, corporations became the equals of American citizens under the law and are protected by the rights of due process, and the Statue of Liberty was found guilty of treason by a military tribunal. Zweibel assumed editorial directorship of *The Onion* in late 1888 after a mysterious series of logjams, paper mill accidents, boiler explosions, and servant uprisings eliminated all other candidates for the post. By 1900, Zweibel had become publisher of *The Onion* following the discovery of his father's headless body at the foot of the staircase in the 680-room Zweibel mansion. Considered a major figure in the history of American journalism, Zweibel changed the face of news reporting in the modern age with a number of bold innovations, such as instituting a policy of deep contempt for a newspaper's readers and eliminating the need for women in the workplace. Although *The Onion* would soon emerge as the most dominant media empire in the world, the demands on Zweibel's health were extreme: by age 60 he was suffering from piles, typhus, worms, Irish blood-vomits, distended scalp, whooping cough, untreated self-inflicted scissor wounds (Zweibel had a profound mistrust of barbers), influenza, the "feathers," smashspleen, dislocated patellas, lead poisoning, cavernous pores, and reversal of the excretory func-

ZIBBY, animated Israeli children's show about a squirrel doctor who performs the same no-anesthesia human experiments on German kids that Nazi physician Josef Mengele performed at the Auschwitz concentration camp during World War II. *Zibby* aired Sunday mornings on the Israeli Broadcasting Authority from 1966 to 1974, delighting children with his gruesome, gore-splattered tests on unwilling blond-haired, blue-eyed 5- to 10-year-olds who had been ripped from their parents' arms, sedated, and pinned to an operating table. Always in a playful mood, Dr. Zibby, along with his sidekick nurse skunk Nentl, performed bone, muscle, and nerve transplants; injected patients with malaria, sulfonamide, and seawater; and had a firing squad execute those who lived for more than a few days afterward. In its most popular episode, "Can't Breathe? Call Dr. Zibby!" a group of German children were locked in a pressure chamber to simulate a high-altitude aircraft ejection, with survivors having their oxygen-depleted yet still-functioning brains cut open for an on-the-spot examination. Later in the show's run, Zibby moved into sterilization experiments, using an untested combination of

Over the years, the wildly popular cartoon featured guest voices from Mel Brooks, Groucho Marx, Buddy Hackett, Estelle Harris, Joan Rivers, and Elie Wiesel.

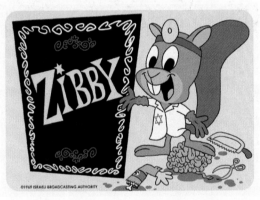

x-rays, surgery, and drugs to ensure Aryan subjects would never be able to reproduce. *Zibby* went into international syndication in 1975 and became a hit in 94 countries worldwide.

T. HERMAN ZWEIBEL: A MAN OF MANY NOTABLE WORDS

"Turn back, filthy vermin! Your desperately toiling fingers are not wanted in our factories and cosmopolitan eateries!"
—**As shouted from a small rowboat off Ellis Island, 1907**

"This will likely end badly for you, but God damn it if I don't admire you."
—**Upon meeting Adolf Hitler at the Berlin Olympic Games, 1936**

"They are huns, brutes, and monstrosities who ought to self-castrate."
—**On *Onion* readers, 2001**

"You can only bury a man alive once."
—**Daily affirmation**

tions. He also became hopelessly addicted to Crawford's Soothing Syrup, a patent nostrum claiming to treat or cure all of Zweibel's ills. After entering the iron lung in which he will be confined for the remainder of his life, Zweibel has spent the autumn of his career penning rancorous editorials concerning the limited subject matter he could see from his bedchamber. Since being launched into deep space in 2003 by his nemesis, the steam-powered robot butler Mr. Tin, Zweibel has only occasionally made contact with the outside world, but his influence can clearly be seen in every aspect of modern journalism, commerce, and politics.

ZZ Top, hit it! Ba-dah-dah-dah-dah-dah-duh-dah-DAH-dah-dah-dah-dah-dah-dah-dah-dah-dah! Ba-dah-dah-dah-dah-dah-duh-dah-DAH-dah-dah-dah-dah-dah-dah-dah-dah-dah! Rumor spreadin' 'round! In that Texas town! 'Bout that shack out-side La Grange—and you know what I'm talkin' 'bout! Just lemme know! If you wanna go! To that home out on the range—they gotta lotta nice girls, ah! Have mercy—a pow, pow, pow, pow, pow, a pow! A pow, pow, pow!

Schedule Of Fees And Charges

In acquiring the knowledge contained in this volume, the reader has implicitly consented to the fees and charges enumerated below. By opening to this page, the reader further acknowledges that these charges are binding and consents to a thorough collections process if payment in full is not received within two (2) business days.

Reader's share of printing costs..$25
Reader's share of research costs...$75
Miscellaneous learnedness fee... *($8 per month for 12 months)* $96
Reader's share of editorial board's retainer at Wilson and Hallerstein, Florida's DUI Specialists.......................$180
Hush money fee..$50
Shush money fee..$100
Late charge..$10
Charge for additional knowledge supplies...$10
Extra fee...$2.50
Copier blood fee..$12.50
You know why, and for what, you sick son of a bitch..$109.96
Extra charge for three Ss right here, SSS...$2
Share of editorial board's monthly "security consultancy" payment to Barnes and Noble, Inc............$9.50
Fee for dabbing finger on tongue before turning page...$50 (all-inclusive)
Steam-cleaning charge...$8.50
Penalty for only reading entry's first sentence and moving on...$2
Adjustment for increase in inflation since you began reading this encyclopedia..............................$1.15
Fee for stealing terry cloth robe from hotel room..$179.95
Penalty for less-than-rapt attention..$7.50
Skipping letter *M* fee...$3.65
Penalty for reading entry before photo caption instead of photo caption before entry.....................$15
Fee for smelling book..$2.50
Reader's generous donation to the Zweibel Center for Knowledge Studies..$25
Penalty for comparing the price of this book to others on "New Arrivals" table.................................$6

Total due...$983.71

Along with your cash payment to the Zweibel Center for Knowledge Studies, please include the following information:

Name _____

Date of Birth _____ / _____ / _____

Race *(check one)* _____Human   _____Irish

Social Security No. ____ - __ - _____

Primary Bank Account No. ☐☐☐☐☐☐☐☐   Routing No. ☐☐☐☐☐☐☐☐

Phone Number Where Customer Service Can Best Reach You (   ) _____ - _____

Address Where Customer Service Can Best Visit You _____
                                                                                STREET ADDRESS

_____   _____   _____
            CITY   STATE   ZIP CODE

What do you fear most in this world? *(Use additional pages if necessary.)*

_____

_____

QUESTIONS FOR DISCUSSION

Despite having now absorbed the sum total of all knowledge, the reader will almost certainly have one of seven questions relating to the material that may form the basis for ongoing discussions.

1. Did I deserve to read this book?

2. Who was I to read this book?

3. Was I not aware of its contents as compared to my level of intelligence?

4. Could I really have expected to fully comprehend this book?

5. Was a book of this magnitude wasted on me?

6. Was it not an act of reckless pride to have read this book?

7. How can I be said to deserve to live after such a humiliating intellectual charade?

HEART RATES

ANIMAL BEATS PER MINUTE

Blue Whale	9
Blue Whale After Morning Run	11
Statue Of Liberty	20
Human (Average)	70
The Floorboards	70
Dog	100
46-Year-Old Curt Johnston Upon Passing Playground	180
Rabbit	200
Duck With Erratic Pacemaker	240/275/200
Canary	750,000

HOW A BRIDGE IS CONSTRUCTED

STEP 1: Two vertical tower pieces are built in the water.

STEP 2: A deck is extended across the tower pieces.

STEP 3: Suspension cables connect the middle of the deck to the towers.

STEP 4: Actually, the cable part in the middle needs to curve, so the tower pieces should probably bend back to make the suspension cables pull the deck up. Does that make sense?

STEP 5: See, the deck still just seems like it's going to collapse without some kind of support. Perhaps a tall beam should be placed under the center to hold it up. Hmm.

STEP 6: You know what? That center beam looks really weird. Pretty sure bridges don't usually have those. Maybe the two leg pieces just need to be closer together?

STEP 7: But that won't work, because then the sides won't be secure and it will just rock back and forth or snap from all the weight.

STEP 8: It is impossible to build a bridge.

PRETTY THINGS

Ballerinas
Baskets
Birdies
Bonnets
Bright Blue Balloons
Bright Red Balloons
Bright Yellow Balloons
Bubbles
Bunnies
Butterflies
Buttons
Caroline
Christmas Trees
Daisies
Decorative Soaps
Doilies
Dolls
Dresses
Feathers
Fireworks
Flowers
Fluffy Bunnies
Freckles
Gems
Gumdrops
Hearts
Kitties
Ladybugs
Mrs. Berkley
Pinwheels
Pixie Dust
Ponies
Posies
Pretty Ladies
Puffy Clouds
Rainbows
Ribbons
Red Bows
Seashells
Snowflakes
Sparkles
Sparklers
Sprinkles
Stars
Sunbeams
Sunsets
Teacups
Tropical Fish

NATIONS OF THE WORLD RANKED BY ꙆONJꙆNꙆIVITY

1. Swaziland (2,450 kg/hr)
2. China (1,125 kg/hr)
3. Spain (1,053 kg/hr)
4. Canada (1,003 kg/hr)
5. East Timor (976 kg/hr)
6. Germany (954 kg/hr)
7. Cook Islands (922 kg/hr)
8. Guyana (880 kg/hr)
9. French Guyana (873 kg/hr)
10. Suriname (871 kg/hr)
11. Israel (825 kg/hr)
12. Turkmenistan (760 kg/hr)
13. Latvia (722 kg/hr)
14. Democratic Republic of Congo (698 kg/hr)
15. Australia (653 kg/hr)

MONETARY CONVERSION CHART FOR INTANGIBLES

Child's sigh as he falls asleep	$62
True love	$9,024.34 (10,987 euros)
Dew-flecked spiderweb, caught just so by the rising sun	$5.12
A sense of identity, of really belonging	$0.05
Respect of one's peers	$147.09
Respect of one's children	$9.16
Sense of accomplishment	$32.17
You know that feeling? When everything is just…you just understand everything so clearly for once and things just make sense—you know what I'm saying, right?	$22.87

FORMER BRITISH PRIME MINISTERS NAMED HAROLD

Harold Macmillan
Harold Wilson

OBSCURE ANIMAL SPORTS

Gorilla Sled Racing
Shrimpfighting
Elk Vaulting
Potato-Sack Horse Racing
Snakeboarding

BEST SEATS AVAILABLE

D 22
HH 15
C 40

SHOWER KNOB POSITION GUIDE

Note: Knob positions intended to help readers achieve average hot shower temperature.

Courtyard Marriott, Bloomington, MN, Room 814

1. Lift knob to begin flow of water
2. Rotate handle 150 degrees so knob's arrow is pointing in the middle portion of the red "hot" line
3. After 25 seconds, water temp. and knob position should be accurately synced
4. If water temp. is not hot enough, rotate knob 3 degrees to left (Do not over rotate, as this particular knob is sensitive and water will rapidly become too hot)

24-Hour Fitness, Chesterfield, MO, West Clayton Road: Men's Locker Room, Third Shower Stall From Left

1. Make sure lever is at 6 o'clock
2. When first turning on shower, stand to left of flow stream, as water comes out extremely hot no matter what
3. Wait 7 seconds for water temp. and knob position to sync
4. To make shower cooler, rotate in opposite direction

Former College Roommate's New Apartment

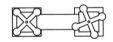

1. Rotate hot water knob all the way to extreme left position
2. Rotate cold water knob no more than 3 degrees to left
3. Water will be extremely hot at this point, but begins to cool almost instantly
4. Wait 10 seconds
5. Rotate cold-water knob 15 degrees to left
6. Wait 10 more seconds as water goes through several quick alternating cycles of icy-cold and scalding-hot temperatures
7. Water temperature and knobs should now be synced
8. Only use cold water knob to alter water temperature (WARNING: Leave hot-water knob alone until shower is complete)

BREAST AUGMENTATION PROCEDURES

Enlargement
Reduction
One-up-one-down
Nipple elongation
Nipple plastification
Implant refill
Mammary recalibration
Winterizing
Popping Martian (Panic Pete)
Cleavage rotation
Dent reversal
Re-rounding
Areola darkening

CIRCLE SIZES *(not to scale)*

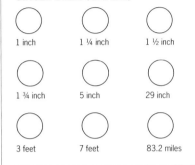

1 inch	1 ¼ inch	1 ½ inch
1 ¾ inch	5 inch	29 inch
3 feet	7 feet	83.2 miles

CLASSICAL COLUMN STYLES

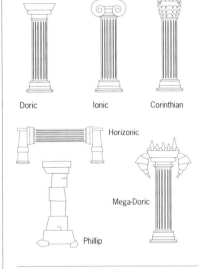

Doric   Ionic   Corinthian

Horizonic

Mega-Doric

Phillip

HOW TO PERFORM AN AUTOPSY

1. Inspect the body externally. Clean it, weigh it, and photograph it, taking note of conspicuous features such as birthmarks and tattoos. In some cases, you may wish to take x-rays.
2. Place a rubber brick known as a "body block" under the back. This will cause the arms and neck to fall and the chest to rise, making it easier to cut and access the organs within.
3. In most cases, you will make a Y-shaped incision in the chest—cuts from each shoulder that meet at the breastbone and continue down the length of the torso to the pubic bone. There will be little bleeding, as a dead body no longer has blood pressure outside that which is generated by gravity.
4. Peel back the skin and use a saw to cut through the sternum and ribs; also cut away the tissue connecting organs to the spinal column.
5. Remove and weigh the organs, making sure to shave off small portions for further analysis. Examine the contents of the stomach and intestines.
6. Take the body block that was used on the trunk and use it to elevate the head. Make an ear-to-ear incision across the head and saw off the top of the skull as a "cap." As with the other organs, weigh the brain and take any necessary tissue samples.
7. Sew up the torso and reattach the cap of the skull before transporting the body to a funeral home.

THE PLAN

1. Leo comes in the front and creates a diversion.
2. Danny, Al, and the boys set up around back.
3. Vlad steps out of the car at the corner of 8th and Topeka and gives the signal.
4. Rick gets on the roof and cuts the power.
5. Otto makes the call.
6. Josephine lets Rick in through the stairwell entrance then goes back up to the old man's room.
7. Rick opens the back door to let Danny, Al, and the boys in with the decoy package.
8. The original package is replaced with the decoy.
9. All rendezvous back at Frank's barbershop.

LITTLE BOY NAMES

Aidan
Brendan
Brian
Brodie
Charlie
Colin
Colby
Conor
Dallas
Dylan
Eli
Ethan
Joey
Kellen
Leo
Logan
Julian
Max

Oberon
Timmy
Toby
Tyler
Tyree
Parker
Percy
Silas
Quinn

LITTLE GIRL NAMES

Ashley

TWO CITIES IN IDAHO

Meridian
Caldwell

FIVE MOST LUSCIOUS U.S. VICE PRESIDENTS (based on the Tothan-Akers scale)

1. Walter Mondale........................987 ta/inch
2. George Dallas .... 52 ta/inch
3. Henry Wilson............................48 ta/inch
4. Dick Cheney/Aaron Burr, Jr. (tie)...45 ta/inch
5. Hannibal Hamlin.........................38 ta/inch

MORE PLACES TO KILL YOURSELF IN UTICA, NEW YORK, AND SUGGESTED METHODS

Utica Boehlert Transportation Center: Stand in middle of tracks, wait for Amtrak to run you over.

Columbia Street: Bash head into asphalt over and over again until dead.

Stanley Theatre Building: Back up car as far as you can on Hopper Street. Put car in drive. Drive as fast as you can directly into building.

Uptown Movie Theatre: You can blow your brains out here before, during, or after a movie.

Government Building: Ask for mayor, tell him his city is a terrible place to live, politely ask him to put you out of your misery.

Valley View Golf Course: Find grounds crew building. Drink every pesticide you can find.

Hampton Inn, Best Western, Days Inn: Perfect places for tourists to check into room and take pills or hang themselves after realizing they are vacationing in Utica.

Utica Zoo: Jump into lion's den, get eaten by lion.

Mohawk River: Tie cinder blocks to feet, jump in.

TOP PIZZA TRADE MAGAZINES
(By Circulation)

Pizza Artisan	231,773
Pizza Tomorrow	207,025
Pizza News Quarterly	202,278
International Pizzeria	199,481
Crust & Mushroom	185,460
Pizza Now	184,092
'Za Times	178,575
Slice	131,718
Pizza Proprietor Monthly	120,988
Deep-Dish Entrepreneur	100,760
Pizza Trend	94,098
Pepperoni Talk	81,768
Saucy!	78,942
Pizza Digest	70,013
Pizza Executive	61,348
U.S. Pizza Report	50,585
Modern Topping	46,380
Brick Oven Professional	31,908

HOW FAR ONE CAN SHOVE THIS ENCYCLOPEDIA UP ONE'S ASS IN RELATION TO HOW BIG A PIECE OF SHIT ONE IS

Huge Piece Of Shit: All the way up your ass
Massive Piece Of Shit: Until you can taste it
Colossal Piece Of Shit: Sideways, and don't stop until you reach your elbow

NUMBER OF SPACE SHUTTLES STACKED END TO END NEEDED TO REACH THE MOON

3 huge space shuttles

SAFFIR–SIMPSON HURRICANE SCALE ADDENDUM (Category 6–10)

Category 6: Beachside homeowner who says he's ridden out tons of hurricanes now floating face down in remainder of living room.

Category 7: All structures crushed except for large steel-frame buildings, which come to think of it, are also crushed.

Category 8: [false alarm…light breeze… drizzle of rain…most outdoor events canceled…due to administrative error…not lasting more than 15 minutes]

Category 9: Nothing noticeable, as all objects become 800-mph projectiles at exactly the same time.

Category 10: Everything natural and man-made ripped from ground and ejected into space, leaving behind only exposed sections of the Earth's mantle.

PROTRACTORS IN POPULAR CULTURE

• Protractor scene in *Brian's Song* (ABC made-for-TV movie, 1971)
• Protractor used to complete some panels of Alan Moore and David Gibbons' acclaimed comic book series *Watchmen* (1986–1987)
• Protractor scene in *When Harry Met Sally* (1989)
• Protractors mentioned 22 times in Paul Simon song "Further To Fly" from Simon's album *The Rhythm Of The Saints* (1990)
• Protractor scene in *The Piano* (1993)
• Protractor appears as "temp" character for recurring gag in one episode of CBS sitcom *Murphy Brown* (1995)
• Protractor scene in *The Thin Red Line* (1998)
• Protractors not mentioned once in Werner Herzog's protractor documentary *Semicircle Of The Gods* (2000)
• Protractor mistakenly referred to as a compass for comedic effect in Edward Albee play *The Goat, Or Who Is Sylvia?* (2002)
• Protractor spotted on set of upcoming film *The Girl Who Played With Fire* (2013)
• Protractor attached to direct untitled Adam Sandler vehicle (pre-production)
• Protractor Boy, a peripheral interface controller accessory for the Nintendo Entertainment System is released, along with a popular series of protractor-based video games (1988)

STEPFATHERS' VIEWS OF THEIR STEPCHILDREN

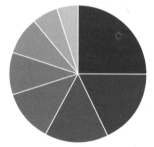

25% - Love Like Own Biological Children

18% - They're 16 And Will Be Out Of The House In Two Years, So Whatever

15% - Still Feeling Each Other Out, But They're Good Kids. Real Good Kids.

12% - An Unbelievable Burden, Naturally

10% - Molestable

9% - They're Pretty Messed Up, But Their Real Dad Is A Total Shitheel, So You Can't Really Blame 'Em

6% - Just Waiting For The Big One To Take A Swing

5% - Molestable, But Barely

SHAPES AND THEIR LAST-KNOWN WHEREABOUTS

Triangle
Buying 40-ounce bottle of King Cobra at a Raleigh, North Carolina, convenience store, August 2003

Rhombus
Boarding a single-engine plane approximately 175 miles northwest of the Seychelles Islands, February 2001

Octagon
At a remote area near Bear Creek, June 1999

Rectangle
Leaving for school Tuesday morning, March 2012

Oval
Outside Nashville, April 1996

Square
Despite numerous false reports, no confirmed sightings of this shape exist

MAXIMUM PAIN THRESHOLD OF PROMINENT AMERICANS

Alexander Hamilton: Rocks to head during speeches
Susan B. Anthony: Peel back fingernails, pour vinegar on wounds
Frederick Douglass: What do you got?
Eileen Chang: Hammer to toes
James Whale: Poking/arm punches
Dorothy Parker: Numerous bat whacks to calves and thighs (drunk); harsh words (sober)
John Wayne: Reduced to tears by noogie
Sandra Day O'Connor: Room heated to 84°
Dakota Fanning: Thumb bent back to forearm
Ira Glass: Can withstand removal of eyes, every tooth, each finger, one knuckle at a time, and still break his bond to slay his tormentor

TYPES OF KNOTS

Bowline: Classic knot that will not slip; if it does slip, one is entitled to $10 from one's government and a written apology from the Secretary-General of the United Nations

Zentangler: Mess  of interlaced strands that often provides spiritual enlightenment when tied properly

Tiny Sonuvabitch: Very small, anger-inducing knot that is impossible to untie with these useless sausage fingers

Flemish Bend Knot: Difficult knot that, if one is really good at tying, means one chose a life path that involves making a lot of these knots, therefore making this person weird and unapproachable

STATISTICALLY LEAST PROBABLE WAYS TO DIE

• Hit by a bus while bending over to pick up a dollar in the street, because how obvious is that
• Mauled by dog, finished off by smaller dog
• Tragic Internet messaging accident
• Herubin overdose
• Blown away by layered performance of James Franco in *127 Hours*
• Finally cornered by Van Helsing
• Murdered by Indiana Pacers basketball team
• Choking on single grain of couscous
• Stabbed by doctor immediately after he tells you your vital signs are looking good
• Courageously
• After discovering that bagels are made from slow-release poison dough
• Shot by completely different coworker than you would have guessed
• Waking up one morning and instinctively traveling to elephant's graveyard in Kenya
• During Great Polio Epidemic of 1916
• Small, sharp-toothed man attaching self to elbow, eating through entire body
• Looking up at sky too fast, Adam's apple protruding through neck
• Swallowed whole by sparrow
• Bleeding out through fingernails
• Turning head to left, head just falling off
• Running out of printer paper
• Getting hit by bus, living, bus turning into very muscular man who beats you to death
• Secondhand stroke
• Respawning into little brother's sniper scope
• Eaten by EMTs
• Unsecured barrel rolling off truck causing car to slam on brakes startling police horse nearby knocking off rider causing gun to fall to ground shooting you in head
• Poisoned underpants
• Non-poisoned underpants: choking
• Being scraped from uterus by a Planned Parenthood doctor
• Surrounded by loved ones
• Dropped by insurance company after major

illness, making it too expensive to engage in preventative medicine, thus letting a small, easily cured ailment spiral out of control until you die
• Exactly like John Barrymore
• Paramedics futilely beating at your chest through the shell of Nutcracker toy soldier costume
• Harry Belafonte vendetta
• Pushed off Days Inn balcony by drunk grandmother
• Choking on own severed fingers
• Quickly spreading flame from burning marshmallow
• Sucked inside powerful vacuum cleaner

UNUSED MATERIAL

The following letters, words, punctuation, symbols, phrases, and images wound up not being needed in the primary text of this reference volume.

w
g
;
g
&
Mycenaean
$
Symptoms include abdominal pain and blurred vision with occasional
/
=
F
bassist Mat Brady
2.65
(
)
$7,360
UU
v
;; ; ; ;
'
.
but what does it matter? What does any of it really matter?
fuck
fuck
Christ
fuck
fuck
d. July 12, 2009
~
hubba hubba
;
;
?

Graphics Credits

G=Getty Images; NC=Newscom; O=Onion; PD=Public Domain; PC=Photos.com; SS=Shutterstock

ii: Ben Grasso; iii: Ben Grasso xiii: D.S.Zweibel-G; M.H.Zweibel-SS; Alcmaeon-PD; H.S.Jong-G; D.B.Hoot-G; P.H.Mirr-SS; J.Karst-Zweibel-SS; R.Mugabe-G ix: G x: O xii: Ben Grasso Page 1: Abdul-Jabbar-NC; Adams-PD Page 2: Abacus-SS; Acupuncture-SS; Adams-PD Page 3: Agriculture-SS; Alcatraz-SS; Alcohol-O Page 4: Al Zawahiri-NC; Ali-G,G; Allen-G; Map-O, Zuckerberg-PD; Alexander the Great-PD Page 5: Amazon-SS; American Civil War, clockwise, from top left-G, PD, PD, G Page 6: Skeletal-S Page 7: Muscular-S; Tuxedal-S; Organs-S Page 8: Antelope-SS; Apple-SS; Amsterdam-SS Page 9: Antietam-R.Sikoryak; Arby's-G; Appalachian Trail-SS Page 10 & 11: Design-Mike Ley; Discipline Icons-PD, Works of Art-PD, Louvre-SS, Centre Pompidou-SS, Outsider Art-PD, Cubism-PD Page 12: Archery-G; Armor-SS; Architecture-O Page 13: Astaire-G, G, PC; Arthur-PD Page 14: Aunt, top to bottom-G,G,G; Audubon-PD; Aztec-G Page 15: Boomers-SS; Ball, top to bottom-SS, SS, SS, SS Page 16: Bank-G; Barbie-PD; L.Ball-NC, G, G, G; Barnum-G Page 17: Bangkok-SS; Bee Gees-G; Basketball-Newscom, PD; Beach-G Page 18: Beefcake-SS; Beer-O; Baseball-SS Page 19: Beethoven-PD; Beaver-Larry Buchanan; Beige-O Page 20: Bicycle-G; Biden-PD; Berkowitz-G; Bible-G Page 21: Big Bang-PD; Big Ben-SS; Beetle-SS, Amoeba-SS, Ficus-SS, Elephant-SS, Caiman-SS Page 22: Birth Control-SS; Towers-SS; Bin Laden-PD Page 23: Black Hills-SS, Note-O; Black Panthers-PD Page 24: Bonsai-SS; Beetle-SS; Boat-All SS; Bonnie & Clyde-PD Page 25: Boxer-G; Booth-S; Bootlegging-G Page 26: Box-SS; Massacre-PD; Boston-SS Page 27: Brian Oster-SS; Buchanan-PD; Bride-Chia & Hon Photography Page 28: Brady-PD; Braille Character-SS; Brothers Karamazov-O; Braille-G; Brothers Grimm-PD Page 29: Buddy Ranch-O; Brains-SS; Breakfast-SS Page 30: Bush-PD; Bull-SS; Burial Icons-PD Page 31: Caesar-PD; Cancer-SS; Cain-PD Page 32: Camel-SS; Caroline-SS; Carter-PD Page 33: Carbon-G; Castro-G, O; Carroll-PD; Casino-G Page 34: Catcher-O; CPR-Pete Sucheski Page 35: Cell-SS; Cert-O; Chainsaw-SS; Challenger-G Page 36 & 37: Sketch-SS, Beaker-SS, Flask-SS, Mortar-SS, Funnel-SS, Pipette-SS, Sep Funnel-SS, Burner-SS, Molecule-SS, Periodic Table-SS, Curies-SS Page 38: Chaplin-NC; Chess-SS; Charlemagne-PD Page 39: Cheney-PD; Chicago-G; Chavez-PD; Ch'i-O Page 40: Chivalry-SS; Christianity-SS Page 41: Evers-G, Robb-G; Cleveland-PD Page 42: Clinton-PD; Coal-Pete Sucheski Page 43: Coolidge-PD; Kane-G; Clown Fish-SS Page 44: Columbus-PD; Communication-O Page 45: Constellation-O; Conch-SS Page 46: Design-Mike Ley, Justice-SS, King-G, Anthony-G, Simpson-G, Borden-PD, Diagram-Mike Ley Page 47: Reef-SS; Cone-SS; Confucius-SS Page 48: Copse-SS; Cracker-SS Page 49: Crumb-SS; Kennedy-G, Khrushchev-G; Crockett-PD; Crowbar-SS Page 50: Cumulonimbus-SS; Dollar-SS, Euro-SS, Crickets-SS, Ruble-SS, Yen-SS, Pound-SS, Renmimbi-SS, Rupee-SS Page 51: Da Vinci-PD; Dali-PD; DDT-SS; Davis-G; Dalai Lama-G Page 52: Dean-PD; Declaration-SS Page 53: Dendrite-PD; De Kooning-G Page 54: Detergent-PD; Dining-O Page 55: Dickens-SS; Graph-O; Dickinson-G; Disney-G Page 56: DNA-SS; DiMaggio-G; Doctors-G Page 57: Alectrosaurus-G; Pterodactyl-G; Saltopus-G; Jake-SS Page 58: Dog-SS; Dolphin-SS Page 59: DEA-G; Chart-O; Donner Party-G; Driftwood-SS Page 60: Dubai-SS; Duncan-NC; Dylan-PD, Album-PD Page 61: Earhart-G; Ear Canal-SS; Edison-G Page 62: Earth-SS Page 63: Eiffel-G, PC; Egg-SS; Aristotle-SS, Frobel-PD Page 64 & 65: Design by Mike Ley; Map-SS, Hieroglyphics-PD, Vase-SS, Mummy-G, Sculpture-G, Sphinx-SS, Pyramid-SS, Nefertiti-SS, Bird-SS, Rosetta Stone-G, Kadesh-G, Cat-SS, Agriculture-G, Pharoah-SS Page 66: Electoral College-G; Elk-SS; Einstein-PD Page 67: Ellis Island-NC Page 68: Embryo-SS, Empire State-SS, End Table-O Page 69: Everest-SS; Ernst-G; Everglades-SS Page 70: Exorcism-PD, Ape-SS, Eye-SS Page 71: Fashion-Mike Loew; Fascism-O Page 72: Photos courtesy of Faded Black Page 73: Fencing-O Page 74 & 75: Wedding-G, Americans-G, Mongolians-G, Inuits-G, Samoans-G, Kenyans-SS, Icon-SS Page 76: Fedora-SS; Fingerprint-SS, G; Fishing Hook-SS; Fireside Chat-G, G, G, G Page 77: Food-SS, SS, SS, SS, SS, SS, SS, SS, SS, SS; Fireplace-SS Page 78: Fillmore-PD; Ford-PD; Football-O Page 79: French and Indian-PD; Frank-PD; Fossil-SS; Trucks-SS, SS, SS, SS Page 80: Franklin-G; Frog-SS; Friedan-G; Friars Club-PD Page 81: Gacy-PD; Galileo-PD Page 82: Gandhi-PD; Gender-O; Gauguin-G; Garfield-PD Page 83: Gettysburg-G; Genie-G; Giraffe-G Page 84: Geography, clockwise, G, PD, NC, G Page 85: God-PD; Golden Gate-SS; Golf-G; Goebbels-G; Goodall-G Page 86: Google-SS; Government-SS Page 87: Grand Canyon-SS; Gotham City-SS; Grant-PD Page 88: Great Wall-SS; Great Depression-G; Greenspan-G, G Page 89: Acropolis-SS, Masks-PD, Coin-O Page 90: Gutenberg-PD; Bust-SS, Ruin-SS; Map-O Page 91: Hannibal-G; Harding-PD; Hard Hat-SS; Harem Pant-NC Page 92: Harrison-PD; Globetrotters-G Page 93: Harrison-PD; Heaven-G; Hayes-PD Page 94: Heisman-G; Hindenburg-PD; Hibernation-G, O Page 95: Hiroshima-G; Hitler-G Page 96: Hoover-PD; Honor-O; Homosexuality-G Page 97: Horsey Sauce-G; HAAC-O; Horn-SS Page 98: Hurricane Katrina-SS; Hussein-G; Houston-SS Page 99: Imagination-O; Ice Skating-SS Page 100: IMAX-PD; Industrial Revolution-G Page 101: Insect-G; Ingrown Hair-Mike Loew; Inverness-PD Page 102: iPod-G; Engine-O Page 103: Istanbul-SS; Iraq-G; Irish-PD Page 104: Ivory-SS; Ixia-PD; Iwo Jima-PD Page 105: Jack the Ripper-G; M.Jackson-G; A.Jackson-PD; J.Jackson-PD Page 106: Camp-G; JAWS-PD; Jaguar-G Page 107: Jefferson-PD; Slavery-G; Jerk-O Page 108: Johannesburg-G; Johns-G; Jesus-PD; Johnson-PD Page 109: Joinery-O; Jordan-NC; Johnson-G Page 110: Juniper-G; Jupsi-O; Juggs-NC Page 111: Kerouac-G; Ke$ha-G; Karate-PD Page 112: Key-G; King Kong-SS; Kennedy-G; Kim-G Page 113: B.J.King-G; M.L.King-G Page 114: Knitting-SS; Kubrick-G Page 115: Ladder-SS; Landfill-SS Page 116: Lava-SS; Lemon-SS; Intestine-SS Page 117: Ahab-PD; Diagram-O Page 118: Libary-SS; Lint-O; Lincoln-PD Page 119: Beatles-G; London-SS; Literacy-SS Page 120: Los Angeles-G; Loop-The-Loop-G; Lyffhauser-G Page 121: Madison-PD; Malcom X-G; Magna-G Page 122: Mail-O; Manhattan-G Page 123: Marshalls-G; Mastodon-G; Mammals-SS; Marshall-PD Page 124: Dolls-SS; Mayflower-G; McCarthy-PD; Maya-Todd Hanson Page 125: Mecca-SS; McGwire l-G, r-G; McKinley-PD; Media-G Page 126 & 127: Design-Mike Ley, Icon-SS, Hippocrates-SS, Body-SS, Jenner-G, Fleming-G, Goldfarb-SS, Salk-G, CVS-G, Rite-Aid-G, Walgreens-G Page 128: Meta-O; Microscope-SS; Bear-SS, Bear Larva-SS, Bear Butterfly-SS, Chicken-SS, Chicken Larva-G, Chicken Butterfly-SS, Human-SS, Human Larva-SS, Cockroach-SS Page 129: Miller-G; Miami-G Page 130: Mitosis-SS; Moccasin-SS; Mister Ed-G; Monroe-PD; Mohonk-NC Page 131: Monsanto-Pete Sucheski; Montreal-G Page 132: Moscow-SS; Mouse Pad-SS; Mosque-G Page 133: Mozart-PD; Muir-G; Mumbai-G; Murdoch-NC Page 134 & 135: Baritone Sax-SS, Bassoon-SS, Kazoo-SS, Trombone-SS, Tuba-SS, Violin-SS, Guitar-SS, Drums-SS, Guiro-SS, Sex Pistols-G, Lynne-G, Harpsichord-SS, Score-SS Page 136: MTV-PD; Murrow-G; Mythology-SS Page 137: NASA-G, SS; Native American-G Page 138: Napkin-SS, Thoreau-PD Page 139: NYC-PD; Nelson-PD; Newton-G Page 140: NYT-G; Newman-G; Nixon-PD Page 141: People-PD; Noah-G Page 142: Nuremberg-PD; Submarine-PD Page 143: Obama-PD; O-Kit-O; Oberon-G; Oakley-G Page 144: Office-SS; Oh Henry-PD; Ocean-O; O'Keeffe-PD Page 145: Olympics-PD; Orb-O; Ono-G; Opal-SS Page 146: Oxford-SS; Opera-SS; Neptune-PD; Playbill-PD Page 147: Parade-SS; Pail-SS; Paris-PD; Pearl Harbor-PD; Parks-G; Pentagon-G Page 148: Penguin-SS; Peter-PD; Peter-PD; Photography, l-r, G, G, G & G, PD, O Page 151: Photosynthesis-Kiji McCafferty; Picasso-G; Philosophers, top to bottom, PD, PD, G; Philtrum-SS Page 152: Pierce-PD; Plant-G; Poe-PD; Pol Pol-G; Pollack-PD; Polk-PD Page 154: Pope-G; Potato-SS; Pompeii-G; Port-O Page 155: Pregnancy-SS; Prairie Dog-PD; Plymouth-PD Page 156: Presley-G; Prison-O; Princip-PD Page 157: Prokaryote-; Prosthetic-G; Prune-SS Pages 158 & 159: Design-Mike Ley; Experiment-Pete Sucheski; Figures, clockwise from top left-PD, G, G, G, G, PD, PD; Mouse-SS Page 160: Puddle-SS; Puberty-Mike Loew; Pulitzer-PD; Pythagoras-G Page 161: Quadrilateral-O; Quarry-SS; Q-PD; Quail-SS Page 162: Quartz-SS; Quill-SS; Quince-SS; Quincy-G; Quiz-PD Page 163: Race, top to bottom, O, O, G; Rasputin-G, Radius-O Page 164: Rattlesnake-SS; Radio-G; Raytheon-G, G Page 165: Reagan-PD; Recycling-SS; Reed-G Page 166: Religion-PD; Tactics-G; Fife-SS Page 167: Retriever-SS; Ridgeway-G; Republic-SS; Rice-Mike Loew Page 168: Roach-PD; Road-Emily Flake; Rio-G Page 169: Robinson-G; Roosevelt-PD; Robots, top to bottom, PD, NC, PD, PD Page 170: Roosevelt-PD; Colosseum-G, Seneca-G, Cretin-G, Map-PD Page 171: Rose-G; Rosie-PD; ROV-G Page 172: Rowboat-SS; Rowling-SS; Rushmore-SS; Ruth-G Page 173: Assisi-SS; Satan-PD Page 174: San Diego-G; Sept 11-G; San Francisco-G; Seneca-PD; Seesaw-SS; Seneca-PD; Serling-G Page 177: Sex-O; Shot Put-G Page 178: Seychelles-G; Shroud-SS; Shakespeare-SS Page 179: Ski-PD Page 180: Snow-SS; Soccer-SS; Socrates-SS Page 181: Sonic-Pete Sucheski; Spector-G; Solar System-PD Page 182: Design-Mike Ley; Javelin-SS; Field-Larry Buchanan, Ref-SS; Stalin-SS; Statue-G; Star Wars-PD; Stringed Bongo Horn-Mike Loew Page 184: String-PD; Geese-SS; Sullivan-TD Page 185: Suburb-SS; Supermodel-G; Swiss-G Page 186: SWAT-SS; Synagogue-SS; Sydney-SS; Gland-O Page 187: Tablet-G; Taj Mahal-Michael Faisca Page 188: Tattoo-Courtesy of Bert Krak; Taft-PD; Taylor-PD Page 189: Tectonic Plate-Ward Sutton Page 190: Telescope-SS; Terracotta-SS; Tehran-SS; Telephone-G Page 191: Time-PD; Theater-G Page 192: This Guy-SS; Titanic-PD; Timeout-G; Toronto-SS Page 193: Tooth-O; Toast-SS; Trafalgar-SS; Tractor-SS Page 194: Trail-PD; Handrail-G Page 195: Truman-PD; Paper-G; Train-SS; Treasury-PD Page 196: Turnip-John Harris; Trojan-G; Truth-PD; Turkury-O; Apostles-SS Page 197: Tyler-PD, Poole-G; Twain-G; Typhoid-G Page 198: Tyson-NC; MKX-PD Page 199: UFO-; Underpants-SS; Unicycle-G; Baby-G Page 200 & 201: Astronaut-PD; Sagan-G; Map-PD Page 202: Uncling Monthly-Charlie Giglia; U-650-G; Utica-PD Page 203: Van Gogh-PD; Tosches-Courtesy of Danny Mulligan; Van Braak-G; Page 204: Flytrap-SS; Van Buren-PD; Venus-PD; Vase-SS Page 205: Running-PD; Fire-PD Page 206: Mary-SS; V-J Day-PD; Venus-G Page 207: Volcano-SS; Krakatoa-G Page 208: Voodoo-NC; Vulture-G; Vonnegut-G; Voyager-PD Page 209: Ʋartin Foster-G; Ʋenstein Map-0, Flag-0 Page 210: Ʋafkenpembülater-SS; Ʋike Fir-O; Ʋipsy Presto's World-David Pagano Page 211: Ʋmanuel Christmas Day-R. Sikoryak; Ʋoeber Square-SS; Ʋrait-SS Page 212: Ʋubi-Clean-PD ; Ʋvvvuʋfevvvsavvet-SS; Ʋwiller Un-Toaster-SS Page 213: Washington-PD Page 214: Watch-O; Washington DC-PD; Martha-PD Page 215: Monument-SS; Water Lilies-PD; Waterfall-SS Page 216: Bombs-G; Computer-G; Saddam-G; Canon-SS Page 217: Illustrations-Mike Loew Page 218: Figures, top to bottom-G, PD, G, PD & O; Letter-O; Poster-G; Mona Lisa-PD; Washington-G; Napoleon-PD Page 219: Photos clockwise from top left-G, G, G; Insignia-O Page 220: West-G; West-O; Western Alliance-O Page 221: Weapons, PD; Photo-PD Page 222: Wilson-PD; White House-G; Whitman-G Page 223: Wind Turbine-Larry Buchanan; Willis Tower-O; Wolf-SS Page 224: WWI: PD Page 225: WWII: Photo-PD, Plane-G Page 226: Woodstock-G; Wright Brothers-PD; Woods-SS; Wright-G Page 227: Xavier-NC; Xs-O; Xylocarp-Kiji McCafferty Page 228: Xanthradel-O; Doctor-G; Drum-SS Page 229: Yellowthroat-SS; Yak-SS; Yalta-G, PD Page 230: Youngstown-SS; Yoga-SS; Yellowstone-SS; Red Velvet-SS Page 231: Zapruder-PD; Zimmer-SS; Logo-O Page 232: Orders-G; GeeseSS; Shark-SS Page 233: All SS Page 234: Zoo-SS; Zeppelin-G; Zodiac-PD Page 235: Zibby Illustrations by Ward Sutton; Zweibel-Ben Grasso; Ready Reference-O, except Page 241: Knots-SS; Mike Bocchetti/O; and Marbles-SS.

ACKNOWLEDGMENTS

Special thanks to Daniel Greenberg; Geoff Shandler and his colleagues at Little, Brown: Liese Mayer, Heather Fain, Mario Pulice, Lindsey Andrews, Kate MacAloney, Ploy Siripant, Matthew Tanner, Rachael Larson, Amanda Tobier, Michael Pietsch, Liz Garriga, and Denise LaCongo; Mike Ley; Larry Buchanan, Mike Loew, Pete Sucheski, Ward Sutton, Emily Flake, Kiji McCafferty, Ben Grasso, Charlie Giglia, R. Sikoryak, and David Pagano; Craig Cannon, Jenny Nellis, Gregory Ronquillo, Maxime Simonet, Gilbert Shi, and William Wiggins; Danny Mulligan; Alyssa Varner; Shira Danan, Mike Drucker, Django Gold, Sam Kemmis, Matt Klinman, Lane Moore, Jill Morris, Andrei Nechita, Michael Pielocik, Zack Poitras, Jocelyn Richard, Anita Serwacki, and Sigmund Stern; Emily Bina, Signe Brewster, Patrick Burns, Marty Cramer, Sam Dean, Leslie Feinberg, Dennis Flynn, Mary Mann, Isaac McQuistion, Rachel Miller, Ali Moran, Matt Powers, Dean Praetorius, Scott Rosenfeld, Lindsay Sanchez, Nicole Schilder, Sophie Song, Caroline Tan, Seena Vali, Chloe Walker, Allissa Wickham, and Robin Wildman; Rachel Arbeit and Anne Johnson; Grace Bello, Renato Bello, and Benito Cereno; Bert Krak; Anne Finn; Dave Rosen; Jun Ueno; The A.V. Club staff

[4]Or all the way back here.